Reading Sport

SPORT
Reading

CRITICAL ESSAYS ON POWER AND REPRESENTATION

Susan Birrell
and
Mary G. McDonald

Northeastern University Press
BOSTON

Northeastern University Press 2000
Copyright 2000 by Susan Birrell and Mary G. McDonald

Library of Congress Cataloging-in-Publication Data

Reading sport : critical essays on power and representation / [edited by] Susan Birrell, Mary G. McDonald.

p. cm.

Includes bibliographical references and index.

ISBN 1–55553–430–9 (cloth : alk. paper) — ISBN 1–55553–429–5 (pbk. : alk. paper)

1. Sports—Social aspects—United States. 2. Sports—Anthropological aspects—United States. 3. Sports—United States—Psychological aspects. I. Birrell, Susan. II. McDonald, Mary G.

GV706.5.R42   2000

362.4'83'0973—dc21   99–088217

Designed by Gary Gore

Composed in Minion by Coghill Composition Company in Richmond, Virginia. Printed and bound by Edwards Brothers, Inc., in Ann Arbor, Michigan. The paper is EB Natural, an acid-free sheet.

Manufactured in the United States of America

04 03 02 01 00   5 4 3 2 1

Contents

CONTENTS

Acknowledgments

We would like to thank Terri Teleen, our original acquisitions editor at Northeastern University Press, for steering us through the crucial stages of this project; Theresa Walton and Joyce Murphy for their help in the preparation of the manuscript; and the authors who contributed their selections to this book.

Reading Sport

SUSAN BIRRELL AND MARY G. McDONALD

Reading Sport,
Articulating Power Lines
An Introduction

● In the past several years our attention has increasingly been drawn to a
new form of critical sport analysis: articles that conceptualize particular
sporting events or celebrities as "texts" and offer "readings" of those
texts.[1] Critical analyses of narratives surrounding events such as the Tonya
Harding and Nancy Kerrigan media circus and such personalities as Michael Jordan, golfer Nancy Lopez, and pitcher Nolan Ryan offer unique
points of access to the constitutive meanings and power relations of the
larger worlds we inhabit. *Reading Sport* features ten essays that provide
interesting insights into that process.

We see particular advantage in overlaying this approach with a critical
theory that foregrounds relations of race, class, gender, sexuality, age, religion, nationality, physical ability, and the like.[2] Too often, mainstream
accounts frame narratives in terms that privilege one identity (i.e., one's
gender or race or class) while ignoring others. Public spectacles such as
the O. J. Simpson double murder case, the shootings at Columbine High
School, and the sexual harassment of Lisa Olson in the New England
Patriots locker room have made it clear that public discourse is limited by
a lack of models that theorize sexism, racism, and classism as interacting
relations of power in our culture. For example, privileging race as a critical
category in, for instance, the O. J. Simpson trial not only marginalizes

contending discourses framed through gender but also runs the risk of making gender disappear altogether. In a similar vein, the Columbine tragedy has been almost entirely depoliticized; in the place of an analysis of violent white masculinity implicated in this and other school shootings, dominant framings focus instead on the individual pathology of the shooters.

Reading Sport is an anthology with a thesis: Structures of dominance expressed around what we call the power lines of race, class, gender, and sexuality (and age, nationality, ability, religion, etc.) do not work independently and thus cannot be understood in isolation from one another. Moreover, because they operate in historically specific ways with identifiable consequences, we must develop theoretical and methodological practices capable of capturing that complexity. The essays in *Reading Sport* provide more complicated analyses of sporting events and people by countering the tendency in the media, and often in social analysis, to organize understanding and action by exploring only one axis of power.

Taken as a whole, the diverse essays represented in *Reading Sport* advance our understanding of the complex interrelated and fluid character of power relations, especially as they are constituted along the axes of gender, race, class, and sexuality. Each cultural incident or personality explored in this anthology offers a unique site for understanding specific articulations of power. The importance of using particular incidents or personalities as points of analytic access is precisely their particularity. Because power operates differently in different places and times, we should avoid the reductive tendencies of arguments over primacy: We cannot settle once and for all which relations of power are always and everywhere most important. What we can say as cultural critics is that at this historical moment, at this particular place, these discourses on race, gender, sexuality, and class were produced around this incident. Thus, the essays in *Reading Sport* traverse the boundaries between lived experience, knowledge production, and political practices.

Exploring Power Lines

Our ideas follow from recent critical work in sport, particularly the theoretical approach known as *critical cultural studies*. The brilliance of this perspective is its engagement with power as a central focus for under-standing social life. Earlier work in this critical genre tended to focus on one means through which power was enacted, such as gender or class. A crucial insight of critical analyses, whether focused on feminist analysis, Marxist analysis, critical race theory, or queer theory, is that they explode forever the myth that sport is an innocent pastime that exists outside the realm of economic and political forces. Moreover, they advance our understandings of race, class, gender, and sexuality by reconceptualizing these identities not as categoric variables but as relations of power.

The specific insights that have been generated by these critical exami-nations provide the basis for the more complicated approach we are ad-vocating. From feminist theory, for example, we know that despite considerable challenges sport is best understood as a male preserve, a major site for the creation of male bonding, privilege, and masculine he-gemony. Feminist analysis also focuses on the patriarchal control of women through the control of women's bodies, seen in a variety of sport-ing practices, most obviously the attempts to exclude women from sport, which, if successful, deny women the opportunity to experience power and physicality in their own bodies.

Marxist scholars have investigated a range of issues that demonstrate that sport is inextricably linked to capitalist practices and ideologies. These include the ways that social class location figures in the distribution of sport resources, opportunities, and experiences; the commodification of sport and sporting personalities; labor issues that make clear the economic base of professional and elite sport; the reinforcement of the myth of meritocracy that justifies and reproduces social class structures; and the increasing move toward global sport markets, with the resultant hybrid and monoculture of sport.

Racial and ethnic relations scholarship begins with the insight that "race" is a social construction and that racial meanings are constantly being refigured in accordance with and in contrast to the fluid new racism of contemporary American popular culture. Earlier studies that focused on the cultural forces that worked to exclude members of racial and ethnic minorities from sport have been joined by efforts to document ways in which raced bodies are represented in sport. One important insight is that sport serves as a central site for the naturalization of race through the discourses that construct African American athletes as natural athletes. Additionally, the privileges of whiteness are increasingly being made visible through critical race relations scholarship.

Originally subsumed within gender analysis, issues of sexuality are now being investigated in their own theoretical right as well. Sport as a male preserve also has deep implications for sexuality. Homophobia works to reinforce gender expectations: Gay men, dismissed as "unmanly," have not been welcome in mainstream sport, and women who insist on their rights to play sport have often been labeled lesbians. Compulsory heterosexuality is thus remade through sport. Queer theory, with its connection to poststructuralist insights, disrupts our commonsense understanding of sexuality as a stable, essential identity. As several scholars demonstrate, the terms "heterosexual" and "homosexual" were invented in the late nineteenth century as a means of differentiating and thus hierarchicalizing particular sexual behaviors.

Critical cultural studies builds on these important insights about sport by expanding on the integrative moves of feminist theories, Marxist theories, critical race theories, and/or queer theory. To many working within those traditions, it became increasingly evident that a focus on only one line of power results in partial analyses that do not adequately capture the complexity of relations of dominance and subordination within culture. One important project of critical cultural studies, as we see it, is to continue this search for sophisticated conceptualizations of the interacting forces of race, class, gender, and sexuality. It is this process of "crossing power lines" that underlies the selections in *Reading Sport* as they focus on particular personalities or stories.

The Limits of Popular Discourse

Stories are always presented within frames, and these frames guide and limit public understandings of events and personalities. This is particularly troublesome when controversial issues such as sexual harassment in and out of sport settings and controversial personalities, such as Dennis Rodman, are presented in a one-dimensional manner. If power is taken into account at all in popular discussions, it is usually through only one point of access such as gender. Thus, inadequate models for understanding and representing the complexity of events prevent even the most well-intentioned critics from speaking in meaningful ways about the intersections and connections between and among relations of oppression. In other words, a considerable problem arises when other relations of oppression are brought into an analysis; somehow the analysis becomes too complex to capture within existing models.

If they engage issues of power at all, mainstream discourses follow one of three options: They privilege one category of oppression; they pit one oppression against another; or they provide a simple additive model of oppression. For example, the media usually present sexual assaults in a one-dimensional way and produce a story that implicates only one category, that of gender. A slightly more sophisticated way to deal with a complex story is to pit one category against another. This was evident in accounts of the Clarence Thomas Supreme Court nomination controversy. Here gender as embodied by Anita Hill was pitted against race as represented by Thomas. No wonder that trial produced little satisfaction for anyone: Few narrative strategies were available to speak about the complicated issues of gender, race, class, and heterosexism that surfaced in the courtroom. A final rhetorical solution is to add a category to a category as in the William Jefferson Clinton sex scandals, where Clinton came to represent male power and class power.

To give prominence to one issue within a frame is necessarily to obscure others. To concentrate on one relationship of power is to produce an incomplete and dangerously simple analysis. We need to look deeper to see what other ideological atrocities are lurking below the surface of these representations: What subtle but equally powerful forms of social control or resistance are at work within the particular frame constructed by the mainstream media, and what stories are only implicitly but still powerfully spoken?

When Power Lines Cross

Applying this school of thought to sport means that athletes are located within a variety of discourses, including those that serve to reify an individualistic worldview and a capitalistic propensity for competition. For example, Nick Trujillo's essay on Nolan Ryan demonstrates that successful athletes are often praised as capitalist workers striving for occupational achievement. Trujillo suggests that just as achievement and productivity are goals of sport and capitalism, these features often are used to glorify an archetypal version of white manhood and thus promote hegemonic masculinity. By further celebrating such characteristics as force, family values, and heterosexuality, the image of Nolan Ryan also helps to reify a sexist gender order in which men are seen to be "naturally" superior to women both physically and socially.

The ideals of masculinity and capitalism celebrated in sport are always complicated by race, as Leola Johnson and David Roediger demonstrate in their analysis of O. J. Simpson. Focusing on the commodification of black masculinity, they show how the image of a sport hero who was originally hailed as the first great African American athlete to transcend race and endorse products for white middle-class consumers relied on white fantasies of black masculinity as stylish, physical, and primitive.

The primitive is also a central image mobilized by Dennis Rodman, as Mélisse Lafrance and Geneviève Rail show. They contend that although the cross-dressing basketball player Dennis Rodman appears to challenge the macho imperatives of mainstream, elite competitive sport, his performance falls short of a disruptive representation of masculinity. Rather, they suggest that the carefully crafted Rodman persona is enabled by a capitalistic consumer society preoccupied with the creation of fresh, different styles and personalities. The marketing success of Rodman is further evidence of the dominant culture's desire to consume the Other, in particular to encounter the alleged "exoticness," savagery, and hypersexuality that are ideologically linked to black sporting bodies.

Lisa Disch and Mary Jo Kane explore the 1990 sexual harassment of *Boston Herald* sports writer Lisa Olson in the team locker room of the New England Patriots. They dispute commonsense understandings of the incident as merely reflective of an issue over equal access to a work space often denied female sport reporters. Rather, Disch and Kane contend that as an authorized critic of male performance with backstage access to the innermost sanctum of elite male sport, the locker room, Lisa Olson was in a position to challenge, even destroy, the fragile status quo of masculine privilege and power. The incident reveals how the players and owner Victor Kiam summoned support for their position by deploying heterosexuality and masculinity as unquestioned norms in order to contain her disruptive presence.

Drawing on the theoretical framework of multiracial feminism, Katherine Jamieson examines the public persona of Nancy Lopez to reveal multiple, contradictory, and intersecting forms of oppression and privilege. Jamieson suggests that too often, women in sport are deemed unwelcome outsiders, and this is particularly true in the case of working-class women of color. Jamieson demonstrates how Lopez's ethnic identity is constructed differently in different cultural contexts. While hailed within the Mexican-American press as a symbol of ethnic pride, Lopez's Mexican-American working-class roots are often ignored or trivialized in mainstream press accounts. However, Lopez's image is redeemed through the celebration of her public pregnancies, which reaffirm heterosexuality as the unquestioned cultural norm while also allaying homophobic fears of a lesbian presence in sport.

If Nancy Lopez is the icon of women's golf, Michael Jordan is the icon of commodified sport, David Andrews contends. In "Excavating Michael Jordan's Blackness," Andrews interrogates representations of Jordan arguing that because race is a social construction, racial meanings are constantly being refigured. In post-Reagan America, Jordan's exceptionalism, his All-American persona, and presumed superior physicality have helped to construct a false image of an open class structure while easing the racial insecurities of white middle-class consumers. Constructed as a hard-working achiever who transcends race in his representation of the American Dream realized, Jordan's marketed persona works to stabilize racist stereotypes of black masculinity as deviant, criminal, and inferior to whites.

Both Abigail Feder-Kane's " 'A Radiant Smile from the Lovely Lady': Overdetermined Femininity in 'Ladies' Figure Skating," and Sam Stoloff's "Tonya Harding, Nancy Kerrigan, and the Bodily Figuration of Social Class," explore figure skating and its most infamous scandal. Both essays document the ways in which the skating spectacle is grounded in notions of white, middle-class, heterosexual ideals of femininity. Feder-Kane also demonstrates that Harding and Kerrigan projected contrasting images of white feminine deviance and elegance long before Harding and her supporters were implicated in the attack on Kerrigan during the 1994 U.S. National Championship.

Shari Lee Dworkin and Faye Linda Wachs explore a different form of "scandal": the public professions of HIV-positive status by basketball player Magic Johnson, diver Greg Louganis, and boxer Tommy Morrison. They show how self-identified heterosexual athletes Johnson and Morrison are framed differently than Louganis, whose gay identity is conflated with his HIV status. Placing their stories in juxtaposition clearly adds to our cultural understanding of the ways that HIV is mobilized within public discourses around sexuality, gender, race, and class.

Finally, Susan Birrell and Cheryl Cole explore the controversy over the entrance of Renee Richards into the women's professional tennis tour. As a male-to-constructed-female transsexual, Richards appears to confound bipolar notions of sex, gender, and sexuality. However, Birrell and Cole show how media representations of Richards end up naturalizing those differences instead, producing the male body as inherently superior. By tracing the lines of support and opposition to Richards, they also show how economic interests in the women's tennis tour work to consolidate masculine privilege.

Each of these essays offers a particular example of the ways that power relations are articulated through sport. In addition to the insights they lend to particular incidents and personalities, they also offer clues to strategies for reading sport critically.

Hints for Reading Sport

Everyone with any interest in sport "reads" sport in some way. For over a century we have had a daily site for the production of sport narratives called the sports page, and that central site has been joined over the years by television and radio broadcasts and commentary, the increasingly popular genre of autobiographies of sport figures, novels and films set in sport settings, web sites devoted to all forms of sport information and dialogue, and of course scholarly analyses of the world of sport. Even attending an event or talking about it to friends and colleagues constitutes a particular reading. "Reading sport" in the sense that we mean it here is built on a familiarity with these popular narratives. But as a methodology for cultural analysis, reading sport compels us to read in a different, more theoretically charged manner. The methodology of "reading" sport—that is, of finding the cultural meanings that circulate within narratives of particular incidents or celebrities—also requires critical attention to the ways that sexuality, race, gender, and class privileges are articulated in those accounts.

An awareness that multiple readings of events and celebrities are always available precedes all critical analyses. We never want to become so confident that we cast our own particular reading as the only authorized version and foreclose the possibility of other contradictory or complementary readings. All texts are polysemic and the site of contested meanings, whether they are seen as dominant, subversive, resistant, transformative, or appropriative. Reading sport critically can be used as a methodology for uncovering, foregrounding, and producing counternarratives, that is, alternative accounts of particular events and celebrities that have been decentered, obscured, and dismissed by hegemonic forces.

Relationships of power structured along the lines of gender, race, class, sexuality, age, religion, and ethnicity are present in all moments and we must search out the form they take in any particular incident. However, all these power relations are not present to the same extent in all incidents, and here our task is to craft an analysis that properly represents the relative salience of each line of power. All the selections in *Reading Sport* show an awareness of the interdependence of lines of power, however different authors necessarily weigh the impact of these relations in the particular incidents or celebrities they analyze, depending on the cultural moment in which the incident takes place.

All the essays are concerned with the reproduction of power through ideological means. The easiest way to get to ideology is through the media, surrounded as we are by mediated accounts and narratives. These include newspapers, magazines, television, radio, autobiographies and biographies, novels and films, documentaries, and other academic papers. The web is an increasingly important source of information. Generally, a reading should include a wide range of accounts, beginning with the mainstream accounts that appear on the wire services (AP, Gannett, Knight-Ridder), are picked up from prominent news agencies (the *New York Times*, the *Washington Post*), or are reprinted throughout the United States in the increasingly large number of local newspapers owned by an increasingly small number of media conglomerates. These accounts tend to be easiest to access, and one might argue that they are the sources most likely to be consulted by popular readers. However, alternative sources must always be included for the different perspective they offer. For example, Katherine Jamieson's article on Nancy Lopez successfully contrasts the mainstream treatment of Lopez with her characterization in two Latino publications. But, of course, all texts are not produced by the media; we can read many aspects of culture as a text, including for example Dennis Rodman's fashion statements, Tonya Harding's athletic body, and the New England Patriots' locker room.

Particular controversial incidents are good points of entry for analysis because they appear to be contained within particular time frames, thus making the initial collection of accounts a more focused task. However, the meanings these events produce are never settled, and they continue to generate new narratives and new meanings. In a similar vein, the cult of celebrity produces personalities who garner significant attention within sport. Dennis Rodman's exuberant presence demands attention since he enters our consciousness constructed—by himself as well as others, as Lafrance and Rail show—as a bad boy. In contrast, Nolan Ryan is an example of how good analyses can make "the familiar strange." Because he is a white, heterosexual man, his race, class, and gender are made invisible. His status is used to confirm silently the "normality" of those identities.

The controversies centered on athletes also require critical analysis. Tonya Harding and Nancy Kerrigan were certainly thrust onto center stage during the Olympics; the double murder case of O. J. Simpson required us to reread the O. J. previously constructed as a hero for whites; and Lisa Olson brought us into the locker room to see the sorts of violent masculine rituals at home there. Their stories require the sort of critical attention Feder-Kane, Stoloff, Johnson and Roediger, and Disch and Kane provide.

Events and celebrities need to be read within their political and historical context. The keys to why a particular event happened at this particular point in time and in this particular place might lie in local politics or in the larger cultural contexts that surround it. In the essays contained in *Reading Sport*, for example, understandings are located within the ideological territory of Reagan conservatism (for example, Andrews), the backlash against women (for example, Disch and Kane), and the economic logics of particular sports. Protecting the women's tennis tour figures in the Renee Richards story; Nancy Lopez is inspected for her impact on golf; and the interests of baseball and basketball are protected by Nolan Ryan and Michael Jordan.

We also need to ask what the dominant framing of particular incidents does in ideological terms. How and why are celebrities made to matter culturally? Examining different accounts of incidents can serve as a point of entry into an analysis of the source itself. How do sources differ from one another, for example, in terms of the central frame used to explain the story? More important, why do they differ as they do? For this reason, it is important to know the background of these sources. How do particular authors or sportscasters tend to present issues or personalities? Who owns the newspaper syndicate, the television network, or the movie studio producing particular narratives? Who owns the products that these athletes endorse? What is at stake for them in the production and circulation of some narratives rather than others? Who benefits?

Taken as a whole, these essays demonstrate that the cultural stakes surrounding sport are greater than they may at first appear. For what is at stake is not just sport as we know it—not just basketball, baseball, women's tennis, or figure skating—but hegemonic masculinity, heteronormativity, economic power, and white privilege.

Notes

1. For an extended discussion of the ontological and epistemological issues that underlie this approach, see Mary G. McDonald and Susan Birrell, "Reading Sport Critically: A Methodology for Interrogating Power," *Sociology of Sport Journal* 16:4 (1999). Some of the ideas in that paper are repeated in this section.

2. *Reading Sport* focuses primarily on the power relations of race, class, gender, and sexuality within U.S. culture. This represents the focus within sport studies in general.

1

NICK TRUJILLO

Hegemonic Masculinity on the Mound
Media Representations of Nolan Ryan and American Sports Culture

● Baseball pitcher Nolan Ryan, in his mid-forties, has become a national phenomenon. Although his major league baseball career spans over twenty-five years, he has received considerable publicity in the last few years following his seventh no-hitter in 1991, his three hundredth victory in 1990, and his five thousandth strikeout in 1989. With national endorsements for Advil, Bic, Nike, Wrangler Jeans, and Major League Baseball itself, he also has become a prominent sports celebrity. Sportswriters have called him "the ageless wonder," "a living legend," "miracle man," and "the last real sports hero."

This essay examines print and television representations of Nolan Ryan as an illustration of how images of male athletes are reproduced in American culture. Specifically, I argue that the media have functioned hegemonically by personifying Ryan as an archetypal male athletic hero. In the next section, I present five distinguishing features of hegemonic masculinity and discuss the general role of mediated sport in reinforcing these features. Following this, the mass media's role in reproducing these features is analyzed.

This essay originally appeared in *Critical Studies in Mass Communication* 8, 280–308. Used by permission of the National Communication Association.

Hegemonic Masculinity and American Sports Culture

As Connell (1990) defined it, *hegemonic masculinity* is "the culturally idealized form of masculine character" (83) which emphasizes "the connecting of masculinity to toughness and competitiveness" as well as "the subordination of women" and "the marginalization of gay men" (94). Connell argued that such an idealized form of masculinity becomes hegemonic when it is widely accepted in a culture and when that acceptance reinforces the dominant gender ideology of the culture. "Hegemonic masculinity," concluded Hanke (1990), "refers to the social ascendancy of a particular version or model of masculinity that, operating on the terrain of 'common sense' and conventional morality, defines 'what it means to be a man'" (232).

Distinguishing Features of Hegemonic Masculinity

Media critics and scholars of gender ideology have described at least five features of hegemonic masculinity in American culture: (1) physical force and control, (2) occupational achievement, (3) familial patriarchy, (4) frontiersmanship, and (5) heterosexuality (see Brod 1987; Connell 1990; Jeffords 1989; Yaufman 1987; Kimmel 1987a).

First, masculinity is hegemonic when power is defined in terms of physical force and control. According to Connell (1983), "force and competence are . . . translations into the language of the body of the social relations which define men as holders of power, women as subordinate [and] this is one of the main ways in which the superiority of men becomes 'naturalized'" (28). In this way, the male body comes to represent power, and power itself is masculinized as physical strength, force, speed, control, toughness, and domination (Komisar 1980; Messner 1988, 1990).

Second, masculinity is hegemonic when it is defined through occupational achievement in an industrial capitalistic society (Ochberg 1987; Tolson 1977; Whyte 1956). Work itself can become defined along gender lines. "Hegemony closely involves the division of labor," wrote Carrigan, Connell, and Lee (1987), "the social definition of tasks as either 'men's work' or 'women's work,' and the definition of some kinds of work as more masculine than others" (94).

Third, masculinity is also hegemonic as patriarchy, "the manifestation

15

and institutionalization of male dominance over women and children in the family and the extension of male dominance over women in society in general" (Lerner 1986, 239). Traditionally, such patriarchal representations include males as "breadwinners," "family protectors," and "strong father figures" whereas females are "housewives . . . sexual objects," and "nurturing mothers." In fact, Segal (1990) argued that modern representations of the so-called "sensitive father" have remained hegemonic insofar as "the contemporary revalorization of fatherhood has enabled many men to have the best of both worlds" because "they are more involved in what was once the exclusive domain of women but, especially in relation to children, they are sharing its pleasures more than its pains" (58). (See also Hearn 1987; Pleck 1987).

Fourth, masculinity is hegemonic as symbolized by the daring, romantic frontiersman of yesteryear and of the present-day outdoorsman. Frederick Jackson Turner's so-called "frontier thesis" (Berquist 1971; Billington 1971; Carpenter 1977) argues that the general U.S. image is so defined. In this context, the *cowboy* stands very tall as an archetypal image reproduced and exploited in literature, film, and advertising (Cawelti 1976; Kimmel 1987b; Maynard 1974; Rushing 1983). As reconstructed in media representations of the western genre, the cowboy is a *white* male with working-class values (see Wright 1975).

Finally, masculinity is hegemonic when heterosexually defined. Rubin (1985) refers to the "sex hierarchy" and predictably, the type of sexuality that rules "is 'good,' 'normal,' and 'natural' . . . 'heterosexual, marital, monogamous, reproductive, and non-commercial' " (280). Thus, hegemonic *male* sexuality "embodies personal characteristics [which] are manifest by adult males through exclusively social relationships with men and primarily sexual relationships with women" and it "requires not being effeminate (a "sissy") in physical appearance or mannerisms; not having relationships with men that are sexual or overly intimate; and not failing in sexual relationships with women" (Herek 1987, 72–73).

Symbolism of male sexuality has received considerable attention from media critics (see Duncan 1990; Dyer 1985; Fiske 1987; Segal 1990) and not surprisingly, much of this symbolism is thought to center on the penis as "the symbol of male potency . . . that appears to legitimate male power" (Dyer 1985, 31). As Fiske (1987) argued, "the phallus is a cultural construct:

it bears a culture's meanings of masculinity and attempts to naturalize them by locating them in the physical sign of maleness—the penis" (210).

Mediated Sport and Hegemonic Masculinity

Perhaps no single institution in American culture has influenced our sense of masculinity more than sport. Throughout our history, dominant groups have successfully persuaded many Americans to believe that sport builds manly character, develops physical fitness, realizes order, promotes justice, and even prepares young men for war (see Dubbert 1979). More recently, American football's hostile takeover of the more pastoral baseball as our "national pastime" has reinforced a form of masculinity which emphasizes sanctioned aggression, (para)militarism, the technology of violence, and other patriarchal values (Real 1975, 1989). The corporatization of sports also has provided far more opportunities for male participants than for female participants and has placed far more emphasis on marginalizing women as cheerleaders, spectators, and advertising images. Indeed, Naison's (1972) conclusion twenty years ago still applies: "as long as the social relations of contemporary capitalism generate a need for violent outlets and a vicarious experience of mastery in American men, the corporations will be glad to finance the sports industry and mold it in their own image" (115).

The mass media, as key benefactors of institutionalized sports (see Jhally 1989), have thus been a powerful site for fashioning hegemony. "Sports tend to be presented in the media," wrote Hargreaves (1982), "as symbolic representations of a particular kind of social order, so that in effect they become modern morality plays, serving to justify and uphold dominant values and ideas" (128). For example, scholars have demonstrated that mediated sports reaffirm mainstream values such as teamwork, competition, individualism, nationalism, achievement, and others (see Duncan 1983; Real 1989; Trujillo and Ekdom 1985).

Media representations of sport reproduce and reaffirm the features of hegemonic masculinity described earlier in important ways. Media representations of sport privilege these features of masculinity when they emphasize these features or link them positively with cultural values and when they ignore and/or condemn alternative features of opposing gender ideologies on preferences such as feminism or homosexuality (see Bennett, Whitaker, Woolley Smith, and Sablove 1987; Bryson 1987). Media representations of sport naturalize hegemonic masculinity when they depict its features as conventional or acceptable and depict alternatives to it as unconventional or deviant (see Nelson 1980; Wernick 1987; Whitson 1990). Finally, media representations of sport personalize hegemonic masculinity when they elevate individuals who embody its features as role models or heroes worthy of adoration and emulation and when they castigate individuals who do not (see Hargreaves 1982, 1986). "To be culturally exalted, the pattern of masculinity must have exemplars who are celebrated as heroes" (Connell 1990, 94). In Texas Ranger pitcher Nolan Ryan, the mass media have found an exemplar to celebrate as a hero and they have reinforced hegemonic masculinity through him in several ways.

Reproducing Hegemonic Masculinity Through Nolan Ryan

Nolan Ryan's major league baseball career has spanned over twenty-five years as he has played for the New York Mets (1966–1971), the California Angels (1972–1979), the Houston Astros (1980–1988), and the Texas Rangers (1989–present). Although Ryan was publicized throughout his career, he became a media hero and celebrity in recent years; he also has become a striking image of American masculinity as well.

This analysis is based on an examination of over 250 articles in popular print media including newspapers (e.g., *New York Times, Los Angeles Times, Houston Post, Dallas Morning News,* and others) and magazines (general ones such as *Life, Time,* and *Gentlemen's Quarterly,* and sports-oriented ones such as *Sport, Sports Illustrated,* and *Sporting News).* The dates of these print materials span the period from 1965, the year before Ryan made his major league debut with the Mets, to 1991, the year Ryan pitched his seventh no-hitter at the age of forty-four. I also examined over one hundred local (Dallas, Texas) and national television news reports, videotaped during the time Ryan first signed with the Texas Rangers until the summer of 1990. Finally, I examined over thirty print and television advertisements featuring Ryan, most of which appeared in the last few years.

Pitching with Power: Ryan as the Embodiment of Male Athleticism

Media representations of Nolan Ryan have reaffirmed the power of the male body. Throughout his career, Ryan has been described as a "power pitcher." Early media coverage during Ryan's career with the Mets focused on his unique ability to throw the ball with force. The *New York Times* characterized him as "the rookie pitcher with the cannonball serve" (Durso 1968, 24) while the *Sporting News* labeled him the "Texas flame-thrower" (Lang 1968, 26). A *Life* magazine article revealed that Ryan had "a fast ball that has been described as faster than Bob Feller's (98.6 mph)—the fastest ever timed" ("Brine for Nolan Ryan" 1968, 78). These earlier articles suggest that Ryan embodied the force of male athletic power.

However, although Ryan had the force, he did not have control. (See Connell's (1983) distinction.) He was described in the *New York Times* as the "tall, slim Texan . . . who has not yet mastered control and consistency" ("These are the Mets" 1969, 57) and "as wild as the spinning Black Dragon ride at Astroworld" (Chass 1970, 59). Reporters presented this lack of control as a challenge to Ryan's athletic success. If Ryan could not control his ability, his "heat" would be just a "flash in the pan" and he would fail as many fastball pitchers had failed before him.

Ryan, though, would not achieve success with the Mets. On December 10, 1971, he was traded to the California Angels. In a *Los Angeles Times* report, Angels general manager Harry Dalton used synecdoche to emphasize Ryan's promise: "We've obtained the best arm in the National League and one of the best in baseball. We know Ryan has had control problems, but at twenty-four he may be ready to come into his own" (Newhan 1971, 3, part III). At this point, Ryan was disembodied power; he was "the best arm" in baseball who might develop into someone complete.

With the Angels, Ryan developed enough control to win and set several pitching records. With success, his status as power pitcher was embellished by the sports media. One feature in *Sports Illustrated* documented that a group of Rockwell scientists timed his pitches during a game at speeds of 100.8 and 100.9 miles per hour, the fastest pitches *ever* recorded (Fimrite 1974). His dominance over batters was ritualized in sportspage clichés, as when power-hitter Reggie Jackson said this about Ryan: "He's faster than instant coffee. He's faster than a speeding bullet and more powerful than a locomotive. He throws wall-to-wall heat" (Newhan 1972, 1, part III). And stories about Ryan's power took on a mythological significance as well, as when a feature in the *Saturday Evening Post*, titled "Nolan Ryan: Whoosh!" made a direct case: "All the while he was leaving a trail of incidents that formed a legend—or myth. The day he tried out with the Mets before signing, his fastball broke through the hands of catcher John Stephenson and broke his collarbone. At Williamsport, Pennsylvania, he bounced a warmup pitch in front of the plate and gave catcher Duffy Dyer a concussion. Not with a fastball, but with a changeup" (Jacobson 1974, 16). Ryan's power—manifested in his force and, in part, in his ability to hurt people—was celebrated as baseball mythology.

In his later years with the Astros and Rangers, Ryan still was portrayed as a fast, power pitcher. One feature in *Gentlemen's Quarterly* put it this way: Ryan "is grateful he can remain true to his singular purpose, which is to rear back, show his numbers and throw a baseball that becomes, in its flight, the approximate size of a ball bearing" (Hoffer 1988, 292).

With age also came media reconstruction of other features of Ryan's masculinity. One article in the *Dallas Morning News*, titled "Pitching with Pain Not New to Ryan," told readers that Ryan had pitched his sixth no-hitter with a stress fracture in his back but that because of his "will power" he was able to "block it out" (Fraley 1990, 6B). A feature in *Sport* magazine even reconstructed his toughness as a child, quoting his mother: " 'I remember when we first came to Alvin, this young wife, a friend of ours, kept pestering me to take Nolan to the doctor,' says his mother, 'because he didn't cry enough' " (Furlong 1980, 68).

Although he came to be portrayed as a complete pitcher, some writers continued to disembody his power. Features in *Gentlemen's Quarterly* (Hoffer 1988) and *Life* (Brewster 1989) presented photographs of Ryan's disembodied right arm; in the former feature, past Dodger pitcher Don Sutton described Ryan's arm as a weapon, as "a howitzer" (Hoffer 1988, 292). Correspondent Dick Schaap concluded his *NBC Evening News* report about Ryan's five thousandth strikeout on August 23, 1989, by providing the length of the appendage: "Nolan Ryan's arm is thirty-five inches long. It will fit perfectly in the Hall of Fame." An article in the *New York Post* noted that Ryan was "blessed with the most remarkable arm in the history of the game" but it cut off his legs as well: "Ryan has a pair of tree trunk legs that supply a great deal of the power behind his fastball" (Hecht 1983, 102). Even in the end, the force—the essence of Ryan's power—remained disembodied.

Pitching Records and Pitching Products: Ryan as Capitalist Worker

If sport and work independently play a role in producing hegemonic masculinity as some have suggested (Fiske 1987), then the construction of sport *as work* is even more powerful. The mass media represent sport as work in at least three ways. First, mediated sport reaffirms the Protestant work ethic. "Athletes," wrote Sadler (1976), "often are aware that what they do is not play. Their practice sessions are workouts; and to win the game they have to work harder" (245). Second, as in American society, there is in sport an overemphasis on success as occupational achievement, defined (and quantified) in terms of team victories and individual records. If "achievement and successful performance (the primary definers of masculinity) are the fundamental requirements of capitalism," as Fiske (1987, 210) argued, then sport is a key arena for displaying exemplars of successful and unsuccessful men in a capitalist society. Finally, sport is commodified inasmuch as leagues, teams, and individual athletes are sold as commodities in a competitive marketplace (see Brohm 1978; Jhally 1989; Rigauer 1981).

Media coverage of Nolan Ryan has reinforced all of these features and, as such, he has been reproduced as a successful male worker in an industrial capitalist society. First, Ryan's work ethic has been exalted throughout his career. When he enjoyed early success with the Angels, one *Sports Illustrated* story quoted former player and then coach, John Roseboro, as saying: "There is no pitcher in baseball today who is in better shape than Nolan Ryan. He knows what work is, and he works" (Leggett 1973, 27). Then, as he continued to achieve success as a power pitcher in his later years, his work ethic was reified in vivid detail when publications such as *Newsweek* and the *Dallas Morning News* printed his entire "rigid workout routine" (see Givens 1989; Ringolsby 1990). Ryan's commitment to this workout was described as so regimented that a *USA Today* reporter wrote that even after throwing his sixth no-hitter, "Ryan was riding the

stationary bicycle in the middle of the Rangers' clubhouse" as "his teammates were either fastening their ties, drinking another beer or driving
back to the hotel. . . . 'You don't deviate from your routine,' he said"
(Shea 1990, 8C).

Second, Ryan's success has been quantified in records of individual
achievement. The Texas Rangers 1991 Media Guide states that Ryan has
set or tied 48 major league records (see Texas Rangers 1991, 71–91). Most
of these records involve two categories of athletic dominance: no-hitters
and strikeouts.

The no-hitter is one of the most dominating forms of pitching performance over athletic opponents. Ryan achieved his record seventh no-
hitter in 1991 at the age of forty-four; Sandy Koufax is second on the list
with four. Ryan's no-hitters were celebrated in media accounts and with
each one, the lore of previous no-hitters grew in significance. One sportswriter for the *New York Times* retold the story of his second no-hitter—
against the Tigers in 1973—on the occasion of his fourth one—against the
Orioles in 1975: "With two outs in the ninth, Norm Cash of the Detroit
Tigers strolled up to the plate in surrender. Instead of a bat, he was carry-
ing a broken-off piano leg. He even got into the batter's box with it before
glancing back at Ron Luciano, the umpire." (Anderson 1975, 39). Through
coverage of Ryan's no-hitters, the media defined complete dominance
over others as ultimate occupational success.

Ryan's strikeout achievements also were praised as records of dominance, especially his record five thousandth strikeout on August 21, 1989,
against Rickie Henderson of the Oakland Athletics. Stories about this
milestone appeared on national news broadcasts and in major daily newspapers across the country while Texas papers published separate sections
with stories, color posters, and "K" sign inserts; *Sports Illustrated* even
ran a complete list of Ryan's 1,061 separate strikeout victims ("K" 1989).
Reporters used testimony from baseball luminaries as well as unknown
fans in attendance to corroborate the historic nature of the five thousandth strikeout; for example, the front page of the *Dallas Times Herald*
quoted a nine-year-old boy, who said, "I'll probably tell my grandchildren
it was the most exciting thing that ever happened in my life" (Henderson
1989, A-1). A report in the *Fort Worth Star-Telegram* indicated that President Bush, father of Rangers owner George W. Bush, watched the game

on television and it published the full text of Bush's brief address which was played on the ballpark's Diamond Vision screen after the milestone strikeout (and which represented state support of Ryan's domination): "Congratulations Nolan Ryan. What an amazing achievement. Indeed, everybody that loves baseball pays tribute to you on this very special record-breaking occasion. Well done, my friend. Well done, my noble friend" ("President's Message" 1989, 6, section 3).

Although all of Ryan's milestone achievements of domination were exalted, some sportswriters still charged that he was mediocre in terms of the occupational bottom line—the win-loss column. For example, Ryan's career record after the 1979 season with the Angels was 167–159; when Ryan became a free agent that year after he and Angels general manager Buzzi Bavasi failed to agree on a new contract, Bavasi told *Los Angeles Times* reporters that he could replace Ryan "with two 8–7 pitchers," a sarcastic reference to Ryan's 16–14 record in 1979 (Littwin 1980, 1, part III); in the same article, the reporter himself critiqued Ryan with the statement, "He's won numerous battles but he keeps losing the war" (Littwin 1980, 1, part III).

In fact, ultimate occupational achievement eluded Ryan until later in his career when, on July 31, 1990, at age forty-three, he won his three hundredth game, becoming only the twentieth pitcher in history to do so. The Associated Press story on Ryan's victory over the Milwaukee Brewers began with this lead: "Nolan Ryan, a pitcher defined by great numbers, finally got the number that defines great pitchers" (see "No. 300" 1990, E1). A reporter for the *Dallas Morning News,* commenting on Ryan's critics, wrote that "No. 300 cuts their vocal chords" (Horn 1990, 2H); a columnist for the same newspaper wrote that Ryan's three hundredth win "represents a triumphant and unarguable validation of the man and his heroic career" (Casstevens 1990, 2B); another columnist for the same newspaper went even further: "God is good. But Nolan Ryan may be better" (Galloway 1990b, 1B). His status as a successful male achiever at last was confirmed. Even so, Ryan's life-long quest for success epitomized the paradox of masculinity in a capitalist society that Fiske (1987) described when he wrote that "men are cast into ceaseless work and action to prove their worth" such that "masculinity becomes almost a definition of the superhuman, so it becomes that which can never [at least rarely] be achieved" (210).

Finally, Ryan has been represented as a valuable commodity with instrumental impacts on his teams. A *Sports Illustrated* feature on Ryan called him "an Angel who makes turnstiles sing" (Leggett 1973, 26).[1] Yankee-owner George Steinbrenner, quoted in *Sports Illustrated,* called Ryan "one of the most desirable quantities in baseball" (Keith 1979, 34). Reporters then bragged for Ryan when he signed with the Astros as the first million-dollar free agent to become "not only the best-paid player in the history of baseball but one of the best paid players in the history of team sports"—at least in 1980 (Furlong 1980, 66).

Reporters bragged for Ryan and his earning power in part because they represented him as a humble, honest man who was not preoccupied with money, unlike many other athletes who have been depicted as greedy, selfish men. One article in the *Sporting News,* titled "Ryan raps pay preoccupation," quoted Ryan, who then was making $125,000, as saying that he had "never seen a ballplayer worth even $250,000" and that he himself was "not bugged over money" because "I feel I have all I can do to keep my mind on conditioning and on pitching" (Durslag 1976, 12). Years later when the Rangers exercised their option to keep Ryan for the 1990 season at an under-market-value of $1.4 million, reporters commended Ryan's refusal to renegotiate as other athletes would have done; as he was quoted in one newspaper report: "That signature on your contract is the same as your word" (Galloway 1990a, IB). Reporters also reinforced Ryan's commodification of himself as an endorser and entrepreneur when they wrote that he was "a good spokesman" because "he uses the products he talks about" (Baldwin 1990, IA) and that he was a smart businessman who recently bought a bank and then "sat in on loan meetings" and "formulated bank policy" (Montville 1991, 124).

In sum, as the media juxtaposed Ryan's values of hard work and modesty with his achievements and his earning power, they reaffirmed his identity as a successful businessman and reinforced the Protestant Ethic and system of American capitalism itself. Ryan has been represented as one who proves the system does work, at least for hard-working men.

Father Throws Best: Ryan as Family Patriarch

The media have reaffirmed hegemonic representations of male-female relations in the family as they have described the relationship between, and respective roles of, Nolan and Ruth Ryan. Predictably, the media chose to present Nolan as the breadwinner. One story in the *Saturday Evening Post* told of the struggles of Nolan early in his career to support the family: "The first year they were married [in 1967], Nolan made $1,200 a month for six months and worked in an air-conditioning shop the other six" (Jacobson 1974, 124). Ryan also has been portrayed as the protecting husband; one reporter for the *New York Daily News* even reconstructed the Mets' trade that sent Ryan to California as motivated by the "fact" that "Ryan personally requested a trade because—says a Mets insider—he feared for the safety of his lovely wife in New York" (Lang 1984, C26).

In contrast, reporters have chosen to cast Ruth Ryan as the attractive woman *behind* the man. Reporters wrote that Ruth chose not to (or failed to) develop her own career interests; one article in the *Dallas Morning News* quoted Ruth's own admission: "I tried to go to college. I tried to keep up with my tennis and my ballet at first. . . . Some of the other wives I knew in baseball tried, but it just didn't work" (Harasta 1990, 17H). Reporters objectified her as the beautiful wife. Finally, reporters wrote that Ruth has experienced satisfaction through Nolan's pitching; one columnist for the *Houston Post* also suggested that she would be lost without Nolan's baseball: " 'At times I get really tired of the hectic pace,' Ruth admits. 'Then I think about how much I would miss it, if he retired, and what I would do when spring training rolls around' " (Herskowitz 1990, B-15).

In these ways, the media reaffirmed the gender-based divisions of labor in the traditional American family through Nolan and Ruth Ryan and they naturalized this division of labor by presenting Nolan and Ruth as the ideal couple. "After twenty-three years, the man is still married to his high school sweetheart," confirmed a *Sports Illustrated* reporter, who then spoke for them when he wrote: "The idea of staying married never came to debate. Why not? Isn't that what you're supposed to do? The idea of raising a family was ingrained. Wasn't that what our parents did?" (Montville 1991, 128).

Additionally, the media reaffirmed the hegemony of family patriarchy by glorifying Nolan's role as actual and symbolic father. The media have emphasized Ryan's relationship with his two sons while they have deemphasized his relationship with his daughter. Dallas station KTVT's live television coverage of Ryan's sixth no-hitter against Oakland on June 11, 1990 focused in as the youngest son Reese, in a little Ranger uniform, sat next to Nolan in the dugout, rubbing his dad's back, which, as later was reported, had a stress fracture. During the 1991 pre-season, Ryan pitched against his eldest son Reid, who then was a freshman for the University of Texas, in an exhibition game. One article in the sports pages of *Austin American-Statesman,* subtitled "Father throws best," noted that "mom Ruth threw out the ceremonial first pitch, her 'nervous fastball' " (Wangrin 1991, C7); however, another article on the front page of the same newspaper deified father Nolan's relationship with his eldest son: "The serious baseball crowd sat huddled against an intermittent evening breeze, watching father and son, concentrating, straining to see if they could detect the signs of greatness passing from the right hand of the father to that of his son" (Johnson 1991, A12).

Ryan also has been represented as the *symbolic* father. "Ryan is providing stability and quiet leadership" to the "young, home-produced talent" of the Angels, wrote one reporter in *Newsweek* (Axthelm 1975, 59). Years later, a report in *Time* extended the father metaphor more specifically: "His second family is the Ranger teammates, who mobbed him after the [sixth] no-hitter. Because some of them were barely in Pampers when Ryan first pitched for the Mets in 1966, the scene also suggested a Father's Day celebration—a bunch of baseball's children swarming around the grandest old man in the game" (Corliss 1990, 68). One *Sports Illustrated* feature revealed that former Astro teammate Harry Spilman "is one of 10 current or former teammates who have named a son after Nolan" (Montville 1991, 127); on Father's Day (June 16), 1991, ESPN "SportsCenter" aired a report which offered video proof of these little Ryans. In these and other ways, the media have reproduced Nolan Ryan as the archetypal husband and father and, in so doing, they have reaffirmed the hegemony of patriarchy.

Castrating Steers in the Off-season: Ryan as Baseball Cowboy

Throughout his career, Nolan Ryan has been portrayed as a rural cowboy who symbolizes the frontiersmen of American history. According to many reports, he grew up and still lives in rural Alvin, Texas (Jacobson 1974; Montville 1991). One feature in the society pages of the *Dallas Morning News* regaled viewers with Ryan's predictable favorites: his favorite music ("country-western"), his personal transportation ("a pickup"), and his hero ("John Wayne") (Jennings 1989, 2E).

Given Ryan's rural Texas roots, the mythic West gave reporters grist for coverage and colorization. The day that Ryan had his first match-up against fastball pitcher and native Texan Roger Clemens of the Boston Red Sox on April 30, 1991, a CNN "SportsNight" sportscaster described the game in his aired report as "the Shootout at the O.K. Corral in the lone star state" where "a native Texan who had taken his blazing arm to New England" was "back in town to face the fastest draw the game has ever known, also a native son." The night that Ryan achieved his seventh no-hitter on May 1, 1991, an ESPN sportscaster described Ryan in this way in his aired report: "He's John Wayne." Of course, as a recent *Sports Illustrated* feature quoted Ryan's longtime friend and business partner, "in Texas he is bigger than John Wayne right now" (Montville 1991, 124).

Advertisers, too, have cashed in on the Western motif. One advertisement for Wrangler Jeans pictures Ryan on the mound, holding a baseball in his right hand and wearing a baseball glove on his left hand, but he is wearing a cowboy hat and Wrangler Jeans; the caption reads: "A Western original wears a Western original" *(Dallas Times Herald,* August 23, 1989, C-10).

However, Ryan is not merely a metaphorical cowboy for stories and advertising: he has been described as a "real cowboy" who owns and works three cattle ranches with hundreds of registered "Beefmaster" cattle. "Ryan is no gentleman rancher," wrote one reporter in a *Sports Illustrated* feature accompanied by several pictures of Ryan riding horseback on his ranch. "In the off-season, he's on horseback, riding herd, 'getting kicked, stomped, and hooked' " (Fimrite 1986, 92). His ranch manager gave more impressive testimony in another *Sports Illustrated* feature, again accompanied by color photos of Ryan in chaps and on horseback: "He helps us castrate the steers, dehorn 'em, everything. Nothing fazes him. I'll see him reach into the chute with that million dollar right arm and I'll say to myself, 'Are you sure you want to do that?' But he'll never buckle" (Montville 1991, 124).

Reporters have used Ryan's status as real and metaphorical cowboy to represent his commitment to several mainstream values of rural America. Unlike another image of the cowboy who, as Kimmel (1987b) wrote, "must move on . . . unhampered by clinging women and whining children" (239), Ryan has been the devoted husband and father, as described in the last section. Representations of his toughness, his hard work ethic, and his fairness also were described earlier. In addition, reporters have written that he is *unassuming.* "As we say in Texas, he is as common as dirt," said his high school principal in a *USA Today* article (Tom 1985, 2C). They have written that he is *loyal.* "Has anyone ever heard him knock a manager, a teammate, an owner, anyone?" asked a columnist from the *Houston Post* (Herskowitz 1988, C-1). And they have written that he is *wholesome:* after his fourth no-hitter, a reporter for the *Los Angeles Times* revealed that "Ryan, who seldom drinks, turned down a glass [of champagne] and said he would celebrate by taking Ruth out for a quiet dinner" (Newhan 1975, 6, part III). In a rare sports-related editorial, the *Dallas Morning News* published this tribute the day of Ryan's five thousandth strikeout:

> Unfortunately, in these times of pill poppers and gamblers, the private lives of too many ballplayers in all sports are hardly fit for prime time. A towering exception is Mr. Ryan. From work habits that have kept his middle-aged muscles fighting trim, to a clean-cut personal life straight out of the rural Texas he loves, Mr. Ryan is a hero for all ages ("Striking example" 1989, 14A).

In short, Ryan has been reproduced as the American hero who embodies the values of our frontier past. This reproduction may perform a bardic function by giving these idealized values a manifest form (Fiske and Hartley 1978) and may perform a compensatory function by helping audiences compensate "for the passing of the traditional dream of success" (Rader 1983, 11).

Finally, the rural cowboy of our frontier past usually is presented as a *white* male. Ryan's identity as a white male athlete was reaffirmed in a powerful, if indirect, way on the recent occasion of his seventh no-hitter on May 1, 1991. Earlier that day, Rickie Henderson of the Oakland Athletics broke Lou Brock's record for career stolen bases. Henderson, who epitomizes the "cool pose" of the inner-city black athlete (see Majors 1986) with his brash, display-oriented demeanor, pumped his fists above his head and, as play was interrupted, told the crowd over a microphone: "Lou Brock was a symbol of great base stealing. But today, I am the greatest of all time" ("A day when" 1991, 6).

Later that same night, Ryan achieved his seventh no-hitter and then told reporters: "This no-hitter is the most rewarding because it was in front of these hometown fans who have supported me since I have been here. This one was for them" ("A day when" 1991, 6).

In the days following these two milestones, sports writers—most of whom are middle-class, white men (see Edwards 1976; Johnston 1979; McCleneghan 1990)—focused their attention on how the two star athletes handled their achievements (see Bodley 1991; Boswell 1991; Lopresti 1991). The *Sporting News* presented the most revealing critique in an editorial ("A day when" 1991). "Too bad Henderson couldn't have handled his moment of renown with similar decorum," read the editorial. "It was a day when Henderson and Ryan displayed two forms of speed, but only one man exhibited class" (6). Although writers of this editorial and of the other stories did not ever mention the race of the two athletes and probably did not intend such metacommentary, they presented an implicit reaffirmation that the hegemonic masculinity embodied by Ryan's white, rural, mainstream values is preferable to the masculinity represented by the counterculture "cool pose" of the black, inner-city athlete. Simply stated, when white reporters exalt white athletes and castigate black athletes, they reinforce racial hegemony whether they intend to or not.

Wearing Balls in His Holster: Ryan as a (Hetero) Sexual Being

In general, "sport," Segal (1990) argued, "provides the commonest contemporary source of male imagery" inasmuch as "the acceptable male image suggests—in its body's pose, its clothes and general paraphernalia—

muscles, hardness, action" (89). In particular, Nolan Ryan has been reproduced as an acceptable image of male sexuality.

Throughout his career, some sports reporters have commented *directly* on Ryan's physical attractiveness. Early in Ryan's career, sportswriter
Ron Fimrite of *Sports Illustrated* described him in this way: "Ryan is tall,
slender, deceptively strong, and certainly one of the handsomest men in
sports—a natural born hero" (1974, 100). One year later, Fimrite (1975)
was even more specific: "Ryan wears his hair short and neatly trimmed
and is a tidy, unflashy dresser, unlike the many peacocks in modern
sports. He is an uncommonly handsome young man with near-perfect
features and a long, lean physique. With his good looks, lanky build and
Texas drawl, he would seem a natural for Western roles in Hollywood"
(36). Ten years later, the same writer included Ryan's high school picture
with the caption: "Most Handsome Senior" (Fimrite 1986, 94). In these
descriptions and images, this white, middle-aged sportswriter directly reaffirmed an image of hegemonic male sexuality, positioning it against
other nontraditional images of male sexuality embodied by flashier sports
"peacocks."

Dave Anderson (1978), another white, middle-aged sportswriter, disclosed this telling revelation when he described Ryan's unnoticed appearance at a restaurant early in his career with the Angels: " 'Table for Ryan,'
he told the hostess. 'Oh, yes, Mr. Ryan,' the hostess, a young brunette,
replied with hardly a glance at the man who is surely one of the most
handsome in baseball. 'Right this way, please.' The waitress, a young
blonde, did not seem to recognize him either. Neither did anybody at the
other tables, not even any of the dozen teenage girls enjoying a birthday
party" (1978, 69).

In this example, the white, middle-aged sportswriter presented a preferred image of male sexuality; however, he revealed unwittingly that the
preference was *his own.* Ryan's physical attractiveness is seen *only* by this
male sportswriter, not by the young blonde or brunette women or by the
teenage girls.

The homoerotic (and narcissistic) implications of these examples notwithstanding, it is unusual for male sportswriters to comment directly on
the physical attractiveness of most male athletes (though they often comment on the attractiveness of many female athletes; see Duncan 1990).

However, in his representation as a wholesome, monogamous, heterosexual, white man, Ryan serves as an acceptable sexual image whose physical attractiveness can be discussed by white male reporters without much risk. Stated differently, Nolan Ryan is a *safe sex symbol,* one that is much safer for white male sportswriters to comment on directly than are white playboys, black beasts, gay blades, and other alternative images (see Hoch 1979; Segal 1990).

As they are wont to do, advertisers have capitalized on Ryan's image of safe sexuality. Some print and television advertisements, including those for Advil, Duracell Batteries, Southwest Airlines, Starter Apparel, and Whataburger, are relatively asexual insofar as they simply show Ryan in his baseball uniform and make reference to his status and athleticism as a major league pitcher. However, other advertisements seem more sexual in their orientation. For example, Ryan wore a fine tailored suit in the BizMart print advertisements (see Baldwin 1990) while he wore a *tuxedo* in the Bic network television advertisements. In the Wrangler Jeans print advertisements, he wears tight-fitting jeans, a cowboy shirt, a cowboy hat, and cowboy boots. Most strikingly, a recent print advertisement for Nike Air in *Sports Illustrated* presents a close-up of Ryan's face and pitching hand, but the top of his balding head is cut out of the picture and his face and hands are moistened so that they glisten in the sepia tones used to color the image. Although these and other images are not overtly sexual, they do reveal the choices that advertisers have made in an effort to exploit Ryan's physical appearance to sell their products.

Perhaps the most intriguing use of sexual imagery can be found in a poster, titled "Texas Ranger," distributed by Nike (see MacCormack 1989). The poster shows Ryan standing in the middle of a dirt street on a Western set: A saddled horse is behind him on his right and a wooden derrick for a water or oil well is behind him on his left, near a sign which reads "Pride, Texas." Ryan is dressed in a white Ranger baseball uniform and his feet are safely on a pitching "rubber." However, Ryan is wearing a long leather overcoat over his uniform and instead of a baseball cap, he is wearing a cowboy hat. Most impressively, Ryan is wearing a holster below his baseball uniform belt; but instead of wearing guns in this holster, he is wearing baseballs, one on each side, though they are not quite symmetrically hung.

For those who are inclined to interpret phallic symbolism, Ryan's "Texas Ranger" poster is fertile with possibilities. Some could interpret the long derrick at Ryan's left, placed next to the "Pride, Texas" sign, as a fairly obvious phallic symbol. Others might see Ryan's hat, especially the longer cowboy hat, as another. Others could see the not-quite-symmetrical baseballs placed in Ryan's holster as symbolic of testicles. Conspicuously absent from the holster is the gun, another phallic symbol, or "penile extender" as Fiske (1987, 210) called it (see also Dyer 1985; Shadoian 1977). But with a (base)ball on each side of his body and a rounded tip on the top of his head, the image is striking, even to those not seduced by psychoanalytic theory. Ryan is the gun; Ryan is the phallus.

"The promise of phallic power," argued Segal (1990), "is precisely this guarantee of total inner coherence, of an unbroken and unbreakable, an unquestioned and unquestionable masculinity (102). Ryan is the hard phallus, conditioned by years of rigorous exercise. He is a true phallus offered only to one woman, his beautiful and devoted wife. Perhaps most importantly, he is the middle-aged phallus with the power still to explode. As another Wrangler Jeans advertisement put it: "300 wins and he still hasn't lost the crease [or, by extension, the bulge] in his jeans" (*Dallas Morning News,* August 2, 1990, 18H). No small wonder that on the day after Ryan threw his sixth no-hitter at age forty-three, *USA Today* ran the front-page headline, "Great Day, To Be 43," and celebrated the fact that "nearly four million forty-three-year-olds woke up feeling young" (see Greene 1990).

In the final analysis, Nolan Ryan represents a white, middle-aged, upper-class, banker-athlete, with working-class cowboy values, who was raised by a middle-class family in a small rural town, and who is a strong father and devoted heterosexual husband. For white, middle-aged, middle-class, beer-drinking scribes interested in maintaining hegemonic masculinity, at least in mediated sports, it doesn't get any better than this.

Concluding Remarks

In professional sport, some challenges have been made to the dominant image of masculinity, including women's sports (especially women's tennis), the public presentation of gays and lesbians, such as tennis star

Martina Navratilova and umpire Dave Pallone (Pallone 1990), and charges of racism in sport such as those by former baseball star Henry Aaron (Aaron 1991). In addition, we have witnessed the demise of the homogeneous mass audience in recent decades and the rise of a fragmented audience composed of heterogenous groups with diverse values and media consumption habits. To the extent that hegemonic masculinity in sport and in other arenas of society continues to be contested by various groups, and to the extent that these various groups continue to constitute fragmented audiences, media critics should study the attempts made in reporting, broadcasting, and advertising to maintain hegemony.

The study of mediated sport should not be taken lightly as a category of academic trivial pursuit. As Bryson (1987) argued, feminists who ignore sport do so at their own peril because "sport is a powerful institution through which male hegemony is constructed and reconstructed and it is only through understanding and confronting these processes that we can hope to break this domination" (349); in fact, Bryson went so far as to say that "sport needs to be analyzed along with rape, pornography, and domestic violence as one of the means through which men monopolize physical force" (357).

Hegemonic masculinity in mediated sport also has negative consequences for men which should be analyzed and critiqued. As Sabo and Runfola (1980) advised, "in a world sadly consistent with the Hobbesian legacy, sports encourage men to forever compete with one another, never trusting and never feeling, and to regard women as frail underlings who are far removed from the panoply of patriarchical pugnacity and privilege" (334–335). Critics should continue to examine how the mass media aid in reproducing these and other values.

Notes

Nick Trujillo thanks Leah Vande Berg and Harry Haines for their suggestions and their encouragement that helped in the development of this article.

1. The media reported that Ryan generated additional revenues for baseball-related businesses inside and outside the stadium as well. To take a few reported exam-

ples, the day after Ryan's five thousandth strikeout: ARA Services, the company which runs concessions at Arlington Stadium, was said to have sold a record six thousand commemorative shirts at $15 each; scalpers were getting several hundred dollars for unauthorized ticket sales; and the value of his rookie baseball card went from $225 to $450 in one day (Tomaso 1989). In a more recent report, Ryan's rookie card was said to have been auctioned off for $5,000 ("Ryan Rookie Card" 1991).

References

A day when crass gave way to class. (1991, May 13). [Editorial]. *Sporting News,* p. 6.

Aaron, H., with Wheeler, L. (1991). *I had a hammer: The Hank Aaron story.* New York: Harper Collins.

Anderson, D. (1975, June 3). For a change, another Ryan no-hitter. *New York Times,* p. 39.

———. (1978, August). The Ryan Express races for the records. *Sport,* pp. 67–71.

Axtheim, P. (1975, June 16). Fastest arm in the West. *Newsweek,* pp. 56–60.

Baldwin, P. (1990, July 10). Pitch man. *Dallas Morning News,* pp. 1A, 6A.

Bennett, R. S., Whitaker, K. G., Woolley Smith, N. J., & Sablove, A. (1987). Changing the rules of the game: Reflections toward a feminist analysis of sport. *Women's Studies International Forum, 10,* 369–379.

Berquist, G. F. (1971). The rhetorical heritage of Frederick Jackson Turner. *Transactions of the Wisconsin Academy of Sciences, Arts, and Letters, 59,* 23–32.

Billington, R. A. (1971). *The genesis of the frontier thesis.* San Marino, Calif.: Huntington Library.

Bodley, H. (1991, May 3). Ryan: Oasis from off-field turmoil. *USA Today,* p. 5C.

Boswell, T. (1991, May 3). Ryan wears age and success with equal grace. *Sacramento Bee,* pp. C1, C4.

Brewster, T. (1989, May). The care and feeding of baseball's greatest arm. *Life,* pp. 86–87.

Brine for Nolan Ryan. (1968, May 31). *Life,* pp. 77–78.

Brod, H., ed. (1987). *The making of masculinity: The new men's studies.* Boston: Unwin Hyman.

Brohm, J-M. (1978). *Sport: A prison of measured time* (I. Fraser, trans.). London: Ink Links.

Bryson, L. (1987). Sport and the maintenance of masculine hegemony. *Women's Studies International Forum, 10,* 349–360.

Carpenter, R. (1977). Frederick Jackson Turner and the rhetorical impact of the frontier thesis. *Quarterly Journal of Speech, 63,* 117–129.

Carrigan, T., Connell, B., & Lee, L. (1987). Toward a new sociology of masculinity. In H. Brod (ed.), *The making of masculinities: The new men's studies* (pp. 63–100). Boston: Unwin Hyman.

Casstevens, D. (1990, July 25). 300th will be Ryan's reply to his critics. *Dallas Morning News,* p. 1B.

Cawelti, J. (1976). *Adventure, mystery, and romance.* Chicago: University of Chicago Press.

Chass, M. (1970, June 11). Pepitone clouts four-run homer. *New York Times,* p. 59.

Connell, R. W. (1983). *Which way is up? Essays on sex, class, and culture.* Sydney: George Allen & Unwin.

———. (1990). An iron man: The body and some contradictions of hegemonic masculinity. In M. A. Messner & D. F. Sabo (eds.), *Sport, men and the gender order: Critical feminist perspectives* (pp. 83–95). Champaign, Ill.: Human Kinetics.

Corliss, R. (1990, June 25). An old-timer for all seasons: For Nolan Ryan, 43, it's no hits, no runs—and no peers. *Time,* p. 68.

Dubbert, J. (1979). *A man's place: Masculinity in transition.* Englewood Cliffs. N.J.: Prentice Hall.

Duncan, M. C. (1983). The symbolic dimensions of spectator sport. *Quest, 35,* 29–36.

———. (1990). Sports photographs and sexual difference: Images of women and men in the 1984 Olympic Games. *Sociology of Sport Journal, 7,* 22–43.

Durslag, M. (1976, April 24). Ryan raps pay preoccupation. *Sporting News,* p. 12.

Durso, J. (1968, July 4). Pirates shell Ryan and rout Mets, 8–1. *New York Times,* p. 24.

Dyer, R. (1985). Male sexuality in the media. In A. Metcalf & M. Humphries (eds.), *The sexuality of men* (pp. 28–43). London: Pluto.

Edwards, H. (1976). Race in contemporary American sports. In A. Yiannakis, T. D. McIntyre, M. J. Melnick, & D. P. Hart (eds.), *Sport sociology: Contemporary themes* (pp. 194–196). Dubuque, Iowa: Kendall/Hunt.

Fimrite, R. (1974, September 16). Speed trap for an Angel. *Sports Illustrated,* pp. 98, 100.

———. (1975, June 16). The bringer of the heat. *Sports Illustrated,* pp. 33, 35–39.

———. (1986, September 29). A great hand with the old cowhide. *Sports Illustrated,* pp. 84–88, 90–94, 96.

Fiske, J. (1987). *Television culture.* London: Methuen.

Fiske, J., & Hartley, J. (1978). *Reading television.* New York: Methuen.

Fraley, G. (1990, June 16). Pitching with pain not new to Ryan. *Dallas Morning News,* p. 6B.

Furlong, B. W. (1980, April). Baseball's best paid pitcher comes home. *Sport,* pp. 66–70.

Galloway R. (1990a, March 29). At all cost, Ryan must be paid to stay. *Dallas Morning News,* p. 1B.

———. (1990b, August 1). Ryan's greatness affirmed. *Dallas Morning News,* p. 1B.

Givens, R. (1989, August 28). Throwing old gracefully: The workout behind the Ryan strikeouts. *Newsweek,* p. 65.

Greene, B. (1990, June 24). Nolan Ryan is newest star of the baby boom set. *Dallas Morning News,* p. 50.

Hanke, R. (1990). Hegemonic masculinity in thirtysomething. *Critical Studies in Mass Communication, 7*, 231–248.

Harasta, C. (1990, August 2). Married to a legend, Ruth Ryan understands sacrifices. *Dallas Morning News*, p. 17H.

Hargreaves, J. (1982). Sport and hegemony: Some theoretical problems. In H. Cantelon & R. Gruneau (eds.), *Sport, culture, and the modern state* (pp. 103–140). Toronto: University of Toronto Press.

Hargreaves, J. A. (1986). Where's the virtue? Where's the grace? A discussion of the social production of gender relations in and through sport. *Theory, Culture, and Society, 3*, 109–121.

Hearn, J. (1987). *The gender of oppression: Men, masculinity, and the critique of Marxism.* New York: St. Martin's Press.

Hecht, H. (1983, April 29). Whatever Ryan does, it never quiets critics. *New York Post*, p. 102.

Henderson, J. (1989, August 23). 5-oh!-oh!-oh!: Heroic Ryan finishes quest for historic K. *Dallas Times Herald*, pp. A-1, A-15.

Herek, G. M. (1987). On heterosexual masculinity: Some psychical consequences of the social construction of gender and sexuality. In M. S. Kimmel (ed.), *Changing men: New directions in research on men and masculinity* (pp. 68–82). Newbury Park, Calif.: Sage.

Herskowitz, M. (1988, October 28). Ryan's loyalty isn't the issue. *Houston Post*, p. C-1.

———. (1990, April 1). A Ruth-less spring training doesn't suit Mrs. Ryan. *Houston Post*, p. B-15.

Hoch, P. (1979). *White hero, black beast.* London: Pluto.

Hoffer, R. (1988, May). Armed and still dangerous. *Gentlemen's Quarterly*, pp. 243–248, 292–294.

Horn, B. (1990, August 2). Expressly Ryan: In honor of 300. *Dallas Morning News*, pp. 1H–2H.

Jacobson, S. (1974, June/July). Nolan Ryan: Whoosh! *Saturday Evening Post*, pp. 14–16, 124.

Jeffords, S. (1989). *The remasculinization of America: Gender and the Vietnam War.* Bloomington: Indiana University Press.

Jennings, D. (1989, March 26). Nolan Ryan. *Dallas Morning News*, pp. 1E–3E.

Jhally, S. (1989). Cultural studies and the sports/media complex. In L. A. Wenner (ed.), *Media, sport, and society* (pp. 70–95). Newbury Park, Calif.: Sage.

Johnson, N. T. (1991, April 3). Dueling Ryans throw fans a curve on loyalty. *Austin American-Statesman*, pp. A1, A12.

Johnston, D. H. (1979). *Journalism and the media: An introduction to mass communications.* New York: Barnes & Noble.

K. (1989, August 28). *Sports Illustrated*, pp. 30–32.

Kaufman, M., ed. (1987). *Beyond patriarchy: Essays by men on pleasure, power, and change.* Toronto: Oxford University Press.

Keith, L. (1979, November 19). It's fishing season for Nolan Ryan. *Sports Illustrated*, pp. 34–35.

Kimmel, M. S. (1987a). Rethinking "masculinity": New directions in research. In M. S. Kimmel (ed.), *Changing men: New directions in research on men and masculinity* (pp. 9–24). Newbury Park, Calif.: Sage.

———. (1987b). The cult of masculinity: American social character and the legacy of the cowboy. In M. Kaufman (ed.), *Beyond patriarchy: Essays by men on pleasure, power, and change* (pp. 235–249). Toronto: Oxford University Press.

Komisar, L. (1980). Violence and the masculine mystique. In D. F. Sabo & R. Runfola (eds.), *Jock: Sports and male identity* (pp. 131–157). Englewood Cliffs, N.J.: Prentice Hall.

Lang, J. (1968, March 30). Ryan whiff saga a fable? Mets wonder. *Sporting News*, p. 26.

———. (1984, May 1). What drove Ryan from NY: Concern for wife led to trade-me-or-I'll-quit demand. *New York Daily News*, p. C26.

Leggett, W. (1973, May 14). An Angel who makes turnstiles sing. *Sports Illustrated*, pp. 26–27.

Lerner, G. (1986). *The creation of patriarchy*. New York: Oxford University Press.

Littwin, M. (1980, April 17). Nolan Ryan: Fastest (and richest?) gun in Alvin. *Los Angeles Times*, pp. 1, 10, part III.

Lopresti, M. (1991, May 3–5). Texas Ranger rides very tall in the saddle. *USA Today*, pp. 1A–2A.

MacCormack, J. (1989, August 22). Alvin's uniform anxiety. *Dallas Times Herald*, pp. A-1, A-10.

McCleneghan, J. S. (1990). Sportswriters talk about themselves: An attitude study. *Journalism Quarterly*, *67*, 114–118.

Majors, R. (1986). Cool pose: The proud signature of black survival. *Changing Men: Issues in Gender, Sex and Politics*, *17*, 5–6.

Maynard, R. M. (1974). *The American west on film: Myth and reality*. Rochelle Park, N.J.: Hayden Book Co.

Messner, M. A. (1988). Sports and male domination: The female athlete as contested ideological terrain. *Sociology of Sport Journal*, *51*, 197–211.

———. (1990). Masculinities and athletic careers: Bonding and status differences. In M. A. Messner & D. F. Sabo (eds.), *Sport, men, and the gender order: Critical feminist perspectives* (pp. 97–108). Champaign, Ill.: Human Kinetics.

Montville, L. (1991, April 15). Citizen Ryan. *Sports Illustrated*, pp. 120–129, 131.

Naison, M. (1972). Sports and the American empire. *Radical America* (July–August), pp. 95–120.

Nelson, M. (1980). Feminism, the jockocracy, and men's liberation: Crying all the way to the bank. In D. F. Sabo & R. Runfola (eds.), *Jock: Sports and male identity* (pp. 239–248). Englewood Cliffs, N.J.: Prentice Hall.

Newhan, R. (1971, December 11). Fregosi "thrilled" by trade to Mets. *Los Angeles Times*, pp. 1, 3, part III.

————. (1972, May 23). Homer lucky blow says Jackson as A's top Angels, 6–3. *Los Angeles Times*, pp. 1, 6, part III.

————. (1975, June 2). Ryan: A hitless wonder for the 4th time. *Los Angeles Times*, pp. 1, 6, part III.

No. 300: Ryan puts final touch on application to Hall. (1990, August 1). *Bakersfield Californian*, pp. E1, E6.

Ochberg, R. L. (1987). The male career code and the ideology of role. In H. Brod (ed.), *The making of masculinities: The new men's studies* (pp. 173–192). Boston: Unwin Hyman.

Pallone, D., with Steinberg, A. (1990). *Behind the mask: My double life in baseball*. New York: Signet.

Pleck, J. H. (1987). American fathering in historical perspective. In M. S. Kimmel (ed.), *Changing men: New directions in research on men and masculinity* (pp. 83–97). Newbury Park, Calif.: Sage.

President's message. (1989, August 23). *Fort Worth Star-Telegram*, p. 6, sec. 3.

Rader, B. G. (1983). Compensatory sports heroes: Ruth, Grange, and Dempsey. *Journal of Popular Culture, 16,* 11–22.

Real, M. R. (1975). Super Bowl: Mythic spectacle. *Journal of Communication, 25,* 31–43.

————. (1989). Super Bowl football versus World Cup soccer: A cultural-structural comparison. In L. A. Wenner (ed.), *Media, sports, and society* (pp. 180–203). Newbury Park, Calif.: Sage.

Rigauer, B. (1981). *Sport and work* (A. Guttmann, trans.). New York: Columbia University Press.

Ringolsby, T. (1990, July 30). Ryan says arm, back recuperated from tiring effort against Yankees. *Dallas Morning News*, p. 5B.

Rubin, G. (1985). Thinking sex: Notes for a radical theory of the politics of sexuality. In C. Vance (ed.), *Pleasure and danger: Exploring female sexuality* (pp. 267–319). Boston: Routledge & Kegan Paul.

Rushing, J. H. (1983). The rhetoric of the American western myth. *Communication Monographs, 50,* 14–32.

Ryan rookie card goes for $5,000. (1991, June 22). *Sacramento Bee*, p. D2.

Sabo, D. F., & Runfola, R., eds. (1980). *Jock: Sports and male identity*. Englewood Cliffs, N.J.: Prentice Hall.

Sadler, W. A., Jr. (1976). Competition out of bounds: Sport in American life. In A. Yiannakis, T. D. McIntyre, M. J. Melnick, & D. P. Hart (eds.), *Sport sociology: Contemporary themes* (pp. 253–261). Dubuque, Iowa: Kendall/Hunt.

Segal, L. (1990). *Slow motion: Changing masculinities, changing men*. Brunswick, N.J.: Rutgers University Press.

Shadoian, J. (1977). *Dreams and dead ends: The American gangster/crime film*. Cambridge, Mass.: MIT Press.

Shea, J. (1990, June 13). Ryan celebrates with bike workout. *USA Today*, p. 8C.

Striking example: Tonight's the night for Ryan to make history. (1989, August 22). [Editorial]. *Dallas Morning News,* p. 14A.

Texas Rangers. (1991). *Texas Rangers 1991 media guide.* Arlington, Tex.: Texas Rangers Baseball Club.

These are the Mets, champions all. (1969, October 17). *New York Times,* p. 57.

Tolson, A. (1977). *The limits of masculinity: Male identity and women's liberation.* New York: Harper & Row.

Tom, D. (1985, July 10). Nolan Ryan smokes only his pitches. *USA Today,* pp. 1C–2C.

Tomaso, B. (1989, August 22). Making a fast buck off Ryan: Tickets to witness pitcher's quest are costly and scarce. *Dallas Morning News,* pp. 1A, 11A.

Trujillo, N., & Ekdom, L. R. (1985). Sports writing and American cultural values: The 1984 Chicago Cubs. *Critical Studies in Mass Communication, 2,* 262–281.

Wangrin, M. (1991, April 3). Big hit: Father throws best. *Austin American-Statesman,* pp. C1, C7.

Wernick, A. (1987). From voyeur to narcissist: Imaging men in contemporary advertising. In M. Kaufman (ed.), *Beyond patriarchy: Essays by men on pleasure, power, and change* (pp. 277–297). Toronto: Oxford University Press.

Whitson, D. (1990). Sport in the social construction of masculinity. In M. A. Messner & D. F. Sabo (eds.), *Sport, men, and the gender order: Critical feminist perspectives* (pp. 19–29). Champaign, Ill.: Human Kinetics.

Whyte, W. H. (1956). *The organization man.* New York: Simon and Schuster.

Wright, W. (1975). *Sixguns and society: A structural study of the Western.* Berkeley: University of California Press.

2

LEOLA JOHNSON AND DAVID ROEDIGER

"Hertz, Don't It?"
Becoming Colorless and Staying Black in the Crossover of O. J. Simpson

> Look at the unprecedented market presence that black athletes have today, what they're called upon (or allowed) to symbolize. Jackie Robinson never made it onto a box of Wheaties.
>
> —*Henry Louis Gates, Jr.*

• Twenty years ago, O. J. Simpson told of his strategy for responding to racial taunts. It consisted of a sharp jab to the offender's chest, followed by a literal punch line: "Hertz, don't it?" The humor rested on the bitter contrast of Simpson's tremendous success as an athlete crossing over to become a corporate icon with his continued facing of racial hurts and desiring to strike back against them. In anticipating the "Hertz/hurts" punning that now is repeated endlessly on "O. J. jokes" web sites, Simpson surely knew that he briefly stepped out of character. He followed the remark with laughing reassurances that such jabbing was of course unnecessary. Referring to himself in the disturbing third-person manner common

40

to toddlers and Republican presidential hopefuls, he pointed out that "the Juice" so transcended white racism that he scarcely faced bigotry. He then shifted discussion to the troublesome African American women who criticized his acting out interracial romances in films and to the insecure African American militants who had tried to draw him into their own wrestling with racial identity. In general, despite the occasional line regarding country clubs flying their flags at half-staff on the days he was their guest, Simpson's pre-1994 self-presentation was as someone for whom racism was not a problem. As early as 1969, he triumphantly reported that O. J. was thought of as a "man," not as an African American. Although he professedly retained a healthy sense of African American consciousness, he later told reporters, the American public happily saw him as "colorless." In making the latter claim, Simpson also invoked Hertz. The marketing division of the firm, he observed, had generated data proving his transcendence of race.[1]

As this is being written, lawyers and trademark bureaucrats are deciding a bizarre conflict regarding who owns the initials "O. J." They are deciding whether, after all, Simpson still might be a colorless commodity rather than a racialized body. Amidst much bad financial news, Simpson has recently prevailed on the orange juice lobby to give up its disputing of his claim to be O. J. Perhaps reflecting a desire not to be much associated with Simpson, the juice industry has ceded claims to the initials, save in direct reference to their product. If the claims of the clothing manufacturer Outer Jock are disposed of, O. J. Simpson will be O. J. He hopes to market a range of products—from apparel to toys—under that trademark. Such connections of Simpson to the sale of things are longstanding and wide-ranging: razors, boots, books, videos, juice, clothing, soda, combination juice and soda, sunglasses, televisions, films, dolls, cars, sneakers, sporting goods, chicken, cameras, aftershave, rental cars, and, as both he and others have long observed, his own "image" and "personality." The length of the list suggests why Simpson could still imagine that the white public might see him as without race.[2]

This essay examines the role of race and the claim of colorlessness in O. J. Simpson's life prior to the 1994 murders of Nicole Brown Simpson and Ronald Goldman. It seeks to understand why Simpson became the first black sports star to massively cross over from athletic hero to corporate spokesman and media personality. We argue that however tragically Simpson believed that such crossover also involved a movement beyond race, his success rested on appeals rooted strongly in his race, in the presence of movements for racial justice, and in the history of race and gender in the United States. While there can be no doubt that Simpson's image became a valuable commodity, commodity and color were consistently imbricated in his appeal.

We address these pre-1994 realities as critical in their own right, murders and trials aside. However, we also realize that all thinking about Simpson now is read as reflecting on "the case"—that books on him are now not in sports or business aisles but in the "True Crime" sections of bookstores. Our writing here obviously intersects with one of the enduring fascinations of that case: the terrifying juxtaposition of slashed, maimed, and lifeless bodies of the victims with the feverish rush of media and markets to sell—and of the public to buy—any and every commodity related to the tragedy. The awful fact that the sales of white Broncos skyrocketed along with sales of the type of stiletto once thought to be the murder weapon; the obscene sensationalizing by the tabloid and mainstream media; the paid-for interviews with witnesses; the seven-figure book contracts; the auditioning for further parts from the witness stand by Kato Kaelin; and the nude photo spread of a Simpson "juror with a difference" in *Playboy* all provoked horror precisely because they showed how quickly and fully the pursuit of dollars displaces and desecrates the memory of the dead. O. J. Simpson, selling his own image from jail (signed, on football cards)—hawking books, videos, medallions, interviews, and even photographs of his children—focused this outrage. Indeed, the prosecution's appeals, from Christopher Darden's warnings against being taken in by high-priced Dream Teamers to Marcia Clark's closing slide show of the victims, offered jurors an opportunity to rescue dead bodies from the lively rush to profit.[3]

The deeply gendered connections of house, home, and community in Simpson's commercial success, which we also will explore, underpin another major narrative regarding the case, one especially found in black reflections on it, from the neighborhood where Simpson grew up to the speeches of Louis Farrakhan. According to this narrative, which has some force, Simpson progressively concerned himself less and less with African

American life, yet was nonetheless unable to transcend racism, and ironically found significant support within a community he had left behind. Simpson's own writing on the case details a growing horror at having to "see race" after a life he characterizes as entirely lived on merit. Understanding O. J. as a seemingly colorless but fully racialized commodity, brilliantly positioned to be marketed to middle-class white men, is thus vital to comprehending his and the public's reaction to the trial.[4]

The Un-militant: Black Revolt and Simpson's Success

So familiar is Simpson's commercial success, along with that of the few African American athletes who followed him to advertising superstardom, that it is difficult to recall how spectacularly improbable such celebrity was. No black athlete, no matter how great, had ever crossed over with anything like such success. In the late 1960s, endorsements remained unavailable to those with substantial professional careers as the greatest in their sport—not Willie Mays, not Hank Aaron, not Bill Russell, not Oscar Robertson, not Wilt Chamberlain, not Jimmy Brown, and, above all, not Muhammad Ali. Nor were African American stars who might have been marketed for their excellence and their youth deluged with offers—not Lew Alcindor, not Lou Brock, not Arthur Ashe, and not Tommie Smith, who in the late 1960s had perhaps the broadest claim ever to the title "world's fastest human." Superstars like Russell and Bob Gibson faced slights and exclusion even in the relatively paltry local markets in which they were the dominant sports figures. Advertising firms, reacting to research demonstrating that commercials overwhelmingly focused on and appealed to whites, stridently maintained that ads should not "look like America" but should look like what advertisers thought white mainstream audiences thought America should look like. They listed products, such as razors and razor blades, for which African Americans were perceived as being too different-looking to ever endorse in ads pitched to those outside the black community. More broadly, as Anne McClintock's work in cultural studies points out, mass advertising since 1900 or before had consistently used racist and racial imagery to sell to white markets. Black images on products were not unknown, but they were often demeaning, servile, and anonymous: Aunt Jemima, the Cream of Wheat man, Uncle Ben, the

Gold Dust twins, and so on. Indeed, McClintock tellingly shows that such "commodity racism" was not just reflective of how the broader society's racism showed up in ads but deeply constitutive of the very ways whites connected race, pleasure, and service.[5]

And then O. J. Simpson, two years out of junior college and not having played a down in the NFL, suddenly entertained so many offers from advertisers that he could turn down any proposals that he appear in individual commercials, insisting on contracting only as an ongoing spokesperson for products. Money poured in from GM, from Royal Crown Cola (for whom Simpson had worked as a deliveryman until shortly before moving to USC), and from so many other sponsors that, as one *Sports Illustrated* writer put it, he was busy just cashing checks. ABC made him a network sportscaster. He soon would impress Schick as not so different as to rule out his appearances in shaving ads. By 1977, he would win polls as the most admired person among U.S. fifth to twelfth graders and as the "most watchable man" in the world. He would garner *Advertising Age*'s "Oscar" as the top celebrity spokesperson in the United States, and he would receive coverage not just as the most successful black athlete in attracting money from beyond his sport but as the most successful athlete of any color.[6]

That this phenomenal success began in 1969, after Simpson's Heisman Trophy–winning season, not in his record-breaking 1973 NFL year, is crucial in beginning to explain his crossover appeal. Then, as now, winning the Heisman had little relation to future professional success, but corporations and the media took a chance on O. J. The sunlit 1968 season of Simpson's Heisman "campaign"—he had chosen Southern Cal in large part because its campaign machinery had functioned so well when Mike Garrett won the trophy—stands out anomalously against the other dramas of that eventful year. But those stormy events constitute an indispensable context for any explanation of Simpson's commercial crossover. His triumph—not in the Heisman race where he had no close rivals, but in the corporate world—lay in the distance Simpson put between himself and those momentous events, quite as much as in the ground between him and would-be tacklers.[7]

Simpson's reception during and after his Heisman campaign unfolded amidst revolt and repression. In 1968, from Paris to Prague to Mexico City

44

to Chicago, protesters faced guns, clubs, and tanks as they campaigned for nothing less than a new society. Vietcong military campaigns reached their turning point in the bloody Tet offensive. The U.S. presidential campaign saw the assassination of Robert F. Kennedy and police riots at the Democratic national convention. Richard M. Nixon won the White House, skillfully deploying a "southern strategy" of appealing to white backlash. The campaign of Memphis sanitation workers for dignity and trade union rights moved Martin Luther King, Jr., to that city and to his death.

Students, African Americans, Californians, and, to an unprecedented extent, athletes played central roles in the struggles of 1968. Thus, Simpson's glorious Saturday afternoons, his disdain for "politics," his ability to socialize one moment with Bill Cosby and the next with John Wayne, and his smiling California and American dreaming stood out in sharp contrast to other televised images and realities of campuses, of the Bay Area, of southern California, of black America, and of the world of sports. Decathlete Rafer Johnson disarmed the assassin of Kennedy, who was shot as he celebrated victory in the California primary. The Black Panther Party, whose roots lay in the Bay Area, also became a significant force and a victim of savage COINTELPRO police repression in southern California. California's campuses continued to be symbols of student revolt, especially in the Bay Area and Los Angeles. California's Governor Ronald Reagan, Senator George Murphy, and San Francisco State University administrator S. I. Hayakawa joined Nixon, yet another Californian, as the most visible figures capitalizing on opposition to campus protests. So extensive was politicization across the ideological spectrum that even Nixon had an African American superstar as an active supporter. Wilt Chamberlain, drawn to Nixon's advocacy of black capitalism, was the tallest delegate at the 1968 Republican convention.[8]

In sports, two symbols dominated what the sociologist and activist Harry Edwards called the "revolt of the black athlete." The first, Muhammad Ali, faced jail in 1968 and suffered suspension from boxing for his refusal to regard the Vietcong as his enemy and to be inducted into the military as a draftee. Pretty, poetic, and seemingly invulnerable in the ring, Ali clearly enjoyed greater recognition, nationally and internationally, than any other American athlete. Just as clearly, he had what the advertisers and pollsters call "high negatives."[9]

The second symbol of black athletes' revolt—the protests surrounding the 1968 Mexico City Olympic games—hit far closer to home for Simpson. The entire summer games carried an immense political charge, from Cold War medal-counting to the gunning down of protesters, which, more tellingly than the lighting of the Olympic torch, marked the beginning of the competition. The struggle over participation in South Africa's reentry to the games invigorated international antiapartheid protest. Fighting for a host of demands, the topmost of which was an end to Ali's victimization and at the center of which were the rights of collegiate athletes, California's Edwards and others built the Olympic Project for Human Rights, which counted Dr. King among its supporters. For a time, the threat of an African American boycott of the games loomed. Lew Alcindor, Lucius Allen, and Mike Warren of UCLA's outstanding basketball team all declined to try out for the U.S. team. Alcindor's gracefully worded demurral did not stop threats against his life. Although he would not adopt the name Kareem Abdul-Jabbar until later, Alcindor converted to Islam in 1968. In Mexico City, California-based sprinters Tommie Smith and John Carlos, both of San Jose State University, protested most visibly, famously clenching their fists in Black Power salutes on the victory stand after the 200-meter race. Simpson, who had run a leg on a world-record-setting 4-by-110-yards sprint relay team earlier in 1968, might well have competed at Mexico City had he concentrated solely on track. Back in California, he publicly denounced the Olympic protests. This denunciation was of a piece with Simpson's generally oppositional stance vis-à-vis the revolt of the black athlete, though his frequently noncombatant response of simply ignoring freedom struggles and his ability to tap into certain aspects of Ali's cultural style and of Chamberlain's black capitalism also are vital in accounting for Simpson's ability to cross over.[10]

Southern Cal, in contrast to UCLA's limited but real progressivism, had an abysmal record of race relations. Even the *Sports Illustrated* reporters who were there to write about Simpson's football exploits commented on the tense, besieged-by-the-city whiteness of the campus. Dean Cromwell, the legendary track coach who engineered many of the school's most significant pre-Simpson triumphs, explained in the 1940s that "the Negro excels in the events he does because he is closer to the primitive than the white man." In the late 1960s, the school's enrollment of nonathlete black students was tiny, a fact the student newspaper complacently explained by noting that this was because tuition was so high. At a time when football success had passed overwhelmingly to large public universities, USC was an oddity: an elite (in terms of tuition) college football power. When a necessarily small black student movement took shape at Southern Cal, Simpson denounced it. He argued that its leaders were rich "Baldwin Hills" kids agonizing over a black identity that they had just discovered, but one that he was "born with" by virtue of his poverty.[11] Whatever the doubtful merits of this analysis of USC's movement, it deserves noting that origins among the working poor hardly kept such leading figures as Ali or Tommie Smith away from protest. Simpson's main competitor for the Heisman, Purdue running back Leroy Keyes, proudly told reporters of his role in militant protests, including the hanging of a banner reading THE FIRE NEXT TIME. Simpson emphasized his "own philosophy" of positioning himself to be able to make charitable contributions and to offer himself as a role model of financial success to black youth.[12]

Simpson carried into the professional ranks an animosity to politics, which meant for him both endorsing candidates and supporting protests. He offered to stay out of politics as long as politicians stayed out of football. At the time, as Nelson George puts it, "Brothers [in sports] were sporting huge Afros, bellbottom pants and gold medallions. They were reading Eldridge Cleaver's *Soul on Ice,* listening to the Last Poets and smoking marijuana instead of drinking beer." Simpson meanwhile disavowed drug use, kept private his feeling that it would be "crazy" to go to Vietnam, and made fun of bearded acquaintances to reporters, referring to them as H. Rap Brown. Buffalo's team had a hair and grooming code during his early career. That Simpson complied made him look different from many athletes of the time. He again connected beards and politics in the late 1970s, in a remarkable, highly public campaign to have Robert Altman cast him as Coathouse Walker, the black entertainer-cum-revolutionary in the film version of E. L. Doctorow's *Ragtime.* Not only did reporters note his sudden interest in African American culture and politics and his new, bearded look, but Simpson himself repeatedly announced that he was changing his image in a frank bid to get a role that would enable him to realize his central acting goal: to become a "bankable" star.[13]

Simpson also weighed in during the mid-seventies on an issue of great concern among antiracist sports activists: the near total absence of black quarterbacks in an increasingly African American National Football League. Coaches continually steered black quarterbacks to other positions—those for which speed and power, rather than intelligence and leadership, figured most prominently in the job description. Discouraged by many college coaches, black quarterbacks were infrequently drafted as professionals and, when they were, needed to deliver solid results much more quickly than white signal callers. James Harris, a young black quarterback who had performed successfully and won no steady starting job, became a focus of the debate. Simpson provoked strong opposition in the black press in 1977 when he unaccountably offered the opinion that an aging and injured Joe Namath could better quarterback the Rams than could Harris, who for a time played on the Bills with Simpson.[14] Only on the issue of freer movement between teams for professional athletes did Simpson flirt with protest movements. But even on this matter his retreats, and the grounds for them, were more spectacular than his advances.

In 1969, Simpson made plans to sue the National Football League, even before he had ever played a down in it. Fresh off his Heisman Trophy–winning 1968 season at Southern Cal and drafted by the Buffalo Bills, Simpson badly wanted to avoid going to a frigid city with a poor team and a small market. He came within an eyelash of emulating baseball's Curt Flood and risking his career to challenge restrictions on the free movement from team to team by players. Like Flood, a gifted St. Louis Cardinal centerfielder much influenced by the black freedom movement, Simpson sometimes cast his personal contractual situation within a broader civil rights framework. His large contracts with General Motors and other corporations, Frank Deford observed in *Sports Illustrated,* made it possible for Simpson to finance legal action and to survive a delay in signing. But the corporate endorsements cut two ways. The negotiator for the Bills, an ex-union lawyer, appealed to Simpson to realize that the real money coming his way would be provided by advertisers, not football owners, and that such endorsements could only continue if he remained in football's limelight. Chevrolet, the negotiator argued, would not fork over another quarter million dollars to a holdout. After much hesitation,

Simpson signed for far less than he had demanded. He admitted that the agreement was a capitulation on his part, but he embraced the logic that his real future lay in advertising and "image." Looking around at all the things he had acquired, particularly his new home, and glorying in his relationship with Chevrolet division head John DeLorean reassured O. J. that he had done the right thing. He would again threaten legal action against the League in the middle 1970s when he charged the NFL with placing itself above the Constitution and supported the 1974 players' strike; he also predicted cooperative ownership of all franchises. But his flirtations with open challenges to the League typically stopped short of decisive action. Simpson's first year with the Bills would be the subject of a book, written with the football journalist Pete Axthelm. Despite his disappointing contract, its title, *Education of a Rich Rookie,* was apt and significant.[15]

Locating Simpson's crossover success within the era of the revolt of the black athlete illuminates two critical ironies of that crossover. The first is that militants in and out of sports both established the preconditions for the advertising and media success of a Simpson *and* ensured that the first athlete to cash in on new possibilities would be anything but a militant. Black Power, as Robert Weems has shown, brought sharply rising interest in African American markets among advertising executives: The ferment of 1968 in particular brought an unprecedented escalation in civil rights lobbying against racism in advertising; mass pressure encouraged sports, media, and marketing elites to search energetically for role models and to trumpet the myth of sport as a "level playing field" so loudly as to deflect attention from inequalities within athletics and from the realities of who owned and ran the industry. The second irony is more subtle. In making his historic crossover breakthrough, Simpson's seeming transcendence of color rested squarely on his racial identity. The epithet "white man's Negro" is noteworthy in this connection, even though we are far more interested in why Simpson's image sold, and in what he bought into, than in the question of whether he sold out. Even the most assimilative crossover strategies rested not only on just pleasing the white (in Simpson's case mainly male) public but in pleasing that public as a "Negro." Being a cheerful athlete who deflected attention from black revolt worked so powerfully in Simpson's case not because he crossed over from black

49

to white; rather, those attributes had meaning largely because he remained an African American as they enabled him to cross over from athlete to advertisement.[16]

Buying and Selling Houses: Home and the Traffic in Style

Simpson's wealth underwrote a Southern California existence that took him far from his roots in inner-city San Francisco to fabulous homes in overwhelmingly white areas. His lifestyle-of-the-rich-and-suburban image reinforced his seeming transcendence of color in a nation in which upper-class whiteness is often cast as the normative experience. However, not only did Simpson's pride in grand homes grow out of his past, but white fascination with his lifestyle and with what flavor he could bring to suburban blandness fundamentally hinged on Simpson's racial identity. At fifteen, and just out of a short stay at a youth detention center, O. J. Simpson got to spend much of a day with the Giants' centerfielder Willie Mays. During this adventure, Simpson later and often related, he was not awed. But the ease of Mays's manner and the absence of any preaching regarding staying out of trouble deeply impressed Simpson. Equally impressive was simply viewing Mays's house and possessions. This visit convinced Simpson of what success could bring. He worshipped Mays not simply for being a great player but for having "a big house to show for it." Fiercely defensive of Mays when the latter was said to pay insufficient attention to using his fame to further African American causes, Simpson argued that his teenage encounter with superstardom provided a model for celebrity role modeling. In Heisman-year interviews and after he emphasized not only a desire to fund a boys' club in the "old neighborhood" of Potrero Hill but to build an impressive house for himself outside of it. He cast *both* acts in terms of aiding black youth. "I feel that it's the material things that count," he told reporters when explaining how to impress lessons on young people. To accusations that he played the "Establishment game" to acquire "the money . . . the big house," he replied that such acquisitions would "give pride and hope to a lot of young blacks." From his early *Sports Illustrated* interviews to the video he has sold after acquittal, Simpson has toured America through his houses. Indeed, prosecuting attorney Christopher Darden has recently complained that Simpson gave such tours when the jury in his murder trial visited his Rockingham home.[17]

Simpson's passion for houses and homes as the symbols of success was not surprising, given his own youth as a resident in housing projects built as temporary shelter for World War II shipyard workers in the Bay Area and his father's absence from the family. Simpson could enthuse, in an interview with *Playboy,* over the projects as "America the Beautiful," and a "federally funded commune," but he seldom looked back after his move to Southern Cal. Although *Time* referred to him as "molded by the slums," reporters and biographers showed little interest in the facts of his youth. (The mainstream press spelled Potrero Hill no less than four different ways, and usually wrong. His own autobiography, with Pete Axthelm doing the writing, offered the least plausible misspelling.)[18] The "old neighborhood" became, not just for Simpson but for the press, a source of a handful of legends, spun out as the occasion required and with much of the ambience of *West Side Story.* Almost all the accounts centered on whether the "gangs" Simpson joined, and sometimes headed, were or weren't tough and criminal. To a remarkable extent, Simpson managed to portray his gang activity as both hard and masculine, and as playful and harmless. Even when he referred to cohorts as a "bunch of cutthroats," the half-seriousness of his account perfectly struck a chord allowing readers to see his youth variously. He described his teenage encounter with marijuana with similarly wonderful ambiguity. Long before President Clinton professed to have "not inhaled," Simpson offered virtually the same account of what happened when he was offered a joint after the "hippie invasion" of San Francisco. Like Clinton, he told the story with a savvy that mixed blamelessness with intimations of a thorough knowledge of the drug culture.[19]

But in the main, Potrero Hill functioned simply as a backdrop to Simpson's real life of stardom. Even when he was just a year out of San Francisco, *Ebony* wrote of Simpson as a "once-tough youngster" who had become "a model of deportment, a B-minus student, a dedicated husband, and an interviewer's dream." Simpson's collaborator on his 1970 book described him as having succeeded in "running from the traps of his ghetto upbringing . . . toward new dreams and images of himself." Simpson married his high school sweetheart and hung out consistently at

Southern Cal and elsewhere with Al Cowlings, a high school teammate. But his visits to Potrero Hill were increasingly infrequent. When publicized, they were mediated by charitable contributions and commodities—most spectacularly when Simpson publicized juices with ads revisiting his youth.[20]

The most significant erasure in accounts of Simpson's youth is that of the 1966 rebellion against San Francisco police violence after Matthew Johnson, a black teenager, was shot dead by a white patrolman in the Hunters Point/Potrero Hill area. For more than five days, "soft" and "hard" antiriot tactics failed to quell the defiance, looting, arson, and vandalism. Damage caused by the rebellion was limited, but police intimidation of the community was not. The authorities' attempts to enlist the aid of ex-gang leaders—the leading study of the neighborhood insists gangs "no longer existed" in Hunters Point in the mid-1960s—failed dramatically. So too did efforts to bring in middle-class "community leaders," largely from other neighborhoods. Police so aggressively "herded" blacks from other public spaces in the city to Hunters Point that "moderately responsible" adults feared that a plan was being implemented in which an aircraft carrier passing in the Bay would stage massive bombings of the neighborhood "like," as one resident put it, "they do in Vietnam." These extremely bitter relations with the police, and the passionate denunciation of "Uncle Toms" and "white Negroes" on Potrero Hill during and after the 1966 events, figure nowhere in accounts of Simpson's youth, though they are vitally important as context to both his triumphs in the sixties and trials in the nineties.[21]

Far more remarkable than the desire to escape poverty, enjoy the fruits of achievement, and secure privacy, which led Simpson to concern himself so passionately with house and home, was the extent to which his hunting for both became a hugely publicized story on America's sports pages. The larger society's obsession with his personal obsession is another key to his crossover appeal and demands an explanation set in the context of the larger racial politics of the period. When Simpson showed reporters his first home going up in Los Angeles's Coldwater Canyon, the focus was on color and housing, but in a way strikingly unfamiliar to readers. At a time when such idols of Simpson's youth as Bill Russell and, significantly, Willie Mays, had recently suffered through highly publicized incidents of racial discrimination in housing in California, and when NFL teams had just begun to break the color line in rooming assignments, Simpson's concern centered on the orange color of Los Angeles's smoggy air. His solution was a fully private one. The house sat, he proudly noted, above the "smog line."[22]

This same sense of the transcendence of concern about race via class mobility ran through the long-running drama of Simpson's attempts to get out of his Buffalo Bills contract and to play at "home." From the start of his pro career, the preferred home was a wealthy section of Los Angeles, not his longtime boyhood home. Simpson's image was not just that of a Californian, but of a wealthy southern Californian. His world was warm, cosmopolitan, lavish, and upscale. Buffalo, known as ethnic and working-class as well as cold, had a team run as a "rinky-dink" operation, and it was a city with nothing going on. Its grime and grit contrasted with L.A.'s splendor and sparkle in a drama in which Simpson's race seemingly mattered little and his class and regional loyalties much. Indeed, in describing what made Buffalo rinky-dink, he told *Playboy,* "In college, I'd played at L.A. Coliseum, which you can see from half a mile away. In Buffalo, you'd be walking through a black neighborhood and suddenly, sixty feet in front of you, you'd see this old, rundown stadium."[23] Simpson so consistently criticized Buffalo that when his salary reached a (mis)reported $2.5 million annually, Johnny Carson joked that the half million was for playing football, the balance for living there. His decisions to renege on refusals to go back to the Bills consistently turned on dollars and on supporting his Bel Air lifestyle. In 1973, he returned to Buffalo, for example, after a hard look at "the material things that I have" in Bel Air. His symbolic value here went quite beyond providing a hopeful scenario regarding fame and wealth as antidotes to racial division. Embodying and very visibly championing the lifestyle of the white upper-middle class in the very region in which its growth and pretensions were most spectacular, Simpson reassured a vital segment of audiences that what they had and wanted, along with the ways in which they related work to consumption, were everybody's dreams—the profound questions raised by the black freedom movement, by hippies, and by the sixties generally notwithstanding. Simpson's race, even and especially when unmentioned, mattered greatly in his providing this reassurance.[24]

A subplot of the "let's rescue O. J. from Buffalo" melodrama more directly focused on race. Almost all of the many stories of his migrations and his threats to stay put mentioned his thorough consideration of family in all decisions. Since Marguerite neither liked Buffalo nor wished to uproot the children twice a year, joining and rejoining the Bills meant extensive separation from his nuclear family (such separations from his mother and other extended family members went largely unremarked). Coverage consistently stressed Simpson's role as a model father and husband who anguished over the decision and recalled his own father's estrangement from the household as Simpson grew up. "Home is always where the heart is," *Parents' Magazine* headlined in a Simpson profile, which allowed that it was often not where he was. The utter responsibility of O. J.'s decision contrasted sharply with the father's apparently unconsidered decision, as did the tremendous financial reward O. J. gained with the lack of support provided by his father. At a time like ours, when single mothers and absent fathers were indicted as the keys to the "pathology" of black families and communities, the "O. J., L.A., and Buffalo" stories did more than offer a positive role model. They portrayed African American success as overwhelmingly hinging on male responsibility, so that Simpson and not Marguerite became the model family member, even as Willie Mays often crowded Simpson's mother out of the success story of O. J.'s youth.[25]

However much Simpson marginalized racism and claimed a colorless appeal, his crossover success very much rested on his race. This was true not only with regard to his anti–Black Power, suburban homeboy positioning, but also with regard to his ability to resonate with familiar racist marketing images and to sell new images of black style. Although his later advertising image came more or less strictly out of the country club, Simpson's early appeals very much drew on the marketing of black athletic style for crossover purposes. He did so at a time when African American "aesthetics" had begun to dominate images of professional basketball, when Maury Wills and Lou Brock had revolutionized base running, and when Muhammad Ali had brought to the public new styles in boxing and voluble reflections on those styles.[26]

Simpson's claims to symbolize stylistic innovation came from a relatively weak position, especially compared to basketball players, since football was not a game nurtured on playgrounds to anything like the extent that basketball was. Played mostly, at least after high school, before white coaches with white quarterbacks calling the signals, football was not so dramatically transformed by African American athletes, though running back was the most changed position. Nor, of course, was Simpson's style anything like as distinctive as Ali's. With neither the power of Jimmy Brown, who more than doubled Simpson's professional touchdowns in a significantly shorter career, nor the breakaway creativity of Gale Sayers, Simpson was a brilliant back largely because of his combination of gifts. But that combination did not rival Brown's.

Nonetheless, Simpson, profiting greatly from increased use of slow-motion photography in sports, did successfully cultivate public interest in his style, which he linked to African American expressive behavior. Although his Heisman campaign stressed the standard elements of grit, aggression, power, and speed, Simpson quickly developed a more distinctive rap about his style. Reporters referred to his "jive patter" regarding descriptions of his own running, replete with references to music and dance. While other backs slashed and ground out yardage, his game plan involved fakes and feints—"juking the tough guys," as he put it, using in "juke" a term that referred to dance halls and evasive swerving as well as to sex. He told *Playboy* that "setting a cat down" with a convincing open-field fake and cut was his greatest football thrill. Stressing his own studied invulnerability, he claimed to have learned to tell the place on the field of all defenders as plays unfolded so that he could avoid crippling hits. Nor, he bragged, even during the hard early years in Buffalo, did he hesitate to go out of bounds to avoid punishing tackles. He never let critics force him to squirm for the last bit of yardage and therefore offered star defenders like Dick Butkus (the linebacker Simpson most delightedly talked of frustrating) slim chances to hit him squarely. On his own description, he hit holes "like a coward" searching for seams.[27]

In his caginess, in his claims of an invulnerability born of intelligence and instinct, and in his ability to evoke comparisons with dancers, Simpson called to mind the ways in which Ali marketed his style. Like Ali, Simpson made individual claims to redefine and transcend his sport. Sportswriters accepted Simpson's claims and the connections to Ali. One major account argued that Simpson's appeal lay in his daring demonstration that "a man can play football just the way he lives." As early as

1968, *Senior Scholastic* clearly made the links to Ali, claiming that Simpson "changed direction like a butterfly and hit with the power of an oil truck."[28]

Echoing the champ's penchant for rhyming self-promotion, Simpson named his deceptive repertoire of fakes, shifts, starts, and pauses the *okey-doke*, again popularizing "jive" black speech. The press bit hard on the term. His 1973 season, *Time* headlined, was the "Year of the Okey-Doke." When Simpson shared a story of fooling high school administrators with playful lies, he was portrayed as perfecting the verbal "*okey-doke.*" Like Will Smith in the recent television comedy hit *Fresh Prince of Bel Air*, Simpson safely brought sprinklings of "the other's" slang to white Americans. He may also have had a sly, complicated laugh of his own in the case of *okey-doke,* which not only meant a "con game" but also sardonically referred to "white values."[29]

Simpson's nicknames offered a further opportunity for white fans to consume the "other." In reflecting on Michael Jordan, breakfast cereal, and McDonald's (which once named a sandwich after Jordan), Michael Eric Dyson has recently argued that the historic consumption of black bodies by Western capitalism is recapitulated in a very different form today via athletics and athletic endorsements.[30] In Simpson's case, the tie between older and newer forms was greatly facilitated by his nicknames. Called O. J. rather than Orenthal James since his youth, Simpson was, according to one journalist, nearly as famous for being dubbed Orange Juice as for his running at Southern Cal. "The Juice," connoting energy, appears to have been generated in Buffalo, where Simpson's blockers were the "Electric Company." As Orange Juice, Simpson came prepackaged as a breakfast staple, recapitulating the impressive history of black advertising icons invited into homes to serve morning pleasure. The Orange Juice image not only contributed to the sunny, cheerful "Southern Californiazation" of Simpson. It also connected him to Aunt Jemima and to the Cream of Wheat man and offered, à la the McJordan sandwich, a direct opportunity for Simpson to be consumed. His runaway fame eventually made "O. J.," originally a "lunch counter" abbreviation, more popular as the familiar reference to orange juice. His earliest and some of his most lucrative endorsements came from juice contracts, especially the "teaming up of two great juices" in Tree Sweet ads. If his big contracts broke with advertising's powerful tradition of "commodity racism," his image was also very much a part of that tradition.[31]

Media-Made O. J.: Race, Speech, and Slow-Motion Supermanhood

As early as 1968, media projections of O. J. Simpson so insistently pegged him as Superman that his first wife, Marguerite Simpson, felt the need to remind the press that there's no such thing.[32] If not quite interplanetary, Simpson's aura of greatness and goodness was distinctly Supermanly, and that aura suffused accounts of his image as being above the racial fray. In his reflections on the trial, none of Simpson's anger runs more deeply than that directed against the press, which he portrays as suddenly seeing him in terms of race, and making him regretfully see race in everyday life. The contrast that Simpson notes was stark. Before 1994, he enjoyed adulation from the sports media's star-making machinery and a quarter-century's work as one of the boys in the booth of television sportscasting. After 1994, he became (literally in the case of *Time* magazine's famous cover) a blackened figure. Executives, who had earlier held that his jobs would likely be waiting for him if a "not guilty" verdict came in, made no gestures toward such reemployment.[33] But to see such dramatic changes as simply a movement from colorless acceptance to race thinking misses the large extent to which Simpson's Superman image was itself about race and the extent to which he remained the black guy in the booth as well as one of the boys there.

Simpson's media image clearly derived from long-standing journalistic traditions and modern television innovations that influenced the public's view of both white and black athletes, though in differing ways. When Los Angeles *Times* sportswriter Dwight Chapin flatly proclaimed "Superman is Orenthal James Simpson" in 1968, he followed a tradition of monumentalizing football heroes dating back almost a century. An 1891 New York *World* football story caught the spectacular flavor perfectly:

Surely, here were the old Roman kings circled about in their clattering chariots gloating over the running fight, and satiated with death. . . . Here were the lovely maidens of ancient days, turning down their pretty thumbs with every mangling scrimmage, and

shrieking with delight at every thrust and parry. . . . Think of Ulysses,
as a center rush, of Menelaus as a guard or of Paris as a quarterback.[34]

The early twentieth century's Walter Camp–inspired reportage on All-
American football role models, mostly from elite colleges, coexisted with,
and by the 1920s gave ground to, emphases on spectacle, violence, and the
alleged racial and ethnic characteristics of minority players. Nor did decades of print journalism on football decide the tension between dwelling
on manly, individual heroism or the competing and equally masculine
narrative of teamwork and male bonding in the trenches. Simpson—a
ghetto kid at an elite private school and the breakaway Juice in the open
field, as well as a back depending on the blocking and loyalty of the Electric Company line in front of him—became the focus of these tensions
and traditions, especially in *Sports Illustrated* reporting. Nowhere did his
distance from the 1968 protest help him more than among sportswriters,
whose opposition to the Olympic boycott was broad and angry.[35]

Ironically, the media's fascination with Simpson's supermanly body
and spirit coexisted with emphases on the abuse that body took from
tacklers and on the inevitability of injury. The "Superman for a day"
narrative of so much media coverage of modern sports finds its best expression in highlight films of football, showing bodies that "can fly," but
which also collide, writhe, and break. Not incidentally, these bodies are
increasingly black and the audience consuming images of their triumph
and destruction is overwhelmingly white.

Growing up with a largely untreated case of rickets, leading to childhood taunts as "Pencil Pins," Simpson was acutely aware of disability.
Sportswriters and opposing coaches often commented on his practice of
getting up very slowly after being tackled, looking absolutely unable to
continue, and then fully bouncing back. This habit, reminiscent of Jimmy
Brown and designedly disheartening to defenses, dramatically suggested
Simpson's vulnerability. His early Ali-like boasts regarding invincibility
backhandedly raised the same concerns. In his many interview references
to endorsements and films as necessary to ensure a career after football,
Simpson increasingly broached the issues of the inevitable brevity of his
career and of the peril to his body. Sportswriters played on the same
theme. Predictably enough, Simpson was in fact chronically hurt by his

later years in the NFL. His murder trial's references to his joint problems only continued a long-running pattern of press coverage regarding the results of the "sacrifice" of Simpson's body. Nowhere was the obsession better reflected than in the *Naked Gun* film series, in which Simpson's acting career came pitifully to rest on the repetition of injuries, culminating in a pratfall from a wheelchair. If part of the humor here arose from the contrast with Simpson's slow-motion grace in the field and in Hertz commercials, the gags also recalled his long career of risking and receiving crippling injuries, of "sacrificing his body" before white audiences.[36]

Print journalists, who consistently emphasized his "mild, warm, and talkative" nature as opposed to the moodiness of Bill Russell or the cerebral qualities of Kareem Abdul-Jabbar, helped Simpson toward crossover salability by making him known as an affable and "inoffensive" football superstar.[37] But it was television coverage and corporate sponsorship that contributed most decisively to the polishing and preserving of his image of easygoing Supermanhood. Both as the football-playing object of the television camera's attention and as the sportscaster covering football and the whole "wide world of sports," Simpson's fortunes consistently intertwined with those of the producer Roone Arledge. Arledge's technical innovations in the filming of sports and his studied blurring of tire lines between journalism and entertainment helped to make a spectacle of Simpson.[38] His reliance on Simpson as a broadcaster helped to ensure that O. J. would not leave the spotlight and would function as one of the boys in sports journalism, largely insulated from serious criticism.

The story of dramatic and seemingly race-neutral technical innovations in the world of televised sports is largely Arledge's story. Arledge began the transformation of television sports coverage seven years before Simpson entered USC. Hired at ABC's sports division in 1960, he immediately set out to cover sporting "events"—as sets of spectacular happenings—off as well as on the field. In 1966, when ABC signed a contract with the NCAA, granting it exclusive college football coverage, Arledge pioneered in the introduction of instant replay during live telecasts. He combined this technique with the extensive incorporation of slow-motion photography. The latter technology, applied to the screening of sports since the early twentieth century and used most effectively by the Nazi director Leni Riefenstahl in the 1930s, had become a staple of Arledge-produced sports telecasts by the time Simpson played his most touted games at USC.[39]

The combination of slow motion and instant replay—along with Arledge's increased use of close-ups, stop action, and sidebar stories on individual athletes—transformed the ways in which sports, and Simpson, were seen. It suddenly became arguable that television viewers could take in more of the action than those at the event. So thoroughly did Arledge come to regard the game as only the raw material from which he would fashion a "show" that his *Wide World of Sports* often featured esoteric sports, with little worry that viewers would be lost.[40] Simpson profited greatly from Arledge's innovations. He smiled not only engagingly, as other athletes had, but in stop action, as they largely had not. Above all, Simpson was among the first great backs to play his full college career with slow-motion instant replay in full use. The effect of such replays cut in two directions. On the one hand, it made couch-bound athletes of all races able to imagine themselves "in his shoes," seeing the holes in the defense and the coming of contact in ways live action precluded. Hertz advertisers appreciated as much in transforming Simpson to a slow-motion rusher through airports. On the other hand, slow-motion replays became vital in the popularizing and even the naming of specifically African American sports performance styles such as the one Simpson marketed with his "jive talk." As Riefenstahl appreciated, slow-motion photography let viewers linger over the "natural" bodies of athletes, making it an effective vehicle for her monumentalizing of Aryan supermen in sports. Before Arledge, slow motion had most frequently been used in the filming of boxing matches, contests in which racially and ethnically typed bodies contested most nakedly and openly.[41] Slow motion also, as Arthur Ashe brilliantly observed, provided the medium that could best showcase highly improvised and visually exciting running styles increasingly seen as hallmarks of African American players, especially Simpson. So thoroughly were race, body, and style entwined in viewers' perspectives that the extent to which intelligence and judgment undergird such rushing went almost unremarked. Instead, the style was seen as natural and Simpson as not only Superman but "supernatural."[42]

Beyond technical innovations, Arledge typified two other important trends in sports television, changes that would influence both coverage of

Simpson as a player and by Simpson as a reporter. The first centered on his further blurring of the line between sports journalism and entertainment. Famously illustrated by Howard Cosell's bitter writings on the battle between professionals (i.e., Cosell) and "jockocrats" (everyone else) on Arledge's *Monday Night Football,* the threat to standards posed by Arledge's allowing stars to report sports was undoubtedly overblown. Ex-athletes had long announced games, and Cosell himself used celebrity rather than qualifications to branch out into reporting on sports about which his expertise was much in doubt. When Arledge's entertainment-first philosophy won him promotion to heading the news division, Cosell steamed because he was not hired to work on the news side, alongside such Arledge discoveries as Geraldo Rivera. Print journalism's standards of objectivity in sports reporting hardly provided an impeccable professional model for television. The broader ethical problems of the cozy, contractual, and mutually rewarding relationships between the networks and the leagues, and between the networks and sponsors who used celebrity spokespersons who were being reported on during the games, raise much more troubling issues than the presence of jockocrats. Nonetheless, Arledge's use of "jocks," including active professional athletes, on telecasts clearly set the stage for Simpson's crossover into media and abetted the sort of nonreporting that caused fraying in Simpson's Superman cape to go unremarked.[43]

The fraternity of jockocrats that Cosell ultimately hated was part of a second contribution of Arledge as a producer. He popularized a sports television style that crafted an appeal designed mainly around gender rather than race or class. Comparing football to bullfights and heavyweight boxing, he hoped to capture some interest from women, but not because they appreciated either the subtleties of football or even the "deftness" of an athlete generally. Instead, he hoped women would tune in to "see what everyone is wearing [and] watch the cheerleaders." He filmed the latter from "a creepy, peepy camera," knowing that "very few men have ever switched channels when a nicely proportioned girl was leaping into the air."[44] Before coming to sports programming, Arledge had hoped his pilot of *For Men Only,* described as a network version of *Playboy,* would move his career beyond the producing of *Hi, Mom,* Shari Lewis's puppet show. Much of his football programming could have also carried the "for men only" tag. Male camaraderie was especially at a premium in the antics of the "teams" of broadcasters, especially the road warriors covering *Monday Night Football*.[45]

Simpson joined the boys on ABC telecasts quite early in his career, very much as both a jockocrat and a black voice. As in advertising, his crossover from the football field to television reporting was precocious and virtually without precedent. He had just left USC when Arledge signed him to a 1970 contract as a very visible freelancer with *Wide World of Sports*. That role, and his reporting on the 1972 Olympics, cast Simpson as an American, abroad and often at sea in the confusing variety of international athletic competitions.[46] But far from colorless, Simpson's easygoing presence as a *Wide World* correspondent bespoke efforts to forget, and to make the world forget, the 1968 Olympics. His more durable career as a "color man" on football telecasts unfolded squarely within a context of race. He succeeded where other great black athletes, such as Bill Russell, floundered. Racism plagued Russell's brief tenure as a superb network basketball commentator and was charged when Fred Williamson was removed after a few pioneering *Monday Night Football* telecasts.[47] However, that Simpson prospered, and became the first African American to work regularly on Monday night games, hardly suggests his transcendence of race. His nonstandard English, so endearing to print reporters, became the object of a running dialogue among critics, who constantly anticipated improvement. During his bitter 1983 feud with Simpson, Cosell began to doubt that his partner's "deplorable diction" and "locution problem" would ever be remedied.[48] Critics also noted his bobbing head, mechanical delivery, and forced smile, but Simpson's highly publicized announcing problems centered on his language, which was heard as insufficiently white English. His 1985 demotion to pre- and postgame coverage of the Super Bowl brought a rare example of contact between Simpson and a civil rights group, with the NAACP vigorously lobbying ABC on his behalf.[49]

Nor was race absent in the highly gendered and economically driven dynamics that led to the failure of the press to investigate and cover stories regarding Simpson's abuse of women and his use of drugs. After the murders, long-standing reports of Simpson's cocaine use, possible violence toward Marguerite Simpson and women at USC, and allegedly compulsive sexual conquests came to light.[50] That these stories had by and large never seen the light of day or been subjected to scrutiny, caused no significant self-criticism. (Indeed, recent accounts of sports reporters buying drugs from New York Giants players in the 1980s have also created little stir.)[51] We raise this issue of nonreporting not out of a commitment to more sensationalist, censorious news about the personal lives of athletes; we would prefer less. But in light of the constant stories on Simpson as family man and role model, the quite negative press on other athletes, and the mania for reporting anything and everything about Simpson after 1994, his insulation from bad press regarding violence, sex, and drugs requires some scrutiny.

That insulation clearly reflected Simpson's role as a commodity valuable to his teams, the NFL, the networks, and major corporate sponsors of games and much else on television. Preserving his image served also to protect the images and profits of powerful interlocking forces. The silence of the press on the difficult, complex relationship of football to male supremacy and to the battering of women suggests how the media and the game protect each other. In Geraldo Rivera's remarkably persistent attempts to combine utter sensationalism with worn-on-the-sleeve concern about domestic violence, you won't hear, for example, the nuanced analysis of gender and football provided in James McBride's *War, Battering and Other Sports.*[52]

Simpson likewise benefited from a more intimate form of journalistic self-protection. When he interrupted filming of a sidebar story on "nightlife" and football to have semipublic sex in the backseat of a car, or when he sought out one-night stands during his marriages, Simpson hardly outraged the norms of sports journalism. Arledge had married the personal secretary of RCA head David Sarnoff in 1953. She typed Arledge's proposal for a pilot on Sarnoff's letterhead and forwarded it to the president of NBC, then an RCA subsidiary, as if it came from on high. This "different brand of cunning" failed, as did the marriage, when Arledge left his wife while on vacation. He subsequently married his secretary, a former Miss Alabama, seventeen years his junior.[53] Cosell, the professional on *Monday Night Football,* "joked" with network secretaries by unbuttoning their blouses "playfully." More broadly, the ABC network had precisely one woman in an executive position.[54] Sexism at the top was neither news nor a topic to be investigated with relish.

But as thoroughly structured by male supremacy and economic self-interest as the nonreporting on O. J. was, the dynamics by which his image was propped up were hardly colorless. The black-star-as-role-model and black-star-as-thug-on-drugs images grew up absolutely in tandem in the press in the last twenty-five years, so that there was little room to cast Simpson in a middle position. Reporters and athletes did not just fraternize via shared drugs, sex, and secrets, but such vices often specifically lubricated more extensive interaction between African American athletes and white journalists. And, of course, the black Superman media image of the 1970s was also Superspade and Superfly, one in which violence, sex, and drugs were assumed to be prominent. Indeed, so important is the extent to which recent discourses on the common manliness of white and nonwhite men has assumed, expressed, and reinforced racial stereotypes that we conclude with an examination of Simpson, gender, and race that extends beyond the coverage of sports.

Hertz and the Buying of O. J.: Company Man, Real Man, Black Man

In a 1994 *Business Marketing* article describing Simpson's genius, a top Hertz executive credited him with having transcended mere sport and "really taken on the persona of a businessperson," impressively "capable of speaking to another businessperson." Aside from its noteworthy assumption that moving from being among the greatest athletes of one's generation to being a "businessperson" represents a steep ascent, the executive's observation is of interest for its framing of Simpson's crossover as one from sports to commerce in a way that both ignores race and renders Simpson's rise in gender-free language.[55]

Such a claim both captures and obscures large parts of Simpson's appeal to the independent entrepreneurs and the corporate salesmen targeted by Hertz's rental car ads. Simpson consistently emphasized his desire to own businesses and to invest. In his initial Buffalo contract negotiations, the one significant concession he did manage to secure was a large bonus for investment purposes. He made films not only as an actor but also as the owner of a production company. His switch from ABC to

NBC was much publicized as resulting from a desire to be a producer.[56] He acquired stakes in many of the corporations he endorsed—enough, as he put it, to be "a player." As time went by, his commitment to being an entrepreneur was increasingly colorless, divorced from any claims to his being a specifically African American role model in this realm, let alone from the sort of ideologically nationalist commitment to black capitalism so much a part of Jimmy Brown's ongoing projects.[57]

By all accounts constantly busy, always moving about along with other men, risking family relationships amidst anguish in order to be a good provider, Simpson served as a perfect symbol with which the business traveler could identify. However, given the fact that his business ventures were plagued by failures born of incredibly bad timing, and given his great prominence as a spokesperson for Hertz and a host of other corporations, Simpson likely wore the label "company man" more fittingly than "businessman." One of the nation's most sought-after motivational speakers at corporate dinners, Simpson could convincingly address his audiences on the importance of being a "team member" in the corporate world. Appealing to both the independent businessmen and the company men who constituted the bulk of the rental car market, Simpson sent Hertz's sales and recognition skyward.[58]

But even Simpson's appeal to white men in meetings, airports, and offices ultimately turned on his status as an acceptable and exemplary black man, not as a colorless fellow worker. In this connection, the recent study of race, gender, and sport by Lisa Disch and Mary Jo Kane especially succeeds in illuminating how the notion of upper middle-class white masculinity both fantasizes important connections with black athletes and retains prerogatives to judge, type, and distance itself from such stars. Employed largely in physically passive jobs, such men cannot claim maleness based on a working body and therefore base such acclaim to an unprecedented extent on the "sovereign masculinity" of sport.[59] Thus, the golf course's male foursome beckons as the reward for choosing Hertz's faster service. The quite passive experience of flying becomes an open field dash through airports. Sporting performance by a few professionals becomes the property of many. As one white male professional puts it in a study by the sociologist Michael Messner, "A woman can do the same job as I can do—maybe even be my boss. But I'll be *damned* if she can go out on the football field and take a hit from Ronnie Lott." Forging pan-male unities, athletic striving particularly shores up male dominance in periods of forward political and economic motion by women so that women's liberation movements as well as Black Power form a critical con-text for Simpson's rise in the late 1960s.[60]

The view that every male middle manager could "take a hit" from Lott is on one level ludicrous, but such a view expresses in shorthand the very real fact that professional team sports are places where women can't play on the field or, by and large, participate in ownership and manage-ment. For black men, during Simpson's career, sports were one of the few realms in which it was possible to be a "player," though the bars to mana-gerial roles, let alone ownership, remained virtually complete. Sport has functioned as a spectacle in which the male body and the white mind are at once exalted, and in which white men feel especially empowered to judge, to bet on, and to vicariously identify with African Americans. Thus, when Simpson, as early as 1969, boasted that his triumph lay in being seen as a "man" and not black, he was half right.[61] The white male target audience had a great interest in claiming his footloose power as male. But in so doing, they could also reserve the right to view his abilities as the natural, easy, and elemental traits of what Messner calls the "primitive other." Time and again, sportswriters, executives, and middle-level man-agers would credit him as a "real man." From fans at corporate dinners to the television executive commenting on why Simpson's "diction" did not get him fired, to the network official who explained why his 1989 domestic violence case did not finish his broadcast career, the judgment was that he was also a "nice guy." Such accolades, we argue, were not colorlessly conferred. At the height of his acceptance, Simpson was a "real black man" and a "nice black guy."[62]

Simpson's crossover success offered white viewers the opportunity to sit in judgment of black manliness at the same moment when they claimed to have gotten past racial thinking. The more marketable appeal was not Simpson's supposed transcendence of race but rather the alleged transcen-dence of race among his audiences. The terrible force of much white reac-tion to both the trial and the verdict grows in no small part out of the dynamics described in this article. Such is most obviously the case with regard to the case with which Simpson's image as a black man could fully accommodate the recrudescence of racist stereotypes. But perhaps more telling has been the outpouring of white rage against the "injection" of the issue of race into the trial—a rage that has consistently blamed a black attorney rather than white police for race's presence in the courtroom. Despite the wholesale change in attitudes toward Simpson himself, his image has remained a vehicle through which white racial ideologies, and the pretense of their absence, can be spun out together.

Notes

Assistance from Tiya Miles, Tom Sabatini, Rachel Martin, and Marjorie Bryer greatly improved this essay.

1. The epigraph is from Henry Louis Gates, Jr., and Cornel West, "Affirmative Reaction," *Transition* 68 (December 1995): 180. See also Rob Buchanan, "18 Holes with O. J. Simpson," *Golf*, December 1990, 100, 106; Lawrence Otis Graham, *Member of the Club* (New York: HarperCollins, 1995), 17; Joe Marshall, "Now You See Him, Now You Don't," *Sports Illustrated*, 19 October 1973, 30–43; Marc Cerasini, *O. J. Simpson: American Hero, American Tragedy* (New York: Windsor Publishing, 1994), 196, 226–227; Beth Ann Krier, "What Makes Simpson Run?" *Ebony*, December 1981, 109; Teresa Carpenter, "The Man Behind the Mask," *Esquire*, November 1994, 84–90; "Harsh Realities Haunt Simpson," *Columbia (Mo.) Daily Tribune*, 25 June 1994, 3-B; and especially, "*Playboy* Interview: O. J. Simpson," *Playboy* 23, December 1976, 92–94.

2. Melanie Wells, "O. J. Agrees to Share Rights to His Initials," *USA Today*, 22 February 1996; Cerasini, *Simpson*, 192; Michigan *Chronicle*, 16 July 1977, B-1; Louis J. Haugh, "O. J. Tops Year's Star Presenters," *Advertising Age*, 20 June 1977, 1; "The Juice Joins the Soda Wars," *Fortune*, 30 September 1985, 9–10; Jack Slater, "O. J. Simpson: The Problems of a Super Superstar," *Ebony*, November 1976, 164; Richard Hoffer, "Fatal Attraction," *Sports Illustrated*, 27 June 1994, 22, 31.

3. See, for example, Hugh Pearson, "Trial by T-Shirt," *Wall Street Journal*, 12 August 1994; "MAD's O. J. Pog Schtickers," *MAD Super Special* 105, July 1995, 31–32; "Enough to Open a Library," *Newsweek*, 25 March 1996, 53; Clifford Linedecker, *O. J. from A to Z* (New York: St. Martin's Griffen, 1995), 37; "Cashing in on O. J., Reluctantly," *Harper's*, October 1994, 21; Adam Hochschild, "Closing Argument," *New York Times Book Review*, 28 April 1996, 14.

4. "The Pack in Search of O. J.'s Roots," *San Francisco Chronicle*, 25 June 1994, A-24; Greg Krikorian and Eric Lichtblau, "A Rising Star," *Los Angeles Times*, 4 October 1995, A-3; Richard C. Paddock and Jennifer Warren, " 'I Was Somebody Who Didn't Care about Anything'," *Los Angeles Times*, 18 June 1994, A-8; Evelyn C. White, "Fallen

Hero Stirs Complicated Feelings," *San Francisco Chronicle*, 4 October 1995, A-6; Craig Marine and Leslie Goldberg, "The Hill O. J. Left Behind," *San Francisco Chronicle*, 26 June 1994, A-1, A-8; Simpson, *I Want to Tell You* (Boston: Little, Brown, 1995), 87–89.

5. Hoffer, "Fatal Attraction," 20. The 1996 HBO film of Arthur Ashe's *Hard Road to Glory: A History of the African-American Athlete Since 1946* (New York: Amistad Books, 1988) makes the point on Simpson's pioneering in crossover advertising most acutely, perhaps because Ashe knew the long odds against such crossover firsthand. On advertising, see Roland Marchand, *Advertising and the American Dream* (Berkeley: University of California Press: 1985), 193; Jackson Lears, *Fables of Abundance* (New York: Basic Books, 1994), 123–124; Stephen Fox, *The Mirror Makers: A History of American Advertising and Its Creators* (New York: Morrow, 1984), 280–284; Harry Edwards, "The Black Professional Athlete," in *Sport and Society: An Anthology*, ed. John T. Talamini and Charles H. Page (Boston: Little, Brown, 1973), 260; Anne McClintock, *Imperial Leather: Race, Gender and Sexuality in the Colonial Conquest* (New York and London: Routledge, 1995), 31–35, 207–231.

6. Louis J. Haugh, "O. J. Tops Year's Star Presenters," *Advertising Age*, 20 June 1977, 1; Deford, "Ready If You Are," 16; Cerasini, *O. J. Simpson*, 84–85, 158–161, 192, 202–203; Edwin Shrake, "The Juice on a Juicy Road," *Sports Illustrated*, 19 August 1974, 36.

7. Teresa Carpenter, "The Man Behind the Mask," *Esquire*, November 1994, 87; James Brady, "Sunlit Afternoons and O. J.," *Advertising Age*, 20 June 1994, 34.

8. The best study of 1968 worldwide is George Katsiaficas, *The Imagination of the New Left: A Global Analysis of 1968* (Boston: South End Books, 1987); on the late 1960s in basketball and Chamberlain/Nixon, see Nelson George, *Elevating the Game; The History and Aesthetics of Black Men in Basketball* (New York: Fireside Books, 1992), 152–178.

9. Edwards, *The Revolt of the Black Athlete* (New York: Free Press, 1970); Talamini and Page, eds., *Sport and Society*, 259–261; Othello Harris, "Muhammad Ali and the Revolt of the Black Athlete," in *Muhammad Ali: The People's Champ*, ed. Elliott J. Gorn (Urbana and Chicago: University of Illinois Press, 1995), 54–69.

10. Edwards, *Revolt of the Black Athlete*; Jack Scott, *The Athletic Revolution* (New York: Free Press, 1971), 86–88; Lee Ballinger, *In Your Face* (Chicago: Vanguard Books, 1981), 34–38; George, *Elevating the Game*, 147–148. See, however, Ashe, *Hard Road to Glory*, 192, for Simpson's brief support of the antiracist boycott of the New York Athletic Club, and Earl Hutchinson, *Beyond O. J.: Race, Sex and Class Lessons for America* (Los Angeles: Middle Passage Press, 1996), 140, 149.

11. George, *Elevating the Game*, 142; Cromwell quoted in Scott, *Athletic Revolution*, 81; *"Playboy* Interview: O. J. Simpson," 94; Dan Jenkins, "The Great One Confronts O. J.," *Sports Illustrated*, 20 November 1967, 33, 38; Herman L. Masin, "All the Way with O. J.!" *Senior Scholastic*, 18 October 1968, 32; Carpenter, "The Man Behind the Mask," 87; A. S. Doc Young, "The Magnificent Six," *Los Angeles Sentinel*, 17 January 1980, A-7.

12. Louie Robinson, "Two Superstars Vie for Heisman Trophy," *Ebony*, December 1968, 173.

13. George, *Elevating the Game*, 164; "*Playboy* Interview: O. J. Simpson," 78-B, 85–90, 98–99; Cerasini, *Simpson*; 56, 145, 177–178; Carpenter, "The Man Behind the Mask," 88–89; Frank Deford, "Ready If You Are, O. J.," *Sports Illustrated*, 14 July 1969, 19; Pete Axthelm, "The Juice Runs Wild," *Newsweek*, 27 October 1975, 10; Simpson with Axthelm, *O. J.: The Education of a Rich Rookie* (New York: Macmillan, 1970), 12–17; Jenkins, "Great One Confronts O. J.," 34–38; Krier, "What Makes O. J. Run?" 110; Peter Wood, "What Makes Simpson Run?" *New, York Times Magazine*, 14 December 1975, 6–38; Ballinger, *In Your Face*, 47–51; Dave Meggyesy, *Out of Their League* (New York: Ramparts Press, 1971), 172.

14. *Michigan Chronicle*, 21 May 1977; Jim Baker, *O. J. Simpson's Memorable Games* (New York: Putnam, 1978), 49.

15. Deford, "Ready If You Are," 16–19; Harry Edwards, *Sociology of Sport* (Homewood, Ill.: Dorsey, 1973), 279–280; Simpson with Axthelm, *Rich Rookie*, 9–17; Shrake, "First Taste of O. J.," 20–22; "*Playboy* Interview: O. J. Simpson," 78–85; Axthelm, "Juice Runs Wild," 72.

16. Robert Weems, "The Revolution Will Be Marketed," *Radical History Review* 59 (spring 1994): 94–107; Fox, *Mirror Makers*, 281–284; on the "level playing field" image, see Mike Marquese, "Sport and Stereotype: From Role Model to Muhammad Ali," *Race and Class* 36 (April–June 1995): 4–5.

17. Cerasini, *Simpson*, 48–49; "Harsh Realities Haunt Simpson," 3-B; Robinson, "Two Superstars," 173; Simpson with Axthelm, *Rich Rookie*, p. 12; Edwin Shrake, "The First Taste of O. J. Is OK," *Sports Illustrated*, 25 August 1969, 20; Darden, "The Bloody Glove," *Newsweek*, 25 March 1968, 57.

18. The most common misspelling, "Portrero," recurs in Pulitzer Prizewinning journalist Teresa Carpenter's recent attempt to tie the murders to Simpson's putatively underclass youth in her "The Man Behind the Mask," 84–100; Simpson's autobiographical (with Axthelm) *Rich Rookie*, 10, comes no closer than "Patero." See also "*Playboy* Interview: O. J. Simpson," 97; "Countdown to Pasadena," *Time*, 11 October 1968, 43; Paul Zimmerman, "All Dressed Up," *Sports Illustrated*, 26 November 1979, 40; "Meet O. J. Simpson: Home Is Always Where the Heart Is," *Parents' Magazine*, February 1977, 42–43.

19. "*Playboy* Interview: O. J. Simpson," 97–99; Carpenter, "The Man Behind the Mask," 86; Warren and Paddock, " 'I Was Somebody,' " A-8.

20. Robinson, "Two Superstars," 173; Brian Lowry, "Adams Turns Up the Juice with O. J. Simpson," *Advertising Age*, 23 December 1985, 6; Axthelm, "Juice Runs Wild," 70–71; "The Juice Joins the Soda Wars," *Fortune*, 30 September 1985, 9–10; Zimmerman, "All Dressed Up," 40; Paddocks and Warren, " 'I Was Somebody,' " A-9.

21. Chuck Wingis, "O. J. Tells How Ads Led to His Tinseltown Success," *Advertising Age*, 20 June 1977, 82.

22. Edwards, "Black Professional Athlete," 263–264; Shrake, "First Taste of O. J.," 20.

23. *Playboy* Interview: O. J. Simpson," 78-A, 78-B; Shrake, "First Taste of O. J.," 20; "Simpson Settles In," *Time,* 8 October 1973, 68; "O. J. to Go," *Newsweek,* 13 January 1969, 76; Jack Slater, "O. J. Simpson: The Problems of a Super Superstar," *Ebony,* November 1976, 164.

24. The Carson joke is in Robert F. Jones, "The $2.5 Million Dollar Man," *Sports Illustrated,* 27 September 1976, 20–21; see n. 23 above, especially for the quote, "Simpson Settles In," 68.

25. "Meet O. J. Simpson," 42, 43; Axthelm, "Juice Is Loose," 66; Joe Marshall, "What's Making O. J. Go?" *Sports Illustrated,* 25 July 1976, 20; Carpenter, "Behind the Mask," 87. On debates over race, family, and pathology in this period, see Lee Rainwater and William Yancey, eds., *The Moynihan Report and the Politics of Controversy* (Cambridge: MIT Press, 1967).

26. On Ali and style, see Jose Torres and Bert Sugar, *Sting Like a Bee* (New York: Abelard-Schuman, 1971); Jeffrey T. Sammons, "Rebel with a Cause," in Gorn, ed., *Ali,* 162–164; see also George, *Elevating the Game,* 132–168.

27. "Year of the Okey-Doke," *Time,* 24 December 1973, 57; Marshall, "Now You See Him . . . ," 37; Axthelm, "Juice Really Flows," 69–70; Bob Oates, "O. J.'s Way," *Los Angeles Times,* 12 October 1975, sec. 3, 1; "Simpson Settles In," 68; Robinson, "Two Supporters," 174; "*Playboy* Interview: O. J. Simpson," 102; Bob Oates, "There's a 'Coward' Loose in the NFL," *Los Angeles Times,* 3 October 1973; on *juke (jook),* see Clarence Major, *Dictionary of Afro-American Slang* (New York: International Publishers, 1970), 72; Robert L. Chapman, *New Dictionary of American Slang* (New York: Harper and Row, 1986), 239–240.

28. "Year of the Okey-Doke," 57; Herman L. Masin, "All the Way with O. J.," *Senior Scholastic,* 18 October 1968, 32; "2003: O. J.'s Odyssey," *Newsweek,* 31 December 1977; on Ali, Simpson, and style, see also Cuda Brown, "O. J. Who?" *Vibe Meanderings* 205 (1995): World Wide Web.

29. See n. 27 above and, on *okey-doke,* Major, *Dictionary of Afro-American Slang,* 87; Clarence Major, *Juba to Jive: A Dictionary of African-American Slang* (New York: Penguin, 1994), 329.

30. Dyson, "Be Like Mike? Michael Jordan and the Pedagogy of Desire," in *Reflecting Black: African-American Cultural Criticisms* (Minneapolis: University of Minnesota Press, 1993), 64–75, esp. 70.

31. Jenkins, "Great One Confronts O. J.," 38; Cerasini, *Simpson,* 61ff; Wingis, "Tinseltown Success," 30; Dan Jenkins, "The Juice Is Turned On Again," *Sports Illustrated,* 13 October 1975, 30; "O. J. Snags Real Juicy Contract with Tree Sweet," *Los Angeles Times,* 14 July 1976, sec. 3, 15; Chapman, *New Dictionary,* 303; Stuart Berg Flexner, *Listening to America* (New York: Simon & Schuster, 1982), 474. See also n. 4 and 5 above.

32. Robinson, "Two Superstars," 173.

33. Gavin Power, "What the Marketing Experts See for O. J.," *San Francisco Chronicle*, 16 June 1994; *Time*, 27 June 1994, front cover.

34. Cited by Michael Oriard, "Order and Chaos, Work and Play," chapter 5 in *Reading Football: How the Popular Press Created an American Spectacle* (Chapel Hill: University of North Carolina Press, 1993), 185. See also Ballinger, *In Your Face*, 33–35.

35. From the beginning of his college career until the time of his trial, O. J. was constantly referred to by reporters as an affable, smiling Negro. For example, "The Great One Confronts O. J.," a 1967 *Sports Illustrated* story about a game between USC and UCLA, described O. J. as "a mild, warm, talkative transfer from City College of San Francisco," 20 November 1967, 37.

36. Shrake, "First Taste of O. J.," 20; Carpenter, "Behind the Mask," 84, 88; Deford, "Ready If You Are," 16, 19; *Michigan Chronicle*, 25 March 1978, B-2; Zimmerman, "All Dressed Up," 38. See also Cerasini, *Simpson*, 196; Jenkins, "Great One Confronts O. J.," 38.

37. Perceptions of O. J.'s affability can be compared to the demonization of Kareem Abdul-Jabbar, who was deeply involved in black protests. See also Kareem Abdul-Jabbar, *Giant Steps* (New York: Bantam Books, 1983), 200: "My adversary relationship with the press started during my second week in the league."

38. Among the many accounts of Arledge's years as head of ABC sports are: Ron Powers, *Supertube* (New York: Coward-McCann, 1984); Marc Gunther, *The House That Roone Built: The Inside Story of ABC News* (Boston: Little, Brown, 1994); Phil Patton, *Razzle Dazzle* (Garden City: Dial Press, 1984); Terry O'Neil, *The Game Behind the Game: High Pressure, High Stakes in Television Sports* (New York: Harper and Row, 1989); Bert Randolph Sugar, *"The Thrill of Victory": The Inside Story of ABC Sports* (New York: Hawthorn, 1978); and Jim Spence, *Up Close and Personal: The Inside Story of Network Television Sports* (New York: Atheneum, 1988).

39. In *Supertube*, Ron Powers reproduces a memo in which Arledge maps out his philosophy of televised sports as spectacle designed to make specific gender appeals, and talks about the role of slow motion in this effort, see pp. 145–146. Patton elaborates on the history of slow motion in television, noting that NBC experimented with the technique before Arledge and CBS perfected the technique of instant replay in the late 1950s. But Arledge perfected its use on live broadcasts, largely because he had access to video technology and especially to the mini-cam. See *Razzle Dazzle*, pp. 63–75. Shortly after the first use of instant replay technology in a college football broadcast in 1963, the technique got its first mass exposure when it was used to replay Jack Ruby's shooting of Lee Harvey Oswald. See Erik Barnouw, *Tube of Plenty: The Evolution of American Television* (New York: Oxford University Press, 1975), 334, for an early example of the use of slow motion in sports, also see Dan Streible, "A History of the Boxing Film, 1894–1915," *Film History* 3, no. 3 (1989): 235–257.

40. Powers, *Supertube*, 160–170; Spence, "The Thrill of Victory . . . The Agony of Defeat: The Incredible Story of ABC's *Wide World of Sports*," in *Up Close and Personal*, 66–79. The concept for *Wide World of Sports* was developed by Ed Sherick, Arledge's

first boss at ABC Sports. But while Sherick developed the idea of covering offbeat sporting events, Arledge executed that idea, figuring out how to make the coverage "up close and personal."

41. Lisa Fluor, "God of the Stadium: National Socialist Aesthetics and the Body in Leni Riefenstahl's *Olympia*" (Ph.D. diss., University of California at San Diego, 1992). Streible, "Boxing Film," 235–257 and n. 39 above.

42. Ashe, *Hard Road to Glory*, 138–139, adds, "In the early 1970s, tickets for NFL games became more sought after than those for any other type of athletic contest. Corporations bought up sections of season tickets and sell-out crowds were the norm rather than the exception. There was a constant demand to make the game more exciting, and fans, especially those watching on television, wanted more scoring; rules were changed to accommodate them, and in nearly every instance black players bene-fited because, aside from the white quarterbacks, they were the most gifted performers on the field." On "supernatural," see Robinson, "Two Superstars," 171.

43. Gunther, *House That Roone Built,* describes some of the panic that struck the ABC news division after Arledge's appointment as its head, noting that one journalist joked that Roone would soon be hiring the likes of Geraldo Rivera. Geraldo, in fact, was one of Arledge's first hires in the news division; see pp. 32, 147. See also Howard Cosell, *I Never Played the Game* (New York: Avon, 1985), 154, 177; and note Axthelm's continuing praises of Simpson in *Newsweek* after the two collaborated on *Rich Rookie.*

44. Powers, *Supertube,* 146.

45. Ibid., 137–141; Spence, "Forever a Man's World? Why Women Sportscasters Are Still So Far from Winning Equal Air Time," in *Up Close and Personal,* 175–188.

46. O'Neill, *The Game Behind the Game,* 262–263.

47. Spence, *Up Close and Personal,* 147–148; Bill Russell, *Second Wind: The Memoirs of an Opinionated Man* (New York: Random House, 1979); Cosell, *I Never Played,* 334.

48. Spence, *Up Close and Personal,* 149–150, Cosell, *I Never Played,* 177–178.

49. Cosell, *I Never Played,* 155, 158.

50. See, for example, Carpenter, "The Man Behind the Mask," 87–101; Hoffer, "Fatal Attraction"; and "Harsh Realities Haunt Simpson," 1-B, 3-B.

51. Interview with former *Newsday* writer Bob Drury, KFAN Radio in Minneapolis, 8 May 1996.

52. James McBride, *War, Battering and Other Sports* (Atlantic Highlands, N.J.: Humanities Press, 1995).

53. Powers, *Supertube,* 138–141. See also Hoffer, "Fatal Attraction," 30–32.

54. Spence, *Up Close and Personal,* 6. Also see Marlene Saunders, "Women in Management," in *Waiting for Prime Time* (Champaign-Urbana: University of Illinois Press, 1988), 158–190, for a discussion of the climate for women at ABC and their struggles to break through the glass ceiling in sports as well as news.

55. Kate Bertrand, "O. J. Simpson Juices Hertz's Image," *Business Marketing,* August 1992, 28.

56. Cerasini, *Simpson,* 180–182; Simpson with Axthelm, *Rich Rookie,* 16–17; "Chalk Up One More Score for 'The Juice,' " *Michigan Chronicle,* 16 April 1977, B-1; Krier, "What Makes O. J. Run?" 106, 110; Gertrude Gipson, "O. J. Signs Exclusive Contract with NBC-TV," *Los Angeles Sentinel,* 5 May 1977, Entertainment-1; Stu Black, "They Call Me Mister Juice," *Los Angeles Magazine,* April 1980, 174.

57. Buchanan, "18 Holes," 100; Lowry, "Adams Turns Up Juice," 6.

58. Deford, "Ready If You Are," 16; Bertrand, "Juices Hertz's Image," 28; *Michigan Chronicle,* 16 July 1977, B-1; Cerasini, *Simpson,* 204; Spangler, "Golf Legends," 26; Wood, "What Makes Simpson Run?" 38; "No Touchdowns," *Inc.,* October 1985, 18.

59. Lisa Disch and Mary Jo Kane, "When a Looker is Really a Bitch: Lisa Olson, Sport and the Heterosexual Matrix," *Signs* 21 (winter 1996): 284, 283–287.

60. Messner, as quoted in Disch and Kane, "Looker," 285.

61. Gates and West, "Affirmative Reaction," 181–183; "Harsh Realities Haunt Simpson," 3-B.

62. Messner, "Masculinities and Athletic Careers: Bonding and Status Differences," in Messner and Don Sabo, eds., *Sport, Men and the Gender Order* (Champaign, Ill.: Human Kinetics Books, 1990), 103; Zimmerman, "All Dressed Up," 39; Shrake, "Juice on Juicy Road," 37; Gates and West, "Affirmative Reaction," 181; Hoffer, "Fatal Attraction," 18, 20.

3

MÉLISSE LAFRANCE AND GENEVIÈVE RAIL

"As Bad as He Says He Is?"
Interrogating Dennis Rodman's
Subversive Potential

• Dennis Rodman has been and continues to be the subject of much consideration in cultural studies (e.g., Barrett 1997; Kellner 1996; Lafrance and Rail 1997; McDonald and Aikens 1996). Rodman's multitudinous personas and often unpredictable interaction with television media have been frequently characterized as disruptive, counter-cultural and/or generally mysterious beyond intelligibility. Indeed, according to many observers, Rodman has radically defied normative convention and conspired, wittingly or unwittingly, to redefine representations of gender, race, and desire within the American cultural imaginary[1] (Barrett 1997; Jefferson 1997; Johnson 1996; McDonald and Aikens, 1996). In this paper, we are interested in elucidating the cultural and economic logics both underlying and propelling the Rodman sensation.

In an attempt to resist binary formulations of the Rodman phenomenon, we will consider those elements of Rodman's subjective productions that may potentially challenge the cultural norms structuring an audience's responses to him. We will argue, however, that Dennis Rodman's extraordinary spectacular enactments produce and consolidate dominant fantasies of race, gender, and desire, and are therefore only problematically subversive. We will show, by means of a critical overview of existing literature as well as an analysis of Rodman's most important promotional

74

strategies, that understanding Rodman's self-presentations as vitally disruptive elicits serious theoretical and conceptual dilemmas.

"This Guy is Something Else!"
Journalists Assess the Rodman Phenomenon

Rodman is significant for daring not to be macho in a milieu that has demanded it.
—*Steve Johnson*

Although varying in their degree of support for his public behavior, most journalists and/or consumers seem to construe Rodman as in some way irreconcilably different from not only the sporting world in particular, but the realm of popular culture in general. For the few journalists able to get beyond their simultaneous disgust and fascination with Rodman's penchant for women's clothing and his highly publicized visits to gay bars, the level of analysis remains enthusiastically cursory nonetheless.

The *Chicago Tribune, New York Times,* and *Sports Illustrated* provide the most consistent sources of both coverage and commentary. In a lengthy and relatively analytical article, *Chicago Tribune* critic Steve Johnson considers Rodman's race, persona, gender, and his alliances to multinational corporations. Disapprovingly, Johnson contends that Rodman's cross-dressing is "the most calculated androgyny since David Bowie vamped his way through the mid-1970s" (1996, 1). Johnson also concludes that this "calculated androgyny" has resulted in a peculiar celebration of Rodman, who has, since his relationship with Madonna, been "remade into a sort of postmodern [Peter] Pan" (1). Questioning the integrity of Rodman's promotional strategies, Johnson stipulates: "The trouble with all of this is that Rodman the persona, a persona, it should be noted, borrowed from the gay nightclub scene, is more interesting than Rodman the personality. . . . Just as putting him on a team less secure in itself would reveal him to be a disruptive force, putting him on TV reveals him to be all action, and little talk" (2). After lamenting Rodman's overwhelming market appeal as well as his swelling television presence, Johnson contradicts the article's earlier assertion that "Rodman is significant for daring

75

not to be macho" through his critical chronicling of one of the more disturbing Rodman exploits:

> Dennis comes out wearing a nurse's uniform and the crowd hoots and hollers as if it were still novel for Rodman . . . to wear a dress. Dennis tells a self-described sports widow to "after the game is over, jump his bones, darlin." The crowd whoops as if it had just heard Dorothy Parker reincarnate. Dennis walks around pushing his stethoscope into women's breasts, he's a medical professional checking their hearts don't you know, and the crowd cheers for what would get one of these women's co-workers a black eye, a pink slip and a visit from flashing blue lights. (3)

Even despite Johnson's sometimes scathing criticism of Rodman's antics, he, like almost all other critics, nevertheless credits Rodman for his progressive politics. Johnson concludes paradoxically:

> Off court, he is an important symbol . . . the first male athlete to gain fame for his willingness to break professional sports' macho code. . . . It is not so much the dress or the nail polish the kids are responding to as the thumb in the eye to convention they represent. . . . The idea that the nation's cul-de-sacs are populated by prepubescent boys who now idolize, for whatever reasons, a sometimes drag queen is both amusing and a relief to those who believe we ought to get going on that testosterone temperance plan. (5)

Using a slightly different approach, *New York Times* critic Margo Jefferson (1997) provides an interesting consideration of Rodman's impact on and engagement with popular culture, calling Rodman a "[feat] of stylistic engineering" (C13). Male athletes, according to Jefferson, have long been known for their tempers and violent tendencies on and off the court. However, she states, "few of them [have been] reprimanded quite as sternly or smugly as Mr. Rodman" (C13). Not only do both opposing team members and referees often set out to aggravate Rodman, but Chicago Bulls management has actually made psychiatric counseling a prerequisite for Rodman if he hopes to continue playing basketball. Jefferson attributes this particularly harsh treatment of Rodman to social prejudices. She keenly observes that

> only since he began talking about bisexuality and dressing up in campy costumes . . . have people been . . . tossing around words like "psychopath." Would there be so many armchair psychiatrists if Mr. Rodman's on-court bullying weren't accompanied by all that off-court cross-dressing and bisexual teasing (those transgressive acts of gender-bending, as academics like to say)? (C13)

And indeed, Jefferson (1997) notes, Rodman has gone further than just bisexual teasing. He has discussed his homosexual fantasies as well as the erotic energy that permeates "even the most heterosexual" (C13) men's locker rooms. Jefferson does not make Rodman out to have transcended sexism or machismo, astutely observing instead that Rodman is the "first star athlete to successfully wed heterosexual macho to drag queen chutzpah" (C20). While not as contradictory as Johnson's (1996) evaluation, Jefferson appears to have difficulty reconciling the paradoxical elements of Rodman's self-presentation and opts, finally, to celebrate him as America's "man of the moment."

The seemingly contradictory nature of both the aforementioned events and their journalistic assessments highlights the dilemma encountered by observers attempting to make sense of the Rodman craze. In fact, Rodman's persona appears to be predicated on the exploitation and reproduction of dominant norms and codes, while paradoxically recognized as rebellious and intelligently nonconformist. Our essay endeavors to address this contradiction in an attempt to understand how the apparently incongruous constituents of Rodman's success seem to at once effloresce and limit his subversive agency. That is, Rodman's enactments of "marketable difference" (Kellner 1996, 459) may indeed destabilize the American semiotic in positively oppositional ways by, for example, mainstreaming superficial aesthetic transgressions such as cross-dressing.[2] However, the white, male supremacist and heterosexist fantasies mobilized by Rodman in order to produce and sustain the popularity of his spectacles reinforce problematic events such as the exoticization of the black sporting body, the commodification of black struggle and the mythification of black physicality (both sensual and sexual). Therefore, our analysis considers Rodman's self-promotional strategies, as well as the intended and unintended discursive effects they produce.

Sex/Gender Reconsidered? Dennis Rodman and the Politics of Identity

Drag and the Limits of Subjective Agency

When journalists, critics, and consumers proclaim that Dennis Rodman is "something else" (Barrett 1997, 106), they are often referring, at least in part, to his enactments of dominant femininity. McDonald and Aikens's (1996) work is one of the most comprehensive academic analyses of Rodman's persona and the politics of his representation. McDonald and Aikens write:

> We consider professional basketball player Dennis Rodman's ever-changing mediated persona as a disruptive force to the ethos of heteronormativity. Specifically, we explore the way Dennis Rodman's appropriation of queer praxis serves to critique dominant heterosexist and gender ideologies by destabilizing binary gender codes. (1996, 97)

These authors suggest that popular representations of Rodman's cross-dressing and his homoerotic interests can work to render intelligible the "fluidity" and "artificiality" of sexual and gender categories, while revealing how masculinities and sexualities are "malleable" systems open to individual and cultural contestation. The latter implies that genders are theatrically performed: That is, subjects have the ability to either enact or not enact their culturally prescribed genders. In fact, according to Harper (1994), those who cross-dress are often seen as bringing into relief the mutability of gender identities and, by extension, the possibility of overhauling such identities. Harper explicates the problematic allure of understanding gender as an instance of theatrical performativity:

> The positing of such an accomplishment is potentially appealing for at least two closely related reasons: (1) it imputes to [drag queens] an

expanded agency whereby they seem to alter apparently fundamental elements of social experience; and it (2) thus recuperates those same personages as active producers not only of political critique but of significant social-structural change. (91)

For Harper (1994), then, to insist on the subject's ability to effect voluntaristic identity overhauls is to become polemically implicated in illusory cultural logics of liberalism and individualism. Indeed, this insistence is seductive as the imagined presence of such agential possibilities signals the success of contemporary liberalism and its corresponding project of providing the individual—and especially the disenfranchised individual—with the tools necessary to shape and determine her own destiny. Harper points out, however, that the latter is questionable. Indeed, to effect a veritable identity overhaul implies that one not only reconstructs her own identity, albeit using always already contaminated psychic resources,[3] but that others attribute the same presumably positive meanings to the overhaul as does she. We would argue, in fact, that rare is the instance wherein agents of mainstream society attribute positive meanings to acts of gender subversion and/or other forms of identity overhaul. More frequently than not, those who "misperform" their prescribed genders are confronted by many different and often dangerous manifestations of cultural disapproval (Bartky 1993; Bordo 1993; Butler 1989). For example, Jefferson (1997) illustrates that Dennis Rodman has also borne the brunt of cultural disapproval for his gender transgressions. Indeed, to both monitor and subdue his apparently undesirable aesthetic tendencies, Rodman has had to undergo mandatory psychiatric consultation at the request of the Chicago Bulls' management. Thus, that which may be considered by an individual in drag as exposing the malleability of gender could be, and often is, simultaneously represented in the popular as symptomatic of individual pathology. In view of such constraints on subjective agency and, contingently, the conditions of its reception, it seems implausible to contend that gender identities are uncomplicatedly plastic or malleable.

Harper (1994) also notes that when viewing drag queens as "active producers not only of political critique but of significant social-structural change" (91), one must closely inspect the scope of these individuals' subjective agency. While it may indeed be possible for an individual to subvert norms of gender, sexuality, and desire microcosmically (i.e., within the realm of her own everyday life), it does not necessarily follow that this agency extends into all (or even most) facets of the public sphere.[4] We argue that the decidedly "public" nature of the violences[5] inflicted upon those who reject and subvert dominant norms of gender, sexuality, and desire seriously undermine the individual's subjective agency as regards identity overhaul. One's ability to refashion her identity in her own image rarely reaches the point of veritable subversion when such refashioning is frequently policed, interrupted, and/or suppressed by public structures designed to maintain dominant cultural processes. To posit that such subversive performances can lead to unrestricted identity overhauls elides the systematic power of public apparatuses working to maintain and consolidate dominant discursive regimes.

In light of the aforementioned, Rodman's mandatory psychiatric counseling and his comparatively stern disciplining by NBA referees might be seen as a particularly apt illustration of how Rodman's ability to "disrupt binary gender codes" (McDonald and Aikens 1996, 97) through "drag queenesque" performances is impelled by the meanings others impute to his enactments and the limits of his subjective agency in the public sphere. Nevertheless, Butler (1993a, 1993b) and Harper (1994) both posit that drag does indeed serve a critical function. That critical function, however, is not related to exposing the essential plasticity of gender. Instead, drag's veritable subversive edge lies in its ability to expose "the mundane psychic and performative practices by which heterosexualized genders form themselves through the renunciation of the possibility of homosexuality. . . . Drag thus allegorizes heterosexual melancholy" (Butler 1993a, 25).

Rodman in Drag: Illusions of Disruption / Articulations of Heteronormativity

> It's hard for men especially to deal with my cross-dressing and my effeminate tendencies, but that's not my problem. Guys, here's a secret: Chicks absolutely love it. Believe me, I know.
>
> —Dennis Rodman

Much like McDonald and Aikens (1996), Barrett (1997) also views Rodman as a disruptive force vis-à-vis regimes of gender and sexuality.

Indeed, Barrett posits that Rodman's cross-dressing "wields an iconoclastic critical remove" (112) and that it "dismisses the relevance of sanitary normativity" (106). Barrett bases such a proposition on both Rodman's public spectacles and statements like the following in his first book, *Bad as I Want to Be*:

> I paint my fingernails. I color my hair. I sometimes wear *women's clothes*. I want to challenge people's image of what an athlete is supposed to be. *I like bringing out the feminine side of Dennis Rodman.* . . . To hang out in a gay bar or put on a sequined halter top makes me feel like a total person and not just a one-dimensional man. (Rodman 1996, 208; emphasis added)

While we concur with Butler's (1993a, 1993b) contention that drag can potentially allegorize the production of normative identities, we hesitate to embrace Barrett's enthusiasm regarding the "iconoclastic" and/or disruptive effects of Rodman's cross-dressing. Admittedly, Rodman's transvestite activities encourage the NBA in particular, and basketball fans in general, to confront a player who neither looks nor acts like the rest of the players. This, however, does not necessarily foreordain Rodman's crossdressing as interrogative of either gender categories or professional sport's gendered economies. We propose, therefore, that construing Rodman as veritably disruptive to dominant gender codes is problematic on three counts: (a) Rodman's cross-dressing strategies rely on heteronormative formulations of gender and thus exploit and confirm male supremacist formulations of femininity; (b) Rodman's comportment, whether in or out of drag, is frequently aggressive, sexist, and/or sexually violent, and therefore reproduces dominant modalities of masculinity; and (c) Rodman's cross-dressing does not veritably confuse perceptions of his sex/gender identity and therefore has little implication for the maintenance and resulting privilege of his dominant masculine persona.

First, let us consider how Rodman's cross-dressing strategies rely on normative gender binaries and thus exploit and confirm male supremacist formulations of femininity. McDonald and Aikens (1996) insist that Rodman mobilizes "queer praxis" to "critique dominant heterosexist and gender ideologies" (97). To understand the implications of the previous statement, a working definition of "queerness" might be instructive. Doty (1993) argues that, fundamentally, "queerness should challenge and confuse our understanding and uses of sexual and gender categories" (xvii). If one accepts that queerness relates to the agitation of normative identity categories, then it becomes difficult to reconcile Rodman's behavior with things queer. This difficulty arises, first and foremost, because Rodman's cross-dressing strategies are undergirded by both the "male gaze" and many male supremacist stereotypes associated with ideal femininity. For Rodman, "doing" femininity includes painting his nails, shaving his legs, and wearing short skirts, wedding dresses, lingerie, and excessive jewelry (Jefferson 1997; Kiley 1996; Luscombe 1996; Rodman 1996, 1997; Seal 1996). Indeed, as revealed in his two books and his numerous spectacles, Rodman's appropriations of the feminine appear to rely wholly on aesthetic exaggerations of culturally sanctioned femininity. Contrary to McDonald and Aikens's stipulation, then, Rodman's behavior does not seem to disarm normative gender binaries.

We argue that Rodman's behavior is neither culturally disconcerting nor individually unnerving precisely because it refuses to "challenge and confuse our understanding and uses of sexual and gender categories." If anything, Rodman's performances confirm male supremacist formulations of femininity while encouraging admittedly conservative audiences to consume banal spectacles of gender transgression. These seemingly unexpected acts of consumption are permissible, even profitable, in the androcentric world of professional sports only insofar as Rodman's "true" gender identity remains unquestioned. Insofar as Rodman's masculinity remains intact, his spectators are encouraged to consume "acceptable" and marketable forms of difference without being asked to rethink and obscure their own conceptions of gender.

Second, let us consider how Rodman's comportment, whether in or out of drag, is frequently aggressive, sexist, and/or sexually violent, and therefore reproduces dominant modalities of masculinity. Rodman's basketball career to date has resulted in numerous suspensions, most of which were attributed to head-butting, kneeing, elbowing, and attacking nonplayers such as photographers and referees (Armour 1996a, 1996b; Jefferson 1997; Smith 1996). In March 1996, Rodman attacked NBA referee Ted Bernhardt and was subsequently accorded the third longest suspension in NBA history (Smith 1996). Although some critics who read Rodman for positive oppositionality disregard his violent propensities (e.g., Barrett 1997; McDonald and Aikens 1996), we argue that Rodman's aggressive behavior reproduces normative modalities of masculinity and therefore cannot be ignored when assessing his subversive potential.

Off the court, Rodman also displays dominantly masculine behavior. Nowhere is this behavior more evident than in his books *Bad as I Wanna Be* (1996) and *Walk on the Wild Side* (1997), which are characterized by measureless themes of aggressive and/or sexist masculine sexuality. Consider the following citations:

> You really can't make love as much as you can fuck. Fucking is so much better, because you let all the aggression out. . . . A lot of guys sit there before and during sex saying, "Honey, I love you, blah, blah, blah. I wish you'd be here forever." Then when they get through with it, the first thought to pop into their head is, "God damn, I'm tired, I don't want to be around your ass." (1997, 75)

> I can have sex anytime I want sex. . . . I'm in charge, I guess you could say. The truth is, I can call a girl and have her over here right now. Give me fifteen minutes and I'll have a gorgeous girl. (1996, 180–185)

> I don't mind pleasing a woman, but I think women in general want to please the man more than they want to get pleased themselves. Or maybe I just think that because I don't particularly enjoy going down on a woman. If I had a tongue-licker that ran on batteries, I would just put it down there and let it go. . . . There's no way I'd ever go down there with my tongue for that long, but the tongue-licker could get the job done. (1997, 86)

> No pussy in the world is worth destroying a team for. (1997, 143)

The above citations illustrate the extent to which dominant formulations of gender and sexuality operate in published accounts of Dennis Rodman's carnal proclivities: His books, his interviews and his abundant media appearances are often suffused with sexist and degrading references to women. Not only does Rodman frequently present women as physically repulsive, but he often likens them to inhuman beings such as fish (e.g., "I'm just gill-filling her" 1997, 87) and trucks (e.g., "I lost my virginity to this wide-body who lived upstairs" 1997, 77). Finally, Rodman's texts position women as sexual objects (e.g., "mostly rent-a-girls" 1997, 81) whose own sexual desires are legitimately subordinated to those of men.

Unfortunately, the aggressive hypermasculinity described above underlies concrete instances of patriarchal violence whose implications extend far beyond the realm of half-witted books and interviews. Surely those eager to point out the innocuous character of Rodman's antics would do well to consider the multiple sexual assault charges recently filed against him (Woman Sues Rodman, 1998).

In view of his attitudes toward gender and sexuality, one must wonder whether, as Rodman (1996, 1997) maintains, his drag spectacles, his ownership of a pink pick-up truck, and his visits to gay bars truly render him different and somehow less masculine than other men. We suggest that Rodman's normative masculinity remains perfectly intact while he carries out allegedly marginal behavior and that, consequently, he neither critiques dominant gender ideologies nor exposes the fluidity of sex/gender categories.

Third, let us consider the final problematic component of construing Rodman as a disruptive cultural force. We argue that because Rodman's sex/gender identity is never veritably troubled, his gender crossing has little implication for the maintenance and resulting privilege of his dominant masculine persona. Rodman, then, garners "a taste of the exotic" (Hall 1992, 23) without having to either participate in the emancipatory struggles of sex/gender "outlaws" or confront the existence of such struggles and the pain, violence, and subordination they imply. hooks (1992) proposes that excursions into Otherness, such as Dennis Rodman's temporary peregrinations to sex/gender outlaw communities, potentially reinforce cultural relations of domination while eliding their effects. hooks posits:

> The desire to make contact with those bodies deemed Other . . .
> assuages the guilt of the past, even takes the form of a defiant gesture

where one denies accountability and historical connection. Most importantly, it establishes a contemporary narrative where the suffering imposed by structures of domination on those designated Other is deflected by an emphasis on seduction and longing where the desire is not to make the Other over in one's image but to become the Other. (25; emphasis added)

Because Rodman does not pollute the boundaries of sex or gender enough to lead people to veritably doubt either his biology or his masculinity, he continues to benefit from forms of heteronormative privilege while profiting, both personally and financially, from his excursions into the Otherness of sex/gender outlaw communities.

Rodman, Sexual Difference, and AIDS

One could argue that Rodman, by discussing his homoerotic fantasies, dying the AIDS red ribbon into his hair, publicizing his visits to gay bars, and asserting the captivating presence of transsexuals and transvestites, is effectively queering mainstream audiences, however temporarily. One could also argue that Rodman's recognizance of non-normative sexualities has the effect of querying dominant regimes of desire. Barrett (1997), S. Johnson (1996), Jefferson (1996), and McDonald and Aikens (1996) have advanced like-natured claims with some success. Although we are not in complete disagreement with the aforementioned authors, we will consider the subversive potential of Rodman's sexual persona within the context of related acts and comments, cultural attitudes toward such acts and comments, and Rodman's stake in their representation.

To begin, let us discuss Rodman's much-publicized homoerotic fantasies. There can be no denying that Rodman appears to be unabashed regarding both his openness toward and his personal interest in gays, lesbians, bisexuals, transvestites, and transsexuals. Doubtless, Rodman's articulation of such openness and interest produces some positively oppositional effects not easily subsumed by conservative sexual politics. Rodman's enthusiasm regarding non-normative sexualities is evidenced in comments such as the following:

I like going to gay bars and hanging out with Queers, transvestites, and transsexuals because I find them a hell of a lot more interesting than the boring-ass dudes I see in the locker rooms and on basketball courts. (Rodman 1997, 20)

Admittedly, the above citation and indeed the majority of Rodman's reflections on queers, transvestites, and transsexuals recall hooks's (1992) and Hall's (1992) discussion of exploring communities of Otherness without taking responsibility for the cultural conditions structuring the Other's marginality. In his book *Walk on the Wild Side* (1997), however, Rodman must be credited with pushing the limits of heteronormative acceptability in at least some narrative instances. Consider the following description of his attraction to a transsexual:

I had been with Mimi a couple of times before I realized that she was a man. It turns out she was on the road to becoming a woman. She took hormones and had a couple of surgeries, and we've stayed close throughout the process. It was intriguing in the beginning. We've kissed before, and I'm not ashamed to say that she turns me on. To be around her, as beautiful as she is, I'd have no problem going further with her. It wouldn't freak me out that she's been surgically altered. To me sex is a vibe, anyway, not some clinical act. (183)

Rodman's unashamed testimonies regarding his desire for transsexuals is not easily reconciled with his dominantly masculine and athletic persona. Such testimonies, then, undoubtedly produce a degree of uneasiness in mainstream readers and might even, to at least a limited extent, prompt some readers to rethink the conventional boundaries of sexual congress. Similarly, Rodman's attraction to other men is the subject of much commentary in both of his published works. Superficially, the utterances characterized by homoerotic sensibilities appear confident and sincere. Rodman (1997) writes:

Since there's one question everyone wants to know, I'll just come right out and answer it. Yes, I'm gay. Feel better? Well, there's a second answer. I'm straight. Confused? Me, too. (174)

I'm not sure whether I'll be with a man in the future, but it's something I've definitely been thinking about for a while. If I ever do decide to have sex with a man, I'll find a guy just like me and love the shit out of him. It'll be like two bulls going at it, bro, I'll tell you that. (179)

When reading his books, however, one discerns significant instabilities in Rodman's allegiance to queerness. While he often appears assertive about his homoerotic desires, he also distances himself from his gay potentiality in many passages. For instance, Rodman declares:

Since I started talking about my fantasies of being with another man, people have assumed I'm bisexual. I don't do much to discourage that, since it fits into my idea of keeping people guessing. I went to a T-shirt shop in West Hollywood during the off-season . . . and I bought two shirts. On one it said, *I don't mind straight people as long as they act gay in public.* The other said, *I'm not gay but my boyfriend is.* I wore the first one out to a club in Newport Beach the next night and a girl came up to me and said "you're cool, you speak your mind and that's what I like about you." Then she said "I'm bisexual too—just like you." *I just laughed at her . . . if I am bisexual it's in my mind only.* (1996, 212; emphasis added)

We do not intend to posit that sexual discontinuities are in any way unique to Dennis Rodman. It is worth noting, however, that Rodman's homoerotic utterances coincide with a cultural moment characterized by the acute fashionability of "queer chic." One might argue, then, that it is precisely these discontinuities that allow Rodman to benefit from the publicity and popular exoticization of queer chic while successfully courting a primarily heterosexual male reader/viewership. Indeed, these instabilities coupled with the overwhelmingly heteromasculine tone of his books and interviews, "[invite] status quo readers to imagine that they too can consume images of difference, participate in the sexual practices depicted, and yet remain untouched—unchanged" (hooks 1994, 15).

Finally, let us turn now to a consideration of Rodman's relationship to queer communities and his engagement with the AIDS epidemic. Rodman certainly appears to be a great supporter of queer communities, projecting an almost paternalistic attitude toward their cultural travails. Whether in books or interviews, Rodman is frequently caught making statements similar to the following:

> When I go to a gay bar, it's not quite as mellow as it used to be, because so many people come up and tell me they appreciate my willingness to stick up for gay rights. But I don't mind the extra attention, because I really enjoy hanging out with gays. They've been through so much that a lot of them are fearless, and they'll do and say anything. (1997, 186)

Rodman's oversimplifications and/or distortions of queer lifestyles in both *Bad as I Wanna Be* and *Walk on the Wild Side* are not necessarily worthy of extensive rumination here. His more mediatized promotional strategies involving the appropriation of specific elements of the gay symbolic, however, are interesting to the cultural critic.

On at least two occasions, Rodman has been widely viewed or photographed with a red ribbon—intended to represent the struggle against AIDS—grafted into the back of his head. In *Bad as I Wanna Be*, Rodman is explicit about what this particular symbol represents to him. Rodman writes:

> Gay men come up to me—and *on* to me—all the time. I think I've done more to recognize them than any other professional athlete. When I put the AIDS ribbon on my head during the play-offs against the Lakers in 1995, I think that opened a lot of eyes. These people were finally seeing somebody openly recognize them. For the first time they saw someone openly show some support—with no embarrassment at all. (1996, 213)

Clearly, then, to Dennis Rodman the red ribbon represents homosexuals and homosexuality in general. This conflation is reproduced in *Walk on the Wild Side*:

> I like being in a position to stick up for gay people. They're the last ones who should be subjected to any shit, because they're getting hit

so hard by the AIDS epidemic. AIDS is such a scary disease, and the worst part is that it can be spread by such a pleasurable activity. (1997, 187)

Without denying for one moment the incalculable trauma suffered by gay men at the hands of the AIDS virus, it should seem curious that queers, an enormous and seriously diverse group of people, would come to be represented by a disease. Although in this instance Rodman's conflation of homosexuality with AIDS is being mobilized for relatively benevolent purposes, it is important to note that many queers have endeavored to eradicate such a conflation from dominant discourses of sexuality. This attempted eradication has transpired for the obvious reason that it both equates homosexuality with disease (Eyre 1997; Patton 1993) and erases the important cultural presence of those queers not widely affected by the AIDS epidemic (i.e., lesbians).

Consider also the semiotic implications of a red ribbon appearing on Dennis Rodman's body—a corporeal sign inscribed, voluntarily and involuntarily, with discourses of pathology, deviance, and in Rodman's words, badness. Since Rodman's success has proven to be virtually contingent on his badness, one must question how the average sports consumer might engage with the superimposition of the AIDS ribbon on the deviant Rodman body. Although we do not contend that Rodman's publicization of the AIDS ribbon was entirely negative, we would like to underscore the possibility that the juxtaposition of the AIDS struggle with a body voluntarily marked deviant produces potentially deleterious representational effects for those infected with the AIDS virus.

Similarly, one must interrogate Rodman's intentions as regards the mobilization of the AIDS ribbon. If Rodman had genuinely wanted to "support gay people" by grafting an element of their symbolic onto his body, then why did he select the red ribbon—a symbol of disease and socially constructed pathology—rather than explicit symbols of gay pride (e.g., the triangle, the rainbow). We propose that Rodman's mobilization of the red ribbon can be alternatively read as a self-marking strategy, wherein Rodman comes off looking more pathological, more different, and quite simply, more "bad."

"Getting a Bit of the Other"
Dennis Rodman and Black Male Sexuality

Heretofore, we have assessed the subversive potential of Rodman's seemingly counter-cultural spectacles of difference (i.e., cross-dressing, homoerotic acts and disclosures, "queer" self-marking). We have not, however, discussed how these spectacles of difference and their representation in the American cultural imaginary relate to—or are interceded by—Rodman's blackness. In this section, we will consider Rodman's blackness in an attempt to evaluate why Rodman's sexuality appears to be a palpable object of popular fascination. Using his success as a yardstick, we will show that representations of Rodman's aggressive, hypermasculine sexuality are always already mediated by his blackness. In so doing, we will also show that these representations are redeployed in order to articulate white supremacist fantasies of savage, phallocentered, and sexually predacious black men.

Rodman as Postmodern Savage
Blackness, Phallocentrism, and Sexuality

I have this fantasy that I can live my life like a tiger in the jungle—eating whatever I want, having sex whenever I want, and roaming around butt naked, wild and free. . . . It sounds difficult and complicated, but it doesn't have to be.

—*Dennis Rodman*

The front and back covers of Rodman's most recent effort, *Walk on the Wild Side* (1997), see him in animal-like poses. On his hands and knees, Rodman is naked, adorned with brown, orange and yellow paint, and covered with black horizontal stripes. One is most likely supposed to gather that Rodman is, in these pictures, a tiger or another wild animal of sorts. Fragments of these pictures litter most pages of the book. Despite its almost unspeakable repetition and contradiction, *Walk on the Wild Side* is characterized by several themes. Of particular pertinence to this section are two predominant leitmotifs: his physicality and his sexuality. Rodman's lengthy discussions of both his body and his sexuality are couched in gratuitous and voyeuristic terms, often consisting of lists and summaries detailing his rawest and most unconventional sexual encounters. These narratives are inevitably framed by Rodman's uncontrollable sexual urges and his basic willingness to entertain sexual relations in any situation.

Walk on the Wild Side is also characterized by detailed autobiographical descriptions of Rodman's penis. In fact, these penis narratives seem to have at least two recurring themes. On the one hand, Rodman's penis is always described as enormous and, most importantly, black. Consider, for instance, Rodman's request that intolerant individuals "beat on [him] for being an uppity N-word who loves to show his big black dong to white women" (240). On the other hand, his penis is often represented in threatening and intimidating terms. Consider, for example, Rodman's meeting with Cindy Crawford at an MTV function: "The highlight was when I put on a G-String. Her mouth got all wide and she looked totally amazed when she saw my big bulge. I told her, 'don't worry—there's a monster in my pants'" (140).

According to hooks (1992), phallic obsessions are particularly frequent among black males. hooks attributes this especially high frequency to white supremacist logics that seek to divert black men away from resistance struggle while preoccupying them with banal and depoliticized questions of genital biology. She problematizes the implications of black men, like Rodman, who embrace a phallocentric orientation:

> Should we not suspect the contemporary commodification of blackness orchestrated by whites that once again tells black men not only to focus on their penis but to make this focus their all consuming passion? *Such confused men have little time or insight for resistance struggle.* Should we not suspect representations of black men . . . where the black male describes himself as 'hung like a horse' as though the size of his penis defines who he is? . . . How many black men will have to die before black folks are willing to look at the link between the contemporary plight of black men and their continued allegiance to patriarchy and phallocentrism? (112; emphasis added)

Indeed, those who read his books are likely left with the impression that Rodman resembles nothing short of a sexually irrational black man whose enormous penis and visceral instincts are directed at and satisfied by apprehensive white women. Rodman, then, presents himself as primitively hypersexual, phallic identified, and racially threatening. We suggest that the aforementioned formulation of Rodman's sexual identity is met with overwhelming commercial success in the popular precisely because it articulates specific white supremacist fantasies of black male sexuality. Historical and cultural contextualizations of Rodman and dominant representations of his sexuality confirm our position. White American culture's complicated interest in black sexuality, and indeed blackness in general, can be traced back to the settlement of the New World (Morrison 1992). For Morrison, young America was a country

> in which there was a resident population, already black, upon which the imagination could play; through which historical, moral, metaphysical and social fears, problems and dichotomies could be articulated. The slave population, it could be and was assumed, offered itself up as surrogate selves for meditation on problems of human freedom, its lure and its elusiveness. This black population was available for meditations on terror—the terror of . . . internal aggression, evil, sin, greed. (37–38)

The elaboration of American identity was thus achieved through not only white culture's suppression of Africanism—"deployed as rawness and savagery" (Morrison 1992, 44)—but also through its highly invested and profoundly troubled engagement with the African Other. This engagement produced, in literary and filmic imaginations, the African Other as the savage, the rapist, and/or the criminal (Davis 1984; hooks 1992, 1994; Morrison 1992; Snead 1994). That is, the African Other was materialized through all of the fictive personages with which whites could not and would not allow themselves to personally identify. Such cultural and historical displacements, resulting in the mythification of African Otherness, allowed and continue to allow dominant groups to consume various modalities of difference (i.e., racial, ethic, sexual), experience fierce pleasure from the consumption of such difference, and maintain white supremacist relations. hooks discusses the problematic nature of white longing for contact with the Other:

To make oneself vulnerable to the seduction of difference, to seek an encounter with the Other, does not require that one relinquish forever one's mainstream positionality. When race and ethnicity become commodified as resources for pleasure, the culture of specific groups, as well as the bodies of individuals, can be seen as constituting an alternative playground where members of dominating races, genders, sexual practices affirm their power-over in intimate relations with the Other. (1992, 23)

White Americans have long been living out fantasies of the Other through the consumption of black literary and filmic images. According to Snead (1994), this consumption is reflective of the cultural moment in which black images are produced as well as actively implicated in the reinscription of dominant norms and codes. We contend that the American mass consumption of Rodman's black physicality and sexuality should be understood in similar terms—as connotative of a crisis in white cultural identity as well as reinscriptive of dominant regimes of race, ethnicity, and sexuality. The next section will consider some particularly acute articulations of white culture's fantasies of the Other's racially coded sexuality, while situating Rodman within this cultural history.

Unbearable Blackness
Rodman's Savagery and the Resurgence of the Racially Coded Monster

In Western culture, the literary and historical tendency to identify blacks with ape-like creatures is quite clear and has been well-documented. A willed misreading of Linnaean classification and Darwinian evolution helped buttress an older European conception (tracing from as early as the 16th Century) that blacks and apes, kindred denizens of the "jungle," are phylogenetically closer and sexually more compatible than blacks and whites.

—*James Snead*

This masculinist preserve of the NBA is further complicated by the stereotypical association that equates people of color with sensuality and physicality. Thus, perceptions of hypersexuality and eroticism persist as

powerful racist undercurrents within the consumer culture and the commodified space of the NBA.

—*Mary McDonald*

We have already delineated the underlying elements of dominant culture's deployment of blackness as rawness and savagery. In so doing, we
have worked toward elucidating the constituents of Rodman's success
with white audiences. To solidify such elucidations, we suggest a comparison of mainstream cultural engagements with two seemingly distinct spectacles of blackness: Dennis Rodman and King Kong. We maintain the
pertinence of considering Dennis Rodman and King Kong concomitantly
for two reasons: (a) both are spectacles evincing hyperaggressive black
savagery; and (b) there has been a resurgence of like-natured, and arguably racially coded, ape spectacles in late twentieth century America—an
epoch, it should be noted, that coincides with Rodman's successes.

We argue that Rodman's successes must be understood within the
context of a cultural imaginary increasingly strewn by awe-inspiring representations of animalistic blackness. This popular cultural resurgence of
anthropomorphic ape images has been materialized by profitable Hollywood remakes of classics such as *Mighty Joe Young* (a *King Kong* sequel)
and *Godzilla*, as well as by television commercials depicting apes wrap-
ping Christmas presents (Fido Cellular Telephones), stealing credit cards
(Visa Credit), intimidating white women in pantyhose (Leggs Hosiery),
watching movies (Blockbuster Video), offering Valentine Day flowers
(Rogers Cantel Inc., AT&T Corp.), and observing circus events (Subway
Submarine Sandwiches). This resurgence has also been evidenced by an
uncommonly significant amount of news coverage pertaining to anthropomorphic ape events.[6] No matter the manifestation, the recent and un-
deniable resurrection of anthropomorphic ape representations in late
twentieth century America might be interpreted as white culture's attempt
to discharge its increased frustration and resentment toward people of
color through popular forms.

Dennis Rodman is an interesting individual to consider within this
analytical context. He is quite obviously not an ape, but his voluntary and
involuntary representation as a primitive, aggressive, oversexed black man
tends to situate him in a semiotic economy shared by other alleged black

savages like King Kong. *King Kong*, the movie, is especially worthy of deliberation in this instance due to its "blatant linkage of the idea of the black with that of the monster" (Snead 1994, 7). Although the Hollywood mobilization of monstrosity is complex in and of itself, many posit that the monster functions as a figurative release of repressed sexual desires that would otherwise threaten social stability and reigning discursive regimes (e.g., Snead 1994; Wood 1979). Snead (1994) remarks: "The Hollywood monster film allows, among other things, a safe outlet of such sexual desires in a surrogate form, and a vicarious experience—pleasurable and horrific—of the chaos that such a release would bring about in reality" (7). Bearing in mind that Rodman is represented, and indeed represents himself, as a primitive, aggressive, irrational, hypersexual, exceedingly "well-hung" black man who dates predominantly white women, consider Snead's recapitulation of *King Kong*'s effects:

> The figure of King Kong would allow the white male to vent a variety of repressed sexual fantasies: the hidden desire of seeing himself as an omnipotent, phallic black male; the desire to abduct the white woman; or the combined fantasy: to abduct a white woman in the disguise of a phallic black male. (24)

It could be argued that mainstream viewers, presumably white and male, might extort from representations of Rodman similar pleasures as those extorted from engagements with King Kong, as both spectacles allow viewers to fantasize about formidable physical prowess, menacing black phallic masculinity, and misogynistic sexual domination. Indeed, both King Kong and Rodman allow white male audiences to consume signs of racial and sexual difference for pleasure-related purposes while, almost paradoxically, rearticulating white supremacist fantasies of black savagery, hypersexuality and deviance. It could be argued, then, that a mainstream spectator's engagement with Rodman's persona, as well as the effects produced by such an engagement, are characterized by affective displacements similar to those produced by the popular consumption of animalistic blackness in other mediatized forms. These events must therefore be understood as highly problematic representations of black masculinity.

Good Black/Bad Black

> [O]n the whole, I believe that [Michael] Jordan is positioned in media culture as the "good black," especially against the aggressiveness and visual transgressions of teammate Dennis Rodman, who with his bleached and undisciplined hair, earring, fancy clothes, and regularly rebellious behavior represents the "bad" Black figure.
>
> —*Douglas Kellner*

Beausoleil (1994) argues that dominant culture formulates simple, monolithic, and often binary conceptions of racial Others in order to justify their sociocultural subordination. This contention, it could be argued, is confirmed through considerations of Rodman's popular representation. Indeed, when contrasted with representations of Michael Jordan—who is constructed as the zenith of "good" blackness—Dennis Rodman is an unmistakable embodiment of "bad" blackness. For Barrett (1997), Rodman's badness renders him incongruous and therefore disruptive to the highly regulated rectitude of the NBA:

> This logic is given the shorthand of "family values" and is deeply implicated in the economic fortunes of the NBA, corporate culture, and the powerful representations they underwrite. An enormous financial return for the NBA depends on the winsome introduction of (primarily African American) "young guys" into what U.S. culture insists on regulating as demure domestic wards. Rodman's unusual appearance and cynicism, on the other hand, interrogate these presumptions. They query the NBA's economic/entertainment monopoly [and] the equally suspect monopoly of moral/ethical discourse in the U.S. (109)

Unlike Barrett (1997), we posit that although Rodman's aggressive refusal of NBA role-model culture and family values subscription may trouble select dominant discourses undergirding professional basketball, his unruly behavior is not culturally and/or economically unproductive. On the one hand, Rodman's badness is culturally productive in that it becomes reformulated to satisfy white fantasies of black savagery and to further mark black (sporting) bodies as deviant. On the other hand, we contend that Rodman's badness is economically productive in that the NBA benefits enormously from Rodman's spectacles. While the former has been asserted at length in this essay and need not be restated here, the latter is echoed by sports journalist Wayne Scanlan (1997). As regards the economic productivity of Rodman's badness, Scanlan observes:

> The scariest notion to reckon with is that the celebrated antics of . . . Rodman have become a financial necessity to major-league sport and the media that present it and cover it. Jim Bouton [suggested that] sports have learned from the John McEnroe example in tennis. Tantrums raise profiles, sell tickets, and even attract sponsors. (1)

Hence, Rodman's appeal to sports fans of the NBA is not irrational, as Barrett (1997) maintains. In fact, we would argue that Rodman's success is entirely logical in that it implies both the consolidation of dominant discursive regimes and the proliferation of NBA economic fortunes. Moreover, Rodman's "badness"—especially when contraposed with Jordan's "goodness"—facilitates mainstream media's dichotomized good/bad representations of black men. Black men are thus locked into a profoundly stereotypical representational politics that denies and even disavows the complexities of their cultural situation and the pluralistic nature of the subject positions they currently inhabit.

Recovery, Transformation, and Transcendence
Rodman, the Failed Black Family, and the American Dream[7]

A lot of times you'll hear somebody ask an NBA player what he'd be doing if he wasn't getting paid to play basketball. The answer they get pretty often is: Dead or in jail. Most of us are from shitty backgrounds: projects, ghettos, no money, no father, no hope. . . . I didn't have a male role model in my life until I got to college and started getting my shit together.

—*Dennis Rodman*

Cole (1996) and Cole and King (1998) have maintained that the success of the black athlete both generates and affirms national fantasies of meritocracy and fluid social mobility while pathologizing the alleged failure of black America. We contend that Rodman's depiction as an African American man who transcended his ascribed situation to finally attain a life of fame and material wealth articulates at least two national fantasy discourses: (a) the failed black family, and (b) America as an open economic system.

The Failed Black Family

Both Rodman and the media that represent him emphasize his fatherlessness in the projects and, subsequently, the white middle-class nuclear family that adopted him when he went off to college. An overwhelming number of articles, in fact, dedicate at least one passage to Rodman's friendship with, and surrogate adoption by, the Rich family after he leaves the projects. His biography is rewritten to appear as though it was only Rodman's inauguration into this white nuclear family that allowed him to excel in his sporting endeavors. Simultaneously, Rodman's biological mother, the struggles she encountered raising and supporting a family of four, and her contribution to his career are effaced.

Rodman's success has also been used to confirm sport as the protector of black masculinity, a discourse contingent on dominant formulations of failed black familialism. Rodman's declaration "I grew up in a house of women . . . I thought when I was growing up that I was going to be gay" has, in fact, been frequently mobilized by the mainstream press to narrate the perverse implications of absent black masculine role models. Moreover, the considerable media attention attributed to this notorious declaration evinces to what extent Rodman's move to a white, middle-class nuclear family and his involvement in professional sports are seen to have saved him from emasculation. In this context, sporting activities become narrated as essential to African American communities as they compensate for the homosocial bonding and paternal role modeling portrayed as inaccessible in black America (Cole 1996; Cole and King 1998).

America as Meritocracy

Rodman's books and interviews host lengthy ruminations on the virtues of American society, the most important of which pertains to every individual's right and ability to better her economic situation. In the aforementioned publications, Rodman offers himself up as proof of American society as an open system, wherein individuals, regardless of race, class, gender, or sexuality, are empowered to transcend their ascribed identities and forge new lives for themselves. Like Barrett (1997), we posit that Rodman's recurring narratives of economic recovery and transcendence, as well as his emphasis on hard work and merit-based achievement, position him as an affirmation of American "rags-to-riches" fantasies. Consider the following citations from *Walk on the Wild Side*:

> Some of my friends think I'm the second coming of Elvis, and I must admit there are some similarities between me and the King. Like Elvis, I'm a southern boy who lifted himself out of a poor upbringing and hit the big-time. When I was growing up in the projects and things seemed bleak, I always look at Elvis as proof that anyone with the right combination of flair, talent, drive, and luck can become important in America. (1997, 26)

> I wouldn't be a strict parent, and I'd make it easy for [my daughter] to appreciate things. But I'd want her to appreciate the value of hard work, because the best way to get your priorities in order is to work for what you get. You've got to work, work, work, work, work, work, work, work. That's what I did, and I've appreciated what it's got me—I still do. (1997, 224)

We conclude, therefore, that the subversive potential of Rodman's utterances relating to the destitution of American inner-city life is undermined, if not annuled, by his meritocratic formulations.

Rodman's apparent hostility toward political explanations of social inequality also ratify dominant depoliticized conceptions of national socioeconomic processes. Silver's (1996) interview with Rodman reveals this hostility:

> There is a fatalistic side to Rodman, but he's more of a '90s dissident than a '60s insurgent. He thinks anything political is *crap* and has adopted a younger generation's everything-is-screwed-up-beyond-

repair resignation. He is drunk on his own ability to do whatever he wants, a rebel without a boss. (23; emphasis added)

The Dallas-based consulting firm Sports Marketing Group confirms this assertion, positing: "The under-29s see him as a rebel with a cause. They appreciate his values. *He doesn't play politics,* he says what he thinks and feels" (Hirsley and DeSimone 1996, 3; emphasis added). In fact, Rodman tends to eschew most explanations of social inequality that posit systemic relations of white domination.[8] Instead, Rodman tends to adopt relativistic positions on questions of race and class:

This is coming from somebody who doesn't see skin color. I'm color neutral. I'm black, but my friends joke about me being a "white" black man. Most of my close friends are white, and I go out with white women. I don't think about color. I try to go beyond that. The problem is, some people won't let you go beyond it. If you're black and a high-profile athlete, you're all of a sudden under pressure to be a spokesman for the race. . . . Sometimes I think: Fuck the race and the people, I'm going to be honest with myself. That way, people—no matter what color—can make their own judgments about me. Everyone has a different experience. Everyone has a different story. When it comes to race, my experiences are different than anybody else's. (Rodman 1996, 166–167)

It is our belief, then, that Rodman has triumphed with mainstream audiences partly because he relieves whites of their responsibility in the reproduction of unequal social relations while simultaneously fulfilling national fantasies of the failed black family and meritocracy.

Rodman's Financial Situation
The Limits of Subversion-Through-Consumption

The claim that Rodman is a destabilizing cultural force can also be evaluated on the basis of his economic location. We argue that because Rodman's alleged subversive praxis is inherently accomplished through consumption, its subversive potential and overall disruptive effects are seriously constrained.

We contend that Rodman's persona is a cultural sensation precisely because it works within and reinforces what queer writer Jeffrey Escoffier (1994) calls "the regimes of the normal" (135). Spectators therefore enjoy Rodman-the-spectacle unproblematically as it allows them to engage with acceptable and marketable forms of difference while residing unchallenged and unchanged (hooks 1994). Indeed, a cursory glance at his financial profile reveals that the kinds of difference for which Rodman is reputed are most certainly marketable and might even be, as Stuart Hall (1992) writes, "a kind of difference that doesn't make a difference of any kind" (23). A brief look at Rodman's economic affiliations sheds light on our skepticism.

Since he first started eliciting substantive media and fan responses, Rodman has made considerable commercial inroads. In the last few years, Rodman has signed contracts with Nike, Pizza Pizza, Converse, Kodak, McDonald's, Oakleys, Victoria's Secret, Mistic Beverages, a national hotel chain, several clothing store chains, multinational computer companies, and has negotiated with Walt Disney Productions and Warner Brothers for the film rights to his book *Bad as I Wanna Be*. On top of Rodman's multimillion-dollar salary, in 1996, his business manager was already expecting a yearly off-the-court income of over $10 million (Armour 1996a, 1996b; Barboza 1996a, 1996b; Hirsley and DeSimone 1996; Johnson, K. C. 1996).

One has to question the fundamentals of Rodman's subversive potential when over ten multinational corporations are involved in his alleged subversion. Most importantly, one has to query Rodman's allegiances to multinational corporations such as Kodak, McDonald's, and Disney—multinationals renowned for their collusion with dominant discursive regimes of race, ethnicity, gender, and sexuality. Surely if these conventional corporations are willing to "risk" their reputations on Rodman, it is precisely because there is very little substantive risk involved. As Kodak's chief marketing officer, Carl E. Gustin, exemplifies: "We did a background check on Rodman and determined that his brand of naughty is benign . . . Rodman is just comically naughty or cartoon naughty—a curious caricature of badness" (cited in Barboza 1996a, D8).

Not only do the corporate think-tanks of popular culture consider Rodman's "counter-cultural" behavior innocuous, but they have and will continue to successfully mark such behavior as pathological. Susan Gianinno, general manager at Thompson New York, the ad agency in charge of Kodak's contract, openly declares: "We're using him [Rodman] *and all he represents* as a foil. The contradistinction between Rodman as the ostensible bad boy seemed an excellent contrast with the goodness and wholesomeness of Kodak" (cited in Barboza 1996a, D8; emphasis added).

Hence, positing that subversive potential can be realized through consumptive patterns is problematic. Bordo (1993) reminds us that "consumer capitalism depends on the continual production of novelty, of fresh images to stimulate desire, [frequently dropping] into marginalized neighborhoods in order to find them" (25). By the very fact that alleged "novelty" or "subversion" is being "produced" for consumption requires that such "difference" be rendered (pleasantly) intelligible to mainstream audiences. Thus, if all representations formulated through consumer capitalism must in one way or another become normalized, then we must seriously doubt the subversive potential of any cultural icon whose image relies on male/heteronormative/white supremacist capitalist market forces. Since consumer capitalism requires a constant flow of new colonies and since consumption is by nature unstable, granted its dependence on market forces, one cannot expect any consumer craze to last—even if it happens to be one with "subversive style."

Concluding Remarks

As previously stated, the far from negligible success of Rodman's persona indicates that mainstream audiences exact a peculiar pleasure from Rodman's communications. We propose that Rodman's success with mainstream audiences is most astutely attributed to dominant culture's desire to make contact with the Other (and to live out its fantasies of savagery, hypersexuality, and deviance through the consumption of black male sporting bodies), and not to its willingness to embrace progressive sociocultural change. Despite a few evanescent moments of significant disruption, we have shown that Rodman, even in the midst of his alleged transgressions, maintains and reinscribes dominant modalities of masculinity, phallocentrism, heteronormativity, white supremacy, and consumer capitalism.

Notes

1. As explicated in Lafrance (1998), the term "American" is fundamentally problematic when mobilized to describe cultural moments specific to the United States. On the one hand, the term "American" effaces other constitutive regions of the Americas (i.e., Canada and the countries of Central and South America) and their distinct experiences. The dominant employment of the term, then, produces homogenizing discursive effects and is, in short, both imperialistic and immaterial. However, we have chosen to use this term when discussing the United States as its very employment (as well as the connotative field within which it is rendered intelligible) discloses many important fictions organizing the American imaginary: namely, that a primordial component of the American identity is based on fantasies of national supremacy.

2. In this regard, Hall (1992) makes an interesting statement about the implications of mainstreaming transgressive acts such as cross-dressing. Hall writes: "I acknowledge that the spaces 'won' for difference are few and far between, that they are very carefully policed and regulated. I believe they are limited. I know, to my cost, that they are grossly underfunded, that there is always a price of incorporation to be paid when the cutting edge of difference and transgression is blunted into spectacularization" (24).

3. In her discussion of the performative, Butler (1993b) explicates the inevitably impure pool of cultural resources from which one works when laboring to oppose dominant discursive regimes: "Performativity describes this relation of being implicated in that which one opposes, this turning of power against itself to produce alternative modalities of power, to establish a kind of political contestation that is not a 'pure' opposition, a 'transcendence' of contemporary relations of power, but a difficult labor of forging a future from resources inevitably impure. . . . For one is, as it were, in power even as one opposes it, formed by it as one reworks it, and it is this simultaneity that is at once the condition of our partiality, the measure of our political unknowingness, and also the condition of action itself. The incalculable effects of action are as much a part of their subversive promise as those that we plan in advance" (241).

4. By public, we understand those dominant social structures, acts, and attitudes that both interpellate and compel the subject.

5. The violences done to those who transgress sexual norms have been described by many as basic human rights violations. In Western countries, for instance, such violences might manifest themselves in the forms of discriminatory immigration policies, heterosexist medicopsychological diagnoses and/or treatments, employment inequities (e.g., wrongful dismissal, denial of spousal employment benefits), queer bashing, as well as censorship and heterosexist legal codes and practices (Burke 1996; Herman 1994; Holmes and Purdy 1992; Lacombe 1994; Oikawa, Falconer, and Decter 1994).

6. This observation, it should be noted, is not based on a rigorous content analysis of mainstream news coverage. It is based merely on the authors' daily engagements with popular cultural forms such as the televised news, newspapers, and magazines.

These engagements have resulted in the authors' conclusion that anthropomorphic ape spectacles seem to preoccupy mediatized space with significant frequency. Although our assertion regarding the consequential amount of news coverage of anthropomorphic apes is based on "soft" empirical evidence, we nevertheless suggest that the ape-centered news story verbatim often displaces moral and cultural panics related to black cultures onto the apes in question. For example, consider the following two headlines that appeared in the *Ottawa Citizen* in early 1999: In " 'Sick gorilla' threatens economy," Beauchesne argues that the recovering Canadian economy is in danger of being knocked back down by the Brazilian economic crisis (represented as the "sick gorilla"), and in "AIDS virus came from chimps," Clover and Highfield report that scientists have discovered that the AIDS virus originated in a sub-species of chimpanzee in the central African rainforest. These examples speak to what could be called a "Return to the planet of the apes," this expression being also the title of an earlier article that confirms our assertion that in this fin-de-millennium, "Apes are in the news again" (Disraeli 1998, A1).

7. The title of this section was inspired by Cole and King's (1998) observation that: "NBA superstars were created through and provided fertile ground for narratives of limited scope that emphasized recovery, transformation, transcendence, and utopic social visions. . . . Indeed, the complex marketing network that territorialized the NBA's celebrity zone privileged seemingly incontrovertible evidence of self-improvement, self-reliance, self-determination, and 'choice' as it simultaneously produced an apparently endless supply of morality and cautionary tales" (52).

8. Rodman has, at times, made astute observations concerning racism on the basketball court and in American society. In *Bad as I Wanna Be*, Rodman states that Larry Bird was "way overrated . . . because he's white. You never hear about a black player being the greatest" (1996, 162). Similarly, in *Walk on the Wild Side*, Rodman proclaims: "The black culture still hasn't recovered from slavery. You can see it in the poverty, the crime, and amount of single-parent families. When you take a proud group of people and whip them and rape them and humiliate them to the point of torture, it's not something they can easily shake off. White people should understand that, but a lot of them don't, and this is still a very racist country" (1997, 233). The trouble is, however, that the resistant value of such race consciousness gets lost, as it were, amidst his carnival of remarks accusing blacks of equally pernicious racism (see Rodman 1996, 1997). In this context, Rodman's comments about "white racism" appear to be just as culturally important, and indeed, just as culturally productive, as "black racism." This discursive tendency is common in "postmodern times" wherein, according to Bordo (1993), "[instead] of distinctions, endless differences reign—an undifferentiated pastiche of differences, a grab bag in which no items are assigned any more importance or centrality than any other. . . . This spectacle of difference defeats the ability to sustain coherent political critique" (258). The incoherent and positively relativistic nature of Rodman's race consciousness "allows American (middle-class) audiences to recognize themselves as compassionate and ethical subjects in 1990s

America" (Cole and King 1998, 54) without forcing them to acknowledge their own implication in systems of oppression.

References

Armour, T. (1996a, May). Nearly broke, Rodman rebounds. *Chicago Tribune* [Online]. Available: http://www.chicago.tribune.com/sports/bulls/belndr/bsrchive/rodbroke.htm.

———. (1996b, March). The Enigma. *Chicago Tribune* [Online]. Available: http://www.chicago.tribune.com/sports/bulls/belndr/bsrchive/rodman7.htm.

Arnold, G. J. (1996). Dennis Rodman: Role model yes! *The Dennis Rodman Connection* [Online]. Available: http://members.aol.com/agencies/homepage/rolemodl.html.

Barboza, D. (1996a, December 19). A star athlete goes from naughty to nice, hoping to earn a Kodak Advantix camera for Christmas. *New York Times*, p. D8.

———. (1996b, March 26). To build basketball sneaker sales, Converse tries a novel double team: Dr. J and Dennis Rodman. *New York Times*, p. D3.

Barrett, L. (1997). Black men in the mix: Badboys, heroes, sequins and Dennis Rodman. *Callaloo, 20*(1), 106–126.

Bartky, S. (1993). Foucault, femininity and the modernization of patriarchal power. In M. Pearsall (ed.), *Women and values: Readings in recent feminist philosophy* (pp. 151–165). Belmont, Calif.: Wadsworth.

Beauchesne, E. (1999, January 16). "Sick gorilla" threatens economy. *Ottawa Citizen*, p. D1.

Beausoleil, N. (1994). Make-up in everyday life: An inquiry into the practices of urban American women of diverse backgrounds. In N. Sault (ed.), *Many mirrors: Body image and social relations* (pp. 33–57). New Brunswick, N.J.: Rutgers.

Bordo, S. (1993). *Unbearable weight: Feminism, Western culture, and the body.* Los Angeles: University of California Press.

Burke, P. (1996). *Gender shock: Exploding the myths of male and female.* New York: Anchor Books.

Butler, J. (1989). Gendering the body: Beauvoir's philosophical contribution. In A. Garry & M. Pearsall (eds.), *Women, knowledge and reality: Explorations in feminist philosophy* (pp. 253–262). Boston: Unwin Hyman.

———. (1993a). Critically queer. *GLQ: A Journal of Lesbian and Gay Studies, 1*(1), 17–32.

———. (1993b). *Bodies that matter.* New York: Routledge.

Clover, C., & Highfield, R. (1999, February 1). AIDS virus came from chimps. *Ottawa Citizen*, p. B1.

Cole, C. L. (1996). American Jordan: P.L.A.Y., consensus, and punishment. *Sociology of Sport Journal, 13*(4), 366–398.

Cole, C. L., & Hribar, A. (1995). Celebrity feminism: Nike style. Post-Fordism, transcendence, and consumer power. *Sociology of Sport Journal, 12*(4), 347–369.

Cole, C. L., & King, S. (1998). Representing black masculinity and urban possibilities: Racism, realism and hoop dreams. In G. Rail (ed.), *Sport and postmodern times* (pp. 49–86). Albany, N.Y.: State University of New York Press.

Davis, A. (1984) Rape, racism, and the myth of the Black rapist. In A. Jaggar & P. Rothenberg (eds.), *Feminist frameworks: Alternative accounts of the relations between women and men*, 2d ed. (pp. 428–431). New York: McGraw-Hill.

Disraeli, B. (1998, January 21). Return to the planet of the apes. *Ottawa Citizen*, p. A1.

Doty, A. (1993). *Making things perfectly queer: Interpreting mass culture*. Minneapolis: University of Minnesota Press.

Escoffier, J. (1994, Fall). Under the sign of the queer. *Found Object*, p. 135.

Eyre, L. (1997). Re-forming (hetero)sexuality education. In L. G. Roman & L. Eyre (eds.), *Dangerous territories: Struggles for difference and equality in education* (pp. 191–205). New York: Routledge.

Hall, S. (1992). What is this "black" in black popular culture? In G. Dent (ed.), *Black popular culture* (pp. 21–33). Seattle: Bay Press.

Harper, P. B. (1994). The subversive edge: Paris is burning, social critique and the limits of subjective agency. *Diacritics*, 24(2–3), 90–103.

Herman, D. (1994). *Rights of passage: Struggles for lesbian and gay legal equality*. Toronto: University of Toronto Press.

Hirsley, M., & DeSimone, B. (1996, May 4). Worm's world: Mainstream clamors for Rodman's next move. *Chicago Tribune* [Online]. Available: http://www.chicago.tribune.com/sports/bulls/belndr/bsrchive/rod04.htm.

Holmes, H. B., & Purdy, L. M. (1992). *Feminist perspectives in medical ethics*. Bloomington: Indiana University Press.

hooks, b. (1992). *Black looks: Race and representation*. Toronto: Between the Lines Press.

———. (1994). Power to the pussy: We don't wannabe dicks in drag. In *Outlaw culture* (pp. 9–25). New York: Routledge.

Jefferson, M. (1997, January 30). Dennis Rodman, bad boy as man of the moment. *New York Times*, pp. C13, C20.

Johnson, K. C. (1996, May). How much is this man worth: Rodman's popularity and bank balance soar. *Chicago Tribune*. Available: http://www.chicago.tribune.com/sports/bulls/belndr/bsrchive/rodman05.htm#top.

Johnson, S. (1996, December). Trash talk. *Chicago Tribune* [Online]. Available: http://www.chicago.tribune.com/sports/bulls/belndr/bsrchive/rod61205.htm.

Kellner, D. (1996). Sports, media culture and race—Some reflections on Michael Jordan. *Sociology of Sport Journal*, 13(4), 458–468.

Kiley, M. (1996, May). Dark and explicit, Rodman's book reveals tortured soul. *Chicago Tribune* [Online]. Available: http://www.chicago.tribune.com/sports/bulls/belndr/bsrchive/bulls02.htm.

Lacombe, D. (1994). *Blue politics: Pornography and the law in the age of feminism*. Toronto: University of Toronto Press.

Lafrance, M. (1998). Colonizing the feminine: Nike's intersections of postfeminism and hyperconsumption. In G. Rail (ed.), *Sport and postmodern times* (pp. 117–139). Albany: State University of New York Press.

Lafrance, M., & Rail, G. (1997, November). Gender crossing in the context of mad capitalism: Dennis Rodman and Madonna as cultural imposters. Paper presented at the annual conference of the North American Society for the Sociology of Sport, Toronto, Ontario.

Luscombe, B. (1996, September 2). Dennis the menace. *Time*, p. 69.

McDonald, M. (1996). Michael Jordan's family values: Marketing, meaning and post-Reagan America. *Sociology of Sport Journal*, 13(4), 344–366.

McDonald, M., & Aikens, E. (1996, November). Damn is he funny: Dennis Rodman and the queer politics of (Ms.) representation. Paper presented at the annual conference of the North American Society for the Sociology of Sport, Birmingham, Alabama.

Morrison, T. (1992). *Playing in the dark: Whiteness and the literary imagination.* New York: Vintage.

Oikawa, M., Falconer, D., & Decter, A. (1994). *Resist: Essays against a homophobic culture.* Toronto: Women's Press.

Patton, C. (1993). Tremble, hetero swine! In M. Warner (ed.), *Fear of a queer planet: Queer politics and social theory* (pp. 143–177). Minneapolis: University of Minnesota Press.

Reilly, R. (1996, October). A nose ring runs through it. *Sports Illustrated*, p. 116.

Rodman, D. (1996). *Bad as I wanna be.* New York: Dell.

————. (1997). *Walk on the wild side.* New York: Dell.

Seal, M. (1996, January). The bad boy of basketball. *Playboy*, pp. 98–102.

Silver, M. (1996, December). The Spurs' no-holds-barred forward gives new meaning to the running game. *Sports Illustrated*, pp. 20–28

Smith, S. (1996, March). Rodman suspended for six games. *Chicago Tribune* [Online]. Available: http://www.chicago.tribune.com/sports/bulls/belndr/bsrchive/rodman.htm.

Snead, J. (1994). *White screens, black images: Hollywood from the dark side.* New York: Routledge.

Weiss, G. (1996, March 31). Rodman's right-hand man. *Chicago Tribune* [Online]. Available: http://www.chicago.tribune.com/sports/bulls/belndr/bsrchive/rodman6.htm.

Wood, R. (1979). *The American nightmare: Essays on the horror film.* Toronto: Festival of Festivals.

Woman sues Rodman for sexual assault. (1998, June 12). *Ottawa Citizen*, p. F8.

4

LISA DISCH AND MARY JO KANE

When a Looker Is Really a Bitch
Lisa Olson, Sport, and the
Heterosexual Matrix

Introduction

● In September 1990, Lisa Olson, a sports reporter for the *Boston Herald*, was sexually harassed in the locker room of the New England Patriots football team. The incident was initiated by one player who walked over to Olson and thrust his penis toward her, asking " 'Do you want to take a bite out of this?' " It escalated quickly as several more players paraded past her, "modeling" their genitals in a mock strip tease while various others shouted: " 'Did she look, did she look?' 'Get her to look'; 'That's what she wants'; 'Is she looking?' 'Make her look' " (Heymann 1990, 15–17). Olson resisted the players' accusations by reporting the incident to her editor. Although she wanted the matter to be handled privately, she refused to dismiss it as insignificant and demanded that the instigators identify themselves and apologize to her. Against her wishes, the story broke four days later in the *Globe*, the more prestigious of the two Boston-area papers. The publicity incited Patriots owner Victor Kiam to call Olson a "classic bitch," adding, "No wonder the players can't stand her" (Mannix 1990, 74).

This essay originally appeared in *Signs: Journal of Women in Culture and Society*, 21 (1996), 278–308. Reprinted by permission of the authors and the University of Chicago Press.

The incident and Kiam's response to it prompted National Football League Commissioner Paul Tagliabue to call for an independent investigation to be conducted by prominent Harvard Law School professor Philip Heymann.[1] It also sparked hundreds of reports and editorials, touching off a national debate over what some characterized as the propriety of having women sports reporters in men's locker rooms and what others defined as a violation of a reporter's gender-neutral right of access to the players. For many commentators, issues of gender difference and sexual tension took precedence over Olson's rights as a professional; they argued that assigning women reporters to cover the locker room "courts disaster" (Hart 1990, 17) and that Olson and the *Herald* had been "asking for trouble" (Mannix 1990, 74). In contrast, others denied the relevance of sex and gender altogether, asserting that women reporters have an equal "right to talk to an athlete, to look for stories, to be treated no worse and no better than men are treated" (Madden 1990b, 49). Strangely, Olson remained a figure in this controversy long after she had been forced to stop covering sports in the Boston area and even left the United States for Australia, where she covers sports for another Rupert Murdoch newspaper.[2] In June 1992, the *Boston Globe* resurrected the controversy by publishing a five-page attack on Olson's character and professional reputation.[3] Her name made the Boston papers again six months later when, after a game between the Patriots and the Miami Dolphins, Dolphins wide receiver Mark Clayton invoked her presence for no apparent reason, shouting to a locker room full of male reporters: "Close the door and keep Lisa Olson outside! Keep that dick-watching bitch outside" (Henkel 1993, 1).[4]

Why this explosion of hostility against a sports reporter engaged in the performance of so routine a part of her job as interviewing a source? It is well known that players spout obscenities in the locker room as a matter of course and pay tribute to women reporters' presence there with hurled offerings of jockstraps, dirty socks, and wads of athletic tape (Huckshorn 1990, 1E). As journalist Mariah Burton Nelson puts it, "Sexual harassment is as familiar to female [sports] journalists as the scent of sweat" (1994, 228). Olson herself was not the first woman reporter to cover sports in Boston. And neither was she the first woman assigned to cover the Patriots nor the first to be harassed by them (Heymann 1990, 6). But by most accounts, what happened to Olson was an unprecedentedly intense, protracted, and collective display of hostility.

The players explained their actions by claiming that Olson was a "looker," a term that one male sports columnist explained as designating a woman "who tended to peek excessively" (Durslag 1991, C3). This term was not unique to the incident between Olson and the Patriots but, according to several women sports reporters, is a common point of contention between them and the players (Heymann 1990, 6). In fact, in the culture of the locker room, this term has the status of a "charge" that the players understand to designate a "crime" that is unique to women reporters.

From a purely legal standpoint, this charge is illegitimate, as a Federal Court ruling in 1978 established women sports reporters' constitutional right of equal access to interviews with the players—even when its exercise would mean entering men's locker rooms.[5] Women currently make up only eight hundred out of ten thousand sports journalists, and most of these are reporters. Only one dozen write regular columns and only four major newspapers have women sports editors (Nelson 1994, 229). In the context of this struggle for gender equity, former sports reporter Melissa Ludtke warns that taking the players' charge seriously would be a step backward, arguing that it deflects attention from the "central question of fairness" to resurrect the specter, of "women . . . who only wanted to gaze at naked men" (Ludtke 1990b, 5). Although we concur with Ludtke that the charge is illegitimate, and that looking cannot be taken literally as a crime, a feminist critical analysis cannot afford to dismiss such claims as a mere rhetorical smoke screen for more central questions of fairness defined as equality before the law. As Olson herself explained two years later, what was at issue in the incident was not rights but power: "We are taught to think we must have done something wrong and it took me a while to realize I hadn't done anything wrong. They resented a woman in their domain and it all became a power issue" (Brown 1993, 1C).

Lisa Olson gauged the stakes in this conflict more shrewdly than did many of her defenders, who tended to position her as a victim of the players' disrespect, bad taste, or "outrageous harassment" (*Boston Herald* 1990, B14). Olson's antagonists also knew precisely what was at stake in the locker room. By the charge of "looking," by their repeated references to Olson as a "classic bitch," and by Clayton's later emendation of that remark to "dick-watching bitch," they designated Olson as a threat. Further, by his gloss on looking as "peeking excessively," sports columnist Melvin Durslag named Olson's alleged crime in a way that unwittingly disclosed her agency.

What can it mean to peek excessively? Literally an oxymoron, this charge points beyond the conventions that govern relations between women sports reporters and players in the locker room to those that govern gender relations more broadly. Drawing on the work of Teresa de Lauretis, we understand *excess* as feminist agency that is made possible by "a *disidentification* with femininity that does not necessarily revert or result in an identification with masculinity" (1990, 126). To put it simply, it is a resistance that goes beyond refusing a particular social role to destablize the very construction of gender as a binary opposition. We contend that a woman sports reporter confounds gender oppositions. In her professional capacity, she is an authoritative critic of athletic performance who enjoys backstage access to cultural heroes and a public forum in which to speak about what she sees. Thus, her profession affords her prerogatives over male athletes that exceed those that can be permitted to her as a woman. Looking, then, is a charge that is deployed by players, management, owners, and—in Olson's case—fans to impute lascivious interest to a woman sports reporter's gaze. An attempt to contain the excess of her professional position, the charge confers a stereotype of envy and desire that reinforces oppositional gender norms. Olson's excess was her refusal to accede to the charge of looking despite months of publicity that would have embarrassed a more conventional woman; in effect, she publicly contested its status as a crime.

What if the problem with a "dick-watching bitch" is not that she is a *dick-watcher* but that she is a *bitch*? *Bitch* is, as Lillian Robinson has observed in a different context, an appellation that a woman earns by her "intrusion into male certainties" (1993, 10). Robinson's observation directs us to re-read this incident not simply as an assault on Olson and on legal principles of equality but as a defensive reaction against a woman in a position of power. As one feminist analyst noted at the time of the controversy, assertions by Kiam and the players that Olson was asking for trouble by entering the locker room deny that power, stereotyping Olson as the victim of a justified attack (Matchan 1990). In contrast, we suggest that it was not Olson's vulnerability as a woman that prompted this confrontation but rather that Olson—as a bitch—had the players at a disadvantage: Hers was an intrusion not just into the locker room but into certainties about gender relations and sex differences that sport serves to guarantee.

It is a commonplace among sport sociologists that professional athletics helps to construct gender as an asymmetrical relation between two mutually exclusive but complementary categories and establishes that social construction as a fact of nature. We take up this commonplace to argue that sport serves as an affirmation of what Judith Butler calls the heterosexual matrix (1990, chap. 2). We mean by this that sport constructs not only the gender order but binary sexual difference as well; in turn, the certainties it affirms go beyond gender complementarity to the more precarious fiction of oppositional sexual orientation. Consequently, we modify Robinson's assessment of what it means to be termed a bitch by viewing the position of the woman sports reporter as an intrusion not just into male certainties but into gender certainties more generally.

Our argument, which rests on Butler's work, will seem counterintuitive to feminists who take for granted that gender is to sex as culture is to nature. Indeed, Butler refutes precisely this assumption that gender is the cultural reflection of a natural sexual binary. Instead, she argues that gender designates the social practices by which that binary is made to seem inherent in nature. Butler introduces the concept of the heterosexual matrix in order to disclose what she calls the "compulsory order of sex/ gender/desire," the cultural logic that makes binary sex difference seem to be the cause of the social effects by which it is constructed, that stabilizes masculine and feminine gender identification, and that regulates the orientation of desire in such a way as to establish heterosexuality as the natural and inevitable outcome of normal psychological development (1990, 6–7). We argue that by calling her a dick-watching bitch, Olson's antagonists disclose the woman sports reporter's potential to break up this logic: By her intrusion into the locker room, she destabilizes the opposition between masculinity as that which is both penetrating and impenetrable, and femininity as that which is receptive and deferential in the face of male power.

Taking the players at their word, this article offers a feminist deconstruction of looking, which we analyze as an excess rather than as a crime. We take as our starting point the words of Jacqueline Rose, who directs a "feminism concerned with the question of looking" to "stress the particular and limiting opposition of male and female which any image seen to be flawless is serving to hold in place" (1986, 232). We argue that sport is a technology for the production of flawless images of gender difference that serve to regulate heterosexual desire and that looking is a technology by which athletic performance organizes ambiguous relations of difference into oppositional gender certainties. The presence in the locker room of a woman sports reporter is an intrusion into these certainties because the access and critical voice that she enjoys as a professional are in excess of that which she ought to enjoy as a woman. The charge of looking is deployed to contain this excess by turning her look of appraisal and her authoritative critical voice into a crime.

Sport and the Construction of White Civility

We have discussed the incident thus far as if gender certainties were the only thing at stake in the Olson–Patriots incident. This is misleading insofar as it leaves unstated the fact that Olson is a white woman, that the players who harassed her were black, and that the men who supported them—the owners, management, players, sports columnists, and probably many Boston area fans—were white. We argue that race, although unmentioned in the coverage and in most of the commentaries, is one key to understanding how this incident played out in public. The controversy exemplified one way that sport, race, and gender work together to the benefit of white masculinity. Analyses of the incident at the time it occurred, which tended to focus either on Olson's perspective or on that of the players, were alike in overlooking this complex of relations. These analyses missed an opportunity to effect a realignment of forces that could destabilize white masculinity, a fragile identity whose articulation is achieved, in part, through sport. Thus, although gender will be our primary lens of analysis, we argue that a feminist deconstruction of this incident must be "race-cognizant" as well (Frankenberg 1993, chap. 6).

It is not often that a sexual assault on a well-educated white woman meets with public congratulations, especially when it is orchestrated by a group of black men. And how often do the media fail to mention race in such a story, especially when the victim is white and her attackers are black? For the sake of comparison, recall the newspaper coverage of the 1989 rape and beating of a woman investment banker in Central Park that conformed to the far more typical pattern of demonizing the attackers and canonizing the victim. In this instance, racial themes were at first invoked implicitly, with the twelve youths involved identified cautiously as part of a "loosely organized gang" from "Upper Manhattan" (Pitt 1989b, A1). Subsequently, race was raised to the central explanatory variable of the incident as the *New York Times* undertook a virtual sociological study of "wilding," which it characterized as a "pastime" by which "packs" of teenagers from "housing projects" "rampage" against "joggers and bikers" in the park.[6] One need not even read beneath the surface of these accounts to get the story they tell of untamed black youths preying on fitness-conscious whites.[7]

Given the way such stories are typically narrated, it is worth asking why a group of black men who exposed themselves to a white professional woman on the job and then boasted—in their own words—of giving her what she "wanted" were not castigated as attackers but celebrated as avengers. Five months after the confrontation, Patriots owner Victor Kiam was still saluting his players when, at an awards banquet for an Old-Timers Athletic Association, he quipped: "Do you know what Lisa Olson has in common with the Iraqis? They've both seen Patriot missiles up close" (Times News Services 1991, C2). Beyond Kiam's predictable support for his team, male sports reporters and fans attacked Olson in numerous columns, letters to the editor, and calls that "deluged" Boston area radio shows (Matchan 1990, 29). What dynamics would be at work to make Kiam, the Patriots management, several white male sports columnists, and scores of fans resist a typical race narrative and side with the players?

In the first place, these are highly paid professional athletes in the employ of a white corporate executive. Further, they are symbols of an ideal of masculinity in which a good deal of cultural capital (literal and figurative) is invested.[8] Historically, professional sport has worked to forge male solidarity around an anachronistic ideal of sovereign masculinity. Sociologist Michael Kimmel has argued that its emergence in the late nineteenth-century United States was prompted by a "perceived crisis of masculinity" among white middle-class males whose autonomy was compromised by political and economic transformations (1990, S7). This presumed crisis was precipitated by the domestication of the frontier by the mechanization and routinization of labor that eroded economic autonomy, by the rise of the women's movement, and by the influx of immigrants into industrial centers. Similarly, Michael Messner has argued that, in the face of the increasing bureaucratization of this society, the professional athlete was an exemplar of irrefutable physical sexual difference and superiority; in the face of social and cultural plurality, athletic performance served as a rallying point for male identity. In football, the most militarist of the sports with which Americans are identified, male athleticism serves, "in the face of women's challenges to male dominance, to symbolically link men of diverse ages and socioeconomic backgrounds" (Messner 1988, 202). To be an exemplar of masculinity puts the black male athlete in an ambiguous position with respect to race by affording him an experience that, in this racist society, is unique: he will be seen first as a man and second as a black man.

This privileged status that the black male athlete enjoys against other black men does not erase his racial identity, however. Sport works paradoxically to forge solidarity in that while it unites men around an anachronistic ideal of masculinity, it also manages to differentiate them by race and class. Messner quotes one white male professional who invoked a black male athlete in just this paradoxical fashion, declaring: "A woman can do the same job as I can do—maybe even be my boss. But I'll be *damned* if she can go out on the football field and take a hit from Ronnie Lott," a black NFL player celebrated for making aggressive tackles (1990, 103). To this man, Lott reaffirms the self-evident natural foundation of male superiority. Thus, he expresses solidarity with Lott as one of the bottom-line guarantors of white professional masculinity in a time of feminist incursions into middle-class occupations. Yet to celebrate Lott as a fearsome hitter is also to denigrate him, as Lott is made to "play the role of the primitive other, against whom higher status men define themselves as modern and civilized" (Messner 1990, 103).

In a different context, labor historian David Roediger has identified such claims to civility as intrinsic to the "pleasures of whiteness" (1991, 13). These pleasures constituted a positive race identity that was addressed to the emerging working class. Over the course of the nineteenth century, whiteness served to reconcile the republican ideal of the independent citizen suited to the elite citizen body of a primarily agricultural nation with the political and economic transformations wrought by industrial capitalism. This pleasure worked both to offset white workers' "fear of dependency on wage labor" and to fortify their dignity against the "necessities of capitalist work discipline" (Roediger 1991, 13). In turn, Roediger argues, blackness was not simply regarded as the other of white racial identity but simultaneously denigrated and admired as a symbol of spirituality and physicality, sources of resistance against the industrial discipline to which white workers had submitted. Insofar as black athletes today are simultaneously celebrated and denigrated as emblems of male potency and explosive physicality, they help to pay middle- and working-class white men what Roediger calls the "wages of whiteness" (1991).

A further paradox for the black male athletes themselves is that they are the least empowered by the idealized masculinity for which they are the standard-bearers. Though sport may appear to be a way to break out of typical patterns of race and class oppression, it actually reproduces them. To begin with, the odds of a black male youth making a living playing professional sports are two in 100,000 (Messner 1990). Harry Edwards puts it starkly: "Statistically, you have a better chance of getting hit by a meteorite in the next 10 years than getting work as an athlete" (Oates 1979, A32). Despite these odds, college talent scouts continue to recruit black teenagers "to out-of-state colleges with dreams not of a degree but of the NBA in their heads. . . . The failure of these players following years of work at (and exploitation by) schools let folks back home know these men were just pawns in a game" (George 1992, 201). For those few black men who achieve professional careers in sport, racially patterned employment discrimination assigns them to the least powerful, least secure, most expendable, and most exploited positions (Edwards 1984). One of the most overt patterns of racial oppression in sport is the distribution of power through control over material resources. In professional sports, black male athletes are disproportionately represented in lower-status occupational positions. In the National Football League, for example, there are no black owners or general managers although 68 percent of all players are black (Lapchick and Benedict 1993). In addition, in 1995 only two out of thirty NFL teams had a black head coach. Sport is so inextricably bound up with the ideology and structure of white male privilege that although it may appear to advantage blacks, in fact it only confirms that privilege. In Edwards's words, "America has progressed from a 'Jim Crow' pre–Jackie Robinson era to a post-Robinson era characterized by . . . 'Mr. James Crow, Esquire' " (Edwards 1982, 20).

White men's responses to the confrontation between Olson and the Patriots conform to the pattern Messner has identified with sport more generally, constructing the black male athlete simultaneously as a rallying point for heterosexual masculinity and as a marker of implicit race and class difference. For example, there was Victor Kiam's remark that the *Herald* was "asking for trouble" by sending Olson into the locker room. Similarly, there was the warning of one male sports reporter that, "traditionally, vulgarity is a part of the locker room scene. It isn't to be recommended, but if one isn't tough enough to brace oneself for the crudeness one is apt to encounter there, one should cover tea dances" (Durslag 1991, C3). Finally, there was the frequently stated suspicion summed up by Patriots running back John Stephens, who demanded: "What kind of woman wants to be in a [men's] locker room?" (Madden 1990a, 66). Such remarks suggested that the locker room is a realm of brute physicality in which women are particularly at risk. In so doing, they implicitly sexualize Olson and the players. She becomes not a professional whose job brings her into the locker room and into contact with other professionals but an adventure-seeker in a domain of unchecked physical and sexual energy.

In sum, we argue that owners, fans, and media professionals sided with the players in celebrating them as avengers of an affront to what Robinson would call male certainties. But this was no simple affirmation of interracial solidarity. Even while rallying in their defense, these onlookers constructed the players' actions as an uncontrolled physical and sexual response. This construction worked simultaneously to confirm the biological basis of male supremacy and to specify elite white males' privileged position over the black men they mark as violent and the white women they mark as inherently vulnerable.

Reconsidering Looking

When the Patriots and their sympathizers charged Lisa Olson with looking, they were defending the certainties that she challenged by entering the locker room. The centrality of looking to the construction of white middle-class gender certainties is something that feminist theorists have long appreciated. As Virginia Woolf has argued, the power of the "patriarch who has to conquer" depends on the "looking-glass vision" of feminine adoration, that magnifying glance "possessing the magic and delicious power of reflecting the figure of man at twice its natural size" ([1919] 1957, 35–36). This is what Naomi Scheman terms the "specular economy of patriarchy," in which woman serves not only as the feminine spectacle who poses as an object of vision but also as the adoring audience who mirrors man's performance in such a way as to exaggerate his potency and overlook his inadequacies (1993, 152). As feminine spectacle, woman defers desire, signaling that she does not desire directly but desires to be desired by man; as adoring audience she defers her own agency, paying him a rapt attention that constitutes "phallocratic reality," that realm in which men's actions, emotions, and values command center stage (Frye 1983, 167). Peeking excessively would violate this specular economy.

Yet Olson's looking was not a simple violation, for most of the men at whom she would have looked, as a sports reporter assigned to cover an NFL team, were black. As bell hooks has argued, in the "phallocentric politics of spectatorship" described by feminist theorists and film theorists, both the adoring woman and the man whose image she magnifies are white (1992, 118). Historically speaking, hooks points out, looking was central to the politics of "racialized power relations" because "slaves were denied their right to gaze" (1992, 115). This proscription of blacks' gaze was imposed most violently on black men, whose looking at white women (real or imagined) was understood by whites to be the ultimate race crime and punished by the ultimate race retribution. Is it possible that in the Patriots locker room this historical relation was reversed? Not exactly. Whereas it is the case that the charge of looking was deployed against a white woman by black men, it makes a difference that the men in this case were athletes and the woman a sports reporter. We shall argue that just as the black male athlete is in an ambiguous position as the standard-bearer of an ideal of masculine supremacy that both celebrates and denigrates his physicality, so is the white woman sports reporter in an ambiguous position with respect to the privileges and prohibitions typically accorded white femininity.[9]

On one hand, then, feminist analyses of the gaze vindicate men's widespread anxieties about looking; on the other, they suggest an interpretation of looking that differs from that of the players in an important way. The players define looking as a sex crime, which constructs Olson as a voyeur and their behavior toward her as a justifiable expression of modesty. Hence the clarion call of defensive player Ronnie Lippert, who, upon seeing Olson in the locker room just before the incident, began handing towels to his teammates and shouting: "Cover your boys, there is a lady in the locker room!" (Heymann 1990, 16). Similarly, Kiam complained (erroneously) that Olson was "sitting on the floor" during the interview, where she "could look at their privates" (Eskenazi 1990, B15). Taken at face value, it appears that the players deployed the charge of looking merely to protect their penises from the untoward curiosity of the female voyeur.

The problem with the players' insistence that looking is a sexual transgression is that this construction is unilaterally contested by the women they accuse of doing it. As sports reporter Christine Brennan put it, "[we] go into locker rooms not because we want to, but because we have to. The locker room is the place where writers interview athletes. It's not exciting or sexy or tantalizing. It's cramped and steamy and messy" (1990, D1). Although they resist being charged with voyeurism, women sports reporters nonetheless understand that the players have a legitimate concern for privacy. Viewed in this light, looking can be interpreted as a kind of occupational hazard for players and women sports reporters alike. The problem, then, is to reconcile the concern over privacy with the sports reporters' equally reasonable expectation of equal access to the players, a legally won right that they must exercise if they are to do their jobs competitively with their male counterparts. Sports reporter Michele Himmelberg put it this way: "The issue for managers, reporters, and athletes is mutual respect. How do you protect the athletes' privacy while respecting a reporter's professional duties?" (1991, 65).

Whereas women reporters contest the construction of looking as voyeurism, the players in turn contest its construction as an occupational hazard shared by athletes and writers who work in locker rooms. They routinely bait women reporters by going out of their way to expose themselves. Mariah Burton Nelson comments: "Talk to women who cover men's sports on a daily basis and you hear about players who walk past, deliberately brushing their genitals against their arm" (1994, 228–229). It appears that what occurred between Olson and the Patriots was not an unusual display but an exaggeration of a normal routine. Moreover, we suggest that neither the women sports reporters nor the players quite get what is at stake in the charge of looking. We counter that looking is neither a perversion to which women sports reporters are particularly susceptible nor a concern that they share with the players but a charge that players use to discipline a woman sports reporter, that is, to render her docile by displacing her from her authoritative position as a reporter who looks critically at players and reassigning her to a sexualized position of wanton femininity (Foucault 1979). The term *looker* is ambiguous in this regard. Where the players use it to suggest that a female reporter is a sex-hungry voyeur, to most it would suggest that she is a feminine spectacle, an exceptionally attractive woman who advertises herself as an object of male desire. Either way, the term sexualizes her and, as such, constitutes a discourse: an ideological construct that delineates the practice of a social relationship in such a way as to anchor and reproduce normal certainties by containing potential transgressions against them (Althusser 1971).

Taken straightforwardly, then, the charge of looking is as misleading as Ludtke suggested. Glossed as peeking excessively, however, the term evinces a profound ambivalence: The players want her to peek but not to look. Where peeking is expected in the specular economy of patriarchy, looking exceeds it. The players' ambivalence directs our analysis beyond their actual privates and the legalistic concern for privacy to something less tangible: cultural anxiety over the precarious relationship of the penis to the phallus, which Joan Scott deems a "veiled and evasive signifier . . . which gains its power through the promise it holds out but never entirely fulfills" (1991, 779). What is the promise of the phallus to which Scott alludes? It is fulfillment of the desire for certainty. This promise can never be made good except in the intangible patterns of linguistic devices and cultural habits that organize ambiguous relations of difference into tidy oppositions.

Scott's conception of the phallus is distinct from that underlying the popular expression "phallic symbol," which is playfully invoked whenever a feature of the physical or built environment appears to pay tribute to male potency—such as a mountain peak or skyscraper, a geyser or rocket launching. In contrast, Scott conceives of the phallus as the paradigmatic instance of meaning-in-opposition; that is to say, it exemplifies the principle of negation whereby any term is defined not by what it is but by its difference from what it is not. Scott calls the phallus evasive, because while it holds out the promise of certainty, it ultimately refers only to otherness and lack, the negations by which meanings are secured in an oppositional system. This means, as Jacqueline Rose observes, that the "status of the phallus is a fraud"; it is not a symbol of potency but instead a contradiction that calls attention to the "precariousness of any identity assumed" on the principle of otherness. This precariousness is due to the fact that sexual difference, the putatively natural binary on which the phallic principle is supposedly based, is merely a "legislative divide" that follows from that principle and therefore cannot serve to ground it. If sexual difference is itself the product of the phallic order rather than its origin, then the promise of the phallus is false: It stands on an opposition of its own making, not on a certainty that is given by nature. Thus, as Rose puts it with undisguised irony, the concept of the phallus is an "impossibility writ large" (1986, 64–65).

We link this argument to sport through the performance of the male athlete, which signifies athletic excellence in the same evasive way that the phallus signifies potency. As sport sociologists have argued, male athletic performance is constructed as commonsense evidence of the superiority of the male body and its absolute difference from that of the female. Like the status of the phallus, however, this superiority is a fraud. Its seemingly irrefutable evidence of male potency is not grounded in the certainties of biology but is, rather, produced by athletic performances that construct excellence in terms of attributes such as muscle mass, strength, and speed in which men typically have an advantage over women (Birrell and Cole 1990; Bryson 1990). Thus, masculine athletic superiority is, like any identity assumed on the phallic principle, precarious.

This precariousness helps to explain the antagonism between players and women sports reporters that prompts the charge of looking. What makes Olson or any other woman sports reporter a potential looker is the fact that she is authorized as a reporter to ask hard questions and as a sports reporter to do so in the locker room. Christine Brennan explained: "When Joe Montana does well, or makes a mistake, the fans . . . want to know why. They can't ask Montana themselves, but I can ask on their behalf" (1990, D2). This means, as one male reporter explained, that the sports "reporter's presence is adversarial," an unwanted intrusion that often comes at the worst possible time: "The players' manliness gets compromised by losing, there's a natural need for a scapegoat, and then to have that intrusion of little people with notebooks?" (Globetti, 1990, 92).[10] When the person with the notebook—and, of course, the pen—is female, this combination of privileged access, critical gaze, and public voice is potentially explosive: She is in a position to demystify the phallic promise of unfailing potency not so much by what she sees but by where she sees and how.

If the performance of the male athlete is, like the phallus, understood be an evasive signifier rather than an unquestionable symbol of potency, it is not difficult to understand why peeking is welcomed in the culture of the locker room and looking—or peeking excessively—is a threat. Peeking is an allowance that players both grant to women sports reporters and expect from them because it stabilizes their precarious identities. It flatters them that their manhood is so overwhelming a curiosity to women that they cannot keep themselves—as one player put it—from "sneaking a peek," but so imposing a force that they dare not look too directly or too long (Nelson 1994, 247). In other words, peeking is not an offense but a ceremonial tribute that confirms the oppositional fiction that the phallus is something possessed by man and lacking from but desired by woman. As a gesture of desire that is appropriately deferential, peeking underwrites the fiction of phallic opposition without threatening to disclose its instability. Thus, the promise of the phallus does not require the proscription of the female gaze but rather "the subtle directing of the allowable lines of [women's] sight" (Scheman 1993, 152).

This care to foster peeking but to prohibit peeking excessively is not unique to relations between players and women sports reporters; to the contrary, it is commonly practiced by filmmakers and the ratings decisions of the Motion Picture Association of America (MPAA). A *New York Times* analysis reported that there is an understood double standard in Holly-wood whereby ratings decisions exhibit a pattern of treating male nudity with greater deference than it does female nudity (Andrews 1992, H13–14). The attitude of the MPAA "seems to be that male nudity is fine as long as it is obscured"—that is, a naked penis can be presented publicly as long as the audience's view of it is masked by night, distance, or some other prop (Andrews 1992, H13). If a penis is directly exposed to the camera for more than a fleeting "peek," the film usually earns the more restrictive NC-17 rating; in contrast, it can linger on an unobstructed female frontal nude and still earn an R rating. Richard Dyer's (1992) study of male pin-ups suggests one further way the camera can commit the crime of looking. Dyer observed that male pin-ups take care to avoid any suggestion that the male body is vulnerable to invasion. In contrast to the inviting and usually passive pose of the female pin-up, the male will be displayed in action or ready for action. If in repose, the backdrop will be one that suggests masculine activity.

The examples of both sport and cinema suggest that the mystique of the phallus requires that public presentations of the male body be carefully orchestrated to produce a flawless image of phallic masculinity. On the movie screen as in the locker room, the presentation of the penis is subtly managed within the parameters of deference. A woman sports reporter is in a rare position to transgress those parameters by virtue of the intersec-tion of her occupation with her gender. Whereas most women who gain access to strongholds of patriarchal power in this society do so at the cost of being able to criticize what goes on there, and certainly at the cost of going public with that criticism, the woman sports reporter is uniquely privileged by a potent combination of insider access, critical vision, and public voice (Kane and Disch 1993). She is a publicly recognized critic of male performance whose profession authorizes her to question athletes in the locker room immediately after a contest in the hope that she will catch them off guard. As an authorized transgression of typical parameters of deference, her looking unsettles the certainties of binary sex, gender com-plementarity, and oppositional sexual orientation on which phallic po-tency is grounded. It is an excess that must be contained by constructing it as a crime.

By calling Olson a looker, the players put a hold on her that enables them to perform what Mary Daly has called a patriarchal reversal (Daly 1978, 79). To carry Daly's felicitous phrase into a sport context, a reversal in wrestling is an oppositional maneuver that is performed from a subordinate position on an opponent who has achieved a position of dominance. It is a defensive strategy to offset the power of the opposition and seize the advantage. As much as it offers a literal picture of power as a physical capacity, this metaphor is also a graphic reminder that power is never the property of an individual but that it is dynamic and shifting, the effect of instabilities in relationships. The patriarchal reversal does not take place whenever a woman challenges the typical gender hierarchy by taking a position in a traditionally male profession; rather, it occurs only when such a challenge to traditional gender roles also destabilizes the certainties on which the conception of gender as a social construction based on a natural binary depends.

The ingenuity of the patriarchal reversal is that the players disciplined Olson by taking the very thing they claimed not to want her to see and—in their words—making her look. By strutting naked in her line of sight, the players asserted their prerogative to orchestrate the way Olson looked at them (cf. Silverman 1983, 231). It is evident from the Heymann report, which reconstructed the confrontation on the basis of interviews with Olson and the players, that this was a contest over looking. Zeke Mowatt made the opening bid in a struggle to catch Olson's eye: "Look at her. She's just watching. I'm going to tell her about herself." The report recounts that Olson "looked up and saw Mowatt walking across the room looking at her [with] what she interpreted as a purposeful look in his eyes." She responded by averting her gaze, "turn[ing] to face Hurst [the player whom she was interviewing] more directly." Mowatt continued across the locker room, narrowing his sights on Olson while other players began shouting: " 'Make her look, make her look,' 'Is she looking? Is she looking?' " When Mowatt reached the area of Hurst's locker, Olson "lifted her head." At this, Mowatt "smiled and purposely displayed himself to her in a suggestive way." Laughter erupted and shouts from other players continued, especially "Is she looking? Is she looking at it?" (Heymann 1990, 16–18).

By getting Olson to look up at him, Mowatt had established a foothold for the patriarchal reversal. Olson's sight lines were precisely described so that if she looked to either side she could be accused of "peeking excessively." There was nothing for her to do but counter with an appropriate gesture: "Embarrassed by Mowatt's action, Olson quickly lowered her head . . . [and] kept her eyes down" (Heymann 1990, 19). This was the moment of reversal and the players celebrated it. They had literally stared her down, displacing her from a position of authority to a posture of deference. Olson was finally a confirmed dick-watcher, but no longer a bitch.

If the gaze of the woman sports reporter unsettles the heterosexual matrix whereby gender and sexual certainties are secured, then the patriarchal reversal reinstates those certainties by turning her prerogative of insider access into an intimidating proximity. When it is read in this way, not as another instance of harassment but in the terms of the patriarchal reversal, this confrontation between Olson and the Patriots magnifies the subtle relations by which the heterosexual matrix is secured, shows how a woman who looks with authority exceeds that matrix, and dramatizes how her agency will be contained. In sum, against the players' protestations about privacy, we contend that this was a performance designed not to teach Olson not to look but to teach her *how* to look.

Exposing the Sport Continuum

To understand why looking is so deeply threatening that it would provoke such a dramatic response by the players and inspire such anger in fans, it is necessary to appreciate the relationship between sport and the apparently compulsory logic of oppositions that Butler calls the heterosexual matrix. We have already noted how professional sport participated in the elaboration of the particular middle-class construction of gender that assigned men and women to oppositional and complementary roles. In 1972, the federal government set the stage for a transformation of the social meaning of sport by enacting Title IX, the statute that prohibits sex discrimination in educational settings. With its passage, which fostered a tremendous increase in women's athletic participation, sport would no longer be a secured stronghold of masculinity but, as Messner put it, "a crucial arena of struggle over basic social conceptions of masculinity and femininity" (1988, 199).

One way that sport is made to hold out against this challenge is, as we have mentioned, by the construction of athleticism in terms of activities and skills that celebrate anachronistic masculinity; such a construction ensures that male performance will serve, like the phallus, as the definitive standard against which all else is compared and fails to measure up. For example, sports that require muscle mass, strength, and speed are more prestigious than those that emphasize beauty and flexibility. Similarly, as athletic accomplishments, physical skills such as hitting or hurling an object are considered vastly superior over tumbling gracefully through space. In sum, sport is the most important public arena for the performance of gender as an asymmetrical, oppositional relation based on natural sexual differences; as such, it helps to reaffirm the belief that a gender order that accords primacy to males is not a mere social construction but a reflection of men's natural physical superiority.

But the practice of sport does more to establish gender certainties than simply providing apparent validation of the physical superiority and social supremacy of males. It also has the far more insidious effect of recasting sexual differences that range along a continuum (Epstein 1990) into a dichotomy. By denying the manifest evidence that physical differences vary along a continuum and thereby perpetuating the assumption that binary opposition is inherent in nature, sport both confirms the logic of the heterosexual matrix and translates it into everyday experience. It is larger-than-life proof that sex differences are dichotomous by nature, confirmation that oppositional gender identities mimic this natural binary, and a commonsense affirmation that heterosexual orientation is normative because it is natural.

Consider that in the world of sport a contestant is never simply an athlete but must be categorized as either a female athlete or a male athlete. In tennis, for example, athletes do not just play tennis, they play men's tennis and women's tennis. Although tennis players compete in mixed doubles, there is no competition for mixed singles. And why not? Because the purpose of these distinctions is to take the continuum of variation among individual characteristics such as strength, speed, and height and construct it as an oppositional sexual binary.

By teaching us how to read athletic performance as incontrovertible proof of binary sexual difference, sport suppresses evidence of a sexual continuum (Kane 1995). As such, it is consistent with the work of feminist theorists who argue that the reproduction of phallic power requires ongoing efforts to organize ambiguous relations of difference into oppositional gender certainties. For sport to admit evidence of a continuum would be tantamount to exposing as precarious the binary sexual difference that gives oppositional gender identity its apparent foundation in nature. Building on the work of Eleanor Metheny, we argue that the suppression of this continuum is accomplished by a variant of sport typing, the concept Metheny introduced to argue that individual athletes are socialized to participate in sports that are consistent with prevailing gender stereotypes (1965).[11] We argue that sport typing is only one of several interrelated devices by which ambiguous relations of difference that are or could be disclosed by athletic performances are organized into oppositional gender certainties. In addition to sport typing, these devices include erasure, re-gendering, and selective gender comparison.

Whereas Metheny understood sport typing as reflecting gender stereotypes, we argue somewhat differently that it works to suppress evidence of a continuum. As Metheny noted, this happens in part by typing some sports as exclusively masculine and differentiating them against others that are typed as exclusively feminine (e.g., football vs. synchronized swimming). While it is not unheard of for women to play football, their participation is treated as an aberration, thereby constructing a potential contestation of binary sexual difference in such a way as to reaffirm it. In sports where both men and women participate, however, typing works instead to segregate their performance into oppositional categories. In the case of gymnastics, for example, women and men compete in entirely different events. Women's events, such as the balance beam and floor exercise, call for movement that emphasizes flexibility and grace, whereas men's events, such as rings and pommel horse, call for movement that emphasizes speed and explosive force.[12]

Erasure, the second device of binary enforcement, comes into play when athletes fail to conform to the prescriptions of sport typing. Erasure occurs through the media's silence about the existence of hundreds of sport clubs and leagues in which women participate in sports such as rugby or ice hockey that have traditionally been typed as masculine.[13] Although theoretically erasure could also be deployed against males who participate against type, there are few sports typed as exclusively feminine because definitions of athleticism have historically been equated with masculinity. Even when males do perform against type, they can usually be made to affirm typical gender certainties, as in figure skating, which provides a clearly delineated masculine role for the male skater. In contrast, women cannot participate in sports such as rugby or football without displaying an athleticism that is typed as masculine. Because their participation cannot be reinterpreted as feminine, it has to be erased.

The third device of binary enforcement, regendering, occurs when a woman athlete displays superior athleticism in a skill or activity traditionally typed as masculine. For example, when a woman hits a baseball exceptionally far, she is typically congratulated for hitting "just like a man." This device both reinforces the equation of superior athleticism with maleness and suppresses evidence of a continuum on which the performances of women and men would be interspersed. Regendering is particularly insidious because it creates the impression that female athleticism is both accepted and enthusiastically supported; in order to receive that support, however, the female athlete must be regendered as male, if only temporarily.

The marathon is a particularly good example of the work that sport does to suppress the continuum because it is a competition in which men and women run on the same course, at the same time, in the same event. With men and women runners interspersed for miles along the same road, the marathon graphically discloses a performance continuum that cannot be reorganized by any of the devices we have discussed so far. This is where selective gender comparison, the fourth device of binary enforcement, comes in. Deployed primarily though not exclusively through media coverage, selective gender comparison recasts this one race as two different contests.

Although it happens throughout the race, selective gender comparison is particularly evident at the end, where the coverage constructs two separate finishes. First, there is the men's finish. Even though typically the first ten runners will cross the line within six or seven minutes of each other, the media constructs a battle between the two or three front-runners. After telling the story of the lead men, the commentators shift their focus to the front-running women, literally editing out that portion of the continuum that lies between the leaders of the so-called men's race and the first women finishers. The first woman to cross the line, typically finishing somewhere in the top sixty runners, will be compared only to the other lead women and to the winner of the men's race. Gender-based comparisons with the remaining male contestants vanish from the media landscape: Neither will we be directed to watch her compete against the men who finish with her nor will we hear that she has just beaten the several thousand men who will cross the finish line behind her.[14] This selective gender comparison ensures that we will never think of women competing against men and prevailing over them, despite the graphic evidence of the marathon where women run interspersed among men and cross the finish line ahead of many of them. Such coverage fits performance differences into approved gender relations by making one sort of gender comparison (the women's winner to the men's winner) and dismissing any other (the women's winner just beat the rest of the men). This articulation serves in turn to suppress evidence of a gender continuum and produce a gender binary.

By virtue of these various devices that serve to reorganize a continuum of difference as a binary opposition and to establish that opposition as natural, we learn from professional sport to see oppositional sexual difference when we look at bodies in motion. This means that professional sport is more than an arena for the display of athletic excellence, more than a mechanism for the accumulation of corporate wealth, more even than an apparatus for the reproduction of race and gender ideology. It is also one of the most visible public institutions by which the cultural logic of Butler's heterosexual matrix becomes everyday experience. Our analysis of these devices, which discloses the precariousness of the gender differences that seem so certain on the playing field, helps to explain how something so apparently trivial as looking could ignite a national controversy. Looking poses a challenge not just to the players but to the cultural truths about sex, gender, and desire that sport makes seem self-evident.

Looking Down: Apologetic Women/Phallic Men

How the public performance of sport invests the male athlete with phallic power and affords a site for contesting that power has been the subject of a great deal of scholarship. There is much less in the way of critical analysis of the men's locker room, however, because it is difficult for scholars to observe it unobtrusively (Sabo and Panepinto 1990; Curry 1991). It is ironic that an NFL team's confrontation with a woman sports reporter over "looking" should facilitate such analysis, but it did. In effect, the controversy served to fling open the very door the Patriots players had so urgently wanted to close against Lisa Olson by generating multiple accounts of locker room culture from diverse perspectives. The players and their sympathizers defended a typical view of the locker room as one of the few men's clubs that ought to stand fast in an era of challenges to gender-based exclusion in other domains. In this hypermasculine culture, even men sports reporters admitted feeling intimidated, as one put it, by having to conduct interviews among "forty-seven people of extraordinary size who question not only your right to question them, but to share the air that they breathe" (Globetti 1990, 92). Despite feeling ill at ease there, both men and women sports reporters contested the players' exclusive claim to the locker room. But as we shall demonstrate, these accounts were striking for the differences they revealed in the way that men and women sports reporters relate to players. These differences emphasized just how far women are from equality with their male counterparts in the locker room, their legal rights notwithstanding.

Patriots owner Victor Kiam reasserted the typical view of the locker room when he declared: "To the players, their locker room is their castle. Every man has a castle" (Freeman 1990b, 25). As Eve Kosofsky Sedgwick has argued, the castle metaphor is an "ideological construction" that "reaches *back* to an emptied-out image of mastery and integration under feudalism" to hold out a promise of sovereignty to men in a time when they no longer rule over the domestic realm (1985, 14). Former Washington Redskins player Dave Butz revealed precisely this desire to return to the gender mores of a more traditional generation when he remarked that Olson's "mother should have told her that if she stepped into a men's locker room, she would be entering a man's world" (Butz 1990, C5). By their use of the castle metaphor, Kiam and the players support our claim that there was more at stake in the locker room than the players' privacy; it signals that the woman sports reporter who enters this so-called castle will be seen as a traitor to its retrogressive image of masculinity. Further, any hostility toward her will be explained as a justifiable reaction to an attack on the battlements. As Kiam put it: "Why not stand in front of her [naked] if she is an intruder?" (Mannix 1990, 74).

But the Patriots' conception of the locker room as a last bastion of male sovereignty did not go uncontested. In a column worth quoting at length, *Washington Post* sports reporter Tony Kornheiser describes the locker room as a realm in which the players are as vulnerable as they are powerful. He begins with images of power: "It's there, directly after a game, when reactions are still raw and unvarnished, that an athlete reveals himself. His nakedness is in a way a metaphor for his honesty, and in another way a symbol of his narcissism; you'd be surprised how many athletes revel [in] being naked there, how many of them strut around in self-idealization of the ancient warrior god" (1990, D6). Although this vision of players naked and strutting is consonant with the ideological construction of the locker room as a domain of anachronistic privilege, Kornheiser reveals an aspect of their nakedness that is at odds with the castle metaphor—honesty.

In contrast to strutting nakedness, naked honesty suggests a lack of protection and a vulnerability to exposure that Kornheiser acknowledges when he writes: "This is the sacred place, the place where the secrets of being an athlete will become known to you. But you go inside and see behind the Wizard's curtain, and realize it's a wind machine and a projector. Disillusioned, staring at bodies puffed and purpled with bruises, you quickly ask yourself, 'What am I doing here?'" (1990, D6). Kornheiser's words are a reminder that the locker room is the place where male athletes prepare for their on-the-field performance and the place where they recuperate after the game. Far from being a castle in which players simply and unquestionably rule, the locker room is the place where their bodies are suited up to be invincible; consequently, it is also a place where those bodies can be vulnerable. While Kornheiser's remarks confirm that the locker room culture celebrates male physicality, they also reveal that this culture is fragile. Its fragility consists of the fact that in the locker room, as on the playing field, male physical superiority is not a biological given but an ideological construct that must be produced by ritual performances that promote male narcissism and exclude male vulnerability.

How do the players sustain a culture of narcissism? By acting out the phallic principle of opposition and defining themselves against what they are not. Sport sociologists identify locker room talk, verbal exchanges whereby male athletes celebrate heterosexual aggression against women, as a common method of oppositional self-definition (Kidd 1987; Curry 1991). In a study of fragments of such verbal exchanges in the men's locker rooms of two Big Ten sport teams, Tim Curry found that players routinely engage in bragging about sexual conquests over women—real or imagined—and in "jokes and storytelling about homosexuals" to enhance their image of themselves as "practicing heterosexuals" (1991, 128, 130). Interestingly, Curry found that in addition to these narcissistic or demeaning types of talk, there was honest talk in which athletes spoke about "women as real people, persons with whom the athletes have ongoing social relationships" (128). Such talk was not broadcast to the entire group, however, but shared in private tones for fear that its public disclosure would be ridiculed as evidence of a vulnerability unbecoming to phallic masculinity.

We argue that a woman sports reporter, a professional who enters the locker room with a gaze of appraisal and publicly recognized critical authority, will be deemed a bitch because her occupation poses a challenge to the very matrix of negation and opposition that stabilizes not just male certainties but heterosexual identity. If this claim is correct, then we should find that intruding into the locker room is unsettling to women sports reporters as well as to players; consequently, we might expect that they might make accommodations to the culture of the locker room, reaffirming their identities as women even as they assert their rights as professionals. We find support for this seemingly paradoxical hypothesis in the accounts of the locker room published by women sports reporters in the aftermath of the confrontation between Olson and the Patriots. The accounts divulged what Ludtke called the "unwritten rules of the road," the code of conduct that women sports reporters routinely follow to brush off the " 'little' bothersome things that happen all the time" but about which they cannot complain for fear of being "dismissed as someone who can't do the job" (1990a, B21).

These rules spelled out the dictates of an apologetic: an overtly deferential posturing that works to reaffirm normal certainties in situations where they are threatened. This apologetic is the women reporters' response to a classic double bind. As reporters, they have nothing to write about if they cannot blend in, but as women they cannot make themselves appear at home in the domain of the locker room without being perceived to invite sexual attentions. Their way out of this dilemma, as Huckshorn describes it, is to "strive for perfect comportment[,] a cross between Miss Manners and Mary Richards," two figures who exemplify desexualized, white middle-class femininity (1990, 1E). In other words, they put on a version of what Butler terms the "female masquerade," a compensatory performance whereby a woman who exceeds the boundaries of her so-cially sanctioned identity makes an exaggerated show of gender propriety to reassure potential antagonists.[15] Butler argues that such posturing "can be interpreted as an effort to renounce the 'having' of the Phallus in order to avert retribution by those from whom it must have been procured through castration" (1990, 51). In other words, it is the strategy whereby a dick-watcher reassures male athletes that she is not a bitch.

The first rule of this apologetic is to expect that you will be hazed and to accept it as the price of admission. As Ludtke puts it, "Tolerate the teasing, since you are after all working in the athlete's locker room" (Ludtke 1990a, B21). Christine Brennan adds that the point is not just to "tolerate" the climate of the locker room but to laugh in the face of ha-rassment. She writes, "Let's face it, I'm an outsider in the players' domain. I have to learn to laugh when Dexter Manley shouts out, 'Hey, Chris, come here. I've got something to show you.' I can't take that seriously" (Brennan 1990, D2). Although looking can be a joke when the players facetiously invite it, the code quite specifically enjoins women reporters to take extraordinary precautions against being perceived as initiating it themselves. To that end, the third rule is to maintain eye-to-eye contact with the players at all times (Huckshorn 1990, 1E). Brennan underscores the importance of the measure, asserting: "I have never, ever been in the shower area of any team, and I avoid the pathway to the shower for obvi-ous reasons. I keep eye contact at all times, and carry an 8-by-11 notebook, so when I look down, I look down at the notebook" (Brennan 1990, D2). Beyond avoiding any behavior that could be interpreted as looking, Bren-nan goes out of her way to show her respect for the players by the visible, elaborate care she takes against doing so.

The injunction governing eye contact is accompanied by a corollary: Remember that you cannot act just like your male colleagues. Ludtke cautions, "A woman reporter never assumed that she could act exactly as male reporters do, which meant lingering around the locker room and conversing in a friendly fashion with the players. If she did that, chances are she would be accused of flirting" (Ludtke 1990a, B21). Sports reporter Leah Secondo is even more emphatic: "I go in there, do what I have to do and get the hell out. I make sure my eyes don't stay anywhere too long so people don't get the wrong idea" (quoted in Cramer 1994).

Several men sports reporters, most of whom sympathized with Olson, gave accounts of how they conduct themselves in the locker room that confirmed that women must be more cautious than their male counterparts in their interactions with the players. Although these men also reported being harassed by players—being showered with buckets of water, punched, or teased about their physical inadequacies—most found the concept of looking incomprehensible and objected to its being leveled at Olson or any other woman sports reporter. Kornheiser described looking as an integral part of any sports journalist's job: "You look at the naked bodies, of course you look—men and women" (1990, D6). Similarly, Madden argued that the idea that any reporter would peek excessively is ludicrous, precisely because a sports reporter sees players' bodies all the time: "The last thing any of us who have been to locker rooms care to look at is athletes' bodies; they are as common to us as a blackboard is to a teacher" (1990b, 49).

How can male reporters be so unapologetic about looking? Mariah Burton Nelson once pursued this question indirectly with Tim Brown, All-Pro wide receiver for the Oakland Raiders, whom she asked whether he "had ever seen a man sneaking a peek." Initially attempting to brush off the question, Brown then denied it: "If somebody saw something like that going on, you'd all know about it 'cause it'd probably be in all the papers." When Nelson pressed the issue, Brown became so agitated that he pushed her (1994, 248). Contrary to Tim Brown, who asserts that a male reporter's looking would cause such a stir as to be widely publicized, we argue that what he reveals by his response is that it is altogether inconceivable that the players would address this charge to another man. For a male athlete to accuse a male reporter of looking—of peeking excessively, that is—would be tantamount to admitting that players want male reporters to peek in the first place. Obviously, for male athletes to admit the possibility of such a desire would amount to a betrayal of the heterosexual matrix by the very standard-bearers who make its compulsory order seem so natural.

Whereas men sports reporters cannot be charged with looking, it seems that the women cannot escape it. If they act just like their male counterparts, they risk being deemed voyeurs who find the locker room a turn-on; yet if they follow its unwritten code, they in effect apologize for looking before they have even been accused of it, thereby legitimating the charge. Do all women sports reporters comply with this code? Given how it mimics others associated with white middle-class heterosexual femininity—the exaggerated propriety of Miss Manners or the flaky vulnerability of Mary Richards—there is good reason to question its generalizability. In turn, it is important to note that all of the women who gave accounts of the apologetic were white and college-educated. Despite this, we maintain that one should not be too quick to dismiss these accounts as purely anecdotal evidence of a phenomenon that is peculiar to white women sports journalists. As we noted earlier, the regulation of looking is not unique to the locker room; films and male pin-ups also model apologetic posturing by the deference that is accorded male nudity and the care that is taken to produce appropriately rugged images of masculinity. Even if such posturing were peculiar to white professional women, we think it unlikely that the codes that were divulged in the wake of Olson's confrontation with the Patriots are confined to the men's locker room, although they may be especially exaggerated there.

Looking Up: How a Bitch Is a Resister

Thanks to the Patriots, whose confrontation with Lisa Olson generated a virtual ethnography of the men's locker room, we can now answer the question we posed at the outset of this article: Why this protracted punishment of a sports reporter who had done no more than engage in the ordinary task of conducting an interview? Because Lisa Olson committed a simple but fundamental crime: She refused to perform the apologetic. Initially, she did not laugh off the attack by the players but demanded that they identify themselves to her and apologize, albeit privately. Once the story broke, she would not back down from this demand despite being harassed by fans. On the contrary, she took an even stronger stand, asserting, "Words are fine, but I want some action. . . . I want the people who did this to be identified and I want them severely punished" (Gee 1990, 62). In addition, she had the self-respect to decry what one sports columnist called Kiam's "backhanded" apology (Madden 1990a, 66), countering, "An apology is not accepted when he is telling blatant lies [about me] on television" (Freeman 1990a, 80).

Further, Olson refused to concede the men's locker room to the athletes, laying claim to it as her professional domain and contesting the players' insinuation that she was a voyeur. Against unwritten rules against lingering and looking, Olson insisted that both of these are part of the job she is expected to do there. In a column published only a few days after the story initially broke, Olson wrote: "I was naive enough to believe the Patriots understood what it meant to be a reporter. That they knew it was my business to look around the locker room. I am not a stenographer. There is much more to reporting than writing down quotes. It is my job to observe who is injured, to see who is throwing chairs, to capture the mood of the day" (Olson 1990, 74). What is striking about this statement is its anger, an obvious violation of the apologetic, and the opposition Olson draws between being a stenographer, typically a female service-sector job, and being a professional reporter. Her assertion that looking marks the difference between the two serves to implicitly (and unintendedly) indict every woman sports reporter who, for fear of being hit with this charge, keeps her eyes down and takes notes. Thus, besides having the obvious effect of challenging the man's castle ideology, this resistance contested the prescriptions of the apologetic.

Perhaps the most eloquent testimony to the force of Olson's disruption of the apologetic came from women sports reporters themselves. Although most of the columns they wrote in the wake of the confrontation expressed support for Olson, the very fact that these women were moved to spell out their previously unwritten code suggests that she inspired uneasiness by transgressing it. Only one woman sports reporter, Kristin Huckshorn, owned up to this uneasiness in a remarkably candid column that began: "Why doesn't Lisa Olson shut up? I admit it. That is what I have been thinking ever since Olson, a Boston sportswriter, began publicly explaining how she was sexually harassed by five New England Patriots in their locker room last month" (1990, 1E). Huckshorn rewrote the story of this confrontation to show that by going public with her story, Olson had not only challenged the players but also women sports journalists who play by the rules. Acknowledging that Olson's act called her to task for her own complicity with a demeaning code of silence, Huckshorn admitted, "I wish she would shut up because I was one of those women who kept quiet." Huckshorn ended the column by exhorting other women sports reporters to stand by Olson, not taking pity on her but joining her in resistance: "By speaking out, Lisa Olson is destroying the fragile status quo. She is bringing an old and dreaded issue back to the forefront. She is reminding us that the battle is not yet won. . . . She makes me wonder: If I had spoken up all along, would this still be happening now? I wish she would shut up. She makes me wish that I hadn't" (Huckshorn 1990, 1E).

As Huckshorn retold the story, Olson's speaking out was a resistance that confronted Huckshorn and others with the fact that winning access to the locker room was an empty victory if women sports reporters are required to engage in a parody of femininity once inside. The nationwide reaction to Olson made it clear that under the terms of this compromise women sports reporters were accorded neither professional respect nor legal equality. And by breaking the rules so publicly, Olson dramatized for these women that they bore some responsibility for accepting it. The broader significance of this analysis of looking, then, is that it not only shows how sport participates in producing the heterosexual matrix on the field and in the locker room, but also that it tells one story of resistance against the apologetic codes in which charges such as looking are embedded and by which they are sustained.

Notes

Earlier versions of this article were presented by Lisa Disch at the Midwest Society for Women in Philosophy in October 1993 and by Mary Jo Kane at the North American Society for Sport Sociology in November 1993. We thank anonymous *Signs* reviewers for their comments. Diana Saco, Jacqueline Zita, and Jonathan Sweet offered suggestions on this work in its early stages, as did Naomi Scheman, who gave it an exceptionally close and generous reading. Special thanks go to Lisa Bower and Jennifer

Pierce for helping us to differentiate penises from phalluses, to Steven Gerencser for his analysis of the marathon, and to Jeanne Barker-Nunn for contributing her expertise in interdisciplinary writing to the final revisions of this article.

1. By November, the Heymann Commission had compiled a sixty-page report confirming that Olson had in fact been harassed and suggesting that the incident may even have been premeditated. Tagliabue then fined three players $2,500 each (approximately one day's pay) and fined the team $50,000, sums that were never collected. When questioned about why the fines were never paid, Tagliabue responded, "At some point, enough is enough," evidently meaning that the players had been adequately chastised (Nelson 1994, 240).

2. Area fans threatened Olson with phone calls, letters containing sexual references and obscene drawings, and even death warnings. Easily recognizable by her long red hair, Olson could not cover a game in Boston without fans shouting at her and even showering her with beer. In hope of defusing the situation, the *Herald* reassigned her to cover basketball and hockey instead of football, but to no avail (Montville 1991).

3. At a panel discussion at the annual meeting of the Association for Women in Sports Media, held in Minneapolis in May 1993, it emerged that the putative expose was based primarily on leaked documents of pretrial depositions from the civil suit Olson initiated against the Patriots. Because of a family illness, Olson settled before these proceedings were completed, although only her opponents had given evidence. The depositions and, consequently, the *Globe* article, told the story of the incident from only one perspective.

4. In contrast to Olson's original harassment, three male sportswriters immediately reported Clayton's remarks, which prompted Clayton to respond by attempting to organize a team boycott against them. Dolphins management countered immediately by forcing Clayton to issue a public apology for the remark (Henkel 1993).

5. Melissa Ludtke, then a sports reporter for *Sports Illustrated*, was refused access to the New York Yankees locker room during the 1977 World Series. She joined suit with Time, Inc. (the parent company of *Sports Illustrated*), claiming a violation of the equal protection clause of the Fourteenth Amendment. In 1978, the Federal District Court ruled that all reporters, regardless of sex, must have equal access to the players (Boutilier and SanGiovanni 1983).

6. These stories quoted experts who theorized "wilding" as a practice engaged in by marginalized youth as a protest against people who "seem to personify unattainable affluence" and as an acting out of a more general aimlessness that comes from having an unsupervised and unstructured lifestyle (Pitt 1989a, 1989c).

7. Such narratives are especially irresponsible given that they perpetuate a kind of "rhetorical wilding" against the demographics of such crimes. As the *Times* itself reported during this same period, the crimes are neither exclusively perpetrated by blacks nor exclusively directed against middle-class whites. And in this particular instance, again as reported by the *Times*, the youths involved, though of color, were not

all black. Neither were they gang members nor habitual delinquents. Contrary to the lurid metaphors and the speculative sociology of "wilding," some of the assailants were "A students" and children of parents whom the paper approvingly characterized as "disciplinarians" (Kaufman 1989, A1).

8. Sport as big business has become so ingrained in our society that teams do not have to play a game or sell a ticket to generate revenue. Billions of dollars are spent annually on licensed sports products (e.g., baseball hats and trading cards). In 1992, retail sales of all licensed sports merchandise totaled $12.2 billion (Gorman and Calhoun 1994). Media rights are another major source of income. In 1994, Rupert Murdoch, the publisher of the *Herald*, purchased the broadcasting rights to cover the National Football League for his Fox Television Network at a cost of $1.6 billion (*Media Week* 1994). These serve as but two examples of the connections among sport, capitalism, and masculinity.

9. Where are black women in the specular economy of the locker room? They are as absent from it as they are from feminist theories that, as hooks has argued, "in no way acknowledge black female spectatorship" (1992, 123). The dozen or so black women covering sports in this country account for approximately 1.5 percent of women sports reporters and for less than one-tenth of 1 percent of sports reporters overall (Nelson 1994, 251). If, as hooks suggests, black female spectators learn to look with an "oppositional gaze" precisely because they are excluded by the specular economy of middle-class whites, then it might be easier for black women sports reporters to laugh off the charge of looking or to refute it in their relations with black male athletes. With so few black women covering sports, however, it is hard to know whether this would be borne out in the locker room.

10. One irony of the Olson–Patriots incident is that Olson's presence could not be deemed an intrusion at a bad time. The interview took place the day after a victory, following a light workout, and she was interviewing a player who had been instrumental in that victory.

11. Of course, sports can also be typed with respect to social class. Participation patterns indicate that members of the upper and upper-middle social strata are more likely to engage in individualized sports such as golf and tennis, which depend largely on access to private facilities and equipment. In contrast, blue-collar workers are more likely to participate in team sports, such as softball, which are typically played on public grounds and often sponsored by a labor union, business, or church (Eitzen and Sage 1984).

12. Gymnastics is one of the more extreme examples of sport typing. In tennis, the typing is more subtle because men and women use the same equipment and are required to perform the same physical skills, the only difference being that a women's match is shorter (three sets as opposed to five). The rules of the sport reproduce a misleading sexual stereotype by suggesting that women's capacity for endurance is less than men's.

13. For example, thousands of women play rugby and ice hockey throughout

North America. Further, their participation is not merely recreational; it is highly structured competition organized into leagues and intercollegiate conferences (Olson 1994).

14. These approximations are based on the 1994 Twin Cities (Minneapolis/St. Paul) Marathon, which is one of the top five marathons in the country. Out of 5,499 contestants who finished, 4,076 were men and 1,423 were women. The lead woman finished sixty-sixth overall, which means that 4,011 men finished behind her.

15. Apologetic posturing is not unique to women. Examples of a black apologetic are plentiful as, for example, the stereotype of blacks' willingness to laugh that Toni Morrison calls a "metonym for racial accommodation" (1992, xiii). For lesbians and gays in the military, the Clinton Administration's "don't ask, don't tell, don't pursue" policy prescribes a homosexual apologetic.

References

Althusser, L. (1971). *Lenin and philosophy* (B. Brewster, trans.) New York: Monthly Review.

Andrews, S. (1992, November 1). She's bare. He's covered. Is there a problem? *New York Times*, pp. H13–14.

Birrell, S., and Cole, C. L. (1990). Double fault: Renee Richards and the construction and naturalization of difference. *Sociology of Sport Journal* 7(1), 1–21.

Boutilier, M. & SanGiovanni, L. (1983). *The sporting woman.* Champaign, Ill.: Human Kinetics.

Brennan, C. (1990, September 30). Jocks, gender, and justice: A woman sports reporter's view from the men's locker room. *Washington Post*, p. D1-2.

Brown, C. (1993, May 31). Reporter still feels pain of harassment. *Minneapolis Star and Tribune*, p. 1C.

Bryson, L. (1990). Challenges to male hegemony in sport. In M. A. Messner & D. Sabo (eds.), *Sport, men, and the gender order*, pp. 173–184. Champaign, Ill.: Human Kinetics.

Butler, J. (1990). *Gender trouble.* New York: Routledge.

Butz, D. (1990, October 7). Respect should keep women out of men's locker rooms. *Washington Post*, p. C5.

Cramer, J. (1994). Conversations with women sport journalists. In Pamela J. Creedon (ed.), *Women, media and sport*, (pp. 159–180). Thousand Oaks, Calif.: Sage.

Curry, T. (1991). Fraternal bonding in the locker room: A profeminist analysis of talk about competition and women. *Sociology of Sport Journal* 8(2), 119–135.

Daly, M. (1978). *GynEcology: The metaethics of radical feminism.* Boston: Beacon.

de Lauretis, T. (1990). Eccentric subjects: Feminist theory and historical consciousness. *Feminist Studies* 16(1), 115–150.

Durslag, M. (1991, April 29). She would be wiser to forget the lawsuit. *Los Angeles Times*, p. C3.

140

Dyer, R. (1992). Don't look now: The male pin-up. In *The sexual subject, ed. Screen,* 265–276. New York: Routledge.

Editors commend Olson. (1990, October 7). *Boston Herald,* p. B14.

Edwards, H. (1982). Race in contemporary American sports. *National Forum 62,* 19–22.

———. (1984). The collegiate athletic arms race: Origin and implications of the "Rule 48" controversy. *Journal of Sport and Social Issues 8*(1), 422.

Eitzen, S., & Sage, G., eds. (1984). *Sociology of American sport,* 2d ed. Dubuque, Iowa: Brown.

Epstein, J. (1990). Either/or–neither/both: Sexual ambiguity and the ideology of gender. *Genders 7,* 99–142.

Eskenazi, G. (1990, September 27). Harassment charge draws NFL's attention. *New York Times,* pp. B11, B15.

Foucault, M. (1979). *Discipline and punish* (A. Sheridan, trans.). New York: Vintage.

Frankenberg, R. (1993). *White women, race matters: The social construction of whiteness.* Minneapolis: University of Minnesota Press.

Freeman, M. (1990a, September 26). Kiam apologizes to Olson, fans, media. *Boston Globe,* pp. 75, 80.

———. (1990b, September 25). Patriots fine player for sex harassment. *Boston Globe,* pp. 1, 25.

Frye, M. (1983). *The politics of reality.* Truman, N.Y.: Crossing.

Gee, M. (1990, October 1). Kiam says he's sorry. *Boston Herald,* pp. 1, 62.

George, N. (1992). *Elevating the game.* New York: HarperCollins.

Globetti, M. (1990, September 26). Locker rooms: Classless ditches. *Boston Herald,* p. 92.

Gorman, J., & Calhoun, K. (1994). *The name of the game: The business of sports.* New York: Wiley.

Hart, J. (1990, October 22). No matter athlete's behavior, women out of place. *Times Herald* (Norristown, N.J.), p. 17.

Henkel, C. (1993, February). Listen carefully to Olson's side. *Association for Women in Sports Media (AWSM) Newsletter,* pp. 1–3.

Heymann, P. B. (1990). *Report of special counsel to the commissioner of the National Football League.* New York: National Football League.

Himmelberg, M. (1991). Hot showers, cold shoulder. *Women's Sports and Fitness 13*(2), 65.

hooks, b. (1992). *Black looks: Race and representation.* Boston: South End.

Huckshorn, K. (1990, October 3). Woman reporter rightfully rocks the boat. *San Jose Mercury News,* p. 1E.

Kane, M. J. (1995). Resistance/transformation of the oppositional binary: Exposing sport as a continuum. *Journal of Sport and Social Issues 19*(2), 213–240.

Kane, M. J., & Disch, L. (1993). Sexual violence and the reproduction of male violence in the locker room: The Lisa Olson incident. *Sociology of Sport Journal 10*(4), 331–352.

Kaufman, M. T. (1989, April 29). Park suspect: Children of discipline. *New York Times,* pp. A1, B24.

Kidd, B. (1987). Sports and masculinity. In M. Kaufman, (ed.), *Beyond patriarchy: Essays by men on pleasure, power, and change* (pp. 250–265). Toronto: Oxford University Press.

Kimmel, M. S. (1990). Baseball and the reconstitution of American masculinity, 1880–1920. In M. A. Messner & D. Sabo (eds.), *Sport, men, and the gender order* (pp. 55–65). Champaign, Ill.: Human Kinetics.

Kornheiser, T. (1990, October 9). A woman's place. *Washington Post,* D1, D6.

Lapchick, R. E., & Benedict, J. R. (1993, summer). 1993 Racial report cards. *Center for the Study of Sport in Society Digest* (Northeastern University), 4–8.

Ludtke, M. (1990a, September 30). Olson harassment a stark reminder. p. B21.

———. (1990b, October 14). What women want: Equal access for interviews, not bad jokes. *Los Angeles Times,* p. 5

Madden, M. (1990a, September 30). Even in his backhanded apology, Kiam misses the point. *Boston Globe,* p. 66.

———. (1990b, September 24). Return to the scene of the grime. *Boston Globe,* pp. 41, 49.

Mannix, K. (1990, September 24). Kiam: "She's a classic bitch." *Boston Herald,* p. 74.

Matchan, L. (1990, October 3). Further abuse of Olson is called typical. *Boston Globe,* pp. 29, 36.

Media week. (1994). *Media Week* 4(1), 13.

Messner, M. A. (1988). Sports and male domination: The female athlete as contested ideological terrain. *Sociology of Sport Journal* 5(3), 197–211.

———. (1990). Masculinities and athletic careers: Bonding and status differences. In M. A. Messner & D. Sabo (eds.), *Sport, men, and the gender order* (pp. 97–108). Champaign, Ill.: Human Kinetics.

Metheny, E. (1965). *Connotations of movement in sport and dance.* Dubuque, Iowa: Brown.

Montville, L. (1991, May 13). A season of torment. *Sports Illustrated,* pp. 60–65.

Morrison, T. (1992). Introduction: Friday on the Potomac. In Toni Morrison (ed.), *Race-ing justice, engendering power: Essays on Anita Hill, Clarence Thomas, and the construction of social reality* (pp. vii–xxx). New York: Pantheon.

Nelson, M. B. (1994). *The stronger women get the more men love football.* New York: Harcourt Brace.

Oates, B. (1979, June 8). The great American tease: Sport as a way out of the ghetto. *New York Times,* p. A32.

Olson, L. (1990, September 24). A lesson from "The Chick." *Boston Herald,* p. 74.

Olson, L. (1994, October). Women's sports continue to grow. *USA Hockey Girls and Women's Newsletter* (USA Hockey Association), 1.

Pitt, D. E. (1989a, April 25). Gang attack: Unusual for its viciousness. *New York Times,* p. B5.

————. (1989b, April 22). Jogger's attackers terrorized at least 9 in 2 hours. *New York Times,* pp. A1, 30.

————. (1989c, April 24), More crimes tied to gang in park rape. *New York Times,* p. B1.

Robinson, L. S. (1993, June). Roving reporter. *Women's Review of Books 10,* 9–10.

Roediger, D. (1991). *Wages of whiteness.* New York: Verso.

Rose, J. (1986). *Sexuality in the field of vision.* New York: Verso.

Sabo, D., & Panepinto, J. (1990). Football ritual and the social reproduction of masculinity. In M. A. Messner & D. Sabo (eds.), *Sport, men, and the gender order* (pp. 115–126). Champaign, Ill.: Human Kinetics.

Scheman, N. (1993). *Engenderings: Constructions of knowledge, authority, and privilege.* New York: Routledge.

Scott, J. (1991, Summer). The evidence of experience. *Critical Inquiry 17,* 773–797.

Sedgwick, E. K. (1985). *Between men: English literature and male homosocial desire.* New York: Columbia University Press.

Silverman, K. (1983). *The subject of semiotics.* New York: Oxford.

Times News Services. (1991, February 7). Kiam apologizes for a joke about Olson told at dinner. *Los Angeles Times,* p. C2.

Woolf, V. ([1919] 1957). *A room of one's own.* New York: Harcourt Brace.

5

KATHERINE M. JAMIESON

Reading Nancy Lopez
Decoding Representations of Race, Class, and Sexuality

● Much like the explosive rise of PGA golfer Tiger Woods, Nancy Lopez burst onto the Ladies Professional Golf Association (LPGA) tour with a bang. Nancy Lopez began playing golf at the age of eight and by age twelve had won the New Mexico Women's Invitational (Chavira 1977). In 1975, prior to graduating high school, Lopez tied for third in the U.S. Women's Open golf tournament, and in the same year, accepted a scholarship to the University of Tulsa, where she won the intercollegiate golf title and was named collegiate athlete of the year (Chabran and Chabran 1996). After two successful years as a collegiate athlete, Lopez joined the LPGA tour. During her first year on the tour (1978), Lopez won nine tournaments, including an unprecedented five in a row, was named Rookie of the Year, Rolex Player of the Year[1] (also won in 1979, 1985, and 1988), Vare Trophy Winner[2] (also won in 1979 and 1985), Golfer of the Year, and Female Athlete of the Year. In 1985, Lopez set an all-time record at the Henredon Classic, recording a 20-under-par tournament total (268), including twenty-five birdies (LPGA homepage 1997). Lopez has amassed forty-seven LPGA victories, and in 1987 became the youngest inductee to

This essay originally appeared in and is reprinted with permission of *Sociology of Sport Journal* 15(4), 343–358.

the LPGA Hall of Fame. Now twenty years after Lopez joined the LPGA, she continues to compete, consistently draws large crowds, and remains the only U.S. Latina on the tour (LPGA homepage 1997).

Moreover, the arrival of Lopez was pivotal for the LPGA, which at that time was experiencing the popularity problems that faced tennis a few years ago. Similar to the rhetoric about Tiger Woods, Lopez's presence supposedly marked an opening up of golf to the masses, especially to "young people" and other unlikely golf fans (Deford 1978). Although this essay centers on the cultural significance of Nancy Lopez's public prominence, Tiger Woods is mentioned to illustrate the continued currency of race, class, sexual, and gender ideologies that operate in U.S. society and permeate all forms of media. Despite two decades of scholarly, political, and institutional progress toward race relations and gender equity, both the Lopez and Woods stories stand out as symbols of persistent, yet shifting inequalities in the lives of all women and men, but especially women and men of color. Clearly, public stories such as these provide cultural material from which we may make sense of our everyday social worlds.

The purpose of this essay is to reveal the social significance of media constructions of Nancy Lopez. The analysis of these specific texts is based in multiple feminist agendas that are best consolidated in what Baca Zinn and Dill (1994, 1996) have labeled *multiracial feminism*. Ultimately, the analytic goal is to reveal several ways that Lopez was upheld as the ideal, assimilated Mexican woman. The essay begins with a discussion of the selected texts and method of analysis. An outline of multiple inequalities in sport is provided and an argument made for the usefulness of multiracial feminism for making sense of Lopez's experiences. The analysis of the selected media representations of Lopez follows, calling attention to constructions of race and ethnicity, as well as constructions of sexualities. Throughout the analysis, the texts are located in particular historical, social, and political contexts within which they were constructed. Specifically, it is argued that dominant narratives about Lopez's family of origin have been constructed out of a deficiency model[3] (Baca Zinn 1992; Zavella 1994) and toward a myth of racial equality, while upholding assimilationist ideals. Moreover, this essay illustrates how the Latina/o print media contested the dominant constructions of Lopez's family of origin and paid little attention to her roles as mother and wife. The essay concludes with a statement about the usefulness of decoding texts from varied and shifting standpoints, as well as the significance of using multiple historical and political discourses to uncover widely varied meanings of a singular event.

The Lopez Texts

It is generally accepted that the media construct and reconstruct particular events in multiple ways and for a variety of purposes (Birrell and Cole 1994a; Duncan 1994; Kane and Greendorfer 1994). Although the power of the media is pervasive (television, radio, print, and electronic options), consumers—real people—make their own meaning of the texts with which they engage (Birrell and Cole 1994a; Duncan 1994). Curiously, nondominant popular texts seldom have been examined regarding the varied meanings they may be constructing about particular events in the U.S. social and political landscape (Messner 1993; Williams 1994). The selected "Lopez texts," which include *Sports Illustrated, Nuestro,* and *Hispanic* magazines, offer powerful and complex examples of the authority of the media to construct and reconstruct the events surrounding Lopez's career. The objective is to apply feminist insights regarding racialized, classed, and sexualized forms of gender to examine the complexity and salience of Nancy Lopez's presence on the LPGA tour.

The focus is on two significant time frames in Lopez's career as a professional golfer: Her bold entry onto the Ladies Professional Golf Association tour (1977–1978), and her pregnancy years (1983–1991). These particular periods of media interest in Lopez do not tell an entire story, but they do offer several texts that construct Lopez in specific racialized, classed, sexualized, and gendered ways. This analysis rests on three articles from *Sports Illustrated,* a cover story and an additional feature article that appeared in *Nuestro,* a popular Latina/o news magazine, and a feature article from *Hispanic,* also a popular Latina/o news magazine. *Sports Illustrated* was selected due to its vast readership, national visibility, and status as a perpetrator of hegemonic ideological story lines. The *Nuestro* publication was selected in part because it claims to be a magazine for Latinos. Additionally, *Nuestro* seems to market itself to middle-class Latina/o readers, many of whom may also be readers of *Sports Illustrated.* Similarly, *Hispanic* offers a middle-class Latina/o take on Lopez's stories, and portrays itself as a magazine "for and about Hispanics." Furthermore, *Hispanic* offered one of very few Lopez texts from the Latina/o popular print media long after her celebrated entry onto the tour. Thus, while these magazines have their unique characteristics, they also may meet at the axis of class with regard to the narrative themes that they have pursued.

The exclusion of some texts and inclusion of others in this analysis appropriately delimits the work, and in some cases reflects a lack of media attention to particular Lopez story lines. For example, it is curious that Lopez's marriages and pregnancies did not fill as many Latina/o print media pages as they did in *Sports Illustrated* and other publications. Moreover, not one of forty texts that were reviewed made a connection to her "inter-racial" marriages and her own racial-ethnic heritage. This particular text may have worked well within an assimilationist argument. Perhaps these authors and publishers felt the effect of marrying non-Latino men made a strong enough statement on its own and required no further textual posturing or deserved no additional attention. This omission is both puzzling and intriguing; however, a detailed critique is beyond the scope of this paper. Nevertheless, the selected texts seemed to be most content-rich and best timed to make sense of the significant events in Lopez's career.

Making Sense of Multiple Inequalities

As though it were unfolding today, the Lopez story provides a fertile field for analyzing the varied consequences of interlocking inequalities. Lopez may be seen as a symbol of false racial equality in the United States, as well as a body coopted in the project of Latina/o pride and social justice. Lopez symbolically straddles several social and cultural borders in her daily life, as do all women and men, but especially women and men of color (Anzaldua 1987, 1990a, 1990b; Baca Zinn and Dill 1994; Pesquera and de la Torre 1995). More to the point, Baca Zinn and Dill (1994) have suggested that for racial-ethnic women, lesbians, older women, disabled women, and lower social class women, gender is but one part of a larger pattern of unequal social relations.

Several studies have suggested that race, class, sexuality, and gender are ever-present as distinguishing characteristics in sport settings, especially in the building of masculinities and femininities (Birrell and Cole 1994b; Foley 1990; Grey 1996; Messner 1992). These studies contest the argument that sport is a natural site for the depoliticization of race, ethnicity, class, or sexuality, as well as a site for the creation and maintenance of community harmony. For example, Foley (1990) suggested that American high school football ritual, such as the homecoming ceremony, traveling to other communities, cheerleading, and pep rallies reflected a hierarchy of privilege based on race, class, sexuality, and gender. Grey (1996) found that for many immigrant and minority students in U.S. educational institutions, sport becomes one of the most visible means to claim one's "American" allegiance. Thus, not unlike Lopez's story, these studies suggest that American sport provides students an opportunity to assimilate but not integrate, both on campus and in the larger community (Foley 1990; Grey 1996). More specifically, persons may be provided opportunities to adopt "American" dominant cultural practices, like Americanized sports and games, but are not able to share their own cultural practices without being labeled "other." This naturalizes a particular "American" culture, while marginalizing all others.

More often than not, sport is a site where dominant cultural groups maintain their power and continue to shape sport and social interactions to reflect their own interests (Birrell 1990; Dewar 1993; Sage 1990). This may be most apparent in elite women's athletics, where it is largely white middle-class men who make significant decisions within sport organizations. For instance, in the case of transsexual Renee Richards, it was men who had the power to decide if Richards was female enough to compete on the women's professional tennis tour (Birrell and Cole 1994b). For the most part, female tennis professionals were left out of the debate about Richards's qualifications as a member of the women's professional tennis tour (Birrell and Cole 1994b). In a similar way, the image of Nancy Lopez was coopted to suit the needs of white, middle-class, heterosexual men and to a lesser extent, women. The images of Lopez as a wholesome, attractive, heterosexual, elite golfer distinguished her from stereotypical images of Mexican women and promoted her as a credentialed middle-class American woman. In this way, Lopez was able to appeal to a diverse audience and provide a much-needed boost in fan support for the LPGA. Clearly, the Richards case and the Lopez case hold material and symbolic significance as they reflect the power of white, heterosexual, middle-class men to construct notions of appropriate womanhood.

In spite of progress toward gender equity in sport, competing equities of race and class continue to impede opportunities for women and men of color in the world of sport (Abney and Richey 1992; Corbett and Johnson 1993). Eitzen and Furst (1993) found that racial preferences exist in the selection of athletes for particular positions in women's collegiate volleyball, while Corbett and Johnson (1993) revealed that stereotypical myths about sport-type preferences among African American women persist, resulting in constricted opportunities for involvement in a wide range of activities. These studies strongly suggest that intergroup contact and increased visibility of minority athletes is not enough to challenge a gender order that is embedded in inequalities.

Moreover, the mere addition of race, ethnicity, or sexuality as variables to existing frameworks has not improved their analytical capacity, which suggests that additive models do not offer the comprehensive analysis necessary to understand the complexity of women's lives (Andersen 1993; Birrell 1990; Collins 1990; Dewar 1993; Smith 1992). As Hall (1996) has suggested, "race does not merely make the experience of women's oppression greater; rather, it qualitatively changes the nature of that subordination" (44). Consequently, African American women, Latinas, Asian, and Native American women do not simply experience increased rates of oppression, their disadvantaged status in sport is qualitatively different from that of their white counterparts (Hall 1996) as well as from that of each other. These analytic limitations have real consequences for women in sport and especially for understanding the cultural currency of particular women in sport. More importantly, they illustrate the need to examine gender as it is mediated by other systems of inequality.

Multiracial feminism offers the analytical rigor needed to comprehend Lopez's varied subordinated and dominant statuses and makes room for multiple standpoints and varied histories in making sense of the Lopez texts. Baca Zinn and Dill (1994) have suggested that:

Multiracial feminism treats racial inequality as a vital shaper of women's and men's lives and advances a powerful and coherent premise—that racial ancestry, ethnic heritage, and economic status are as important as gender for analyzing the social construction of women and men. (11)

Creative tensions in multiple feminist frameworks (i.e., Chicana feminisms, black feminisms, and white feminisms) have revealed what Collins (1990) has referred to as a "matrix of domination" operating in the lives of all women and men. For example, Lopez's multiple social statuses as a raced, classed, and sexualized woman intersect to locate her differently than white, heterosexual women or Latina lesbians. All women and men fit within this matrix, but they are situated at different intersections depending on their multiple statuses as raced, classed, and sexualized individuals. Moreover, these "intersecting forms of domination produce both oppression and opportunity" (Baca Zinn and Dill 1996, 12). More explicitly, the intersecting forms of domination in Lopez's experience offer her privilege as a professional athlete, a financially secure woman, and a heterosexual woman, but oppression as a person of Mexican heritage and working-class heritage. These experiences directly point to the fluidity of privilege and oppression that come with varied locations within a web of inequalities (Baca Zinn and Dill 1994, 1996; Collins 1990, 1991).

The relational nature of domination and subordination is also a significant focus within multiracial feminism. That is, the significance of race is visible in "patterns of relations among minority women and white women" (Baca Zinn and Dill 1996, 12) as well as among Latinas of different social classes or of varied sexual identities. For Lopez, the relational nature of gender was apparent as she came on the tour at a young age and as the only U.S. Latina on the tour. She was set apart by her brown skin, unique looks, age, and Mexican working-class heritage. Cultural ideology suggested that Lopez fell outside of the ideal woman status, and yet her golf skill gave her entrée to social and cultural locations that other twenty-one-year-old Mexican women would not experience. Although Lopez earned entrée, her presence was constantly constructed in relation to an ideal type of woman and to an ideal type of athlete (i.e., male).

The comprehensive framework of multiracial feminism provides a lens through which Lopez may be seen as both oppressed and oppressor, especially in relation to other women on the tour. For Lopez, as it is for all women, gender is but one axis in a matrix of social structural domination. The intersection of these multiple axes (i.e., race, class, gender, ethnicity, sexuality) situates Lopez and other Latinas differently than it would white women, and yet Latinas take up diverse and dynamic locations within the matrix. That is, they are situated by more than racial or ethnic identities. Thus, the significance of the texts relied upon for this analysis lies in their ability to construct Lopez as a cultural marker of particular racialized, classed, and sexualized statuses in U.S. society and sport.

Constructing Race and Ethnicity

In the textual analysis that follows, I suggest that Lopez is constructed in various ways across axes of race, ethnicity, and class. An overarching purpose in these texts seems to be to differentiate Lopez from other Latinas. In reality, Lopez is different from other Latinas in many ways. For example, in contrast to nearly half of all U.S. Latinas, Lopez graduated from high school (U.S. Department of Commerce 1996). Moreover, unlike many Latinas/os who are compelled to leave college due to financial constraints, family needs, or feelings of isolation on campus (Nieves-Squires 1993), Lopez left to join the tour—a career move that would further differentiate her from other Latinas. Perhaps most striking is the disparity between Lopez's earnings during her first full year on the tour (LPGA 1997) and the median earnings of Hispanic women nearly twelve years later. In 1978, Lopez earned $189,817 on the LPGA tour, yet the median earnings of Hispanic women in 1990 were a mere $10,999, 21 percent less than that of non-Hispanic women (Mexican American Women's National Association 1993). In spite of these visible differences in power and privileges, a variety of distinguishing characteristics were constructed or reconstructed in order to exploit Lopez in the particular project of each text. A large majority of these projects were connected to ideologies of race and ethnicity.

Culture as Villain[4]

Despite several advances in analytical and intellectual depiction of Mexican families (Baca Zinn 1976; Ybarra 1988), a *Sports Illustrated* (July 1978) article relied on a deficiency model to describe Lopez's father and family resources. Early in the article, Lopez's father is described as "Domingo, who has a third grade education and an auto-body shop in Roswell, New Mexico" (Deford 1978, 24). The statement about his "third grade education" suggests that Domingo Lopez stopped learning when his formal education came to an end. Intended or not, this may be read as code for a popular stereotype that most Mexicans do not value educational attainment and are content to operate at a lower educational level than others. Therefore, by choice, Domingo stopped his own education and, consequently, is no longer suitable to guide his daughter's social, professional, and educational development. In fact, Deford (1978) suggested that Lopez's father was:

> a natural athlete who could teach her golf, but however street-smart he may be, there is no way he can educate her in the school of marketing and six figure affiliations that she has been ushered into. (31)

The obvious message is that Lopez's family of origin has taken her as far as it can. Lopez must now leave her father's care in order to learn how to succeed in the more legitimized world of big contracts and big money deals. In a larger context, the coded message reinforces a belief in social mobility through sport. Clearly, Lopez's social ascent is symbolic of the American ideal of pulling oneself up by one's own bootstraps. The suggested separation of Lopez from her family of origin goes even further in solidifying a model for assimilation and social mobility. As Sage (1990) has suggested, the well-publicized success of a few individuals aids in the maintenance of a belief in social mobility among the masses. Despite the limited extent of actual social mobility through sport, Lopez serves as a symbol to promote and sustain hegemonic ideology about widespread social climbing in the American social structure (Sage 1990). Although Nancy Lopez was the 1980s "poster child" for Latina/o upward mobility, the careful distinctions made between her and her family of origin made this mobility one of individual assimilation rather than institutional transformation.

Culture as Rational Response

The Latina/o publications took a different perspective on Lopez's family of origin and it's significance. The *Nuestro* publication suggested that "on a deeply personal level, [Lopez's] story is a tribute to the integrity of a Mexican American family" *(Nuestro* 1978, 23). In contrast to the subordinated status attributed by the dominant media, the Latina/o media suggested that this is a family that maintained their Mexican pride, and yet made it in U.S. society. In the same publication, Nancy's father is described in the following manner, "Domingo was once a field hand who picked cotton under the broiling sun of west Texas. His education ended after the third grade" *(Nuestro* 1978, 23). This information about Domingo symbolically solidifies Nancy Lopez's Mexican working-class heritage, and as we learn later in the article, illustrates her father's upward mobility from field hand to small business owner. This is a sharp contrast to the deficiency model used to construct the mainstream narrative about Lopez's family of origin.

In reality, the educational status of Domingo Lopez is but one example of the varied consequences of multiple inequalities facing immigrant and colonized Latinas/os in the United States. Segregated schools, anti-Mexican sentiment, and the need to earn a wage forced many Latinas/os of Domingo's era to curtail their formal education. During Domingo's school-age years, Latinas/os in the Southwest fought segregation and demanded equality in the provision of educational resources (Meier and Ribera 1993). In fact, in 1931, the Lemon Grove, California, lawsuit marked the first successful legal challenge to school segregation (Meier and Ribera 1993). Thus, low educational attainment is not an inherent Mexican deficiency, but rather a consequence of the social and political landscape during the early 1900s in the southwestern United States (Meier and Ribera 1993).

The longstanding estrangement from formal educational institutions, however, continues to have consequences in the lives of all Latinas/os in the United States. For example, despite significant growth in numbers, U.S. Latinas/os face lower college attendance and graduation rates, lower than average family annual income, and higher than average rates of poverty (Rumbaut 1995). Inequalities such as these further restrict participation in various social institutions (i.e., education and sport) and predispose Latina/o youth to greater negative consequences during economic and political shifts in the social structure (Baca Zinn 1992). The inequalities discussed above are a striking contrast to the "successful" life of Nancy Lopez and are simultaneously representative of her family of origin. It is these contrasts that *Sports Illustrated* relies upon to construct Lopez herself as different from the unnamed white status group, but also different from other Mexicans. *Nuestro,* on the other hand, claims an understanding of Lopez's struggle as well as a vested interest in her achievements.

Resisting Ethnicity

After carefully constructing Lopez's father and family of origin in their respective manners, the *Sports Illustrated* text turned directly to Lopez for symbolic representations of racial, ethnic, and class statuses. For example, Deford (1978) noted that Lopez "put on" an accent when speaking to her sister on the phone, and uttered the following words, "It's my seester" (25), and "Hey beeg seester, I love you" (25). The fact that Lopez "put on" the accent suggests that she may not actually speak Spanish, thus further removing her from her Latina/o heritage and solidifying her status as an appropriately assimilated Mexican. In yet another example of constructing Lopez as "other," her own public relations handler refers to her in a racially derogatory manner. During the course of a discussion regarding how and when to get Lopez to her next LPGA event, Lopez's public relations handler asked her caddie, "When are you going to get Taco Belle's car to Indianapolis?" (Deford 1978, 25). In the very least, this is reflective of a lack of insight to white privilege and fails to acknowledge the potential for offending Latina/o readers. More specifically, this passage simultaneously constructs Lopez as the racial-ethnic other, and trivializes the significance of her Mexican heritage (Birrell 1990; Dewar 1993). A final touch to this construction of Lopez is obvious as her caddie refers to her as "Lopes" (rhymes with *ropes)* rather than calling her by her correct surname.

These particular examples of text suggest that Lopez's accent is make-believe and that her ethnicity is appropriately described by calling her "Taco Belle." Moreover, the failure to call Lopez by her name marks another form of resistance to her ethnicity. More than a casual nickname, "Lopes" symbolizes the desire of a dominant culture to de-race Lopez and erase the political, historical, and cultural struggles of Latinas/os in the

United States—struggles that are deeply rooted in rights to culture, language, and naming of one's self. Together, these narratives construct Lopez as different from other Mexicans, especially those in her family of origin. This particular text also naturalizes the dominant status of Lopez's caddie and public relations man in relation to Lopez's subordinated status (i.e., as a woman, as a person of Mexican working-class heritage). The combined effect of these media representations is to render Lopez subordinate in the social construction of her own racial-ethnic identity and status, and to simultaneously uphold a white, male, middle-class status as the ideal.

Resisting Resistance

Nuestro made careful distinctions between Lopez's ethnic identity and social structural inequalities, rather than collapsing these two distinct categories of analysis into one culturally deterministic model. For example, Chavira (1977) suggested that Lopez "made it" despite the fact that "sex discrimination, lack of professional training, and money problems all stood in her way" (34). Moreover, he acknowledged community financial support of the up-and-coming golfer when he suggested that "the chamber of commerce has raised money to help her enter tournaments" (Chavira 1977, 35). Lopez reflected on economic difficulties and familial sacrifices, as she told Chavira, "My dad pays the expenses. He's not rich so it's a real sacrifice. I've been very lucky my father has been willing to go all the way to help me make it" (Chavira 1977, 35). This type of familial sacrifice and perseverance described in *Nuestro* reflects the reality of various forms of inequalities faced by Latinas/os in the United States. In fact, *Nuestro* magazine suggested that part of Lopez's appeal among Latinas/os is the fact that Latinas/os can relate to many of her challenges. *Nuestro* (1978) suggested that "perhaps we can identify more closely with this particular star's rise. Lopez has known the sting of discrimination too well to forget it" (23).

Throughout the majority of Latina/o media accounts, Lopez is often named as Latina or Mexicana, her surname is spelled with an accent, and her family of origin is presented in a positive and significant light. The authors express a collective pride in Lopez's achievements, which they believe to be true for most of their readers. The *Nuestro* authors suggest that Lopez

> is a symbol for us. She symbolizes the increasing reality of crossing over into the American mainstream and making it. Hers, moreover, is a crossover accomplished without rage, without controversy, without (so far) selling out. *(Nuestro* 1978, 23)

Reflective of Lopez's connection to multiple historical and political debates during the late 1970s, this text may be decoded in a number of ways. For example, the fact that Lopez has made her move into "mainstream" without "rage" or "controversy" may be read as discontent with radical and separatist tactics used by both the Chicano movement of the 1960s and 1970s and the predominantly white feminist movement of the 1970s (Meier and Ribera 1993; Zavella 1994). Many Chicanas were highly critical of white feminists' anti-male sentiment, particularly because they were aware that, like themselves, their own Latino brothers were facing varied and systemic subordinated statuses (Meier and Ribera 1993; Zavella 1994). Thus, rather than make a political scene about the patriarchal aspects of sport, Lopez moved quietly and yet noticeably into the "mainstream."

Yet, woven into this textual embrace of Lopez's ascent is an expectation that Lopez will achieve a balance between her Latina/o heritage and her status as a member of a socially and financially elite class of U.S. society. *Nuestro* connects Lopez's struggles to the struggles of all Latinas/os; therefore, her successes are also collectively owned and experienced. Despite Lopez's public closeness to her father and maintenance of her Spanish surname, the *Nuestro* text warns of the potential for Lopez to relinquish her ties to working-class Mexicanas/os. Speaking about Lopez's financial advisors and the commercialization of Lopez, *Nuestro* (1978) writers stated the following, "Many people already call her 'Lopes' (to rhyme with dopes), thus making her less Latina, less foreign. And so far, Nancy seems to be accepting it all" (26).

Although Lopez is revered for her quiet, sophisticated move into the mainstream, she is simultaneously admonished for not resisting attempts at making her "less Latina." In reality, Lopez's "bridge-building" is no different than that of other women of color who are consistently bridging cultural divides in the daily-ness of their lives (Anzaldua 1987, 1990a, 1990b; Baca Zinn and Dill 1994; Pesquera and de la Torre 1995; Zavella 1994). That is, Latinas are constantly involved in a dynamic process of maintaining ties to their working-class backgrounds, ethnic heritage, cultural heritage, and yet to prove their allegiance to social, economic, and educational progress in U.S. society (Anzaldua 1987, 1990a, 1990b; Baca Zinn and Dill 1994; Pesquera and de la Torre 1995; Zavella 1994). Lopez once again is co-opted, this time in the project of constructing and maintaining a particular Latina/o identity.

Constructing Sexualities

Additional examples of intersecting inequalities of race, ethnicity, class, gender, and sexuality lie in the stories of Lopez's marriages and pregnancies, especially as they became badges of middle-class and heterosexual status. In 1979, prior to returning to the tour for her second season, Lopez married the Cincinnati sportscaster Tim Melton. The marriage did not last; moreover, the marriage the media has come to celebrate is that between Lopez and the major league baseball player Ray Knight. Lopez and Knight have been married since 1982 and have three daughters who were born in 1983, 1986, and 1991. As mentioned earlier in this essay, Lopez's marriages and parenting have been curiously absent or limited in coverage in the Latina/o popular print media, especially in the late 1980s. Consequently, this analysis focuses primarily on the *Sports Illustrated* texts.

Masculinities and Femininities

The stories about Lopez's marriages and motherhood provide examples of a modern-day apologetic (Felshin 1981). The media countered Lopez's potentially emasculating skill with stories of her talents as wife and mother. The pregnancy comebacks were veiled forms of trivialization of Lopez's athleticism (Griffin 1996), and her talent on the golf course was deemed "natural" (Newman 1986, 38). For example, the *Sports Illustrated* author compared Lopez and Knight in the following manner: "Knight may have lacked her natural skills, but he was celebrated enough in his own right to have played in two All-Star Games" (Newman 1986, 38). The naturalization of Lopez's talent not only disregards her hard work but also that of her only pre-professional coach, her father. In contrast, *Hispanic* magazine (Alvarez 1989) acknowledged the discipline and hard work of Lopez and her family in the quest to build a career as a professional golfer.

Alvarez (1989) makes it clear that Lopez worked diligently to develop her skill in golf. In one passage, Lopez stated the following: "You're only going to be as successful as what you are willing to give. . . . I gave up a lot. I loved golf so much, and I just wanted to win. It wasn't given to me. I worked hard" (Lopez in Alvarez 1989, 16). This acknowledgment of hard work and love for the sport contradicts the dominant attempts to trivialize Lopez's talent. Yet when flanked by the marriage and motherhood narratives, Lopez's hard work was annihilated.

The union between Lopez and Knight was constructed as the "very model of a modern marriage" (Newman 1986, 34), despite the obvious hegemonic conceptions of masculinity and femininity that were operating. In fact, much of the text constructed Knight as a "new age," maybe even "profeminist" husband, who was not at all threatened by his wife's obvious ability to live independent of him. Lopez colluded in exalting Knight's willingness to support his professional, financially independent female partner as she stated: "After I married Ray, I felt that golf was second. He made me happier than golf did. But he never pressured me not to go anywhere to play golf, and I had often felt that pressure from Tim" (Lopez in Newman 1986, 38). Thus, by comparison, Knight is less rigid in his gender role accomplishments. That is, Knight is able to be both husband and elite athlete without facing gender role conflict or questions of sexuality. In fact, he is so "modern" that he expresses support for Lopez's career goals in this way:

I allow her to play golf because she has never put it ahead of me. I've never asked her to come home, and I never would. . . . It never entered my mind as a problem that she needed to play golf, as long as it doesn't affect my standing with her. But I married her as a woman; I didn't marry the LPGA tour. (Knight in Newman 1986, 39)

Not only do these texts naturalize Lopez's and Knight's roles as feminine and masculine subjects, they also serve to promote their heterosexual marriage as a bastion of equality, while inadvertently offering examples of embedded inequalities between women and men. Moreover, the last line in the above quote is especially interesting as it is a striking contrast to an earlier *Sports Illustrated* construction of Lopez as a "baseball wife" (Newman 1986, 34). In concert with the role conflict theme, Alvarez (1989) pointed out that, "While at home . . . Nancy refuses to pick up a golf club. It is more important to devote herself to home and family in a traditional sort of way, cleaning, cooking, and playing with the kids" (16). Yet, the *Sports Illustrated* article suggested that Knight built a batting cage in their backyard and that Lopez would feed the pitching machine while he took batting practice. So at home there was space for Knight's athletic pursuits, but Lopez supposedly left golf at the course to attend to Knight and the children.

This is a construction that is difficult to believe, especially in light of the *Hispanic* text that recognized Lopez's love for golf. Regardless, it works to perpetuate a model of family life, divisions of labor, and household power that benefits men and subordinates women. As Kane and Greendorfer (1994) have suggested, "Gender *difference* is translated into gender *hierarchy,* because in existing social arrangements women are defined not only as 'other than' but also as 'less than' their male counterparts" (29). The underlying message is that even in this "modern" model of marriage, the socially constructed organizing principle of gender hierarchy reigns supreme.

Compulsory Heterosexuality

Not surprisingly, Lopez's marriages and pregnancies have also resulted in a social construction of her as a heterosexual woman. This was important, not only to the media, but also to the LPGA as it worked to market women's golf to a vast audience (Diaz 1987). The representations of Lopez as a bona fide heterosexual woman maintain a sexist and heterosexist status quo and continue to co-opt sport in the service of compulsory heterosexuality. More significantly, they serve a larger project, which is to divide and silence women through fear tactics (Griffin 1996; Lenskyj 1987).

For example, Lopez's marriages and pregnancies were cleverly juxta-posed to the hidden social and sexual lives of other LPGA members, thus further silencing lesbians on the tour (Griffin 1996). Much of the article in *Sports Illustrated* about the rivalry between Lopez and Pat Bradley was constructed around Lopez's pregnancy comeback and Bradley's psycho-logical comeback. The subtext here is that Lopez's heterosexual married life is so good that the strength she gains from it enhances her game. In contrast, Bradley, presumably unmarried, needs professional help to keep her game up to par. The contrast was stated in this way:

> While Bradley was tearing up the tour [1986], Lopez had her second child . . . and played only four tournaments. . . . As she did in 1985 [after her first pregnancy], Lopez is drawing strength from her life away from competitive golf. (Diaz 1987, 84)

Regardless of actual sexuality, this subtext suggests that heterosexual life is fulfilling and tantamount to a healthy lifestyle, while being unmar-ried (for whatever reason) is unfulfilling, and has obvious consequences in one's personal and professional life, including the opportunity to choose motherhood.

Moreover, Lopez's pregnancies are symbolic of a type of reproductive control that white, heterosexual, middle-class women exercise at much higher rates than do women of color, especially lower-class Latinas (MANA 1993). Thus, Lopez's pregnancies stand out as a dominant cultural symbol of reproductive freedom, a freedom that is not yet enjoyed by all U.S. women. Carefully woven into this text about Lopez's pregnancies is a class-based construction of motherhood. That is, Lopez's ability to "balance" family life and a career further legitimizes her as a "good mother." In actuality, because of her financial status, Lopez has been able to employ a nanny to help care for her children. Additionally, the fact that Lopez does motherhood within the credentialed status of heterosexual marriage puts her at less risk for losing her rights to reproduction and parenting as compared to most single, poor, lesbian, and non-white women (MANA 1993).

Taken together, these texts use Lopez to project sexist, heterosexist, and homophobic images of women in sport. Griffin (1996) has argued that homophobia is manifested in women's sport in several distinct ways, two of which are silence and heterosexy images. The rhetoric underlying the Lopez–Bradley rivalry is that lesbians in sport are "nasty secrets that must be kept locked tightly in the closet" (Griffin 1996, 394). The power of the media to "out" Lopez as a heterosexual makes the silence surrounding the personal life of Bradley (and others on the LPGA tour) even more deafening. Constructing texts that uphold Lopez's heterosexuality and inclination toward motherhood as *natural* works to confer privilege and normalcy on particular social groups while holding others in contempt (Griffin 1996). In this way, dominant texts such as *Sports Illustrated* and *Hispanic* support and aid in the maintenance of existing social arrangements.

Conclusion

Perhaps what is most informative about decoding *Sports Illustrated, Nuestro,* and *Hispanic* media accounts of Lopez is the complexity of Lopez's multiple statuses—the very real experience of intersecting statuses of race, class, sexuality, and gender. More specifically, when the various Lopez texts are analyzed in the historical context from which they emerged, they offer insight to the pervasiveness of the project of white male superiority. When the histories of "others" are relied upon to decode mediated texts, a more complex, yet clarified analysis of multiple inequalities is possible (Messner 1993).

Nuestro and *Hispanic* in some ways offered what Gorelick (1991) called "a view from below," and what Collins (1991) termed the perspective of the "outsider within." These differentiated perspectives may offer a less partial view of the social world and perhaps a more accurate picture of what is really shaping social life (Collins 1990, 1991; Gorelick 1991). Anzaldua (1987) suggested that those persons who are most marginalized in any society have the potential to offer a more accurate view of the power structures and hierarchies that operate within the social system. Pronger (1996) echoed this perspective when he suggested that gay men are estranged in sport, and therefore offer a differently informed view of the social structure of sport. Taken together, these scholars make a strong argument for valuing multiple perspectives and standpoints in making sense of the social world. There is no one accurate perspective, but there are perspectives that are less partial than those that we have come to accept as the standard in sociological analyses of women's sport. The texts analyzed here offered varied perspectives on the significance of Nancy Lopez in the elite, primarily upper-class, and very white sport of golf.

In a complementary way, these textual constructions of Lopez provide insight into the fluid nature of gendered statuses and identities. They reveal the simple reality that gender is never the only appropriate category of analysis, nor can it be the most significant, because it is always mediated by other systems of inequality (Andersen 1993; Birrell 1990; Collins 1990, 1991; Dewar 1993; Smith 1992). More than that, gendered identities fit within cultural and historical contexts that shape all women's lives but have different consequences for different groups of women (e.g., working-class women, heterosexual women, white women) (Zavella 1994). If one looks closely and simultaneously applies a broad framework, it is apparent that all women and men are in the process of traversing borders. It is our work as social scientists to develop the tools to make sense of these border crossings and to do so with regard to relevant historical, cultural, and political contexts.

Notes

I am greatly appreciative of the comments by the reviewers of the *Sociology of Sport Journal* and Cynthia Hasbrook. Thanks also go to Diana Rivera, Lillian Castillo-Speed, Richard Chabran, and the journalism class at Goddard High School in Roswell, New Mexico, for their assistance in locating nondominant print media on Nancy Lopez.

1. LPGA tour players earn the Rolex Player of the Year by amassing points for "top 10" finishes.

2. LPGA tour players earn the Vare Trophy by posting the lowest scoring average per 18 holes for a minimum of 70 rounds.

3. A deficiency model locates the cause for social distress in the values and morals of individuals and groups. The culture of poverty thesis of the 1960s held that poor people had "distinctive values, aspirations, and psychological characteristics that inhibit their achievement and produce behavioral deficiencies likely to keep them poor not only within generations, but also across generations through socialization of the

young" (Baca Zinn 1992, 72). This type of model was often misapplied to explain the structural challenges facing Mexican families.

4. This term is used by Baca Zinn in 1989.

References

Abney, R., & Richey, D. L. (1992). Opportunities for minority women in sport: The impact of Title IX. *Journal of Physical Education, Recreation & Dance*, *63*(3), 56–59.

Alvarez, A. (1989, June). Nancy Lopez: Balancing family and golf. *Hispanic*, *2*(5), 15–16.

Andersen, M. L. (1993). *Thinking about women: Sociological perspectives on sex and gender*, 3d ed. New York: Macmillan.

Anzaldua, G. (1987). *Borderlands/la frontera: The new mestiza*. San Francisco: Spinsters–Aunt Lute.

———. (1990a). Haciendo caras. una entrada. In G. Anzaldua (ed.), *Making face, making soul: Haciendo caras: Creative and critical perspectives by feminists of color* (pp. xv–xxviii). San Francisco: Aunt Lute.

———. (1990b). En rapport. in opposition: Cobrando cuentas a las nuestras. In G. Anzaldua (ed.), *Making face, making soul: Haciendo caras: Creative and critical perspectives by feminists of color* (pp. xv–xxviii). San Francisco: Aunt Lute.

Baca Zinn, M. (1976). Chicanas: Power and control in the domestic sphere. *De Colores*, *2*(3), 19–31.

———. (1989). Family, race and poverty in the eighties. *Signs*, *14*(4), 856–874.

———. (1992). Family, race and poverty in the eighties. In B. Thorne & M. Yalom (eds.), *Rethinking the family: Some feminist questions* (pp. 71–90). Boston: Northeastern University Press.

Baca Zinn, M., & Dill, B. T. (1994). Difference and domination. In M. Baca Zinn & B. T. Dill (eds.), *Women of color in U.S. society* (pp. 3–12). Philadelphia: Temple University Press.

———. (1996). Theorizing difference from multiracial feminism. *Feminist Studies*, *22*, 321–344.

Birrell, S. (1990). Women of color, critical autobiographies, and sport. In M. A. Messner & D. F. Sabo (eds.), *Sport, men, and the gender order* (pp. 195–199). Champaign, Ill.: Human Kinetics.

Birrell, S., & Cole, C. L. (1994a). Media, sport and gender. In S. Birrell & C. L. Cole (eds.), *Women, sport and culture* (pp. 245–248). Champaign, Ill.: Human Kinetics.

———. (1994b). Double fault: Renee Richards and the construction and naturalization of difference. In S. Birrell & C. L. Cole (eds.), *Women, sport and culture* (pp. 373–397). Champaign, Ill.: Human Kinetics.

Chabran, R., & Chabran, R., eds. (1996). *Lopez, Nancy. The Latino encyclopedia* (Vol. 3, pp. 915–916). New York: Marshall Cavendish.

Chavira, R. (1977, August). Three to cheer. *Nuestro*, *1*, 34–35.

Collins, P. H. (1990). *Black feminist thought: Knowledge, consciousness, and the politics of empowerment.* New York: Routledge.

———. (1991). Learning from the outsider within: The sociological significance of Black feminist thought. In J. E. Hartman & E. Messer-Davidow (eds.), *(En)gendering knowledge* (pp. 41–65). Knoxville: University of Tennessee Press.

Corbett, D., & Johnson, W. (1993). The African-American female in collegiate sport: Sexism and racism. In D. D. Brooks & R. C. Althouse (eds.), *Racism in college athletics: The African-American athlete's experience* (pp. 179–204). Morgantown, Va.: Fitness Information Technology.

Deford, F. (1978, July 10). Nancy with the laughing face. *Sports Illustrated, 49*(2), pp. 24–26, 31.

Dewar, A. M. (1993). Would all the generic women in sport please stand up? Challenges facing feminist sport sociology. *Quest, 45,* 211–229.

Diaz, J. (1997, February 9). Time for the Pat and Nancy show. *Sports Illustrated, 66* (16), pp. 84, 87.

Duncan, M. C. (1994). The politics of women's body images and practices: Foucault, the panopticon and *Shape* magazine. *Journal of Sport and Social Issues, 18*(1), 48–65.

Eitzen, D., & Furst, D. (1993). Racial bias in women's collegiate volleyball. In A. Yiannakis, T. D. McIntyre, & M. J. Melnick (eds.), *Sport sociology: Contemporary themes,* 4th ed. (pp. 327–330). Dubuque, Iowa: Kendall-Hunt.

Felshin, J. (1981). The triple option . . . for women in sport. In M. Hart & S. Birrell (eds.), *Sport in the sociocultural process* (pp. 487–492). Dubuque, Iowa: Brown.

Foley, D. E. (1990). The great American football ritual: Reproducing race, class, and gender inequality. *Sociology of Sport Journal, 7,* 111–135.

Gorelick, S. (1991). Contradictions of feminist methodology. *Gender & Society, 5,* 459–477.

Griffin, P. (1996). Changing the game: Homophobia, sexism, and lesbians in sport. In D. S. Eitzen (ed.) *Sport in contemporary society: An anthology,* 5th ed. (pp. 392–409). New York: St. Martin's.

Grey, M. A. (1996). Sport and immigrant, minority, and Anglo relations in Garden City (Kansas) High School. In D. S. Eitzen (ed.), *Sport in contemporary society: An anthology,* 5th ed. (pp. 295–312). New York: St. Martin's.

Hall, M. A. (1996). *Feminism and sporting bodies: Essays on theory and practice.* Champaign, Ill.: Human Kinetics.

———. Her drive to win. (1978, September). *Nuestro, 2,* 22–23, 26.

Kane, M. J., & Greendorfer, S. L. (1994). The media's role in accommodating and resisting stereotyped images of women in sport. In P. J. Creedon (ed.), *Women, media and sport: Challenging gender values* (pp. 28–44). Thousand Oaks, Calif.: Sage.

Lenskyj, H. J. (1987). Female sexuality and women's sport. *Women's Studies International Forum, 10,* 381–386.

LPGA. (1997, July). LPGA player biographies: Nancy Lopez (5 pages). LPGA (World Wide Web page). Available: <http://www.lp2a.coni/touribiosibiohtml/lopez. html>.

Meier, M. S., & Ribera, F. (1993). *Mexican Americans/American Mexicans: From conquistadors to Chicanos.* New York: Hill & Wang.

Messner, M. A. (1992). *Power at play: Sport and the problem of masculinity.* Boston: Beacon.

————. (1993). White men misbehaving: Feminism, Afrocentrism, and the promise of a critical standpoint. *Journal of Sport and Social Issues, 16,* 136–144.

Mexican American Women's National Association (MANA). (1993). *In search of economic equity.* Washington, D.C.: Author.

Newman, B. (1986, August). The very model of a modern marriage. *Sports Illustrated,* 65(5), pp. 34–41.

Nieves-Squires, S. (1993). *Hispanic women in higher education: Making their presence on campus less tenuous.* Project on the status and education of women. Washington, D.C.: Association of American Colleges.

Pesquera, B. M., & de la Torre, A. (1993). *Building with our hands: New directions in Chicana studies.* Berkeley: University of California Press.

Pronger, B. (1996). Sport and masculinity: The estrangement of cave men. In D. S. Eitzen (ed.), *Sport in contemporary society: An anthology,* 5th ed. (pp. 410–423). New York: St. Martin's.

Rumbaut, R. (1995, April). Immigrants from Latin America and the Caribbean: A socioeconomic profile. Statistical Brief No. 6. Michigan State University, Julian Samora Research Institute.

Sage, G. H. (1990). *Power and ideology in American sport.* Champaign, Ill.: Human Kinetics.

Smith, Y. (1992). Women of color in society and sport. *Quest, 44,* 228–250.

U.S. Department of Commerce, Economics and Statistical Administration, Bureau of the Census. (1996). *Statistical abstract of the United States 1996: The national data book* (No. 241, p. 159). Washington, D.C.: Author.

Williams, L. D. (1994). Sportswomen in black and white: Sports history from an Afro-American perspective. In P. J. Creedon (ed.), *Women, media and sport: Challenging gender values* (pp. 45–66). Thousand Oaks, Calif.: Sage.

Ybarra, L. (1988). Separating myth from reality. In M. Melville (ed.), *Mexicanas at work in the United States* [Mexican-American Studies Monograph, no. 5]. Houston, Tex.: University of Houston Press.

Zavella, P. (1994). Reflections on diversity among Chicanas. In S. Gregory & R. Sanjek (eds.), *Race* (pp. 199–212). New Brunswick, N.J.: Rutgers University Press.

DAVID L. ANDREWS

Excavating Michael Jordan's Blackness

● The fact of Michael Jordan's blackness, to paraphrase Frantz Fanon
(1967), is without doubt one of the most pivotal, yet strangely overlooked
questions posed by contemporary American culture. In spite of the pervasiveness of the crass color-blind credo so gleefully expressed by Jerry
Reinsdorf, owner of the Chicago Bulls, "Is Michael Jordan black? . . .
Michael has no color" (quoted in Kornbluth 1995, 26), close examination
of Michael Jordan's popular signification reveals a complex narrative in-
corporating many of the historically grounded racial codes that continue
to structure the racial formation of the United States. Far from his racial
identity being nonexistent, or extraneous to his social and cultural significance, the imaged persona of Michael Jordan represents an important
site of mediated popular culture at which particular racial ideologies are
publicized and authorized in support of the multiple inclusions and exclusions that delineate the post-Reaganite American imaginary. Jordan's
image exemplifies what Reeves and Campbell (1994, 49) identified as "a
spectacle of surveillance that is actively engaged in representing authority,
visualizing deviance, and publicizing common sense" in a way which has

This essay is a revised version of D. L. Andrews, "The Fact(s) of Michael Jordan's
Blackness: An Excavation in Four Parts," *Sociology of Sport Journal*, 13 (2) (1996),
125–158.

profound implications for the structuring, disciplining, and experiencing of race in contemporary America. For this reason, Michael Eric Dyson was wholly correct in contending that Jordan is "a supremely instructive figure of our times" (1993, 71).

While asserting the central importance of Jordan's racial identity, it is also necessary to underscore that his covert racial signification has displayed a distinct lack of uniformity, a condition of instability which clearly corroborates Grossberg's post-structuralist leitmotif that "no element within the cultural field has an identity of its own which is intrinsic to it and thus guaranteed in advance" (1992, 39). As Hall noted, anticipating his notion of a conjunctural "Marxism without guarantees" (Hall 1983), there are no necessary correspondences, or for that matter noncorrespondences, between meanings and cultural symbols:

> The meaning of a cultural form and its place or position in the cultural field is not fixed once and forever. . . . The meaning of a cultural symbol is given in part by the social field into which it is incorporated, the practices with which it articulates and is made to resonate. (Hall 1981, 235)

As a cultural construct, Jordan's mediated racial identity is neither stable, essential, nor consistent; it is dynamic, complex, and contradictory. Thus, it is perhaps more accurate to refer to the facts of Michael Jordan's blackness, and to assert his status as a floating racial signifier who, in Derridean terms, is constantly under erasure (Derrida 1978). As such, the aim of this essay is to provide a contextual interpretation of the dominant racial discourses that have fashioned the mediated icon, Michael Jordan, in accordance with the shifting imperatives of the reactionary post-Reaganite cultural agenda. More specifically, this essay examines how the racial meaning and significance of Michael Jordan is perpetually being deferred in light of the endless chain of racial signifiers that have been attached to his signified image, through the conjunctural and intertextual machinations of the popular print and electronic media. Consequently, I hope to develop a critical understanding of Michael Jordan which highlights "the elasticity and the emptiness of 'racial' signifiers as well as the ideological work which has to be done in order to turn them into signifiers in the first place" (Gilroy 1991, 39), and thereby disrupts the notion of essential systems of racial differentiation, and instead confronts race as a conjuncturally informed, and materially manifest, discursive construct (see Smith 1994). In Callinicos's terms, the examination of any racial discourse must be engaged within the contextually specific realms of culture and politics, because "they [racial discourses] emerge as part of a historically specific relationship of oppression in order to justify the existence of that relationship" (1993, 18). Certainly, the racial signification of Michael Jordan can be characterized by five distinct yet overlapping moments. Each one of these stages in Jordan's semiotic evolution is contingent upon the climate in racial and cultural politics, and each, in differing ways, represents the conjunctural appropriation and fleeting curtailment of the endless play of signifiers that have historically contributed to the violent racial hierarchy (Derrida 1981) of American popular culture in general, and that of the NBA in particular. As is the responsibility of any example of critical cultural pedagogy (Giroux 1992, 1994; Kellner 1991, 1995; McLaren 1993, 1994), the goal of this essay has been to formulate the type of knowledge and understanding which would encourage people to interrogate their engagement with racially oppressive mediated discourses. In framing the articulation of cultural texts such as Michael Jordan, these popular discursive tracts inevitably contribute toward the construction of the multiple inclusions and exclusions through which the American racial formation continues to be structured, disciplined, and experienced. Hence, in excavating and reconstructing the evolution of Michael Jordan as a racial sign, paraphrasing Grossberg (1992), it has been my modest aim to develop a better understanding of the popular politics of racial representation within contemporary culture's "empire of signs" (Dery 1993), which will inform where *we* have been, and where *we* are, in order that *we* can get somewhere better.

The Natural Athlete: "Born to Dunk"

Nineteen eighty-two marked the year in which Michael Jordan first came to the attention of the nation's sports media. His promising rookie collegiate season was capped off by hitting the winning basket in North Carolina's defeat of Georgetown in the NCAA championship game. Given the frequency with which this shot has been replayed in the ensuing years, it would be easy to fall into the trap of thinking that Jordan's celebrity status at that time was somewhat similar to its current level. On the contrary, at that time, Jordan was a relatively anonymous figure in the minds of the American viewing public. At this fledgling stage of his career in the national media spotlight, Jordan's identity was primarily influenced by his membership on the North Carolina team, and the championship game became the context for the revealing engagement of contrasting racial signifiers to distinguish the competing teams. The media fabricated the event as an intriguing battle between the methodical strategies devised by Dean Smith (the North Carolina coach), and the hyperactive physical frenzy encouraged by John Thomson (the Georgetown coach): "Carolina was," as Smith put it, "the hunted," and Georgetown, quicker, ravaging, downright frightening in its full court press was, "the hunter" (Kirkpatrick 1982, 16). Black players on either side, who comprised the dominant racial grouping in the contest, were cast in stereotypical fashion as the contest became an exposition of the mind-body dualism that has historically informed racial discourse.

Closely tied to the stereotypical media representation of the pathologically violent and criminal black body is the popular fascination with the supposed natural athleticism of the African American Other (see Davis, 1990). Mercer described this as "that most commonplace of stereotypes, the black man as sports hero, mythologically endowed with a 'naturally' muscular physique and an essential capacity for strength, grace and machinelike perfection" (1994, 178). In his infamous televised remarks, Al Campanis, the onetime Los Angeles Dodgers vice president for player personnel, voiced these stereotypical views, which many Americans probably would not even have questioned were it not for his subsequent firing:

> They are gifted with great musculature and various other things. They're fleet of foot, and this is why there are a lot of black major league ballplayers. Now as far as having the background to become club presidents, or presidents of a bank, I don't know. (Al Campanis remarks to Ted Koppel on ABC's *Nightline*, quoted in Omi 1989, 112)

These remarks neatly captured the mind-body dualism that has dominated popular racial discourse related to males of African descent. Similarly, but seemingly less offensively, the popular media's trite celebrations of some inherent African American sporting prowess also draws from the same reservoir of racial signifiers that characterizes black urban youth as being habitually violent and therefore threatening. Both the contemporary construction of the pathologically criminal and naturally sporting black body are founded upon a common assumption of the innate physicality of the black body, a racist discourse whose genealogy can be traced back at least to the era of systemic slavery:

> Classical racism involved a logic of dehumanization, in which African peoples were defined as having bodies but not minds: in this way the superexploitation of the black body as a muscle-machine could be justified. Vestiges of this are active today. (Mercer 1994, 138)

In this vein, and with specific regard to the 1982 NCAA championship game, the media alluded to the fact that the white coach, Smith, infused his players with a sense of his superior knowledge of the game, whereas his black counterpart, Thomson, merely assembled a group of players and allowed them to do what came naturally, that is, to rely on their natural physical attributes. It was hardly surprising, therefore, that Dean Smith was lauded more widely for his basketball acumen than James Worthy, Sam Perkins, or Michael Jordan were celebrated for their input into the victory. When praise was extolled on the North Carolina players, it was usually meted out in recognition of the degree to which they had successfully executed the coach's masterful game plan (Vecsey 1982a, 1982b).

The racial discourse which underscored the media's narration of the 1982 NCAA championship game clearly displayed aspects of the racial context out of which Michael Jordan, the promotional sign, was initially constructed. Furthermore, throughout the construction of his mediated identity, Michael Jordan's imaged persona has been configured either in congruence with, or in opposition to, the economy of signifiers (as depicted by Lanker [1982]) pertaining to the physical comportment of the African American male. As a collegian, the media portrayed him as the latest in a seemingly endless supply of naturally talented and exuberantly physical black bodies. He was, in Cashmore's damning terms, yet another media celebration of "that black magic of nature" (1982, 42). This ubiquitous narrative accompanied Jordan throughout his successful collegiate career, which reached its zenith with him co-captaining the USA team to a gold medal triumph at the 1984 Los Angeles Olympics, where Jordan was referred to in familiar refrain, "The flashiest men's player was Jordan, the 6-ft. 6-in. University of North Carolina senior who has won six awards designating him America's best collegian. *Born to dunk*, he penetrated the zone defenses of opponents to slam at least one goal in each of the eight games" (Henry 1984, 50, emphasis added). Having decided to forgo his senior year at the University of North Carolina, Jordan had already been drafted by the Chicago Bulls in the June 1984 NBA draft. This occasion warranted the *Chicago Tribune* sports columnist, Bernie Lincicome, to sarcastically (due to the rumored interest shown by the Bull's management in making a trade for Jordan) introduce his readership to the Bull's potential "savior" (Logan, 1984):

> They [the Bulls] got stuck with Michael Jordan of North Carolina, maybe the greatest natural basketball talent, inch for inch, in this young decade. Nothing they could do. They want you to know that. They tried to avoid Jordan, tried hard. But nobody wanted to trade with them, swap some big fossil of a center for the third pick in the draft. It was like they were under quarantine or something. So they were forced to do the intelligent thing Tuesday.
>
> They had to take Jordan, even though he is already famous, has had quality coaching, is not a social disgrace and may likely become the next Julius Erving before the old one is in the Hall of Fame. (Lincicome 1984, 1)

Not only did Lincicome identify Jordan's natural ability and his respectable social standing (in contrast to the way many NBA players were perceived at the time), he also provided him with a pertinent professional basketball ancestry. Although Jordan entered into an NBA which had been revitalized by the Johnson and Bird multi-faceted rivalry and the marketing strategies which nurtured it (see Cole and Andrews 1996), Jordan's already acknowledged televisual presence, "his sinewy combat [which] demanded close-ups and super slo-mo," would generate an identity out of difference to the full court "mark-of-Zorro ricochets" orchestrated by

Magic Johnson and Larry Bird (Plagen 1993, 48). Lincicome traced Jordan's basketball lineage, and by inference his racial identity, not to the athletic and indeed racial anomaly represented by the genial Magic Johnson, the Laker's 6-ft. 9-in. floor general, but to the natural, uninhibited, free-form grace and artistry of Julius Erving (Plagen 1993). By advancing Jordan as a possible successor to the aging, but revered, Julius Erving, Lincicome engaged the dubious project of basketball social Darwinism. Others subsequently exalted Jordan as the "highest order of basketball's evolutionary chain," a chain beginning with Elgin Baylor, and comprised of Connie Hawkins, Julius Erving, and ending up with the supreme basketball being, Michael Jordan (Ryan 1993, 28).

On entering the league, Jordan took the NBA by storm. He scored twenty-five points in ten of his first fifteen games, including thirty-seven in his third game. Less than a month into Jordan's first NBA campaign, Larry Bird described him as the "Best I've ever played against" (quoted in Ryan 1993, 27), and he was compared on national television to Julius Erving, who appeared more than comfortable with the comparison (*ABC Nightly News*, November 4, 1984). However, there was a marked difference in the popular racial articulation of Jordan and Erving. Although both were primarily racialized by their supposed natural physical attributes, Jordan's image was not identified in the popular memory for sporting the 1970s black statement, "bushy Afro," or for being one of the "airborne brothers who defined ABA ball" (George 1992, 181), overt identifications with black identity which inhibited Erving's popular acceptance, not as a supreme sportsman but as a national icon. His imaged identity having been fermented within a very different racial climate, that of the color-blind Reagan Revolution, Jordan necessarily emerged as a racially under-stated version of Julius Erving. As such, even more than Erving, he was always likely to become "the kind of [non-threatening] figure who goes down easily with most Americans" (Shelby Steele, quoted in Naughton 1992, 137).

Although Jordan's stellar rookie performances during the 1984–85 NBA season garnered him considerable national publicity, his initial popular identity was crystallized through the innovative promotional initiatives engaged by Nike. In the previous fiscal year, Nike had experienced an alarming decline in sales and sought to redress this by confronting its anonymous presence in both collegiate and professional basketball. In the spring and summer of 1984, the company surveyed the incoming crop of collegiate players and set their sights on Jordan. To Sonny Vaccaro, Nike's intermediary with the collegiate game, Jordan "was brilliant. He was charismatic. He was the best player Vaccaro had ever seen. He could fly through the air!" (Strasser and Becklund 1991, 535). Vaccaro's enthusiasm for Jordan went as far as admitting "I'd pay him whatever it takes to get him" (Strasser and Becklund 1991, 536). On Vaccaro's recommendation, Jordan was pinpointed as the figurehead who could reassert Nike's position as the sport shoe industry's market leader. Such confidence in Jordan's playing and marketing potential was confirmed when the company signed him to a $2.5 million contract. Nike was ridiculed for taking such a financial risk on an untried player at a time when it was experiencing considerable economic troubles. In retrospect, such concerns seem almost laughable, as the Air Jordan phenomenon grossed $130 million in its first year (Strasser and Becklund 1991, 3), a financial boost which reasserted Nike as the preeminent sports shoe manufacturer, and elevated the company to the position of an American corporate icon.

Given the exhilarating telegenicism of Jordan's play, Nike's advertising company at the time, the Los Angeles based Chiat/Day agency, chose to develop an innovative campaign for the equally innovative signature Air Jordan shoes. This involved saturating the electronic media with strategically coded images of Michael Jordan wearing Air Jordan shoes. Hence, during early 1985, the first Air Jordan commercial was aired, a slot entitled "Jordan Flight," in which a slow-motion Jordan executed a dunk on an urban playground to the sound of jet engines accelerating to take off. With this commercial, and especially his parting salvo, "Who said a man was not meant to fly?" Michael Jordan's identity was constituted in the minds of the American populace as Air Jordan, "the Nike guy who could fly" (Katz 1994, 7). The locus of Nike's Air Jordan initiative keyed on Jordan's physical prowess, and thus corroborated the taken-for-granted assumptions pertaining to the naturalistic element of black corporeality. Jordan's repeatedly valorized sporting body thus became a prominent, if underscored, signifier of racial Otherness: a seemingly material vindication of what popular racist discourse had extolled all along.

Transcendental Mediation: Reagan's All-American

The early stages of the Air Jordan promotional phenomenon were evidently dominated by the signification of Jordan's *naturally* athletic *black* body. Although racial signifiers pertaining to black physicality have provided a backdrop for the promotional discourse which narrated his stellar career, to a large degree they have been subsumed by a more obtuse relationship to popular racialized codes. In accordance with the prevailing racial politics of the American New Right—founded upon a paranoid defensiveness toward overt expressions of racial difference and a concomitant dismissive attitude toward the existence of race-based discrimination—Nike's subsequent Air Jordan campaigns inspired the multifarious segments of the American mass culture industry (who subsequently invested in Jordan) into nurturing an intertextually informed identity, which explicitly invested in the affective epidemics which delineated Reagan's America (see Grossberg 1992). Thus, Jordan's carefully scripted televisual adventures on the corporate playground were designed to substantiate an All-American (which in Marable's terms means white) hardbodied identity (Jeffords 1994), which would appeal to the racially sensitive sensibilities of the American mass market. Jordan's phenotypical features could not be overlooked, but his imaged identity could be distanced from the racial signifiers which dominated popular representations of African American males. Corporate image makers recognized that if he was to become "America's player" (Sakamoto 1986, 10), they could not afford to explicitly associate him with the threatening expressions of black American existence.

To facilitate this evolution from mall America's flavor-of-the-month to enshrined All-American icon, Jordan's marketing directors realized he had to be packaged as a Reaganite racial replicant: a black version of a white cultural model who, by his very simulated existence, ensures the submergence and subversion of racial Otherness (Willis, 1991). As David Falk, Jordan's agent at ProServ surmised, the intention behind the Jordan project was to promote an "All-American image . . . Not Norman Rockwell, but a modern American image. Norman Rockwell values, but a contemporary flair" (quoted in Castle 1991, 30). This process was initiated by Nike's decision to move away from Air Jordan campaigns that solely displayed his physical talents, to slots which furnished Jordan with an identifiable, if superficial, personality. Thus, Nike's move from Chiat/Day to the more innovative Wieden and Kennedy agency saw the introduction of a series of ground-breaking advertising campaigns in which Jordan interacted with Mars Blackmon, Spike Lee's cinematic alter ego from the film "She's Gotta Have It." The apparent willingness of the basketball hero to spend time with his bicycle messenger fan/friend demonstrated that for all his success, fame, and fortune, Jordan was reassuringly just another "down-to-earth guy" (*New York Times*, February 20, 1989, section D, p. 7). In true Reaganite fashion, Jordan's self-evident wholesome humility, inner drive, and personal responsibility "allow us to believe what we wish to believe: that in this country, have-nots can still become haves; that the American dream is still working" (Naughton 1992, 7). In other words, through his comedic interludes with Mars Blackmon, Jordan was inextricably articulated as a living, breathing, and dunking vindication of the mythological American meritocracy. Through subsequent creative associations (see Andrews 1998) with McDonald's, Coca-Cola (latterly Gatorade), Chevrolet, and Wheaties—all significant All-American corporate icons—Jordan was similarly cast as a "spectacular talent, midsized, well-spoken, attractive, accessible, old-time values, wholesome, clean, natural, not too Goody Two-shoes, with a bit of deviltry in him" (David Falk, quoted in Kirkpatrick 1987, 93).

Unlike the stereotypical representations of deviant, promiscuous, and irresponsible black males which punctuated the ubiquitous populist racist discourse of the New Right, Jordan was identified as embodying personal drive, responsibility, integrity, and success. The flight metaphor which dominated the articulation of his imaged persona graphically encapsulated Jordan's decidedly individualistic and *American* demeanor, "striving for agency, self-determination, differentiation from others and freedom from control" (Langman 1991, 205). Here was the prototypical simulated Reaganite hard body (Jeffords 1994), lauded by the popular media for being living proof of the existence of an "open class structure, racial tolerance, economic mobility, the sanctity of individualism, and the availability of the American dream for black Americans" (Gray 1989, 376). This ideology, and indeed the very image of Jordan, cruelly posited that anyone in America could realize the dream regardless of race, color, or creed, the only variable being the individual's desire to take advantage of the opportunities afforded by this *great* country. For, as Herman Gray identified, the repetitious celebration of this color-blind credo within the popular media does little more than reinforce the notion, propagated within more explicit channels of political communication, that the material and economic failure of the African American constituents of the urban underclass is "their own since they [*apparently choose to*] live in an isolated world where contemporary racism is no longer a significant factor in their lives" (1989, 384).

By creating an opposition between Jordan and *them* (the failing and thereby threatening African American throng), the concerted promotion of Jordan as the "embodiment of [Reaganite] American virtue" (Naughton 1992, 154) had the desired effect of downplaying his racial Otherness in a way that mirrored the signification of his equally hard-bodied media contemporary, Heathcliff Huxtable (see Jhally and Lewis 1992). According to the novelist John Edgar Wideman, Jordan "escapes gravity" and "makes us rise above our obsession with race" because he leaps the great divide between races and classes by being a down-to-earth, middle-class, and apolitical hero (1990, 140). This notion of Jordan as a figure who transcends race (and indeed sport) was certainly a common theme, voicing as it did the strategic evacuation of race which characterized the Reagan Revolution (Jeffords 1994). As David Falk avariciously conceded, "He's the first modern crossover in team sports. We think he transcends race, transcends basketball" (quoted in Kirkpatrick 1987, 93). An extended article that astutely deconstructed "The Selling of Michael Jordan" (Patton 1986), concentrated on the marketing of Jordan as an individual possessing "uncanny moves on the court and 'a charisma that transcends his sport,'" a personal attribute which turned him into "basketball's most lucrative property" (Patton 1986, 48). Likewise Donald Dell, the chief executive of ProServ, commented that Jordan was a rare commercial property because he "has a charisma that transcends his sport. He belongs in a category with Arnold Palmer or Arthur Ashe" (quoted in Patton 1986, 50). Clearly, the use of sport in this context (specifically Jordan's sport, basketball) is a euphemism for race. Jordan is the figure who has *transcended* the black identity of professional basketball, and thus garnered a widespread and inclusive simulated appeal that resulted in him becoming

America's favorite athlete, a status which no black man before him had achieved (Naughton 1992, 137). In doing so, Jordan played a crucial role in making the NBA accessible to the white American populace who had previously been turned off, and turned away, by the game's overtly black demeanor (see Cady 1979; Cobbs 1980; Cole and Denny 1995; and Cole and Andrews 1996).

Michael Jordan's carefully engineered charismatic appeal (Dyer 1991), which had such an impact on popularizing the NBA to corporate and middle America alike, is not an example of racial transcendence. Rather, it is a case of complicitous racial avoidance, facilitated through the displacement of racial signifiers. Jordan's hyperreal image was charismatic in as much as it set him apart from the popular representations of *ordinary* black males, by endowing him with "supernatural, superhuman or at least superficially exceptional qualities" (Weber, quoted in Eisenstadt 1968, 329). The most pertinent of Jordan's "exceptional qualities" related to his understated racial identity, as opposed to his superlative basketball displays. After all, there was nothing about demonstrations of African American physical excellence that the popular imagination would have considered exceptional. Hence, Jordan's image was coveted by the media primarily because of its reassuring affinity with the affective investments associated with America's white-dominated national popular culture. Although the media could not escape the fact that Jordan is of African American descent, his identity has been shrewdly severed from any vestiges of African American culture. Some black superstars, the most prominent being Jordan, have been able to pander to the racial insecurities and paranoia of the white majority primarily because of their ability to shed their black identities in promotional contexts. In doing so, these black mediated icons have achieved a degree of popular approval which superficially would seem to legislate against the presence of race-based discrimination within American society. As Marvin Bressler, the Princeton sociologist, noted, "It has always been possible in the history of race relations in this country to say that some of my best friends are X. Such people are very useful in demonstrating our own benevolence. We must be good people—we love Michael Jordan" (quoted in Swift 1991, 58). Nevertheless, the compulsion for African Americans to disavow their blackness in order to successfully harness rather than alienate popular opinion is indicative of the ingrained hegemonic racism within American society. American culture simply does not tolerate individuals who are, to put it plainly, too black.

The notion of acceptable, racially understated representations of black America was vividly illustrated in a scene from Spike Lee's 1989 film *Do The Right Thing*. In the scene in question, Mookie (a pizza delivery man played by Spike Lee, the African American lead in the film) confronts Pino (the Italian American son of the pizzeria's owner) about his bigoted but contradictory attitude toward black people:

Mookie	Pino, who's your favorite basketball player?
Pino	Magic Johnson.
Mookie	Who's your favorite movie star?
Pino	Eddie Murphy.
Mookie	Who's your favorite rock star? Prince, you're a Prince fan.
Pino	Bruce!
Mookie	Prince.
Pino	Bruce!
Mookie	Pino, all you ever talk about is "nigger this" and "nigger that," and all your favorite people are so called "niggers."
Pino	It's different. Magic, Eddie, Prince, are not "niggers." I mean they're not black. I mean. Let me explain myself. They're not really black, I mean, they're black, but they're not really black, they're more than black. It's different.
Mookie	It's different?
Pino	Yeah, to me its different.

In this brief interchange, Spike Lee expressed the racial double standards within American society. Many of the white population are *gracious* enough to accept, even adulate, African Americans, but only if they do not explicitly assert their blackness: If you're black, you are not expected to harp on it; if you do then you are, to use the racist vernacular, a "*jumped up nigger*." African Americans are tolerated, and even valued, if they abdicate their race and are seen to successfully assimilate into the practices, value system, and hence identity, of white America. Moreover, African American membership in this exclusive club requires constant affirmative renewal. Any fall from grace (ranging from the judicial severity of a criminal misdemeanor, to the tabloidic scandal of sexual impropriety, to even the supposed democratic right of asserting one's racial identity) canceled membership, and recast the hitherto American person as a criminally deviant, sexually promiscuous, or simply threatening racial Other, exiled to the margins of American society with the bulk of the minority population. The ability of certain black celebrities to downplay their blackness was the reason for Pino's lauding of Magic Johnson and Eddie Murphy. Spike Lee could have easily substituted Michael Jordan, Bill Cosby, Bo Jackson, or Arsenio Hall, as Pino's favorite stars (Swift 1991). Conversely, the outspoken championing of black civil rights issues by figures such as Reverend Al Sharpton, Minister Louis Farrakhan, and Reverend Jesse Jackson, greatly disturbed Pino. These radical black activists with *"chips on their shoulders,"* they were *"niggers."*

Like the reactionary color-blind cultural politics which nurtured it, the very notion of racial transcendence, supposedly embodied by Jordan and alluded to by Pino, was a seriously flawed and contradictory concept. Racial discourse is never transcended; it is in a Derridean sense, *always already there* (see Smith 1994). Jordan is not an example of racial transcendence; rather, he is an agent of racial displacement. Jordan's valorized, racially neutered image displaces racial codes onto other black bodies, be they Mars Blackmon, Charles Barkley, or the anonymous urban black male whom the popular media seem intent on criminalizing. Nike's promotional strategy systematically downplayed Jordan's blackness by contrasting him with Spike Lee's somewhat troubling caricature of young, urban, African American males, Mars Blackmon. Borrowing from Pino's discriminatory discourse, Jordan was Jordan, he wasn't *really* black. Mars was a "nigger." The contrast fortified Jordan's wholesome, responsible, All-American, and hence nonthreatening persona, and became the basis of his hyperreal identity which was subsequently embellished by the multiplying circuits of promotional capital which enveloped him.

With specific regard to Nike, having been deified (initially in opposition to Mars Blackmon) as the All-American paragon of virtue, Jordan assumed the role of centrifuge of a racial sign system which the company subsequently built around him. According to Phil Knight, the Nike chairman, the company compartmentalized basketball into distinct playing styles in order to create an expanding network of ties with the buying public:

> We thought about it, we realized that there are different styles of playing basketball. Not every great player has the style of Michael Jordan, and if we tried to make Air Jordan appeal to everyone, it would lose its meaning. We had to slice up basketball itself. (quoted in Willigan 1992, 96)

However, the stylistic differences utilized by Nike engaged contrasting elements of embodied racial discourse. In essence, Nike mobilized stereotypical racial codes in order to fashion identities for the Air Force and Air Flight endorsers/product lines, which would provide ways of demarcating between them, and also set them apart from the Air Jordan phenomenon. Within Nike's ever-expanding economy of larger-than-life basketball icons (exemplified by the emergence of promotional figures such as Charles Barkley, David Robinson, Scottie Pippen et al.), Jordan's identity was continually reasserted out of (racial) difference to predominantly African American figures, once again confirming his imperious racial transcendence, while displacing dominant racial codes onto the bodies of his Nike underlings (see Andrews 1993).

Without question, Charles Barkley represents the most problematic of Nike's racial caricatures expounded within their basketball campaigns. Unlike David Robinson, whose physical force and aggression were encased in a veneer of humor and moral fortitude within the parodic "Mr. Robinson's Neighborhood" campaigns, Barkley's image promotes sheer, unadulterated aggression. As Knight enthused, "It's not just Charles Barkley saying buy Nike shoes, it's seeing who Charles Barkley is—and knowing that he is going to punch you in the nose" (quoted in Willigan 1992, 100). In his earliest commercial slot, a black and white commercial inspired by the musical "Hell's-a-Poppin'," Barkley was initially surrounded by a line of chorus girls. He was then confronted by a group of journalists and photographers, one of whom he ends up punching. The ensuing newspaper headline predictably reads "Charles-a-Poppin'." Even in the renowned Barkley vs. Godzilla commercial, the humorous nature of the narrative cannot detract from the fact that Barkley is being portrayed as little more than an overtly physical and aggressive, almost animal-like individual. Likewise, the recent "The Barkley of Seville" commercial, which lampoons the excesses of operatic expression, still has Charles killing the referee. While these narratives are undoubtedly amusing, they do little but reinforce the popular perception of African American males. Despite their humorous overtones, they merely feed the widespread paranoid hostility created by the media's routine use of stereotypically violent and threatening images of young black males.

The pathological signifiers mobilized by Nike to delineate their embodied racial economy were negatively reinforced by Michael Jordan without impinging upon (indeed they augmented) his racially transcendent image. Thus, in stark contrast to Nike's creation of Barkley as an antihero (an image designed to appeal to sizeable sections of the consuming public), Michael Jordan was portrayed as a paragon of American virtue. The positive identification of Michael Jordan's image in opposition to those of Barkley, and to a lesser extent, Robinson, Pippen et al., strategically downplayed his African American identity by engaging binary oppositions between Jordan and the dominant discursive formations of African American Otherness. In this way, Jordan's atypical black body deflects and reinscribes stereotypical signifiers of racial Otherness onto the pathologized black bodies which dominate the media's representation of African American males, ranging from the demonized black male urbanite (ably represented by Mars Blackmon) to the equally problematic caricaturing of Jordan's Nike basketball brethren.

"Look, a Negro!": The Devil Inside[1]

The majority of Michael Jordan's tenure in the media spotlight has been characterized by his portrayal as a figure whose singular virtuosity differentiates him from, and hence underscores, the demonized soft-body signifiers of African American Otherness. Nevertheless, there have been occasions when Jordan's racially neutered identity has been severely questioned by the popular media. Although explicitly referring to British sporting culture, Kobena Mercer provides insights into the Jordan phenomenon, and explicitly the scrutinizing of his identity:

As a major public arena, sport is a key site of white male ambivalence, fear and fantasy. The spectacle of black bodies triumphant in rituals of masculine competition reinforces the fixed idea that black men are all "brawn and no brains," and yet, because the white man is beaten at his own game—football, boxing, cricket, athletics—the Other is idolized to the point of envy. This schism is played out in the popular tabloid press. On the front page headlines black males become highly visible as a threat to white society, as muggers, rapists, terrorists and guerrillas: their bodies become the image of a savage and unstoppable capacity for destruction and violence. But turn to the back pages, the sports pages, and the black man's body is heroized and lionized; any hint of antagonism is contained by the paternalistic infantilization of Frank Bruno and Daley Thompson to the status of national mascots and adopted pets—they're not Other, they're OK because they're our boys. (Mercer 1994, 178–179)

While Jordan conformed to the role of wholesome, nonthreatening, hard-bodied hero, he was deified for being one of "America's boys." However, once his behavior, especially off the court, was deemed to be transgressing the boundaries of what was considered acceptable for the prototypical All-African American male (George 1992), the specter of racial Otherness reared its demonized head.

The interrogation of Jordan's Reaganite hard body was virtually inevitable because, although his very symbolic existence indicated that images of African American athleticism are not necessarily representations of black men misbehaving (Clarke 1991), the new cultural racism was prefigured on the virulent assumption that these *innately* physical males would be misbehaving were it not for the involvement of their natural physical attributes in the disciplinary mores and stringencies imposed by the dominant (sporting) culture. According to this spurious logic, within sporting activity African American males have found salvation (if only temporary, i.e., Mike Tyson and O. J. Simpson) from themselves. Such reactionary thoughts were echoed by a *Chicago Tribune* columnist, Bernie Lincicome, in a startlingly offensive summation of the O. J. Simpson case: "Arguments that sports is responsible for O. J. Simpson's present situation must begin with concessions that without sports, O. J. Simpson is sitting in that chair thirty years ago" (1994b, 1). Renouncing such racist diatribes, Giroux (1994) ably illustrated how contemporary American culture is dominated by a fascination with the assumed superior physicality of the black male body, and a simultaneous fear of the ever-present threat which it poses. Such mass mediated appeals to middle America's racial paranoia and insecurities dared American popular consciousness to confront the potentiality of Jordan's deviant racial Otherness and, in doing so, posed the unthinkable question, "Perhaps Michael Jordan is black (i.e., pathologically flawed) after all?"

During the 1991–92 season, and for the first time, Michael Jordan experienced "The underside of stardom" (Isaacson, 1992a, 14). As Sullivan noted, "After seven years of nearly perfect marriage with the media and his fans, Jordan endured a season of criticism" (1992, 3). At the hands of a salacious mass media, Jordan was: rebuked for failing to attend George Bush's honoring of the Chicago Bull's NBA championship win at the White House; castigated for gambling large sums of money on his golf game (Jackson 1992); criticized for the ruthless and hyper-competitive side of his nature (outlined in Smith's [1992] controversial book *The Jordan Rules*); attacked for his initial reluctance to compete for the United States team in the Barcelona Olympics (Cronin 1991); and chided for his wrangling with the NBA over the commercial rights to his likeness (Banks 1992; Hiestand 1992; Mulligan 1992; Vecsey 1992), that also led to the ignominious "Reebok flap" at the Olympic medal ceremony (Myslenski 1992, 8). In other words, for the first time Jordan's "faults and foibles were chronicled, along with his dunks and doggedness" (Sullivan 1992, 3).

Even though Jordan was able to sidestep the controversies which arose during the 1991–92 season, media interest had been sparked in a new and seemingly profitable spin-off industry from the Jordan phenomenon. Jordan's new-found human frailties represented big business for the tabloid sections of both the electronic and print media. Much to the delight of the salacious media, within a year the undermine-Jordan industry was given fresh impetus. On May 27, 1993, it was reported that Jordan was seen gambling in Atlantic City late into the night, on the eve of Game 2 of the Chicago Bulls Eastern Conference Final series against the New York Knicks (Anderson 1993). In light of this incident, and arguably for the first time, the media began to seriously re-evaluate Jordan's imaged identity.

The catalyst which initiated this reappraisal was undoubtedly his repeated association with gambling, which had first come to national attention in 1992, when it was revealed that Jordan had gambled and lost a considerable amount of money on a golf game played with one Slim Bouler, who turned out to be a drug dealer (Isaacson 1992b). The Atlantic City sighting thrust the open secret of Jordan's love of gambling into a racial discourse from which his image had previously been disassociated (Jackson 1992). In the immediate aftermath of the Atlantic City visit, Jordan's identity as a figure who transcended (displaced) race was disturbed by the questioning accusations of certain sections of the media. The most inflammable account of the incident predictably came from the New York press, and specifically Dave Anderson's intentionally provocative piece "Jordan's Atlantic City Caper" (1993, 11), which first broke the story and pilloried the "best player in basketball history" for letting down his teammates and coaches by gambling until 2:30 A.M. (an hour later refuted by a variety of sources, including Jordan). In a sardonic tone, Anderson identified this display of inappropriate behavior as turning the Knicks' "home-court advantage" into their "home-casino" advantage (1993, 11), and conclusively linking Jordan to the NBA's deviant lifestyle:

> Apologists for the NBA lifestyle argue that players are accustomed to staying up until the early hours, then sleeping late or taking a nap after the shootaround. Some NBA players enjoy frequenting the Atlantic City casinos when their teams visit Philadelphia for a game. (Anderson 1993, 11)

The NBA had never been completely separated from its popular, and racially charged, connotation as an aberrant domain. Yet this was the first time that Jordan's imperious image had been tainted with the festering detritus of this implicitly racial discourse. However temporarily, Jordan became an imaged sign whose impending fall from grace appeared destined to reinforce the historically inscribed racial discourses that cast African American males as pathologically deficient individuals, whose weaknesses are manifest in addictive and obsessive lifestyles (see Reeves and Campbell 1994).

Anderson's column not only granted the gambling story a degree of legitimacy because it originated in the august pages of the *New York Times*, it also ignited a furious debate within the popular media—a debate whose underlying current centered on the scrutiny of Jordan's racial identity. In Jefford's (1994) terms, Anderson disrupted the dominant articulation of Jordan's strong and decisive (unraced) hard body à la Reagan, by insinuating that he actually possessed a pathologically weak and corruptible (raced) soft body à la Bernard King, Eddie Johnson, or Terry Furlow, or for that matter Len Bias (see Cole and Andrews 1996; Donohew 1989; and Reeves and Campbell 1994). The *ABC Nightly News* on May 27, 1993, ended with a segment on the story, introduced with a marked solemnity by Peter Jennings. Within the piece, Dick Schaap identified how, in the first quarter of the game against the Knicks, Jordan played like what he was, "The greatest best basketball player who ever lived." By the last quarter, Jordan "looked human, he looked tired." Schaap then asked the audience to consider whether Jordan was worn down by the Knick's aggressive defense, or was he himself to blame for his own demise, "worn down by a visit to this Atlantic City hotel on the eve of the game." Once again, Jordan's iconic stature was questioned for violating "people's expectations," and, without condemnation, Schaap offered some advice, "The most famous and richest active athlete in the world is not supposed to go to a gambling casino and stay out beyond midnight. He is too easy a target." Jordan's status as an exceptional human being and role model (Mariotti 1993), founded as it was on his imaged identity in opposition to the media's vision of the archetypal black male, was now in doubt. The nation's eyebrows were raised, as the media suggestively implied that Jordan was perhaps human (a less than subtle euphemism for being black) after all (Mariotti 1993; Miklasz 1993).

The raging debate concerning Jordan's gambling habits was given further stimulus in early June with the hastened release of Richard Esquinas's book, *Michael & Me: Our Gambling Addiction . . . My Cry for Help!* (Esquinas, 1993). The author maintained the book was circulated sooner than planned because, in the wake of the Atlantic City story, "We wanted to stay in control of information . . . we felt we were losing confidentiality" (Esquinas, quoted in Isaacson 1993, 7). It seemed more likely that the book was distributed in order to take advantage of the popular interest already generated around Jordan's alleged gambling problem. As a result of the popular media's rabid coverage and circulation of the debate over Jordan's alleged predilection for gambling, the story took on "a life of its own," evidencing the "media's apparent inability to put on the brakes when a story is spinning out of control" (Fainaru 1993, 68). In the wake of Jordan's gambling exposé, the media gleefully censured him, and in doing so stimulated popular interest in the story. For this reason, Jordan's attempt to exonerate himself was always likely to elicit a skeptical response from the more avaricious sections of the media:

> I think that was Michael Jordan behind those dark glasses, though it might have been a candidate for the witness protection program. Did he know the camera was on? Was he wired to a polygraph we couldn't see? Jordan's first step back as icon and wonder symbol looked more like testimony than conversation . . . the network did him no favors, lighting him like a criminal all the while Jordan was insisting a criminal is exactly what he isn't. (Lincicome 1993, 1)

Despite the proliferation of stories related to Jordan's penchant for gambling, the currency of mediated narratives within a postmodern culture engorged by information is unavoidably brief. The gambling story which temporarily dominated the media's coverage of Michael Jordan and threatened to seriously discredit his All-American image had within a matter of days become a residual and largely neutral aspect of his mediated identity. This process was hastened by the Chicago Bulls' victory over the Phoenix Suns in the NBA Final Series. Once more Jordan's on-court exploits took center stage, as the "Bull's three-peat" relegated the gambling issue to the status of a minor problem that was overcome during the course of the team's ultimately triumphant "season of endurance" (Cardon 1993, 5). Jordan's appearance on CBS's *Eye to Eye with Connie Chung* (July 15, 1993) seemed to finally lay the ghost of his gambling problem to rest, as he talked candidly about his life, family, and the gambling controversy. To all intents and purposes, Jordan's gambling had become a nonstory, and from being packaged as a role model, a "walking image onto which gambling simply does not project" (Fainaru 1993), Jordan had been reinvented as the All-American hero "who loves motherhood, apple pie and *games of chance*" (emphasis added, Heisler 1993, 1).

Question marks surrounding Jordan's personal integrity did not stay dormant for long. The gambling narrative became violently reactivated around the murder of his father in August 1993. Once James Jordan's body had been positively identified, the media immediately and enthusiastically alluded to a connection between the father's murder and his son's gambling, which implied that the murder was a pay-back for Michael Jordan's gambling debts (Dobie 1994). As Margaret Carlson noted, speaking on an edition of CNN's *Reliable Sources* program which examined the popular media's proclivity for reporting conjecture rather than fact:

> I think there was another thing at work in the Jordan murder which was that people were looking for a reason, and they went back to the last story, the last big story, which was this—these gambling charges, and they took the death, and they took the gambling, and they linked the things without any evidence at all, but there's this human desire, I think, here that newspapers pick up on which is to find a reason. They—we don't want to believe that there's absolute, total, random violence, especially when it's someone famous. (August 28, 1993)

In terms of semiotic analysis, once again, the constant erasure and deferral of Michael Jordan's racial signification resulted in the conjunctural rearticulation of Jordan's image. From the relative tranquility of post-championship euphoria, the signification of Jordan "the obsessive gambler" was exhumed and widely attached to the sign of his murdered father. For example, Michael Janofsky, writing in the *New York Times*, appeared to presume a connection between Jordan and his father's murder, and seemed most disappointed with Sheriff Morris Bledsole's failure to corroborate it, "The absence of clues, Bledsoe said, made it impossible for him to speculate on the possibility that Jordan's death was connected to any gambling activities of his son" (1993a, 25). Writing in the same paper, Ira Berkow added to the speculation:

> and now that James P. Jordan is dead, we don't know whether the father is paying for his son's celebrity in some bizarre way. . . . We don't know all the circumstances behind the death of James Jordan . . . but the police are calling it homicide. (1993a, 25)

Perhaps the most irresponsible, and certainly the most hypocritical commentary on the murder came from Jay Mariotti. Writing shortly after James Jordan's body had been identified, Mariotti (1993b, 2A) opined, "it would be the height of irresponsibility to start speculating or suggesting factors that may not be factors. Whodunit commentary is impossible until more is unearthed in the Carolinas." And yet, within the same article Mariotti blithely stated, "There are concerns about his gambling habits . . . Now there is the possibility that his fame may have contributed, in some way, to his father's murder" (1993b, 2A).

The reportage of unfounded conjecture and sensationalist supposition was by no means confined to the print media, as television coverage of James Jordan's murder also revisited and reinscribed the gambling narrative. The *CBS Evening News* of August 13, 1993, covered the breaking news of the Jordan murder as its lead story. A somber Connie Chung opened the program in dramatic fashion:

> Triumph. Turmoil. And now, tragedy. Michael Jordan has seen it all this year. Today police in North Carolina confirmed the worst fears about the basketball star's missing father. James Jordan shot to death. Killer and motive unknown.

The story then moved into a film segment narrated by Diana Gonzalez, a correspondent situated in North Carolina. She described a "devastated" Michael Jordan's return to North Carolina following his learning of the "mysterious" death of his father. Gonzalez then recounted the events leading up to James Jordan's disappearance/murder, and the closeness of the relationship between father and son. She concluded with a revealing commentary on the case:

> The body of James Jordan was found in a area known for a lot of drug-related crime, but as of now police say they have no obvious motive. Authorities have not said whether they will consider the *possibility* the killing *might* be connected to the family's gambling activities. Other possibilities include kidnapping for ransom, or simply random crime. (emphasis added)

This coverage represented a clear example of what Margaret Carlson (appearing on CNN's *Reliable Sources*, August 28, 1993) referred to as the media's need for immediate gratification, in terms of instantaneously providing a motive for any action within their gaze. The police may have been unwilling to identify an obvious motive; however, CBS News was more than happy to do so. In one fell swoop, Gonzalez's less than subtle inferences provided the viewing public with a seemingly compelling rationale for the murder, one which clearly implicated Michael Jordan, without any direct reference to him. Connie Chung, with a picture of James Jordan now providing a backdrop, then contextualized his murder within the narrative of his son's career, "Jordan's murder adds another bitter twist to the darker side of an All-American success story"—a narrative which seemed to be realizing Jordan's dreaded metamorphosis from "Michael Jordan the person to Michael Jordan the black guy" (Michael Jordan, quoted in Breskin 1989, 396)

Back to Basics? Michael Jordan as Gingrichite America

Media speculation related to Jordan's potentially deviant (racial) identity abated with the arrest of James Jordan's alleged murderers, one of whom was an African American male. In light of this development, the accusatory and racist vectors of the popular media became directed at another black body, that of the indicted African American assailant, Daniel Andre Green. The media's casting of Green as an embodied and highly visible racial sign of "the kind of random violence that all the public was concerned about and afraid of" (Jim Coman, quoted in Janofsky 1993b, 1), neatly absolved Jordan of any responsibility, however indirect, for his father's death. As Janofsky pointed out:

> Today's arrests brought to a swift conclusion a sad and somewhat bizarre case that drew nationwide attention because of the fame of Michael Jordan, the National Basketball Association's premier player, and speculation that the death might be in some way related to Jordan's highly publicized gambling activities. (1993b, 1)

With Daniel Andre Green assuming the mantle of a latter day Willie Horton (see Feagin and Vera 1995), his demonized racial presence provided a semiotic space for, and inverted unity with, the revitalization of Michael Jordan's All-American sign value. In essence, the strategic mobilization of corporeal pathologies associated with the deviant African American Other necessarily resuscitated Jordan's atypical racial persona.

Following the arraignment of his father's alleged murderers and his subsequent retirement from the NBA in October 1993—which was widely reported as being at least partly attributable to the stress and anxiety resulting from his father's murder and the media's reporting thereof (McCallum 1993)—the articulation of Jordan's simulated existence became infused with a sense of familial sympathy, sorrow, and understanding. As with Wayne Gretzky's "defection" from Canada in 1988 (Jackson 1993, 1994), Jordan's retirement resonated as a catalyst for the popular expression of national loss and mourning (Jones 1993; Madigan 1993; Thomas 1993). In Bill Clinton's funeral terms, "We may never see his like again. We will miss him—here and all around America, in every smalltown backyard and paved city lot where kids play one-on-one and dream of being like Mike" (quoted in *Inside Sports* special issue "The End of an Era," October 1993, 7). However, unlike the Gretzky scenario—which proved a catalyst for intersecting debates related to Canada's perceived national decline—Jordan's retirement also provided a platform for the national popular celebration of the *American way*, as seemingly vindicated by the very nature of his imperious being. Ira Berkow enthused, "His wholesome image, his broad smile and his basketball achievements made him the embodiment of the American dream" (1993b, 17). John Leland, in the *Newsweek* special issue "The Greatest Ever," which marked Jordan's retirement, continued this romanticized celebratory narrative of contemporary America *through* Michael Jordan, a discourse which for so long had dominated the populist articulation of his career:

> There is a clip of Michael Jordan that we Americans will be replaying in our heads well into the next century. It is a part of our shared cultural experience, a flash of the American Dream bright enough to join us all momentarily in its promise. It begins with Michael swooping toward the basket. His tongue is out, the ball a willing appendage at the end of his long, muscular right arm. He takes one stride, and then he begins to rise.

It is a magnificent thing, his rise, as articulate a refutation of the forces that hold humankind earthbound as the drawings of Leonardo or the joyous music of Louis Armstrong. His legs start to churn in midair, mocking gravity, and he begins, at his apex, to climb even higher: he begins to fly. Jordan made this move scores of times; television multiplied it a hundredfold. And each time he went up he held out the hope that this time—for the sake of all who believe themselves slaves to gravity—he would never come down. (1993, 9)

Despite the prevalence of such self-satisfied nationalist discourse surrounding the spectacle of Jordan's retirement, some journalists would not let the rumors surrounding Michael Jordan's personal indiscretions dissipate. In the *Newsweek* special issue, Mark Starr resurrected "that gambling thing" (1993, 39) in a particularly indicting manner. After chronicling his varied gambling habits, Starr accused Jordan of being a compulsive gambler, a personality flaw which had rendered his basketball legacy, "sadly, a slightly tarnished one" (1993, 39). Likewise, Harvey Araton's barbed summation of Jordan's career chided him for a hypocritical lack of personal integrity and responsibility:

For even as Jordan was saying goodbye, his bitterness over his name being dragged through gambling headlines was obvious. He kept referring to the news media as "you guys," you problem makers, as if the news media had dug up Slim Bouler and Richard Esquinas and every other controversy that dogged Jordan the last two years.

That's the troubling part of the Jordan legacy, his lack of public acknowledgement that the persona he marketed so brilliantly, so lucratively, did not come with responsibility, with accountability. (1993, 1)

Evidently in the wake of his retirement, the popular media's representation of Jordan was in a state of flux, polarized by the oppositional signifiers of All-American greatness and African American pathological depravity.

Within four months of his retirement from the NBA, Jordan embarked on his highly publicized baseball odyssey. This somewhat improbable venture resolved the semiotic ambiguity and exorcised the specter of racial contamination implied by the media's prolonged discussion of Jordan's numerous *indiscretions*. Despite the ever-increasing presence of African American, Hispanic, and Latino players within the game, baseball continues to be a touchstone of white (sporting) culture. Hence, with Jordan pursuing his, and what is frequently and often uncritically assumed to be *every* true-blooded (white) American male's (sporting) dream, the threat posed by his emergent deviant identity to his racially transcendent image almost inevitably subsided. Once again he could be portrayed as the near-mythic All-American hero.

Although there were some notable examples to the contrary (for example Mariotti [1994], and most controversially Wulf [1994]), Jordan's sojourn into minor league baseball was largely characterized as being beneficial to the game as a whole. Perhaps even more important than the direct economic boost that Jordan was expected to bring to the game (Banks 1994; de Lissier and Helyar 1994; and van Dyck 1994a), his very presence in a baseball uniform was felt to have improved the game's image by association (Crain 1994; Lincicome 1994a; van Dyck 1994b; and Verdi 1994a). Jordan was even anointed as the "savior" of the strike-curtailed 1994 major league baseball season: "All he has done since putting on a baseball uniform is bring positive attention to a sport in dire need of it, and dignity to himself by risking his athletic reputation on this baseball fantasy" (Burwell 1994b, 3C). As Burwell intimated, the Jordan-baseball couplet proved to be a mutually beneficial alliance.

When braced with Jordan's revitalizing All-American aura, baseball's residual identity as the national pastime provided the media with a synergetic narrative context, which almost compelled the discursive appropriation of the valorized personal attributes associated with successful engagement with the American dream, most pertinently naked innocence, hard work, commitment, and desire for success (Verdi 1994b). Jordan was valorized for being "just a guy who chased his dream" (Myslenski 1994, 1), and someone who was "not afraid to fail" (Michael Jordan, quoted in *Chicago Sun-Times*, February 8, 1994, 88) in the pursuit of his dream. The discursive emendation of the explicitly American competitive individualism which engulfed Jordan's fledgling baseball career reached its zenith within the crass popular psychology which comprised the inspirational tome, *I Can't Accept Not Trying: Michael Jordan on the Pursuit of Excellence* (Vancil 1994). Most of the text for this discussion of Jordan's personal philosophy was garnered from the pictorial coffee table book, *Rare Air* (Vancil 1993), which was published the previous year. However, the timing of the later book's release, its very title, and thematic organization proved an effective intertextual reinforcement of the Algeresque articulation of Jordan's baseball odyssey.

Perhaps wary of the negative publicity which could potentially be accrued if Jordan struggled in baseball (as he plainly did), his coterie of corporate affiliations were initially reticent to develop "Jordan baseball tie-ins" (Jensen 1994). Soon, however, Jordan's baseball trials and tribulations proved too good a marketing opportunity to miss. Having retired the anthemic "Be like Mike" campaign, during Jordan's tenure with the Chicago White Sox's Double-A affiliate, Birmingham Barons, Gatorade introduced a television commercial which overtly played on his baseball travail. Over grainy, black and white, nostalgia-inducing sequences drawn from his imperious basketball career, Jordan—bedecked in baseball garb—solemnly declared, "I always wanted the ball, and I got it where it should go. And, I always drank Gatorade because nothing's better." Switching to color, baseball, and the contemporary, the visual narrative displayed images of Jordan diligently practicing his hitting, base running, and throwing, over which he announced, "Now I'm playing baseball. I still drink Gatorade. I still want the ball. I still know where it should go. And sooner or later, I'm gonna get it there [he smiles] . . . I hope. It's got to be Gatorade!" This commercial keyed on the self-conscious and whimsical admission of Jordan's fallibility with regard to his baseball abilities and ambitions, and admiration for the strength of character required for putting himself in a position where failure was a very real and public possibility, simply to pursue his dream. Such a theme also provided the impetus for Nike's somewhat belated (especially since the television commercial was made redundant after less than a week following Jordan's decision to return to the NBA in March 1995) contribution to the fabrication of Jordan's baseball-related identity. Within this television spot, baseball icons Stan Musial, Willie Mays, and Ken Griffey, Jr., were shown surveying Jordan's baseball prowess and admitting to the attendant Spike Lee (resurrecting the Mars Blackmon character), that while Jordan cannot

be considered their equals in terms of playing ability, there was no doubt-
ing his sincerity, or the fact that "he's trying." Following footage of the
ball rolling through Jordan's legs, Bill Buckner, the ex-Boston Red Sox
player remembered for committing precisely such an error at a crucial
point during the 1986 World Series, wryly noted, "He ain't no Bill Buckner. . . . But he's trying." Nike pursued this parodic overture within their
next Air Jordan commercial which first aired in May 1995. The spot, which
Hiestand (1995, 3C) identified as being reminiscent "of your grammar
school fiction efforts," reprised images and scenarios drawn from previous
Nike commercials, his NBA comeback game against the Indiana Pacers,
Bobby Ewing's (Patrick Duffy) resurrection in *Dallas*, and most importantly from Jordan's baseball detour, which was now cast in a surreal light:

> I had this dream . . . I retired . . . I became a weak hitting Double-A
> outfielder with a below average arm . . . I had a $16 meal per diem
> . . . I rode from small town to small town on a bus . . . and then I
> returned to the game I love, and shot 7 for 28. . . . Can you imagine
> it . . . I can't.

This commercial simultaneously brought Jordan's baseball career to a satirical conclusion and effectively announced his return to the NBA.
Through the use of parody and self-deprecating humor, it positioned Jordan's relative failure in baseball as a platform for reasserting his humility,
steely determination, and desire to realize even the most challenging goals.
Despite a .202 batting average at the Double-A level, Jordan's status as
an All-American icon was conclusively reaffirmed. As Grant poignantly
summarized, Jordan's "improbable quest" fell short of his goal, "but it
wasn't for lack of effort" (1995, 110).

Evidently the maturation of Jordan's popular identity in the mid-to-
late 1980s was both influenced by and contributed to the prevailing climate in popular racial politics. So, his significatory resurrection in the
mid-1990s was contingent upon the hyperreactionary, and necessarily racist traditionalism of the new populist Republicanism which engulfed public space. According to John Dempsey, writing in *Variety*, the loss of
marquee players, impending contract talks, and the rise of overly physical
play had all contributed to the situation where "the NBA's image dribbles

away" (1994, 27). This questioning of the NBA's exemplary image, which Jordan had played such a large part in cultivating, intensified following his retirement from the league in October 1993. Thereby, and by disassociation, Jordan's image was further revitalized. The neo-Reaganite climate of racial retrenchment—concretized within the Newt Gingrich orchestrated "Contract with America," which swept the Republicans to a landslide victory in the November 8, 1994, elections for the House of Representatives (see Mollins 1995a, 1995b, 1995c)—rendered the high profile and overt African American constitution of the Jordanless NBA a semiotic space that inevitably became implicated in the rise to ascendancy of the *new* New Right's accusatory regime of racial signification. In the wake of the semiotic ambiguity created by Jordan's departure, the NBA became targeted by the reactionary popular media as yet another site for representing African American males as signifiers of danger and social depravity. The process of honing the NBA into a racially acceptable semiotic space, initiated by Bird–Johnson and consolidated by the transcendent persona of Michael Jordan (see Cole and Andrews 1996) was derailed by reactionary diatribes which condemned the new generation of NBA stars for being self-centered, spoilt, brash, arrogant, and irresponsible (Boeck 1994a, 1994b; Burwell 1994a; Dempsey 1994; Diefenbach 1995; Graham 1995; Swift 1994; Taylor 1995). According to Burwell, here was

> an entire generation of slammin', jammin', no jump-shooting, fundamentally unsound kids who have bought into NBA's and Madison Avenue's shallow MTV-generated marketing of the game. People with no soul for the essence of the game turned the poetry into gangster rap. (Burwell 1994a, 3C)

The much publicized dissension of players such as Dennis Rodman, Chris Webber, Derrick Coleman, and Isaiah Rider became widely characterized as being indicative of the "league's discipline problems mirror[ing] those of society" (Taylor 1995, 23). Using the NBA as a euphemism for the American nation, the racial paranoia and insecurity which pervaded popular discourse depicted the unruly and disrespectful behavior of these *young* African American males as being as threatening to the stability of the NBA, as the criminal irresponsibility of the *young* urban African

American male was to American society as a whole. According to Taylor, "A form of insanity is spreading through the NBA like a virus threatening to infect every team in the league" (1995, 19). Or, as Diefenbach described it, "In the NBA, at least for the time being, it is evident: The animals control the zoo" (1995, 31). Perhaps Graham most succinctly placed the entire debate within its neo-conservative political context, "The players are just the most visible example of what's happening in sports and, in a larger sense, in society: The decline of old-fashioned values" (1995, 10). Upholding old-fashioned values, and thereby distinguishing the young deviants, were the residual and ever-revered images of Bird, Johnson, and Jordan (Boeck, 1994a; Diefenbach, 1995). Thus, despite his commitment to baseball, Michael Jordan's sign-value continued to influence the racial representation of the NBA, the only difference being his imperious, but absent, image was now used in an almost nostalgic sense to distinguish what the league had become. Even in absentia, Jordan's image was a potent agent of racial displacement, which deflected stereotypical racial signifiers away from his atypical black body and onto those of the youthful African American miscreants who now dominated the popular representation of the NBA. This explains the relevance of, and inferences behind, the pointed question asked on the front cover of the December 1994 issue of *Inside Sports*, "Why can't Shaq be like Mike?"

Despite the ubiquitous and intrusive presence of Michael Jordan, his separation from the NBA created the semiotic space for, indeed his physical absence almost necessitated, the creation of a more immediate embodied oppositional referent within the turgid maelstrom which the NBA now represented. Grant Hill, the Duke forward, was posited as a future NBA star long before his entry into the league (Wolff 1993). Having debuted in the Jordan-less NBA in November 1994, Hill produced the type of on-court performances which allowed the popular media, and his expectant commercial sponsors, to legitimately capitalize upon the Jordan-like off-court demeanor which had been manufactured for Hill during the course of his successful collegiate career. Almost overnight Hill was sucked into the vortex of promotional culture. This meant that as well as being a regular performer on NBC's, TBS's, and TNT's NBA game coverage, Hill was featured in numerous television (even playing the piano on CBS's *Late Show with David Letterman*), newspaper, and magazine profiles, and appeared in commercials for Fila, Sprite, and General Motors, all of which created an economy of mutually reinforcing texts which expedited the signification of Hill as the new Michael Jordan (DuPree 1994a, 1994b; Feinstein 1995; Junod 1995; Lewis 1995). As a result he became "Everybody's new NBA favorite [who] is admired not just for the greatness of his game, but for the content of his character" (Feinstein 1995, 58). In a matter of months, Hill was touted as "the savior" of a league which had become "replete with hoodlums" (Junod 1995, 170, 172) because, like Jordan a decade before him, he had been shrewdly promoted as

> a harbinger of the day when the value police will finally break down the laws of the locker room and make all those muscled miscreants toe the line in the name of God and country . . . [someone who is] said to "act white" and "play black," he makes a black man's game more palatable to the white folk who have started imputing a connection between "in your face" and "in your house." (Junod 1995, 172)

Or, as Feinstein identified, "To marketers, Hill is a dream come true. He's the anti-Shaq" (1995, 59). The promotional juggernaut which propelled Hill to the top of the 1995 NBA All-Star balloting, and to being co-recipient (with Jason Kidd) of the 1994–95 NBA Rookie of the Year award, was temporarily interrupted by Jordan's decision to resume his NBA career in March 1995. With the more immediate proximity of Jordan's sign-value, actively redeeming the league's tarnished image, Hill was relegated to the status of an apprentice Jordan, the "Heir Jordan" (Johnson 1995, 38), ready to assume the paragonic mantle when his forebear decides to retire once and for all.

Whereas Charles F. Pierce, somewhat prematurely, described Grant Hill as "our first post-Gingrich superstar" (quoted in Junod 1995, 172), Jordan could be considered America's first Gingrichite superstar who epitomized the "back to basics" (to borrow a term from John Major), ideology espoused by the new New Right. Jordan's comeback provided the popular media with a context for accenting the neo-Reaganite personal traits and characteristics that originally framed his mediated identity, implicated him as lustrous vindication of Reagan's color-blind ideology, and thus set him apart from popular stereotypes of the African American male:

> In this season of Jordanmania, we are celebrating excellence, which is all to the good. With his fierce work ethic, his insistence on practices as competitive as games, and his refusal to concede a defeat until the buzzer sounds, Jordan is a role model and then some. Even the ad slogans most widely associated with Jordan—"Be like Mike" and "Just do it"—remind us of how much we can achieve if we simply make a real commitment to our dreams. (Kornbluth 1995, 22)

The reassertion of "SuperMichael" (*Sports Illustrated*, front cover, March 20, 1995) inevitably positioned Jordan in opposition to the NBA's vilified "spoilsports and malcontents" (Leland 1995, 54), thus reinforcing both poles of this racially charged binary opposition. In remarks made during the post-game press conference which followed his comeback game, Jordan obligingly adopted this crusading role:

> I really felt that I wanted to instill some positive things back to the game. You know, there's a lot of negative things that have been happening to the game, and I guess in terms of me coming back, I come back with the notion of, you know, Magic Johnson and the Larry Birds and the Dr. Js—all those players who paved the road for a lot of the young guys. And the young guys are not taking care of their responsibilities in terms of maintaining that love for the game, you know, and not let it waste to where it's so business-oriented that the integrity of the game's going to be at stake. (CNN News, March 19, 1995)

Even Scoop Jackson, writing in *Slam*, the youth-oriented and self-styled "In Your Face Basketball Magazine," toed this reactionary line, "Just when the NBA's salvation is in question, Air Jordan returns to save our souls . . . Michael Jordan's return to the NBA is more like Jesus or Dr. King returning to save our souls, rather than a brotha coming back to shoot hoops" (1995, 43). With Jordan engaged in his stated mission of "reclaiming his throne," and righting the wrongs perpetrated by the NBA's "gimme gimme Generation X'ers" (Araton 1995, 6), it remains to be seen whether a series of sub-par performances, which eventually led to the Chicago Bull's second round playoff defeat at the hands of the Orlando Magic, will lead to a serious re-examination and reconstitution of his popular racial identity. There is a distinct possibility that prolonged evidence of Jordan's physical decline and sporting fallibility may be couched in terms which mobilize residual and deep-rooted racial anxieties around his imaged persona. However, the only thing that can be conclusively forecast is that the perpetual dynamism and ephemerality of mediated popular culture demands that, as this chapter has hopefully shown, the racial [dis]-articulation of Jordan's imaged persona will not achieve any degree of enduring stability or permanence.[2]

Notes

This project has been greatly informed by Cheryl Cole, as an influential author, enthusiastic collaborator, supportive colleague, and valued friend. Therefore, I would like to take this opportunity to publicly acknowledge my great debt of gratitude to her. I would also like to thank the anonymous *SSJ* reviewer who provided a particularly rigorous and helpful critique.

1. This section is an elaboration of a position introduced within Cole and Andrews (1996).

2. The October 2, 1995, trade which sent Dennis Rodman to the Chicago Bulls appears certain to represent yet another new chapter in the popular signification of Michael Jordan, with Jordan being positioned in opposition to "Dennis the menace" (Bickley 1995, 92).

References

Andrews, D. L. (1993). The cult of sporting personality: Nike's affective basketball economy. Paper presented at the annual meeting of the North American Society for the Sociology of Sport, Ottawa, Ontario, Canada.

Andrews, D. (1998). Excavating Michael Jordan: Notes on a critical pedagogy of sporting representation. In G. Rail (ed.), *Sport and postmodern times* (pp. 185–220). New York: State University of New York Press.

Anderson, D. (1993, May 27). Jordan's Atlantic City caper. *New York Times*, p. B11.

Araton, H. (1993, October 7). A legacy as Jordan departs: Stars as corporate heroes. *New York Times*, p. A1.

———. (1995, May 15). Be like No. 23, and don't dare say a word. *New York Times*, p. C6.

Banks, L. J. (1992, February 4). Powerful Jordan packing plenty of promotional pop. *Chicago Sun-Times*, p. 78.

———. (1994, February 6). Baseball can earn, learn from MJ, NBA. *Chicago Sun-Times*, p. 14.

Berkow, I. (1993a, August 14). Jordan's haunting words. *New York Times*, p. 25.

———. (1993b, October 7). Suddenly, Michael doesn't play here anymore. *New York Times*, p. B17.

Bickley, D. (1995, October 3). Rough childhood root of problem. *Chicago Sun-Times*, p. 92.

Boeck, G. (1994a, December 1). Spoiled—and rotten? "Attitudes" of players worry some. *USA Today*, p. 4C.

———. (1994b, December 1). Magic: Game needs stars off court. *USA Today*, p. 4C.

Breskin, D. (1989, March). Michael Jordan: In his own orbit. *Gentlemen's Quarterly*, pp. 318–323, 394–397.

Burwell, B. (1994a, June 3). Pacers' victory could end ugly ball. *USA Today*, p. 3C.

———. (1994b, October 7). Get real, purists: Jordan is baseball season's savior. *USA Today*, p. 3C.

Cady, S. (1979, August 11). Basketball's image crisis. *New York Times*, p. 15.

Cardon, B., ed. (1993). *Chicago Bulls three-peat!* Chicago, Ill.: Chicago Tribune Souvenir Issue.

Castle, G. (1991, January). Air to the throne. *Sport*, pp. 28–36.

Clarke, S. A. (1991). Fear of black planet. *Socialist Review*, 21(2), 37–59.

Callinicos, A. (1993). *Race and class*. London: Bookmarks.

Cashmore, E. (1982). *Black sportsmen*. London: Routledge and Kegan Paul.

Cobbs, C. (1980, August 19). NBA and cocaine: Nothing to snort at. *Los Angeles Times*, p. C1.

Cole, C. L., & Denny, H. (1995). Visualizing deviance in post-Reagan America: Magic Johnson, AIDS, and the promiscuous world of professional sport. *Critical Sociology*, 20(3), 123–147.

Cole, C. L., & Andrews, D. L. (1996). "Look—It's NBA *ShowTime!*": Visions of race in the popular imaginary. *Cultural studies: A research volume* (Vol. 1, pp. 141–181).

Crain, R. (1994, February 28). Baseball to learn to "Be like Mike." *Advertising Age*, p. 24.

Cronin, B. (1991, July 31). Olympics don't fit MJ to a tee. *Chicago Sun-Times*, p. 114.

Davis, L. R. (1990). The articulation of difference: White preoccupation with the question of racially linked genetic differences among athletes (review essay). *Sociology of Sport Journal*, 7(2), 179–187.

de Lissier, E., & Helyar, J. (1994, April 8). Is a baseball club with Michael Jordan still minor league? *Wall Street Journal*, pp. A1, A6.

Dempsey, J. (1994, June 27–July 3). NBA's image dribbles away. *Variety*, pp. 27–28.

Derrida, J. (1978). *Writing and difference.* London: Routledge & Kegan Paul.

———. (1981). *Positions.* Chicago: University of Chicago Press.

Dery, M. (1993). The empire of signs. *Adbusters Quarterly: The Journal of the Mental Environment*, 2(4), 54–61.

Diefenbach, D. (1995, June). Disturbing the peace. *Sport*, pp. 24–31.

Dobie, K. (1994, February). Murder by the roadside in Robeson County. *Vibe*, pp. 72–78.

Donohew, L., Helm, D., & Haas, J. (1989). Drugs and (Len) Bias on the sports page. In L. A. Wenner (ed.), *Media, sports, & society* (pp. 225–237). Newbury Park, Calif.: Sage.

DuPree, D. (1994a, October 26). Hill has 'em talking: Pistons rookie stirs Jordan comparisons. *USA Today*, p. 7C.

———. (1994b, December 6). Impact draws comparisons to Jordan. *USA Today*, pp. 1–2C.

Dyer, R. (1991). Charisma. In C. Gledhill (ed.), *Stardom: Industry of desire* (pp. 57–59). London: Routledge.

Dyson, M. E. (1993). Be like Mike: Michael Jordan and the pedagogy of desire. *Cultural Studies*, 7(1), 64–72.

Eisenstadt, S. N., ed. (1968). *Max Weber on charisma and institution building.* Chicago: University of Chicago Press.

Esquinas, R. (1993). *Michael & me: Our gambling addiction . . . My cry for help!* San Diego, Calif.: Athletic Guidance Center Publications.

Fainaru, S. (1993, June 6). Jordan's actions speak louder than words. *Boston Globe*, p. 68.

Fanon, F. (1967). *Black skin, white mask.* New York: Grove Press.

Feagin, J. R., & Vera, H. (1995). *White racism: The basics.* New York: Routledge.

Feinstein, J. (1995, May). Grant the good. *Inside Sports*, pp. 58–59.

George, N. (1992). *Elevating the game: Black men and basketball.* New York: HarperCollins.

Gilroy, P. (1991). *"There ain't no black in the union jack": The cultural politics of race and nation.* Chicago: University of Chicago Press.

Giroux, H. A. (1992). Resisting difference: Cultural studies and the discourse of critical pedagogy. In L. Grossberg, C. Nelson, & P. Treichler (eds.), *Cultural studies* (pp. 199–212). London: Routledge.

Giroux, H. (1994). *Disturbing pleasures: Learning popular culture.* New York: Routledge.

Graham, S. (1995, June). The heroes take a fall. *Inside Sports*, pp. 10, 12.

Grant, R. E. (1995). Running down a dream. In *Beckett great sports heroes: Michael Jordan* (pp. 110–114). New York: House of Collectibles.

Gray, H. (1989). Television, black Americans, and the American dream. *Critical Studies in Mass Communication, 6,* 376–386.

Grossberg, L. (1992). *We gotta get out of this place: Popular conservatism and postmodern culture.* London: Routledge.

Hall, S. (1981). Notes on deconstructing "the popular." In R. Samuel (ed.), *People's history and socialist theory* (pp. 227–240). London: Routledge & Kegan Paul.

———. (1983). The problem of ideology: Marxism without guarantees. In B. Matthews (ed.), *Marx 100 years on* (pp. 57–86). London: Lawrence & Wishart.

Heisler, M. (1993, May 28). Jordan's cards under the table. *Los Angeles Times,* p. C1.

Henry, W. A., III. (1984). Faster, higher, stronger. In *Olympic Games 1984: The pictorial record of the XXIII Olympic Games* (pp. 49–51). Upper Montclair, N.J.: ProSport.

Hiestand, M. (1992, January 30). Jordan cuts out of NBA apparel deal. *USA Today,* p. 1C.

———. (1995, April 27). Baseball marketing schemes tardy but not on target. *USA Today,* p. 3C.

Hoekstra, D. (1993, October 7). Jordan feeds media dose of own medicine. *Chicago Sun-Times,* p. 16.

Isaacson, M. (1992a, June 15). 2nd world championship is "more" to Jordan. *Chicago Tribune,* p. A14.

———. (1992b, October 17). Jordan leaves gambling story up in air. *Chicago Tribune,* pp. B1, B5.

———. (1993, June 4). Jordan mum on book's gambling allegations. *Chicago Tribune,* p. D7.

Jackson, D. (1992, March 29). Jordan's acquaintances in shadowy world. *Chicago Tribune,* pp. A1, A16–A17.

Jackson, S. J. (1993). Sport, crisis and Canadian identity in 1988: The issue of Americanisation. *Borderlines: Studies in American Culture, 1*(2), 142–156.

———. (1994). Gretzky, crisis, and Canadian identity in 1988: Rearticulating the Americanization of culture debate. *Sociology of Sport Journal, 11*(4), 428–446.

Jackson, S. (1995, July). The new testament. *Slam,* pp. 42–48.

Janofsky, M. (1993a, August 14). Man shot to death is identified as father of Jordan. *New York Times,* p. A25.

———. (1993b, August 16). Two men are charged with murder of Jordan. *New York Times,* p. C1.

Jeffords, S. (1994). *Hard bodies: Hollywood masculinity in the Reagan era.* New Brunswick, N.J.: Rutgers University Press.

Jensen, J. (1994, March 21). Nike, Gatorade resist Jordan baseball tie-ins—For now. *Advertising Age,* pp. 4, 42.

Jhally, S., & Lewis, J. (1992). *Enlightened racism: The Cosby Show, audiences, and the myth of the American dream.* Boulder, Colo.: Westview.

Johnson, B. (1995, April 10). Adages. *Advertising Age,* p. 38.

Jones, C. (1993, October 7). Jordan about to become last year's role model. *New York Times*, p. B20.

Junod, (1995, April). The savior. *Gentlemen's Quarterly*, pp. 170–175, 238–240.

Katz, D. (1994). *Just do it: The Nike spirit in the corporate world*. New York: Random House.

Kellner, D. (1991). Reading images critically: Toward a postmodern pedagogy. In H. Giroux (ed.), *Postmodernism, feminism, and cultural politics* (pp. 60–82). Albany: State University of New York Press.

———. (1995). *Media culture: Cultural studies, identity and politics between the modern and the postmodern*. London: Routledge.

Kirkpatrick, C. (1982, April 14). Nothing could be finer. *Sports Illustrated*, pp. 14–16.

———. (1987, November 9). In an orbit all his own. *Sports Illustrated*, pp. 82–98.

Kornbluth, J. (1995, April 22). Here comes Mr. Jordan. *TV Guide*, pp. 22–26.

Langman, L. (1991). From pathos to panic: American national character meets the future. In P. Wexler (ed.), *Critical theory now* (pp. 165–241). London: Falmer Press.

Lanker, B. (1982, December 27). Pieces of '82. *Sports Illustrated*, pp. 52–69.

Leland, J. (1993, October/November). Farewell, Michael . . . and thanks . . . for the memories. *Newsweek: Collector's Issue—The Greatest Ever*, pp. 4–23.

———. (1995, March 20). Hoop dreams. *Newsweek*, pp. 48–55.

Lewis, D. (1995, January). Who got "next"? *Slam*, p. 12.

Lincicome, B. (1984, June 17). Apologetic Bulls "stuck" with Jordan. *Chicago Tribune*, p. D1.

———. (1993, June 10). Jordan's TV appearance criminal. *Arizona Republic*, p. E5.

———. (1994a, March 9). Jordan's majesty is safe, despite baseball's efforts. *Chicago Tribune*, p. D1.

———. (1994b, July 8). Suspicions, guesses and knowledge too good to suppress. *Chicago Tribune*, p. D1.

Logan, B. (1984, June 17). Bulls hope Jordan's a savior. *Chicago Tribune*, pp. D1, D6.

Madigan, C. M. (1993, October 7). Gloom in the cathedral of the sneaker. *Chicago Tribune*, pp. A1, A7.

Mariotti, J. (1993a, June 4). Hoopla: What's up Michael? *Newsday*, p. 181.

———. (1993b, August 15). The ultimate challenge awaits Michael Jordan. *Chicago Sun-Times*, p. 2A.

———. (1994, February 8). Michael at the bat was too painful to watch. *Chicago Sun-Times*, p. 87.

McCallum, J. (1993, October 18). The desire isn't there. *Sports Illustrated*, pp. 28–35.

McLaren, P. (1993). Border disputes: Multicultural narrative, identity formation, and critical pedagogy in postmodern America. In D. McLaughlin & W. G. Tierney (eds.), *Naming silenced lives: Personal narratives and the process of educational change* (pp. 201–235). London: Routledge.

———. (1994). Multiculturalism and the post-modern critique: Toward a pedagogy of resistance and transformation. In H. A. Giroux & P. McLaren (eds.), *Between borders: Pedagogy and the politics of cultural studies* (pp. 192–222). New York: Routledge.

Mercer, K. (1994) *Welcome to the jungle: New positions in black cultural studies*. London: Routledge.

Miklasz, B. (1993, June 4). Jordan gambling with reputation, not poker chips. *St.Louis Post-Dispatch*, p. 1D.

Mollins, C. (1995a, April 17). The politics of disgruntlement. *Maclean's*, pp. 34–35.

———. (1995b, April 17). Man of the house. *Maclean's*, pp. 36–37.

———. (1995c, April 17). Newt's agenda. *Maclean's*, p. 38.

Mulligan, M. (1992, January 30). Nike gets rights to Jordan apparel. *Chicago Sun-Times*, p. 91.

Myslenski, S. (1992, August 5). Now you see it, now you don't: Reebok flap finally resolved. *Chicago Tribune*, p. D8.

———. (1994, May 1). Jordan: Remember me as just a guy who chased his dream. *Chicago Tribune*, p. C1.

Naughton, J. (1992). *Taking to the air: The rise of Michael Jordan*. New York: Warner Books.

Omi, M. (1989). In living color: Race and American culture. In I. Angus & S. Jhally (eds.), *Cultural politics in contemporary America* (pp. 111–122). New York: Routledge.

Patton, P. (1986, November 9). The selling of Michael Jordan. *New York Times Magazine*, pp. 48–58.

Plagen, P. (1993, October/November). Turning hoops upside down. *Newsweek Special Issue: The Greatest Ever*, p. 48.

Reeves, J. L., & Campbell, R. (1994). *Cracked coverage: Television news, the anti-cocaine crusade, and the Reagan legacy*. Durham, N.C.: Duke University Press.

Ryan, B. (1993, December). Courting greatness. *Sport*, pp. 26–30.

Sakamoto, B. (1986, December 16). Jordan's glamor fills league arenas. *Chicago Tribune*, p. D10.

Smith, A. M. (1994). *New right discourse on race and sexuality*. Cambridge: Cambridge University Press.

Smith, S. (1992). *The Jordan rules: The inside story of a turbulent season with Michael Jordan and the Chicago Bulls*. New York: Simon & Schuster.

Starr, M. (1993, October/November). That gambling thing. *Newsweek Special Issue: The Greatest Ever*, p. 39.

Strasser, J. B., & Becklund, L. (1991). *Swoosh: The unauthorized story of Nike and the men who played there*. New York: Harcourt Brace Jovanovich.

Sullivan, P. (1992, June 18). MVP Jordan credits Chicago fans. *Chicago Tribune*, p. D3.

Swift, E. M. (1991, August 5). Reach out and touch someone: Some black superstars cash in big on an ability to shed their racial identity. *Sports Illustrated*, pp. 54–58.

———. (1994, June 20). Hot . . . Not: While the NBA's image has cooled, the NHL has ignited surprising new interest in hockey. *Sports Illustrated*, pp. 30–40.

Taylor, P. (1995, January 30). Bad actors: The growing number of selfish and spoiled players are hurting their teams and marring the NBA's image. *Sports Illustrated*, pp. 18–23.

Thomas, R. M. (1993, October 7). Across the globe, expressions of regret and gratitude. *New York Times*, p. B21.

Vancil, M., ed. (1993). *Rare air: Michael on Michael*. San Francisco: HarperCollins.

———. (1994). *I can't accept not trying: Michael Jordan on the pursuit of excellence*. San Francisco: HarperCollins.

van Dyck, D. (1994a, February 7). Better believe it: Baseball banking on MJ as "savior." *Chicago Sun-Times*, p. 85.

———. (1994b, February 25). MJ's charisma lesson for baseball. *Chicago Sun-Times*, p. 108.

Vecsey, G. (1982a, March 30). Dean Smith finally makes the final one. *New York Times*, pp. B9, B11.

———. (1982b, March 31). Kicking the habit. *New York Times*, pp. B7, B9.

———. (1992, November 20). Owning a likeness. *USA Today*, pp. 1C, 4C.

Verdi, B. (1994a, February 10). Question is: Can baseball learn from Jordan style? *Chicago Tribune*, p. D1.

———. (1994b, February 15). Jordan's baseball bid a fantasy, but his work ethic isn't. *Chicago Tribune*, p. D1.

Wideman, J. E. (1990, November). Michael Jordan leaps the great divide. *Esquire*, pp. 140–145, 210–216.

Willigan, G. E. (1992, July/August). High performance marketing: An interview with Nike's Phil Knight. *Harvard Business Review*, pp. 91–101.

Willis, S. (1991). *A primer for daily life*. London: Routledge.

Wolff, A. (1993, February 1). The son is shining. *Sports Illustrated*, pp. 58–64.

Wulf, S. (1994, March 14). Err Jordan: Try as he might, Michael Jordan has found baseball beyond his grasp. *Sports Illustrated*, pp. 20–23.

7

ABIGAIL M. FEDER-KANE

"A Radiant Smile from the Lovely Lady"
Overdetermined Femininity in
"Ladies" Figure Skating

• A casual observer of the figure skating coverage at the 1994 Olympics might have supposed that in the figure skating world Nancy Kerrigan had always been the princess and Tonya Harding the white trash whore. In a limited sense they would not have been wrong: Kerrigan and Harding were contrasted in figure skating coverage, especially television coverage, long before the attack on Kerrigan at the 1994 U.S. National Championships. But what might surprise some is that the contrast did not always favor Kerrigan. In the shorthand of figure skating identification, Kerrigan was the elegant lady, Harding the "tough cookie." The ubiquity of this shorthand identification was remarked on by Frank Deford: "everybody who makes reference to Harding, like her or not, is bound to say: 'a tough cookie.' It's like an official part of her name, a position, like: Tonya Harding, shortstop; or Tonya Harding, soprano; Tonya Harding, tough cookie" (1992, 52). While Kerrigan had more "tel-appeal" as a skating personality, a stereotypical "ice princess," Harding had more legitimacy as an athlete, especially among sports writers who usually cover men's sports.

This essay was originally published in *Women on Ice: Feminist Essays on the Tonya Harding/Nancy Kerrigan Spectacle*, edited by Cynthia Baughman, 22–46. New York and London: Routledge, 1995. An earlier version of this article appeared in *TDR 38*, 1 (T141), Spring 1994.

Femininity and athleticism are mutually exclusive concepts in American culture. Even in recent years, when the fitness craze extended to both sexes, women were constantly reminded that all signs of their athleticism must be kept invisible. In an Arid deodorant commercial that ran extensively in the mid-1990s, the young man says to the camera, "To me, it just isn't sexy when a woman sweats"; the young woman says, "Sure, a guy is going to sweat sometimes, but who wants to be close to a guy who smells?" In our culture "it is assumed that sports success *is* success at being masculine. Physical achievement, and masculine activity, are taken to be the same" (Willis 1982, 123).

I became interested in exploring singles figure skating when I observed that, although the athletic requirements do not appear specifically gendered, the narrative surrounding the women's competition is sickly sweet in its presentation of the competitors' femininity. I discovered, as I will detail below, that in the original (short) program, for which the requirements are set by the International Skating Union (ISU), gender differences are built in. However in the free (long) program, for which the athletes choose their own material, there is little difference between the skills performed by men and women. Both are required to perform complex footwork and a variety of spins and jumps; no competitor would be taken seriously who does not have several triple jumps, and for both men and women the triple Axel is the most difficult jump performed (although two male competitors and one female have performed a quadruple jump). Judging ranges from the fairly objective to the extremely subjective: Jumps are judged on height and clean take-offs and landings; skaters are judged on how well they "relate" to their music. They are awarded two sets of marks, for technical merit and artistic impression.

Perhaps it is because of the equality of the skills performed that the narrative surrounding competition is so overdetermined in its construction of the women skaters' femininity. "Even if ideology cannot totally submerge itself as common sense, it can at least forward plausible suggestions for the reinterpretation of events. Ideology can never afford to let contradictory interpretations of reality go free from at least a crippling ambiguity" (Willis 1982, 127). The almost hysterical assertion of gender difference presented in coverage of figure skating is not very commonsensical, but it does succeed in tangling the ideological issues until they are almost beyond debate. The idea that men may not have a "natural" physical superiority is no longer out of the question: Evy Scotvold, the coach who trained U.S. skaters Nancy Kerrigan and Paul Wylie, once said of Japan's Midori Ito, "The only man I've ever seen outjump her is [1988 Olympic gold medalist] Brian Boitano" (Swift 1992, 20), an opinion echoed by former Olympic champion Scott Hamilton during CBS coverage of the 1992 games (see also Deford and Starr 1992, 52). Boitano himself said of Tonya Harding, "She jumps like a male skater. . . . There's an incredible strength and control in her jumping" (Swift 1992a, 63). When physical capabilities no longer distinguish men and women, femininity is overdetermined to keep female athletes from being labeled as masculine or lesbian. This phenomenon can be observed elsewhere in women's sports from the obsession with tennis player Monica Seles's latest "do," to the late Florence Griffith-Joyner's long nails and lace stockings, to professional golfer Jan Stephenson posing for a Marilyn Monroe style pin-up poster. "The more successful a female athlete, the more she tries to embody the culturally appropriate gender role . . . a role essentially at odds with her athleticism" (Faller 1987, 154). This is, of course, assuming that the athlete wishes to avoid such a label; an out lesbian, such as Martina Navratilova, did not need to bother.

"Femininity," wrote Susan Brownmiller, "must constantly reassure" (1984, 15) that, no matter their accomplishments, women athletes are still "just girls" underneath. Successful women athletes risk being labeled "mannish," with generally unspoken implications of lesbianism close to the surface. The connection between femininity and reassurance was made explicit in a 1982 *Sports Illustrated* article on the above-mentioned Stephenson. "Stephenson did a lot for the image of women's golf in 1981. That was the year in which Billie Jean King admitted she'd had a lesbian affair and almost knocked a wheel off the apple cart of women's sports. And all during that perilous time, there was Stephenson out front on the sports pages, looking good and playing better" (McDermott 1982, 31). Women must precariously negotiate their societally contradictory roles of woman and athlete. Nancy Therberge summarizes one strategy, Jan Felshin's theory of the female apologetic in sports:

> Felshin characterized the social dynamic of women in sport as an anomaly. . . . As an extension of this, women in sport advance an

apologetic for their involvement. The apologetic affirms a woman's femininity despite her athletic endeavors and thus "legitimates the woman's role in sport by minimizing the anomaly." This legitimation is not complete, however, and social conflict over the contradictions inherent in women's sport activities persists. (1981, 344)

Figure skating's "apology" is actually incorporated into the competition, where costume, makeup, and gesture feminize and soften the athletic prowess required for executing triple jumps and flying sit-spins. The fact that the female competitors are still officially called "Ladies" under U.S. and International Skating Union rules (a fact which even the typically unselfconscious U.S. television reporters felt the need to explain to their audience) is only the beginning (ABC, January 11, 1992). Television coverage is framed in vignettes featuring soft-focus lights, stars in little girls' eyes, glittery costumes, and flowers from adoring crowds. "A dream is a wish your heart makes when you're fast asleep" is the music accompanying shots of a little girl falling asleep surrounded by stuffed animals wearing skating medals which introduced ABC coverage of the 1992 U.S. National Championship; "You look wonderful tonight" sang Eric Clapton over close-ups of the 1992 female Olympic medal hopefuls before the finals. In contrast, the framing device that introduced the men's finals played the percussive background to a Genesis song which has accompanying lyrics: "I can feel it coming in the air tonight," while computer animated lightning signaled each explosive editing cut. While the women were shown in flowing movement, in worried close-ups or applying makeup, the men were pictured doing their most difficult jumps, raising their hands in gestures of triumph. Spots publicizing the 1994 men's Olympic competition featured more explosive shots of men jumping or pumping their arms in triumph to rock music, while the voice-over punched out their names: "Boitano. Petrenko. Browning. Elvis . . . The battle will be epic!" The teaser for the ladies final featured Frank Sinatra singing, "Yes, you're lovely, with your smile so warm, and your cheeks so soft, that there's nothing for me but to love you, and *The Way You Look Tonight*" over shots of the women spinning, smiling, bowing, waving, and hand-kissing to the crowd.

There is always an emphasis on the women skaters' physical beauty (and a corresponding denigration of the sport), which is related to their exchange value and the commodification which is the ultimate reward of Olympic victory. An insidious duality is established by labeling some women as athletic and others as artistic, with the artistry associated with physical beauty and a slender body type. Finally, the women competitors are never allowed to own their success, but are always identified in relationship to family, either biological or their extended skating family; they are especially identified with their mothers.

The anxiety about the success of women athletes is most obviously symbolized by the Olympic practice of sex-ID testing, which proves how closely sports success and masculine identity are connected in our culture.

> The idea of certifying female athletes as females originated more than twenty-five years ago. Athletic directors said they were trying to guard against male impostors, but a more subtle message was also being sent, said Alison Carlson, a member of the athletic federation's committee and a tennis coach. A successful female athlete "challenges society's notion of femininity," Ms. Carlson said, so both the athletic directors and the women themselves felt it important to prove they were real women. (Kolata 1992, E6)

In order to compete, women athletes must strive for strength, speed, and competitiveness—all those qualities which our society codes as masculine. "As an athlete becomes even more outstanding, she marks herself out as even more deviant. . . . To succeed as an athlete can be to fail as a woman, because she has, in certain profound symbolic ways, become a man" (Willis 1982, 123). So in order to avoid being coded as overly masculine or a lesbian, the athlete will participate in her own construction as a hyperfeminine creature. This is more true in figure skating than in any other sport. Because of its element of theater, figure skating provides more opportunities for adornment and display, those familiar tropes of femininity with which the American public is comfortable. But even as they have become embraced as stars, female skaters have often been negated as athletes.

Women in figure skating are caught in a trap that Naomi Wolf could have labeled "the bind of the Beauty Myth": A woman must live up to popular notions of beauty in order to compete successfully, both on the ice and in the commercial endorsement sweepstakes. The spectacle of their beauty is one factor in the fabulous popularity of women's figure skating, and why the women's competition is one of the few that is more popular than the men's equivalent. (The valorization of male athletes is reversed in those sports "whose 'aesthetic' properties encode them as suitably 'feminine' [Whannel 1984, 104].) "When Katarina Witt won her second gold in '88, the prime time ratings . . . topped out past 35, the sort of number that baseball and basketball never fetch and that football obtains only for the Super Bowl itself" (Deford 1992, 46). But the sport is taken less seriously precisely because its competitors are beautifully dressed and made-up women. "The preservation of youthful beauty is one of the few intense preoccupations and competitive drives that society fully expects of its women, even as it holds them in disdain for being such a narcissistic lot" (Brownmiller 1984, 167). One particularly overwrought male columnist wrote, "Figure skating—should be dropped altogether. What used to be a genuine competition is now what 'Cats' is to musical comedy, a costumed, overwrought, pretentious joke. And what kind of game is it where the winner gets to wear cosmetics and skate on tour?" (Lincicome 1992, 1).[1]

The concern with spectacle can be seen in the obsessive attention to women's costumes. In 1992, skating fashion found its way from the sports pages to the "Living Arts" section of the *New York Times*, because top fashion designers, including French haute couture designer Christian LaCroix, were making skaters' costumes. Vera Wang described the outfits she designed for Nancy Kerrigan: "Nancy wanted me to translate the look of couture evening wear to the ice" (Louie 1992, 1). What was not pointed out is that all these costumes, in addition to sequins and tiny skirts, have some simulated nudity, whether it is a plunging neckline, a cutout back or "sheer illusion sleeves" (Louie 1992, 1). "Appearance, not accomplishment, is the feminine demonstration of desirability and worth. . . . Feminine armor is never metal or muscle, but paradoxically, an exaggeration of physical vulnerability that is reassuring (unthreatening) to men" (Brownmiller 1984, 51).

"So why do they play into it?" a male friend asked me. "What if they competed in full body coverings like the men?" As it turns out, both men and women are limited in their choice of costumes by the rules. Debi

Thomas, who won the bronze medal at the 1988 Olympic games, skated her short program in a sequined body stocking rather than a short skirt. Although she skated her program "flawlessly," according to a Canadian magazine ([O'Hara 1988, 49] which might be expected to be free from U.S. partisanship), she received low artistic impression marks. If, as speculated, artistic impression for women skaters is connected to a particular kind of unthreatening femininity, perhaps the scores were connected to her costume and to gold medalist Katarina Witt's, which made her look "like a member of the Rockette's chorus line" (O'Hara 1988, 49). After this competition, the ISU adopted new rules on costuming which specified that "Costumes for Ladies cannot be theatrical in nature [?!]. They must have skirts . . . covering the hips and posterior. A unitard is not acceptable" (USFSA Rulebook 112). This rule eliminates the most sensible (and unisex) costume available to all skaters, the unitard.

Dick Button, a former Olympic gold medalist who has covered skating for ABC for decades, commented in a 1992 interview about the women's Olympic competition: "The dress helps. The easiest thing is to get here. The hardest is to get that last 1 percent. You can't have anything out of place. Tonya Harding's dresses don't help" (*New York Times* 1992, B13). Harding's 1992 Olympic costumes, although they had the ubiquitous short skirt and a cutout back, were also high necked with shoulder pads and a faintly military air about them, the kind of power lines usually reserved for the men (in fact, in 1988, both gold medalist Brian Boitano and silver medalist Brian Orser wore outfits with military shoulders and trim). At the 1992 World Championships which followed the Olympics, Harding had softened both her music and the lines of her costume for her short program: Her artistic impression scores went up.

Women find their greatest popular acceptance in sports that are considered "feminine" and then are denigrated as lesser athletes. Nancy Kerrigan, according to numerous print and television profiles of her family, wanted to play ice hockey like her older brothers. But there were no teams for girls and her parents "felt figure skating would be more appropriate": "You're a girl. Do girl things," her mother recalled telling her (CBS, February 29, 1992). Women are ghettoized into certain sports, then the sports are seen as less serious because mostly women participate in them. The coverage of the sports identifies the competitors as women first and then

212

athletes. When Nancy Kerrigan took to the ice to skate her free program at the 1992 U.S. Nationals, Dick Button said, "Doesn't she look elegant," and Peggy Fleming agreed, "She looks like a little angel," thereby framing her program not as the competition of a serious athlete, but as the display of a beautiful woman. Verne Lundquist, commentator for CBS coverage of the Olympics, said of Kerrigan, "She has such an elegant presence . . . and then to skate that well," as if the beauty were natural and the skating skill an unexpected surprise in an Olympic athlete. An interview in *Gentlemen's Quarterly* with two-time Olympic gold medalist Katarina Witt pointed out this practice (even as it presented Witt in a centerfoldlike pose): "Coverage of the 1988 Winter Olympics at times degenerated into an overheated symposium on Katarina's sex appeal—from the shape of her legs to the lush arrangement of other body parts, most notably those that Katarina refers to matter-of-factly as her boobs and her butt" (Cook 1991, 130).

Witt may be able to laugh at her objectification. In fact, she has laughed all the way to the bank, with several highly lucrative commercial endorsements, ice shows, and TV sports commentary jobs. But the message that women, no matter how accomplished, will always also have to live up to highly unrealistic standards of physical beauty, harms women and girls far from the spotlight of the Olympic winner's circle. An article in *People* magazine dropped the comment that 1992 Russian pairs champion Natalia Mishkutenok looked a little "chunky"; the following week *People* ran a cover story bemoaning the tragedy of a young TV star who, after years of being the butt of fat jokes in the context of the show, now suffers from anorexia. Somehow, they seemed to have missed the connection. Objectification is about power.

> [T]he female athlete is rendered a sex *object*—a body which may excel in sport, but which is primarily an object of pleasure for men. A useful technique, for if a woman seems to be encroaching too far, and too threateningly, into male sanctuaries, she can be symbolically vapourised and reconstituted as an object, a butt for smutty jokes and complacent elbow nudging. (Willis 1982, 122)

Although the coverage of the 1992 Olympics seemed to tend closer to the worshipful than the smutty, the latter is hardly unknown in skating:

"In Europe, anyway, by far the most popular photograph of any skater in recent years is not of anybody jumping, but of Witt coming completely out of the top of her outfit after a simple spin" (Deford 1992, 50). In 1994, the frequent reiterations of the story of Harding's costume coming undone, combined with tabloid broadcasts of Harding stripping out of her wedding dress at a party on home video served as signs of her "sluttishness" and sloppiness.

In a lecture on sports photography, University of Washington professor Diane Hagaman emphasized the need for sports photos to be a "good quick read . . . eyecatching . . . able to entice readers to read the text" (1992). They must also reinforce the image conveyed by the text, be it winning or losing, endurance or conflict. Therefore, sports photography depends on "highly conventionalized images" (Hagaman 1992). For example, the narrative surrounding Nancy Kerrigan in 1992 always emphasized her beauty and elegance; she could not step onto the ice without the commentators, male or female, remarking how "lovely-elegant-angelic-sophisticated" she was. Not surprisingly, therefore, many different newspapers and magazines caught her in the same arabesque pose (called a spiral in skating) from the end of her program, one long leg extended out behind her, arm extended out front, a very balletic pose.

Television editing can also manipulate our perception and lend credence to narrative. An impression of speed and choppiness can be emphasized by use of cuts, which instantaneously switch from one shot to another, while flow and grace can be emphasized by use of dissolves, which gradually replace one shot with another. Kerrigan's 1992 Olympic long program was broadcast with nine dissolves and eight cuts; in contrast, the program of French skater Surya Bonaly, a former gymnast who is commonly described as a choppy skater and dynamic jumper, had only four dissolves to thirteen cuts. Hagaman, who was looking at particular gestures representing victory, defeat, injury, and endurance in sports photography did not observe gender differences in these particular gestures. But in figure skating, despite the similarity in skills performed, certain poses and gestures are gendered female. The most obvious is the forward layback spin, a move meant to show the flexibility of female skaters. Back arched, eyes closed, mouth slightly open, arms extended as for an embrace—in still photographs it looks like nothing so much as popular conceptions of female sexual climax. The same pose is often used in fashion photography or "beauty pornography," as described by Naomi Wolf. "Beauty pornography looks like this: The perfected woman lies . . . pressing down her pelvis. Her back arches, her mouth is open, her eyes shut . . . the position is female superior, the state of arousal, the plateau phase just preceding orgasm" (1991, 132). In figure skating a layback spin is a requirement in the women's original program; men rarely perform this skill. There were more pictures of Yamaguchi in this position than in any other in 1992. The repetition of this image presents a disturbing convergence of racist and sexist images, playing into stereotypes of the sexually submissive Asian beauty. The virginal, elegant Kerrigan, in contrast, is rarely represented this way. In my review of two years worth of skating articles in newpapers and magazines leading up to the 1992 Olympic games, I never saw one photograph of Kerrigan in this pose, although all the other top skaters (Harding, Ito, and Bonaly) were pictured this way at least twice. The notable exception was the picture of Kerrigan which was a prominent part of the cover montage for "*Life* Remembers '92" (1993a). An irate reader wrote in response to that cover, "Did you guys forget Kristi Yamaguchi was the gold medal winner for the U.S.A.? 'Racist' is a very harsh word, but I can't think of any other word to explain this inexcusable slight." The editors replied, "All the cover images were chosen for their complementary shape, composition, and perspective" (1993b, 30). My research indicates that *Life* would have had to pass over many representations of Yamaguchi in a layback spin in order to put an atypical Kerrigan photo on its cover.

It is not only the narrative surrounding skating which favors "feminine ladies." The rules and judging are also skewed to reward such skaters. Skating is judged in two categories, technical merit and artistic impression. A maximum technical merit score is predetermined by the difficulty of the program, and then deductions are made for each error. There is a range of possible deductions, making the technical merit score far from objective. By far the most straightforward part of the program to judge is the jumps, because the order of difficulty is agreed upon and the success or failure of a jump is usually obvious. In the original program, for which the requirements are set, the men are expected to do at least two and perhaps three triple jumps, while the women are only *allowed* to do one triple jump.[2] This requirement reduces the most objective end of the scoring—how difficult was the jump and was it landed cleanly—and gives far more emphasis to the more subjective areas of judgment that fall under "technical merit," along with the already nebulous category of "artistic impression."

The 1992 Olympic competition was filled with soul-searching debate over the direction the sport was going: Would it lose all its artistic beauty and become just a "jump-fest"? The Yamaguchi gold and Kerrigan bronze were hailed by many commentators and sportswriters as a clear victory for artistry over athleticism (see Deford and Starr 1992); this debate undercut the athletic abilities of "artistic" skaters. "Although figure skaters train hard, they are schooled to make the difficult look easy. . . . [They are] 'athlete[s] in disguise' who [skate], with unimpaired femininity, into hearts closed" to less feminine athletes (Guttman 1991, 200–201). Few athletes were more skillful at disguising their athleticism than Yamaguchi, whose jumps at the 1992 Nationals were described as "beautiful, effortless, soft. . . . She does indeed float like a leaf" (ABC, January 12, 1992). Katarina Witt said Yamaguchi "represents the sport in the right way. Because it's figure skating and it's not only sport, there's a big part of artistry involved. And her jumps look just so effortless, so easy and they're still so difficult" (CBS, February 19, 1992).

Kerrigan is another athlete who has managed to make the signs of her athleticism all but invisible. None of the stereotypical signs of the athlete—grunting, sweating, bulging muscles—ever seemed to disrupt the ladylike Kerrigan package. She was known not for her strong jumps (although, in fact, she is quite a strong jumper), but for her elegance and her line. In contrast, Harding, with her huge jumps, speed, and muscular body was aggressively athletic. Her incompetence as a woman, whether it was her choice of costumes, her hobbies (shooting pool, hunting, fixing cars, and drag racing), or her controversial behavior (firing coaches, her rocky marriage, fighting with a fellow motorist on a Portand street) marked her as deviant. Because she was such a strong jumper, she threatened the very notions of sexual difference which to a large extent define masculinity. This "deviance" reduced her value as a television entertainer and commercial spokeswoman long before she was connected to the Kerrigan attack.

What is always close to the surface, but rarely acknowledged, in the narrative of the artistry vs. athleticism debate is that for the women, artistry is indistinguishable from physical beauty. Japan's Midori Ito came the closest to expressing this when she explained why she relied on her athleticism over artistry: "All I can really do is jump. Figure skating is a matter of beauty, and Westerners are so stylish, so slender. I wish I could be beautiful like them" (in Deford 1992, 51). According to a report in *USA Today*, compiled from interviews with coaches and various books on skating techniques, Ito had the ideal body for figure skating: "a compact body with a low center of gravity" (*USA Today* 1992, 10). It did not question this apparent contradiction, but assumed that because she was not "beautiful" she could not be artistic. As Willis said about interviews with female weight-lifters, "the (at least reported) responses of the women . . . either collude in the sexualisation of the topic or reinforce the standards of male comparison" (131).

Why are artistry and athleticism considered mutually exclusive in ladies figure skating? A baseball player can be called poetry in motion; the balletic grace of Michael Jordan's jumps was admired without implying that he was less of an athlete. Comments on male skaters make it clear that the younger skaters are expected to grow into their artistry—which is related to elegance, showmanship, playing the audience, and choreographic maturity—and become "complete" skaters.[3] Yamaguchi, on the other hand, grew into her artistry and, according to many, out of her athleticism. "Poor Yamaguchi. Paradoxically, in the past, she had always been labeled 'the athlete' in comparison to the artistic Jill Trenary. . . . Then suddenly Yamaguchi found herself written off as some kind of a bush leaguer just because she couldn't hit the triple Axel; never mind she can land all the other triples extant" (Deford 1992, 47, 50). Only Ito and Harding among the women have completed the triple Axel in competition. Although most of the top men had incorporated the triple Axel into their programs by the early 1990s; those who had not, such as Christopher Bowman (who won the 1992 U.S. Nationals without a triple Axel), and 1992 Olympic bronze medalist Peter Barna, were not considered nonathletes, simply less advanced. There were no reporters worrying over the future of the men's competition because some athletes were acquiring new skills. In fact, the idea of a man being called "too athletic" is simply ludicrous.

A woman's athleticism is belittled, often undercut in commentary which calls attention away from her athletic ability and right back to her physical appearance. After Kerrigan completed a complicated triple-double combination in 1992, Scott Hamilton commented, "Perfectly done!" and Verne Lundquist chimed in, "That brings a radiant smile from the lovely lady." After Yamaguchi's double Axel, Hamilton said, "Look at the height and flow," and Lundquist added, "And then look at the smile." Says Brownmiller: "A major purpose of femininity is to mystify or minimize the functional aspects of a woman's mind and body that are indistinguishable from a man's" (1984, 84). Yamaguchi's coach, Christy Ness, complained about her athlete not being taken seriously: "Kristi doesn't lift weights to be called fluff" (in Swift 1992b, 19); yet her weight-lifting was treated with fluffy, patronizing humor. *Sports Illustrated* reported that she had begun to lift "(very, very small) weights" to increase her strength (Swift 1991, 18); while a TNT reporter joked that after getting off practice Kristi thought about "things girls think about—weights!" as if a world class athlete lifting weights was the most unexpectedly comical thing he had ever encountered (TNT, February 20, 1992). "Frequently, reporting of women's sport takes its fundamental bearings, not on sport, but on humour, or the unusual. The tone is easy to recognise, it's a version of the irony, the humour, the superiority, of the sophisticated towards the cranks" (Willis 1982, 121).

Newsweek presented its version of the athlete vs. artist debate as a fairy tale, with an insidious, antifeminist moral:

> Surely, there must be a fairy tale that fits here. . . . It'd be the one about the two stylish gorgeous creatures—swans or butterflies, take your pick—competing against the stronger, more daring beings for the favor of the gods. And, of course, the stronger, more daring beings are certain to win, because spectacular is always better ever after. Only, the stronger, more daring beings reach for too high a sky . . . and so the stylish gorgeous creatures glide to victory—and, probably, here comes a handsome prince or two, as well. . . . Oh, truth be told, it wasn't all that neat. The athletes weren't quite that klutzy, and the

artists weren't quite that wimpy, but let's not louse up a good fairy tale. (Deford and Starr 1992, 50)

In fact, one of those "daring beings," Midori Ito, took the almost unheard of risk of adding a triple Axel late in her long program after she had missed it twice in the competition; her daring was rewarded when she vaulted over Kerrigan to win the silver medal. But "let's not louse up a good fairy tale" with the facts. The moral that America seems most comfortable with is that "ladies" will be rewarded for being "stylish and gorgeous" and punished for being too daring. *Sports Illustrated* had a different take on the same event: "This was a competition incorrectly billed as the athletes vs. the artists. . . . Yamaguchi and Kerrigan were plenty athletic. They were just minus one jump: the triple Axel" (Swift 1992b, 19). The athlete vs. artist dichotomy was even clearer in the 1988 competition, where preview articles such as one in *Time* magazine set up the competition between Debi Thomas and Katarina Witt as "steely resolve" vs. "stylish allure," with accompanying pictures showing the former lifting weights and consulting with her coach, while the latter flirted with the judges and pouted at the camera (*Time* 1988, 44–46).

"I always tell my girls: think like a man, but act and look like a woman," says former skater turned coach Carol Heiss (in Deford 1992, 6). What does it mean to "think like a man?" Men are supposed to be competitive, focused, and ambitious. They can even be cocky, if they have the skill to back it up—witness the popularity of Charles Barkley and Andre Agassi. Proper masculinity is by definition ambitious and competitive: Canadian skater Kurt Browning had a "job to do," which was winning the gold medal, while of Kristi Yamaguchi it was said, "she would skate even if they didn't give out medals." He was lionized for being a "big game" skater (although, in fact, he did not skate his best at either the 1992 or 1994 Olympics); she was patted on the head for being very steady, consistent. She was allowed ambitions as long as they were couched in terms of little girl dreams, creating a continuity with past champions such as 1976 gold medalist Dorothy Hamill. This connection was made by television interviewers who asked Yamaguchi, "Have you been dreaming of this moment?" and by television visuals which caught Yamaguchi talking to Hamill backstage before her free skate. It all seemed to lend credence to the "A dream is a wish your heart makes" framing device of the 1992 U.S. National Championships that I described above. To win the men's final, a competitor would need "all the ammunition you can fire" (CBS, February 15, 1992), while Ito, the "Queen of the triple jumps" was going to have to be "on her toes" to win (February 19, 1992).

The emotions that make for a good competitor do not necessarily fit those that make for a feminine woman. Kerrigan's monumental success in the endorsement game, which dates back to before the attack, was always based more on her ladylike demeanor than on her prowess as an athlete. She was admired as a genuine girl who, her father said, has "got all the emotions of anybody. If she's watching TV and something is sad she'll cry, if it's laughter she'll laugh" (CBS, February 19, 1992). This image of Kerrigan was contrasted to that of the poised (read inscrutable?) Yamaguchi. Women aren't supposed to have the nerves and ambition to compete. TV is always searching for signs of women's instability, sure that they are always about to crack under the pressure. The framing device for the 1992 Olympic pairs final focused exclusively on the women, with the implication that the men were a given, stable and solid as rocks:

It's a tale of two women [close-up of Natalia Mishkutenok]. One who has always exemplified grace under pressure [tape showing Mishkutenok lifted, spread-eagled, above her partner's head]. And one who wants so much to win it's sometimes gotten the best of her [close-up of Yelena Bechke looking up into her partner's eyes]—until it was the Olympic games [Bechke receiving a kiss from her partner after a successful original program]. . . . It's also the story of another woman who flew so high [Isabelle Bresseur being thrown by her partner], but couldn't land [Bresseur falling on her double Axel, then a cut to Bresseur backstage in tears]. Three different women, who with their partners tonight share one common purpose. (CBS, February 11, 1992)

Coverage of women skaters always seems to emphasize women's vulnerability, both emotional and physical, rather than their strength and accomplishments. This vulnerability was one of the most common descriptions of Nancy Kerrigan even before the attack that cast her as the nation's number one victim of greed-motivated violence. Along with a reputation for elegance and niceness, Kerrigan built a reputation for crumbling under pressure. At the 1992 Olympics, "Kerrigan . . . botched her long program . . . , gasping for air and nearly crying afterward" (Deford and Starr 52). She dropped from second to third and held on to the bronze only because the other top competitors also fell. The same was true of her silver at the 1992 Worlds and even her performance when she won the 1993 U.S. Nationals. Although this did not win her much respect as an athlete—after the 1993 Worlds, Filip Bondy, writing in the *New York Times*, said flatly, "Kerrigan has not come up big in the long program at a major competition since the Nationals in 1991, and she fell apart again today" (1993a, 6)—it did not seem to affect her marketability. In fact, her vulnerability may have made her more appealingly feminine and less threatening. After the January 1994 attack, Kerrigan and her public relations people seemed to have borrowed a page from Tonya Harding's press book, describing her as "tougher" than people gave her credit for. About two weeks after the attack, Kerrigan's coach Evy Scotvold was quoted as saying, "since the incident, she has become a different cat. She has a different look in her eyes—a peaceful determination with the confidence of a gunslinger" (Hersh 1994).

I find Frigga Haug's notion of "slavegirl competence" a useful framework for thinking of the way in which women both use and are victimized by the figure skating system. It "allows us both to grasp the relation of structural domination within which femininity is subordinated to masculinity, and at the same time to portray women as active, albeit in the context of given constraints" (Haug 1987, 131).

> Women are made both supplementary and subordinate to men, they are abused as objects of sex and pleasure. . . . Yet women also know from their experience that skill is involved in conforming to prevailing rules and orderings. Among other things, we take pleasure in acquiring and endorsing the requisite skills.
>
> Our active appropriation of the rules makes us more self-confident in our activities; in availing ourselves of the existing order by actively "exhibiting" our own bodies, we participate in our own construction as slavegirls. (Haug 1987, 144)

During the 1992 Olympic coverage, there was one interview with Yamaguchi while she was being fitted by her costume designer. She stood in
a red body suit while another woman measured and pinned her, saying:
"I think it's important to create the entire mood of the program. . . .
People come to watch you because, you know, it's supposed to be a beautiful sport and the costumes are just part of it" (CBS, February 21, 1992).
She was actively participating in her own construction as a passive object
of beauty. Yamaguchi's original program, much praised for the beauty of
its choreography, was described by her choreographer Sandra Bezic as the
moment when a girl looks in the mirror and realizes she's a beautiful
woman. The beauty of Yamaguchi's program played into popular concepts
of what Brownmiller describes as "preoccupied gestures that are considered sublimely feminine because they are sensuously self-involved" (1984,
73). This sensuous self-involvement was admired by Martha Duffy in an
article in *Time*:

> They are at their most beautiful, these rarefied athletes, in the six-
> minute practice session where competitors warm up, a few at a time.
> Done by a Kerrigan, the waltz jump, a mere half revolution, is a
> perfection of grace. A double Axel is clear and open, not the
> whipped-up whir a triple must be. Yamaguchi and Harding may land
> perfect leaps in tandem. . . . All the women are intently absorbed,
> and their jumps look less like stunts than whitecaps bubbling out of
> waves. (1992a, 56)

The model of the "slavegirl" is especially useful when thinking about
Kerrigan. During the 1993 Worlds, before Kerrigan skated her long program, NBC broadcast a piece on how her life had been changed by the
pressures of fame. The theme was "everyone wants a piece of her." Her
mother commented, "It's almost too much. Every once in a while she
becomes emotional. And then she'll cry, like, 'I just can't do this, I just
can't do any more. All I want to do is skate.' " It was as if she had no
choice when it came to signing contracts, filming commercials, and posing
for magazine spreads. The NBC report on the pressures of fame included
tape of Kerrigan being prepared for filming. She wore a white flowing
dress and long loose hair, but she was harnessed, so that she could be

flown in front of a backdrop of a gorgeous sky. The illusion constructed was that she was flying when, in fact, she was restrained. This was Nancy Kerrigan as the perfect slavegirl: soaring success, completely confined.

Another way in which the figure skating coverage emphasized the femininity of its ladies was by constantly defining them in the context of their families, either their biological families or their skating family. Biographical sketches of each of the three 1992 U.S. Olympians contrasted the three as being from different worlds, but the story worked like the classic family picture: Kristi Yamaguchi as first-born, businesslike, an overachiever, out on her own—the bio featured shots of Yamaguchi in her work environment and with her coaches. By foregrounding Yamaguchi's move to Canada to train, television was able to portray her as an outsider without ever referring to her race. Tonya Harding was the troubled middle child, firing and rehiring her coach, referring to her coach as her "employee," breaking up and reuniting with her husband, all evidence of a lack of values in the skating world; rebellious and unconventional, she was shown behind the wheel of a truck. Kerrigan (although actually the oldest of the three at twenty-two) was the much-beloved baby of both this skating family and of her biological family in Massachusetts, with whom she was shown in happy domestic settings, ending at the dinner table toasting with milk (you could almost hear the dairy industry chortling with glee).[4] In subsequent newspaper and television coverage, these themes were picked up again and again: stories about Yamaguchi emphasizing her wonderful working relationship with her coach and choreographer, her poise, her consistency ("Kristi's greatest strength is her lack of weaknesses," said Scott Hamilton before her original program); stories about Harding emphasizing her personal troubles, her foolish stubbornness; and stories about Kerrigan always emphasizing her family, especially her "mother and best friend Brenda [who] is legally blind" (ABC, January 12, 1992), an appealing human-interest story that TV milked for all it was worth.

Kerrigan's family was the most overplayed at the 1992 Olympics, but hers certainly wasn't the only family put on display. Families are big in Olympic coverage. Families sell. The U.S. Postal Service brought over a number of athletes' families to see the games in exchange for product endorsements. "Pride and profit, that's why we're in it," said Postmaster

General Anthony Frank (CBS, February 19, 1992). The commercial appeal of family is linked to the commercial appeal of femininity. Before the pairs were to free skate, Charles Kuralt and Scott Hamilton did a special on the mothers in the stands—but only the mothers of the women. Said Hamilton, "Especially for the women in the pairs team the mother must really go through a lot because of the danger involved. . . . If I was a mother of a child and my little girl was out there and somebody dropped her . . ." (CBS, February 11, 1992). Women skaters are little girls. Kuralt finished up, "Skaters' mothers pull for their children." By only showing the mothers of women skaters, they reinforced the assumption that the women are children.

Of course, this same touching portrayal can take on the ugly stereotype of the stage mother, who Hamilton calls the "nightmare mother . . . [who] thinks they know everything about skating, they know more than any coach. . . . Everybody in the building is against them, everyone hopes their child falls." This seemed to be the case with French skater Surya Bonaly and her mother Suzanne: "the Olympic gold medal . . . is clearly the tangible object of her adoptive mother's desire. . . . With apparent manipulative encouragement from her mother, Bonaly has turned into . . . a chippie . . . the sort of school kid who would pinch the other students or pull their hair" (Hersh 1992b, section 4:2). A woman's success is not her own but a collaborative effort between the skater and her biological family or her surrogate family of coach and choreographer. On the "CBS Morning" program preview of the 1992 Ladies Original Program, Harry Smith asked Kerrigan's parents, "Tell me a little about what it takes to get a daughter on the ice in the Olympics. How much work is it? Dad?" When Daniel Kerrigan would have given all the credit to Nancy—"[It's] all her work. She does it all. . . . She came here on her own"—Smith turned to her mother and persisted: "Doesn't it really take a family commitment, Brenda?"[5] What this coverage never mentioned were those skaters whose families were less than supportive, such as Harding's. Women must be portrayed in relationship; only men can thrive as lone individuals.

And women will be punished for not being good girls. Coverage of Yamaguchi emphasized her steady, professional, but also close and loving working relationship with her choreographer and coach: "Says U.S. coach Don Laws: 'Kristi has the ideal temperament for a skater. She trusts her coach, her parents, and her program'" (Duffy 1992b, 49). Coverage of Kerrigan made her the perfect loving, obedient daughter and best friend of her blind mother. Harding was portrayed as recalcitrant and head-strong; she publicly regarded her coach as an employee rather than as a surrogate parent or friend and she was "rightfully" punished for not "honoring her mother":

> Harding's fourth-place finish in France was not surprising, given how erratically she had trained and her strong-willed decision to defy jet lag and travel fatigue by leaving Portland only three days before the competition began. . . . Teachman [her fired coach] said "I'm looking forward to working with other skaters who are hard workers, respectful of their coaches and are a joy to work with. I wish Tonya and her new 'employee' all the best." (Hersh 1992a, section 3:2)

Many sports writers who normally cover men's sports are dismissive of figure skating. But Harding was different and therefore, for a while at least, admired. She was called "dynamo," a "blond hotspur," "the gallant asthmatic" who had been through so much, who would never give up, and (my personal favorite) "the tough little American buzz-bomb" (Vec-sey 1992) These writers could barely contain their excitement in 1991, when Harding won the National Championship:

> In one energized four-minute free skating program, Harding leapt from nowhere into history as she became the first American woman to land a triple Axel in competition . . . Forty-five seconds into her routine, Harding stroked the length of the ice, coiled and sprang to an improbable height. Her ponytail became a blur as she spun. Upon landing, she cried out, "Yes!" The crowd, recognizing history in this 5'1", 105-pound package of fist-clenching grit, roared. (Swift 1991, 19)

In her only major national commercial, which ran extensively in 1992, Harding skated in an ad for Texaco as a demonstration of the company's "boundless energy." *New York Times* columnist George Vecsey used his admiration of Harding as a backdoor way of insulting skater Todd El-dredge. Eldredge did not choose to compete in the 1992 U.S. Nationals because of a back injury, but was named to the Olympic team anyway because he was the world bronze medalist; Harding, who was also injured, chose to compete, although as the world silver medalist she also would have been given a spot. "She did not get this far by being afraid of falling. Harding did not want to qualify for the Winter Games by the whim of a committee. Drag racers don't do it that way." The obvious implication was that Harding was more macho than Eldredge.

Harding's reputation for athletic prowess survived the attack on Kerrigan somewhat intact. What may surprise readers far more in retrospect is how many writers in 1991–92 described Harding as a refreshingly unaffected presence in the figure skating world, even an innocent. Janofsky admiringly described Harding playing pool in a bar after she won the 1991 National Championship "[w]hile hundreds of everybodys-who-are-anybodys in skating were in the hotel's ballroom attending a huge party."

In a world of lavish costumes, haunting music, and obsessive discipline, where millions of dollars await the very best the sport can produce, Harding seems to be an anomaly, a baby-faced, twenty-year-old skater either unfamiliar with or unready for what lies beyond the moment. "She doesn't even have an agent," said a woman associated with a production company based in New York, her tone one of astonishment.

In 1992 Swift catalogued Harding's hard-knock life—which up until then had been virtually unknown and even after this article was rarely mentioned before the Kerrigan attack—and looked for the fairy tale ending:

> Lord knows she's trying. Problem is, when life has been dealing you cards from the bottom of the deck for most of your twenty-one years, the aces and jacks all start to look marked, and it's kind of hard to trust the dealer. Even after winning a couple of hands.
>
> But Tonya Harding, the reigning U.S. women's figure skating champion, is trying . . . Trying to fulfill a preposterous childhood dream in which a hardscrabble, dispossessed kid from Portland, Ore., hoists herself above a troubled past and wins the most refined gold medal of the Olympic Games—the women's figure skating title—propelling her toward a happily-ever-after she has never known.

It could happen, and wouldn't it be rich if it did? An ice princess who has her own pool cue . . . an interloper in the realm of pixies and queens who's as at home doing a brake job as she is performing an arabesque. Aspirant to the throne of some of the most elegant women in the sport . . . who can curse like a sailor, bench-presses more than her weight and drag races in the summer for kicks.

Harding shatters all stereotypes of the pampered and sheltered figure skater who has spent his or her youth bottled in an ice rink, training. At twenty-one, she has seen a lot of life, and she is unapologetic if the experience has left her just a little rough around the edges. (1992, 54–55)

Harding's rough edges were admired when she was at the height of her success; later these same qualities would be identified as the cause of her downfall. For a woman, strong-willed behavior is obviously wrong, and punishment is the "not surprising" outcome. Long before she became connected with any criminal behavior, Harding's rebellion was contained in the moral of her "punishment," her fourth-place finish in 1992; in contrast, quite similar erratic relationships with various coaches by U.S. skater Christopher Bowman (and more serious allegations of illegal drug use) were treated, at least among TV commentators, as just a part of his unconventional personality. Bowman laughed at his own bad boy reputation, nicknaming himself "Hans Brinker from Hell" and skating in exhibition to Buster Poindexter's "I'm Just a Bad Boy," mugging for the cameras with a showmanship that commentators treated with slightly exasperated but affectionate amusement.

Similar showmanship nearly led to an international incident when French skater Surya Bonaly performed a back-flip during warm-ups the morning of the 1992 Olympic original program. She was castigated on television and in the press for intimidating poor Midori Ito—"an illegal trick," all gasped with horror. "Intimidation," they murmured. "What are the ethics involved?" asked Tim McCarver. "I was a little shocked. . . . I heard that Surya Bonaly did this already the third time this week," reported Witt (somewhat disingenuously, as she was herself legendary for her ability to intimidate competitors during warm-ups). It was only added as an afterthought that Bonaly always does a back-flip during her warmup, that although it is illegal in competition, it is a popular part of her exhibition routines, that as the local favorite in France she was naturally playing to the crowd, and that when she heard that she might have distracted Ito, she apologized. Her "active flamboyance" did not win over the press. In contrast, Ito won widespread sympathy on American television when she apologized to her whole country for falling during her ladies original program. American audiences could both admire her humble shyness and implicitly bash the Japanese for putting so much pressure on such a sweet girl. It was almost as if Ito was a poor child being held hostage by the power- and glory-hungry Japanese. Coverage of Ito's slip under pressure was handled much more sympathetically in the U.S. press than Harding's.

In large measure, the Olympics are an audition for future commercial endorsements. One of the many ironies of being a successful woman athlete is that the most marketable and potentially lucrative images are those that are farthest removed in the public's mind from associations with filthy money. In 1994, Tonya Harding was repeatedly chastised for saying she had dollar signs in her eyes; meanwhile, Kerrigan flew to California in the middle of her rehabilitation to film a Reebok commercial. Harding was condemned as a hotdog seeking the limelight, while Kerrigan was given sympathy because no one would leave her alone, despite the fact that Kerrigan was being paid by Seiko and Reebok to wear their products to each excessively photographed press briefing and Olympic practice. Kerrigan signed a multi-million dollar deal with Disney before the competition began and was featured in not one but three commercials which aired during the finals, adding yet another nail to the coffin of the concept of the Olympics as an "amateur" competition.

If Kerrigan and her agents took great advantage of her image as gallant lady athlete up until the Olympics, the post-Olympic backlash demonstrated how frail that image was. Beginning with her impatience before the medal ceremony, when she misinterpreted the delay in locating the Ukrainian national anthem as gold medalist Oksana Baiul redoing her makeup and snapped, "Oh, give me a break, she's just going to cry out there again. What's the difference?" to her endless comments of "I was perfect" in interviews about the competition to her "this is so corny" remark during the Disney parade in her honor, Kerrigan displayed an awkward streak that sent her image plummeting in the week following the competition. Her critics felt that she should have taken her money and shut her mouth; the "brutal attack" of January was now a "whack on the knee."

Arguing referree calls is a respected skill in Major League Baseball, and post-game criticism of the officiating is accepted practice in the NBA. But being scrappy and pugnacious is one acceptable model of masculinity to which "ladies" do not have access. Allen Guttman writing on the history of women in sports noted that "advertisements are here to stay and that most advertisements will use physically attractive rather than unattractive models" (1991, 263), ignoring the fact that advertisements not only reward but also determine what is attractive in our society. Frank Deford, in his preview of the 1992 games, predicted the possibility that a Yamaguchi win would touch off feelings of racism: "And now: what's a good ole boy to do if there's not only a Toyota in the driveway and a Sony in the bedroom and a Mitsubishi in the family room—but on the screen there, as the band plays the 'Star-Spangled Banner,' is the All-American girl of 1992, and her name is Yamaguchi?" (1992, 53). An article in *Business Week* after the Olympics stated that Yamaguchi was not getting the offers a white champion would have gotten ("The environment to 'max out' on her earning potential is not enhanced by the present mood of the country toward Japan," said one agent [1992, 40]). Subsequently, Yamaguchi's agent denied the story, telling reporters that they simply had no time to sort through offers.

Yamaguchi has appeared on boxes of Kellogg's Special K, a cereal marketed to dieters. Several months after the Olympics, E. M. Swift wrote in *Sports Illustrated*, "Post-Olympic endorsements were down for all athletes in 1992, probably due to the sluggish economy. Still, Yamaguchi did pretty well. She signed lucrative deals with Hoechst Celanese Corporation, which makes acetate fabric for fashion designers, and DuraSoft contact lenses" (Swift 1992b, 75). Yamaguchi's television commercial for DuraSoft was especially interesting. She tells us that ever since the Olympics, people have been encouraging her to change. A series of comic vignettes follows, with Kristi taking up tennis and hosting a talk show. But when she really wants to change, she goes "blue, green, violet": in other words she changes the color of her eyes, changes them to colors an Asian woman would not normally have.

Post–1992-Olympic endorsements may have been down, but not for bronze medalist Nancy Kerrigan. Long before the attack which made her a household name, Kerrigan had been tagged by Campbell's Soup, Seiko, Reebok, Northwest Airlines, and Xerox to tout their products. Campbell's cited Kerrigan's "all-American charm and her grace and beauty on the ice," (Reisfeld 91) (all-American as opposed to Japanese American?). In naming Kerrigan one of the "50 Most Beautiful People in the World" in 1993, *People* magazine wrote, "Kristi Yamaguchi may have won the Olympic gold last year, but bronze-medal winner Nancy Kerrigan got the gasps for her Grace Kelly gleam." The article also confirmed that Kerrigan had six-figure endorsement contracts (1993, 138). She was labeled the "Irish Katarina Witt" during the 1992 Olympics. Witt was then Diet Coke's poster girl, and Diet Coke–NutraSweet was a major sponsor of ladies figure skating. Kerrigan was the only 1992 Olympic skater to have a prior commercial relationship with Coke, having done a Coke Classic commercial in 1988 (playing the character of a Russian skater, not herself). Because of these circumstances, I was not surprised that the coverage of the Nationals and the Olympics focused on Kerrigan to a degree that might have seemed out of proportion to her chances of winning a gold medal.

What are the images of femininity we are presenting for young girls to emulate and for young boys to expect of women? What does it do to a girl's self-image when she is told that Midori Ito, Tonya Harding, or Debi Thomas are not beautiful enough, that Natalia Mishkutonek is chunky? Such rhetoric extends to sports other than figure skating. Speed skating gold medalist Bonnie Blair was shown a few mornings after she finished competing in 1992 being "made over." Her "wholesome image and nice smile" made her attractive as a possible product pitcher, but only with a "new do" and makeup, only when she could conform as closely as possible to societal norms of beauty. The female newscaster reporting the story observed, "I'm not sure if she liked that makeover" (CBS, February 19, 1992). But like it or not, there she was, reassuring the public that despite her lightning speed, she's still "just a girl." The metaphor that Greg Faller uses to describe romance could also apply to commercial endorsement:

The promise of romantic union [or commercial success?] works like the three golden apples Melanion rolled in front of Atalanta. They will be seduced from their position of culturally unacceptable power and dominance in a masculine pastime to a culturally demanded position of submissive femininity within the patriarchal family. (1987, 157)

Notes

1. This is the same writer who wrote a subsequent column disguised as his own brother because he was so embarrassed that most of America's 1992 medals had been won by women.

2. Rules applicable as of the original publication date of this article.

3. This is not to say that the male skaters completely escape the stigma of being involved in a "feminized sport." In his autobiography, four-time world champion Kurt Browning felt the need to write, "Let me just say, 'I like girls.' " Pairs skater Rocky Marval's mother said in an interview, "It was hard to accept a figure skater which is of course known for tutus and ballet."

4. In hindsight, the author proved less than precient in this remark: when the dairy industry began its highly successful milk mustache campaign, Yamaguchi was one of the first subjects (the campaign began in November 1994; Yamaguchi was photographed in January 1995). The ad fits nicely into the construction of Yamaguchi as sexual object. She is photographed wearing white skates, a sleeveless dark leotard and sheer dark stockings, bent over from the waist so that her face is in the lower left corner, on level with her skates and her buttocks are in the upper right. Although the ad agency says they chose this pose in response to the "challenge" of "show[ing] someone from head to toe, er . . . head to skates, and still be close enough to see her face" (Schulberg et al. 22), the layout and lighting make Yamaguchi's buttock and hip much more prominent than her face. (Ironically, in the introduction to *The Milk Mustache Book*, the Yamaguchi shot is reproduced in the margin of a page to the left of the sub-head "A Face That Makes You Smile"; because of its layout, Yamaguchi's backside is closer to the subhead than her face.)

5. Men's parents are mentioned sometimes, but rarely is a man's success attributed to his parents. One Russion skater was said to be supporting his mother and grandmother on his small stipend. Hamilton gave a eulogy for his mother, who died of cancer before he won his Olympic medal, describing her as "perfect." But her perfection seemed to lie not in active influence, but in unquestioning support: "She always let me be me" (CBS, February 11, 1992).

References

Bondy, F. (1993, March 14). Ukraine's rising star sets worlds ablaze. *New York Times.*
———. (1993a, March 24). Yamaguchi figures: Gold, not gold medals. *New York Times.*
Brownmiller, S. (1984). *Femininity.* New York: Linden Press/Simon & Schuster.
Capozzola, L. (1992, March 2). Photo. *Sports Illustrated, 76,* p. 8.
Cherney, C. (1992, February 20). Photo. *Chicago Tribune.*
Cook, A. (1991, July). Das Kapitalist. *Gentlemen's Quarterly, 61,* p. 7.
Deford, F. (1992, February 10). The jewel of the winter games. *Newsweek.*
Deford, F., & Starr, M. (1992, March 2). American beauty. *Newsweek.*
Duffy, M. (1992, February 10). Spinning gold. *Time, 139,* p. 6.
———. (1992b, March 2). When dreams come true. *Time, 139,* p. 9.
Faller, G. S. (1987). The function of star-image and performance in the Hollywood musical: Sonja Henie, Esther Williams, and Eleanor Powell. Ph.D. dissertation, Northwestern University.
Guttman, A. (1991). *Women's sports: A history.* New York: Columbia University Press.
Hagaman, D. (1992, March 6). The joy of victory, the agony of defeat: Stereotypes in newspaper sports feature photography. CIRA lecture, Northwestern University.
Haug, F., ed. (1987). *Female sexualization: A collective work of memory.* London: Verso.
Hersh, P. (1992, March 8). Adulation on hold for Tonya Harding. *Chicago Tribune.*
———. (1992a, February 21). French flip stirs tempest in figure skating's teapot. *Chicago Tribune.*
———. (1992b, January 20). Coach says Kerrigan way ahead of schedule. *Chicago Tribune.*
Janofsky, M. (1991, February 18). Wearing crown minus the glitz. *New York Times.*
Just this once, Button makes call from couch. (1992, February 21). *New York Times.*
Kolata, G. (1992, February 16). Who is female? Science can't say. *New York Times.*
Life. (1993, January). Cover montage. *16,* 1.
———. (1993, March). Letters to the editor. *16,* 3.
Lincicome, B. (1992, February 20). Here's a sure cure for winter blahs. *Chicago Tribune.*
Louie, E. (1992, Feburary 17). Women's figure skating puts couture on the ice. *New York Times.*
Mackson, R. (1992, March 2). Photo. *Sports Illustrated, 76,* p. 8.
To marketers, Kristi Yamaguchi isn't as good as gold (1992, March 9). *Business Week.* (March 9).
McDermott, B. (1982, January 18). More than a pretty face. *Sports Illustrated, 56,* p. 2.
O'Hara, J. (1988, March 7). Stars in the spotlight. *Maclean's.*
Reisfeld, R. (1994). *The Kerrigan courage: Nancy's story.* New York: Ballantine Books.
Shulberg, J., with B. Hogya & S. Taibi. (1998). *The milk mustache book: A behind-the-scenes look at America's favorite advertising campaign.* New York: Ballantine Books.

Silverman, B. (1992, February 22). Photo. *New York Times*.

Swift, E. M. (1991, February 25). Triple threat. *Sports Illustrated, 74*, p. 7.

———. (1992, January 13). Not your average ice queen: A troubled past hasn't stopped Tonya Harding from becoming a figure skating champion. *Sports Illustrated, 76*.

———. (1992b, March 2). Stirring. *Sports Illustrated, 76*, p. 8.

———. (1992c, December 14). All that glitters. *Sports Illustrated, 77*, p. 25.

Therberge, N. (1981, December). A critique of critiques: Radical and feminist writings on sport. *Social Forces, 60*, p. 2.

USA Today. (1992, January 28). Winter Olympics: Figure skating.

United States Figure Skating Association. (1993). The 1994 official USFSA rulebook. Colorado Springs, Colo.: The United States Figure Skating Association.

Vecsey, G. (1992, January 12). Skating's double standard. *New York Times*.

Whannel, G. (1984). Fields in vision: Sport and representation. *Screen*, p. 25.

Willis, P. (1982). Women in sport in ideology. In J. Hargreaves (ed.), *Sport, culture and ideology*. London: Routledge and Kegan Paul.

Wolf, N. (1991). *The beauty myth: How images of beauty are used against women*. New York: W. Morrow.

Television Coverage

"The Olympic Games" on CBS, February 1992.

"Olympic Highlights" on Turner Network Television, February 1992.

"The 1992 U.S. National Championships" on ABC, January 11, 1992.

"The 1992 World Championships" on ABC, March 29, 1992.

8

SAM STOLOFF

Tonya Harding, Nancy Kerrigan, and the Bodily Figuration of Social Class

● Recollection will sieve the Tonya/Nancy affair until only the large pieces remain—the good girl vs. bad girl confrontation, Kerrigan clutching her knee and howling "Why me?" and Harding frantically fixing her skate lace in the corridor behind the Hamar rink. But how rich in symbolic silt the story was, in pathos and absurdity: Shane Stant crashing through the plexiglass; Eckardt the would-be spook in a trenchcoat, playing his tape recording for a minister classmate in a fit of conscience or bravado; Eckardt's father bragging of his son's exploits to his phone-sex partner; the tale which surfaced of Tonya brandishing a baseball bat at a woman after a traffic mishap; the incriminating napkin discovered in a dumpster outside a Portland restaurant; Tonya's mother singing a maudlin song to "her baby" on *A Current Affair,* and then collapsing on a talk show; the eerie symmetry when Tonya twisted her ankle, as if making a bid for a share of the sympathy Kerrigan had won—and then Oksana Baiul too skating on an injured leg, after she crashed with another skater in practice (Tania Szewczenko of Germany, another Tonya!); Nancy complaining to Mickey Mouse that Disney World was "corny."

This essay originally appeared in *Women on Ice: Feminist Essays on the Tonya Harding/ Nancy Kerrigan Spectacle,* edited by Cynthia Baughman, 225–239. New York and London: Routledge, 1995.

The Tonya Harding/Nancy Kerrigan episode had everything to make it sensational: fascinating characters, personal rivalry, violence, villainy, and buffoonery, intrigue and cover-up, investigative drama, legal strategy, a distinct dramatic climax, sports spectacle, high stakes, and moments of exquisite foolishness. But absorbing as these qualities were, they do not in themselves explain why the episode riveted our attention—why, in fact, the affair assumed the proportions of national myth. Why did it produce such emotional extremes? Why did it inspire expressions of such revulsion and dismay, as well as glee? Why did it become a drama, not merely of personal ambition, but of national corruption and moral ruin?

It will be my argument here that, more than anything else, the episode tapped profound contemporary anxieties about social class in the United States. These anxieties were most discernible in the newspaper and magazine commentary that surrounded the events, spanning the range from sermon to satire. The anxieties focused in particular on Tonya, on her personal history, her persistence, her speech, her habits, her hometown, her friends and husband, and, not least, her body. But these anxieties were rivaled by other emotions, which signaled a different kind of investment in the affair—a pleasure in the up-ending of the outwardly decorous world of figure skating, and in Tonya's brash challenge to the reigning proprieties.

Of course, it's not news that the Tonya/Nancy affair concerned social class; even where class was not an explicit theme of the commentary, it provided a subtext, an allusive ground, or the material for ridicule.[1] Still, as an analytical category, social class suffers from a thorough confusion about its functioning, its significance, and even its existence in the United States, and the Harding/Kerrigan commentary was mired in this confusion. Only occasionally was the centrality of class in the affair directly addressed; for example, writing in *Rolling Stone*, Randall Sullivan argued that class was in fact the basic category for understanding the furor:

Nearer to the heart of the matter was America's profound denial of (and subterranean fascination with) social class. A cultural apparatus that had substituted race for class was engaged in a willful indifference to the millions of fair-skinned Americans who work for a living that is meager at best. Tonya Harding was the skeleton in the country's closet.[2]

Although I am arguing for the priority of class over gender in the way the media constructed the Harding/Kerrigan episode, the two should not really be seen as exclusive categories; rather, it was their entanglement that was one of the affair's most absorbing qualities. The categories were confused, mapped onto one another, reversed and exchanged. Just to cite the most obvious example, Tonya, when placed in juxtaposition to Nancy, was perceived to be rather stocky, therefore unfeminine, therefore low class. All of the epithets used to describe Tonya participated in this slippage: She was a smoker, a pool player, a truck driver, and so on, and all of these terms were markers of both class and gender. However, it's not as simple as saying that the lower term in one binary can be exchanged for the lower term in another, although this certainly happens; femininity, for example, while a signifier of female weakness when opposed to masculinity in men, may function as the higher term in a class binary. In the Tonya/Nancy episode, femininity appeared as an element of figure skating's "classiness," where femininity is signified by graceful motion and certain forms of balletic gesture. Femininity, in this context, reveals itself as a class style—as a signifier of leisure and cultural capital. To the commentators, Tonya revealed her class origin, in part, through her failed attempts at "high-class" femininity.

The axis on which all these terms hinged, in both their gender and their class connotations, was the body.[3] Tonya's apparent density, in opposition to Nancy's slenderness, evoked carnality, and especially a sense of bodily excess, or lack of bodily discipline. In the terms of cultural hierarchy, the controlled body figures the superior position in binarisms of class, gender, and race, while the excessive or uncontrolled body figures the lower position. The deployment of this kind of body imagery in the Tonya/Nancy episode suggested fierce anxieties, particularly on the part of the middle class (represented by most of the mainstream media) which the commentary served to manage.[4] But what we must also not forget is that this same body imagery can convey a very different set of social implications when viewed, not "from above," but "from below." In the remainder of this essay, I will try to sort out some of these competing class readings of the Harding/Kerrigan affair, exploring first the middle-class view, then an alternative view that might be called the carnivalesque, and finally the class configuration of commercial spectator sport, and how Tonya and Nancy adopted roles within that configuration.

White Trash and Blue Collar

The opposition between Tonya and Nancy was frequently construed as a class rivalry.[5] Such commentary focused on the different class cultures from which the two skaters had come: Harding as low-class, defined in terms of cultural attributes, and Kerrigan as her opposite (although what that opposite term consisted of varied). A long litany of vaguely pejorative or mocking expressions were attached to Harding: She was a "tough cookie," "trailer park honey," a "bad girl," "terminally tacky," etc., while Kerrigan was "elegant" and "classy." In fact, although some writers acknowledged that Harding and Kerrigan were both "daughters of the working class,"[6] much more attention was focused on Harding's class than on Kerrigan's. Harding was from a class culture which required explication, while Kerrigan seemed to come from a culture more familiar to the imagination of the middle class. Both as an object of scorn and of fascination, Harding was the stronger emotional pole in the drama, because, for the middle class, she represented the class Other.

For the middle-class commentators, the land from which Harding came was paradoxically both familiar and strange. It could be dismissed with the flick of a stereotype ("trailer park," "K-Mart"), but it was also *terra incognita*, requiring the services of an interpreter. There was, for example, Susan Orlean's essay in the *New Yorker*, which explored Clackamas County, Oregon, with the following lead: "People who say that Tonya Harding lives in Portland have missed the point. She comes from a place that's tougher and more intractable."[7] The essay's tone was distinctly anthropological, as it described the physical geography of Clackamas in dismal colors. At the margins of the article were advertisements for Italian vacation homes and "country club living in Santa Fe," the more familiar habitats of *New Yorker* readers.

Descriptions of Tonya relied heavily on the bodily register to figure such class categories, dwelling on the ways in which Harding satisfied the stereotypes of the undisciplined lower classes, their lack of bodily containment and control. Consider, for example, the matter of the asthma inhaler. The image of a breathless Tonya sucking on an asthma inhaler was popular in the media, but because it was connected to images of her smoking, the message was not that Tonya had a disability (which might have been seen as an obstacle overcome by heroic tenacity), but that she lacked self-control. Cigarette smoking in itself has rapidly become a *signifier* of low social class, suggesting a carelessness about the body as well as ignorance about well-documented risks, but in Harding's case that signification of lower-class improvidence was compounded by the way her breathing problems apparently hurt her ability to compete.

Similarly, Tonya's costumes generated a good deal of disapproving commentary, not only because they were judged to be tacky, but because they failed to properly contain her. The story of Tonya "popping a snap" and nearly coming out of her halter at the 1993 national championships suggested poor quality of construction, but more importantly, a sense of bodily surfeit—a grotesque sense that Tonya was swelling beyond the capacity of her clothing to hold her.[8] This sort of thinking led to some rather monstrous images of a gargantuan Tonya bestriding the earth: "*Playboy* offered Tonya $250,000 to pose for the magazine with her tool kit. True story. Ohmigoodness! Can you picture that? I mean, Tonya is wider than I-93."[9]

On the other hand, there was considerable confusion about what class Kerrigan should be assigned to. Was she "middle class," "working class," or (since she wore expensive designer outfits and stood to make a lot of money, and because she was on the threshold of joining the media aristocracy) "high class"? Or was she moving from one class to another? And if so, from which, to which? Confusion about Kerrigan's class provides a good illustration of the ideological filters through which class is perceived in the United States.[10] Without formal markers of class distinction, the white population is seen as a vast undifferentiated social body called "the middle class," with only the obviously indigent and, perhaps, the shadowy "rich" defining the wafer-thin excluded margins at bottom and top. There are gradations within this vast middle, based on income, occupation, place of residence, education, taste, and so on, but since all of these things are theoretically alterable, they are assumed to be voluntary, and thus they do not define essential attributes of persons. The gradations, therefore, may score the national body, but they do not divide it. Anything outside of this body is perceived to be a threat, but almost everything within the nation is part of this undifferentiated body.[11] Even those who are "lower class" may be contained within it, since the circulation within this body is assumed to be free. Anything that threatens to block the circulation, however, or which asserts that the body is in reality partitioned-like "white trash," which is tantamount, in this figurative case, to saturated fat, will be the object of revulsion and anger. Harding's apparent attack on Kerrigan was just such an assertion of division.

While this vision of a classless United States has deep cultural roots, the particular configuration described here is of fairly recent vintage, a product of post-war prosperity in the 1950s and 1960s. The model is a middle-class view, and one which becomes increasingly parochial as it less and less accurately describes contemporary social reality. The ideal of classlessness rationalizes the position of the successful stratum which can still be called "middle class" with some justice—what the Ehrenreichs call the "professional-managerial class," more colloquially referred to as "the upper-middle class." This class, which is in fact a relatively small minority, dominates the means of social representation, including (most importantly for present purposes) television and journalism.

Kerrigan, although she comes from a working-class family, was thus presumptively middle class, and therefore included within the national body. The telltale expression in her case is "blue collar," which is not precisely synonymous with "working class," but instead has come (in the Nixon-Reagan era) to represent that *faction* of the skilled working class which is understood to be socially conservative, and comfortably if shabbily well-off; the blue collar belongs, in effect, as the bottom bracket of the middle class, and represents the post-war fantasy of universal prosperity, with home ownership for all, and families supported on a single industrial income.

It's possible that ethnicity also plays into this idea of the blue collar—the Kerrigans were identifiably Irish, while the Hardings were "white trash," i.e., ethnically indeterminate. Tonya's mother's many marriages probably also contributed to the idea of mongrelization and ethnic decay, signified by Tonya's being called a "mutt," fallen away from the white ethnic purity which is a classic ingredient of the integrationist trajectory of upward mobility.[12] (This, however, is a contradictory view, since integration itself implies the decay of isolated ethnic identity, and its incorporation into the undifferentiated national body.)

What commentators found most distressing was Harding's putative attack on the supposedly superior athlete: the threat she posed, therefore, was to the natural aristocracy of talent, i.e., the assumption of free circulation within the social body. This, too, is paradoxical, since the undifferentiated body should not admit of a concept like "aristocracy." But, on the contrary, it is precisely because of the absence of *a priori* classes that something like a "natural aristocracy" can theoretically emerge. This is why such a fuss was made about Harding's remarks concerning money. Her open declaration of pecuniary interest violated the sham conventions of amateurism which give figure skating its veneer of aristocracy (such declarations have always gotten athletes in trouble; Harding is by no means the first to transgress norms of amateur idealism). Kerrigan, on the other hand, made sure to recite the athlete's media credo: "Take any of [the endorsements] away and I would still do it. I didn't know there was any money to be made in the sport except for teaching until two or three years ago, when I got a couple of endorsement contracts. I had no idea. I do it because I love it."[13]

The more the blue-collar reality erodes in the "post-industrial" United States, the more hysterically attached to the idea of the blue collar the middle class has become. Harding and Kerrigan represented competing middle-class fantasies of the poor—Harding the threatening fantasy of a resentful lumpenproletariat, something outside and beneath the national corpus, and Kerrigan the reassuring fantasy of the conservative, assimilationist blue collar. According to Joe Klein, in a *Newsweek* column: "Tonya and Nancy are made-for-TV versions of two dominant, American working-class predispositions. It's not just lady and the tramp; it has more to do with assimilation and rejection, faith and resentment. Assimilation— the possibility of upward mobility—is the bedrock of American faith. Nancy's faith."[14] These are not only "working-class predispositions," however, but middle-class fantasmatic projections. This is not to deny the class realities of cultural disparities. On the contrary, class anger and resentment really seem to have motivated the assault on Kerrigan, and to have defined the emotions of some of Harding's supporters. It is merely to observe the emotional and ideological investment that middle-class commentators have in believing the country is full of Kerrigans, while being occasionally attacked by a lone-gun Harding—in believing, in other words, that their own privileged position is a matter of justice, not accident.

So far I have considered only what I'm calling the middle-class view, which by and large sided with Nancy, even if sometimes reluctantly. But there was another view, one that I've hinted at, and one which was poorly represented in the mainstream press. Following Mikhail Bakhtin and those who have developed his ideas, I will call this the carnivalesque view.[15] Some qualification of Bakhtin's vision of the popular, festive, utopian mode of carnival must undoubtedly be made for the contemporary U.S. context, in which the middle class assumes the dominant position, at least in popular ideology, against the extremes of high and low. The carnivalesque will have a different charge when it is addressed to the dominance of the fantasmatic middle-class body which claims an all-encompassing universality rather than claiming a class exclusivity (as a formal aristocracy would). Liberal political ideology in the United States does not allow much of a position for alternative cultures of any sort, but particularly not those of class. There has also undoubtedly been considerable attenuation of the carnivalesque mode in modern commercial culture: Class cultures are absorbed, mitigated, diluted, and dissected in commercial popular culture. Where, after all, could an autonomous class culture reside within the totality of the media? The fragmentation of broadcasting by cable notwithstanding, television is still the foremost medium of, and figure for, the undifferentiated social body.

But the carnivalesque persists nonetheless, if not as a coherent class culture, then as the vestigial remnants of a festive world view which Bakhtin traced back to the European middle ages. That view emphasizes the grotesque body, especially the lower bodily strata—the feet, the legs, the organs of sexual reproduction and defecation, the belly and the rump, as opposed to the head and heart; it prefers the animal to the angelic; it elevates the low, and diminishes the high; it revels in reversal, in obscenity, in the open and the excessive. This kind of cultural repertoire was evident throughout the Tonya/Nancy affair, in its satirical subversion of the class hierarchies in skating, sport, and U.S. culture generally. Tonya represented the carnivalesque, although sometimes in a somewhat disappointing fashion. The same recklessness, trash-talking, and bodily excessiveness that the moralists found repugnant are the stuff of which carnival is made.

To get this view, you had to read between the lines of newspaper reports, or watch the tabloid TV programs instead of the network news. Even there, you would have to read carefully. As Barbara Ehrenreich notes, "Ideas seldom flow 'upward' to the middle class, because there are simply no structures to channel the upward flow of thought from class to class."[16] The flow is one-way, down: The middle-class media represent their views as universal, while in fact they circulate and recirculate information and opinion among themselves.

But the carnivalesque view comes bubbling up, betraying its presence even in the middle-class media. The "man in the street" gets his say; the tabloid programs include all sorts of odd ephemera; the networks have moments of inadvertent hilarity. (Of course, there would not have been so much comic potential if the attack on Kerrigan had been more damaging. The carnivalesque took root in the attack's failure, and flowered more fully as the misadventures of the perpetrators became public. After the initial shock of the attack had worn off, and once it was clear that Kerrigan was only superficially harmed, there was greater license to laugh at the clumsiness of the conspirators.)

Harding was thus a pole of identification as well as an object of repudiation. Given that the carnivalesque version of the affair was poorly represented in the media, this assertion of Tonya's appeal has to remain somewhat hypothetical. While it is clear that Tonya had her fans, and while it is also clear that the affair expanded the class base of the normally "upscale" audience for Olympic figure skating, it would require empirical research to establish certain class allegiances to Harding.[17]

It should also be pointed out that there were those among the journalistic commentators who sided with Harding, most conspicuously in the progressive press.[18] Although I have been attributing a unified ideological perspective to the middle class, a less reductive account would have to acknowledge what Erik Olin Wright calls the "contradictory locations within class relations" that characterize the middle class.[19] The middle class, situated as it is between the high and the low, between capital and labor, occupies a peculiarly ambivalent position, and does not have a simple, unified class interest. But those in the media who allied themselves with Tonya were a distinct minority, vastly outnumbered by the revilers.

The Legs of the Skater: Sport and the Carnivalesque[20]

In the remainder of this essay, I want to explore the particular ways in which competing class cultures are invested in the field of popular sport, and the ways in which Harding and Kerrigan came to represent those cultures.

It shouldn't be a surprise that such a conflict erupted in sport, and particularly in ice skating. Sport is a fertile field for such conflicts; it inherits rival traditions of the classical and the carnivalesque, and the two traditions, figuring different cultural attitudes, are bound to clash. Among sports, skating is particularly well suited to manifestations of the carnivalesque, because of its open connections to other fields of commercial "show" culture.

Cultural commentary in the United States has both celebrated and dismissed sport, when it has regarded sport at all; to some it is civil religion, to others it is pacification of the masses by a capitalist elite.[21] In fact, of course, neither celebration nor condemnation offers a suitably complex account of sport, which is a widely various cultural field, a vehicle for different ideological investments—not indoctrination, but conflict. John Hargreaves, a historian of British sport, for instance—arguing against a Marxist, determinist position which holds that contemporary Western sport is necessarily an instrument of capitalist hegemony—describes the ideological heterogeneity of sport in this way:

> There is no sense [in the strict Marxist position] in which people might quite consciously value sports as meaningful and beneficial aspects of their lives, while at the same time being aware that ruling groups attempt to use sport as an instrument of control. In [the determinist] approach sport has to be the exclusive possession of one class rather than another, and so there is no room for conceiving that it might be an arena of uneasy accommodation and conflict between them.[22]

Sport, in other words, is an open field of social representation, and not a set of fixed social meanings.

Having said that, however, it must be admitted that in the United States, mass spectator sport has frequently served as a vehicle for conservative ideologies.[23] It has served to rationalize hierarchy, through its reinforcement of the ideas of the career open to talent, and of natural aristocracy. It has served as a vehicle for nationalist sentiment, and it functions as a primary discursive field for the establishment of the "imagined community" of the nation.[24] And, perhaps most important, it has functioned to signify "tradition" in a culture in which "everything solid melts into air"—it is very often marketed as an exercise in nostalgia for a pre-industrial, precapitalist past (despite its clear historical relation to capitalist development). "Tradition," in turn, signifies a fantasized former national body which was not socially differentiated by racial upheaval, immigration, gender conflict, and so on.

However, this is only half of the picture. As Stallybrass and White caution:

> When we talk of high discourses—literature, philosophy, statecraft, the languages of the Church and the University—and contrast them to the low discourses of a peasantry, the urban poor, subcultures, marginals, the lumenproletariat, colonized peoples, we already have two "highs" and two "lows." History seen from above and history seen from below are irreducibly different and they consequently impose radically different perspectives on the question of hierarchy.[25]

Commercial popular culture, I would argue, is peculiarly a mixture of the two discourses, the classical and the carnivalesque, the high and the low. Even when sport seems most to reinforce conservative ideologies, it may retain popular, utopian, subversive meanings for those who watch.

Sport is in particular an arena of bodily representation, and so is an especially apt carrier of the kinds of bodily figuration of class and gender I've discussed in relation to Tonya and Nancy. There is a strand of thinking about sport which gives it a firmly aristocratic heritage of ascesis, or training of the body.[26] Spectator sport inherits some of this sense of training, but it contains another, competing strand which emphasizes performance for others. This tension can be described as one between *play* and *dis-play*, sport performed in itself, and sport performed for others, with "play" furthermore suggesting nonpecuniary amateurism, and "display" suggesting the commercial exhibitionism of professional sport.[27] These terms, of course, are highly gendered. Display of the body for visual consumption has been an almost exclusively feminine function in Western culture, and for this reason, in "masculine" sports, the display element is covert; male athletes are reluctant to acknowledge their audience, preferring the fiction that their performance is something they do for its own sake. Sport is supposed to have the status of "event," not "performance," and the sporting body is not an object but an instrument. Only at moments of extreme spectatorial demand will a baseball player tip his cap, for example, and then only grudgingly, in a shrug of embarrassment. By acting as if the crowd did not exist, and therefore as if the sport were worth pursuing merely for its own sake, male athletes subscribe to the aristocratic ideal of ascesis, and the classical masculine ideal of bodily self-containment. The display element in spectator sport is often held to be a contamination, often in gendered terms that are reminiscent of modernist condemnation of popular culture earlier in the century.[28]

But play and display are also terms that are clearly class-coded. To the extent that sport contains these two tendencies, it combines elements of the classical body with those of the grotesque body—the high discourses of the nation and the state, with the low discourses of the carnivalesque.

Ice skating, even more than other spectator sports, is not a "pure" sport, but a hybrid cultural form. Skating thus has a decidedly mixed range of class associations, and contains a greater than usual tension between play and display—a more explicit display component than in other sports. One way in which skating manifests this is in the tension between "athleticism" and "artistry." These terms are openly gendered, and thus reveal the gendering already latent in the terms play and display, classical and grotesque body. But there is also a class coding involved. For sportswriters, figure skating is suspect because it isn't "pure" sport—it's contaminated by the elements it borrows from other forms of entertainment, such as musical accompaniment and spangled costuming. In other words, high-class sport is degraded by adopting elements of popular spectacle.

The attack on Kerrigan and its aftermath, then, which were perceived to be outside the arena of skating proper, in fact revealed tendencies and contradictions already contained within the sport, and within sport in general. Harding was accused of turning the "dignified" sport of skating into a "circus," but circus—or the carnivalesque—is the inherent flip-side to spectator sport, especially but not only in those sports that emphasize display. We might call skating's tendency to the classical its "balletic" quality, and its tendency to the carnivalesque its "circus" quality. Skating is frequently associated with both ballet and circus in public commentary; reference to ballet is usually an approving association, which tries to align skating with high culture, while reference to circus is usually disapproving, aligning skating with low culture. But this overlooks the ways in which all three cultural forms are mixed.

Like the ballet, and like the circus, skating has incorporated elements of spectacle: costume, music, and fragments of dramatic narrative. Like dance and circus, it is partly a drama of transcendence, and like those other cultural forms, it codes its spaces and bodies according to social class hierarchies. Within the circumscribed rinks, stages, and arenas, a vertical axis organizes the spectacle, with elevation of the body as the figure for transcendence. The axels and toe loops of figure skating have their counterparts in ballet's dancing on pointe, and trapeze and high wire acts in the circus—in all these bodily expressions, the emphasis is on the lifting of the body, and therefore on its denial, or the denial of its weightiness.

But in all these cases, there is the weighty counterpart to the ethereal leap. Ballet was transformed in the late nineteenth and early twentieth centuries into "high culture," as cultural hierarchies were established in the United States, and so tried to suppress the lower bodily elements, but it is useful to remember that at the moment of its transformation into a commercial form of entertainment, ballet was as much about the display of dancers' bodies as about an aesthetic sublime. The cult of the ballerina emerged historically with the perfection of the technique of dancing on pointe, which served both to figure transcendence and to emphasize the legs of the dancer. The display of the leg specifically served to suggest sexual availability, a suggestion which could increasingly be taken literally as ballet shifted from court patronage to the commercial sphere, and female dancers were no longer protected from the sexual predations of their male audience. At the same time, therefore, as the romantic ballet appealed to a sense of the spiritual, it was practicing a barely tacit form of prostitution.[29] In the circus, the trapeze and high-wire artists, who adopted the ballerina's costume, had their counterpart in the clown, with costumes that exaggerated the body into grotesque caricature. The clown represented the materiality of the flesh, emphasizing bodily excess and miraculous bodily reproduction. The clown was earthbound, where the highwire walker defied gravity; the clown was carnal, while the trapeze artist denied incarnation.

And in skating, there was Tonya. Much of the emphasis on Tonya's "athleticism" covertly referred to Tonya's very fleshiness, and the physical effort she displayed which highlighted that embodiedness. When Kerrigan was described as "graceful," that in turn suggested a feminine concealment of bodily labor, indeed of the body itself. While Tonya wore costumes that seemed to gape open, Nancy wore costumes that were notably discreet. While Tonya fussed with her skate laces, thereby calling attention to the apparatus of her work, Nancy was wearing "Sheer Illusion," a material which in a peculiar way produced a sense of bodilessness (not exactly the illusion intended by the name of the fabric). If Kerrigan was skating's highwire act (at least until she was trumped by Oksana Baiul), then Tonya was the clown.

Skating's mixed cultural heritage is marked by its emphasis on the legs of the skater, which echoes the carnivalesque emphasis on the lower bodily strata. As one sportswriter noted in the *New York Times:* "Harding-Kerrigan has more legs than a centipede."[30] Tonya in particular called attention to the lower body, to the turned ankle and the clubbed knee, to the broken lace and the loose blade; Tonya's remark about "kicking Nancy's butt" was tacitly juxtaposed to the often-repeated image of Tonya falling on her own butt after attempting a difficult jump. All skaters fall, but Tonya's falls were happily, ruthlessly detailed.

What we saw acted out in the early months of 1994, culminating in the winter Olympic skating competition, was thus a traditional class drama, of a kind that is formally embodied in various types of commercial culture. Partisans of skating's aristocratic pretensions rely on the association with ballet, on ballet's constricted status as signifier of "high culture." For them, Tonya represented an invasion of trash into this sanctified sphere, and the intrusion of class difference into the fantasy of the classless social body. Tonya's admirers, too, appreciated her challenge to the snobbery of skating's high-cultural ambitions. What detractors and admirers alike misunderstood was that Tonya was no invasion; she was always already there. The carnivalesque continues to be embedded in popular culture, despite efforts at purification.

But already there or not, Tonya came to define an emerging class conflict that is increasingly going to be played out in the fields of culture. In that sense, the middle class is right to be worried. "The nineties finally have their defining figure—and he hates your guts" writes Tad Friend in *New York's* cover article on the "White Trash Nation." But although the pronoun was "he," it was Tonya who was singled out as "the ultimate icon" of white trash.[31]

Notes

My thanks to Peter Stallybrass, for several enlightening conversations on the subject of Harding and Kerrigan; and to Burl Barr, Paul Downes, Rebecca Egger, Julie Hilden, Naomi Morgenstern, Laura Murray, and Ed White, for their thoughtful comments.

1. However, there was, too, an occasional denial of its significance, such as one writer's claim that "this has nothing to do with class, manners or 'dysfunctional' families." Dan Shaughnessy, "Don't Fall Victim to Twisted Thinking," *Boston Globe,* 6 February 1994, 49. However, what Shaughnessy is really complaining of is the use of class as an exculpation.

2. Randall Sullivan, "The Tonya Harding Fall: The Transformation of a Young Figure-Skating Champion into the World's Most Visible Villainess," *Rolling Stone 686/ 687,* 14–28 July 1994, p. 114.

3. For an interesting account of the social significance of body management, see Susan Bordo, "Reading the Slender Body," in Mary Jacobus, Evelyn Fox Keller, and Sally Shuttleworth, eds., *Body Politics: Women and the Discourses of Science* (New York: Routledge, 1990); for work on how the body serves social symbolic functions in general, see Mary Douglas, *Natural Symbols* (New York: Pantheon, 1982), and *Purity and Danger* (London: Routledge, 1966).

4. The term "middle class," however, needs to be specified; I attempt this specification below.

5. More often, commentary on Tonya/Nancy was merely connotative in matters

of class. This was in part because class as a causal frame was taken for granted by the moralists: The argument buried in such commentary took the form *post hoc ergo propter hoc*: She did it and she is low-class, therefore she did it because she is low-class. In this sense, social class was merely assumed, at the same time as it was, for other purposes (particularly in perceptions of Kerrigan), denied.

6. See the *Washington Post*, editorial, 5 February 1994, A1 6.

7. Susan Orlean, "Figures in a Mall," *New Yorker*, 21 February 1994, 48–63.

8. See Abby Haight and J. E. Vader, *Fire on Ice: The Exclusive Inside Story of Tonya Harding*, (New York: Times Books, 1994), 66–67.

9. Mike Barnicle, "Media Wobbles on Skater Story," *Boston Globe*, 15 February 1994.

10. The necessarily brief discussion of class which follows is influenced in parts by Barbara Ehrenreich and John Ehrenreich, "The Professional-Managerial Class," in *Between Labor and Capital*, ed. Pat Walker (Boston: South End Press, 1979), 5–45; Barbara Ehrenreich, *Fear of Falling: The Inner Life of the Middle Class* (New York: Harper Perennial, 1989); and Richard Sennett and Jonathan Cobb, *The Hidden Injuries of Class* (New York: Vintage, 1972). See also Benjamin Demott, *The Imperial Middle: Why Americans Can't Think Straight About Class* (New Haven: Yale University Press, 1990).

11. This may help to explain the particular reliance of Americans on foreign villains, since, to deny internal division, we require external threat to maintain the bodily integrity of the nation.

12. Richard Cohen, *Washington Post*, 3 February 1994, A27: "Harding stands in contrast not only to her rival but to her sport itself. She's a mutt among supposed purebreds." The disclaimer implied in the word "supposed" does not, it seems to me, mitigate the straightforward assertion of Tonya's mongrel status.

13. Quoted in Christine Brennan, "Kerrigan Can't Wait to See What Happens; Interested in Harding Saga, But Intent on Ice," *Washington Post*, 13 February 1994, D1.

14. *Newsweek*, 14 February 1994, 57. Klein's conclusion, however, is that Nancy's faith is justified, while Tonya's class resentment is just the bad faith of a sore loser. Of course, winning justifies the faith of the winners. But for losing not to justify the broken faith of the losers, a belief must survive in the rules by which winners and losers are chosen. In skating, the notoriously arbitrary criteria for judging give good grounds for suspicion on this score.

15. Mikhail Bakhtin, *Rabelais and His World* (Bloomington: Indiana University Press, 1984); see also Peter Stallybrass and Alton White, *The Politics and Poetics of Transgression*, (Ithaca, N.Y.: Cornell University Press, 1986).

16. Ehrenreich, *Fear of Falling*, 139.

17. For a useful discussion of the audience for figure skating and the internal politics of Olympic broadcasting, see John Powers, "The Crying Games," *Boston Globe Magazine*, 30 January 1994.

18. See especially Katha Pollitt, "Subject to Debate," *The Nation,* 7 March 1994, 297.

19. Erik Olin Wright, *Classes* (London: Verso, 1985).

20. My title for this section is drawn from Abigail Solomon-Godeau's discussion of nineteenth-century photographic fetishism, "The Legs of the Countess," *October* 39 (winter 1986).

21. For the celebratory view, see Michael Novak, *The Joy of Sports: End Zones, Bases, Baskets, Balls, and the Consecration of the American Spirit* (New York: Basic Books, 1976); for the condemnation, Noam Chomsky's statement about sports in the recent film "Manufacturing Consent" is representative if cursory: "Take sports. That's another crucial example of the indoctrination system. It offers people something to pay attention to that's of no importance, that keeps them from worrying about things that matter." Quoted in "Out in Leftist Field," *The Village Voice,* 13 July 1993, 137.

22. John Hargreaves, "Sport, Culture and Ideology," in *Sport, Culture and Ideology,* ed. Jennifer Hargreaves (London: Routledge, 1982).

23. I would argue, however, that it often does so as a defensive measure—sport wraps itself in a conservative mantle to ally itself with vested power.

24. Benedict Anderson, *Imagined Communities: Reflections on the Origin and Spread of Nationalism,* (London: Verso, 1983).

25. Stallybrass and White, *The Politics and Poetics of Transgression,* 4.

26. Pierre Bourdieu, "Sport and Social Class," *Social Science Information* 17:6 (1978), 819–840.

27. Gregory P. Stone, "American Sports: Play and Display," *Sport: Readings from a Sociological Perspective,* ed. Eric Dunning (Toronto: University of Toronto Press, 1972), 47–65.

28. See, for example, Andreas Huyssen, *After the Great Divide: Modernism, Mass Culture, Postmodernism* (Bloomington: Indiana University Press, 1986), especially Chapter 3, "Mass Culture as Woman: Modernism's Other," 44–62.

29. Lynn Garafola, "The Travesty Dancer in Nineteenth-Century Ballet," *Dance Research Journal* 17:2 and 18:1, (Fall 1985/Spring 1986), 35–40.

30. Jere Longman, "A Pause in Scandal: Now They Will Skate," *New York Times,* 23 February 1994, B9.

31. Tad Friend, "White Hot Trash," *New York,* 22 August 1994, 22–31.

9

SHARI LEE DWORKIN AND FAYE LINDA WACHS

"Disciplining the Body"
HIV-Positive Male Athletes, Media Surveillance, and the Policing of Sexuality

Hegemonic Masculinity, Sport, and "Normal Sexuality"

• In the United States, sport and success at sports signify masculinity, and particular sports are linked to the "right" kind of masculinity. Connell applies the term hegemonic masculinity to this form of masculinity. He argues that hegemonic masculinity is the most valued form of masculinity, which is defined hierarchically in relation to what is feminine and to subordinated masculinities (1987).[1] At the turn of the twentieth century, changes in men's and women's roles challenged social ideologies of male physical superiority. Competitive team sports were popularized in the United States as a means of symbolically reaffirming male physical superiority over women and socially subordinated men (Crosset 1990; Kimmel 1990; Messner 1988).[2] From these early influences, modern sport has evolved as a bastion of masculinity in which one particular form of masculinity (white, middle class, heterosexual, and physically dominating) is constructed as the most highly valued (Connell 1987, 1990; Davis 1997; Messner 1988).

Participation in particular types of sport, especially collision sports

This essay originally appeared in and is reprinted by permission of *Sociology of Sport Journal* 15 (1), 1–20.

and often team sports, is understood as "masculine appropriate." For example, sports like basketball, football, and boxing are coded as masculine appropriate sports (Kane 1988; Kane and Snyder 1989; Metheny 1965). These sports are not merely "masculine appropriate" in the sense that they are considered inappropriate for women, but they reinforce the ideologies of hegemonic masculinity. As a general rule, the sports in which men dominate or display the elements linked to ideologies of masculine physical superiority are those most valued by our culture (Messner 1988). These sports are the ones which garner the bulk of television and print media attention (Duncan, Messner, and Jensen 1994). By extension, the men who participate in these sports are constructed as heroes.

Sport may be highly adored and valued in U.S. culture, but it has not gone without its critics. While some applaud the role of sport in reproducing masculinity, others are distinctly apprehensive about what type of masculinity is valued and reproduced. Often, male sports stars are excused from wrongdoing by the phrase *boys will be boys* and are valorized for their sexual conquests of women (McKay 1993). Ironically, the media often frame these events so as to privilege and protect "excessive" male heterosexual activity through the classification of women as the aggressors, the "problem," or the temptation upon which any "normal" man would act (McKay 1993; Wachs and Dworkin 1997; Wachs and Dworkin, in press). The media can be said to carry out ideological repair work which protects sports heroes in a gender regime that privileges heterosexual manhood and pathologizes gay male and female (hetero)sexuality (McKay 1993; Wachs and Dworkin 1997).[3]

An interesting scenario arises when valorized sports heroes, or icons of hegemonic masculinity, contract HIV/AIDS. In Western thought the athletic male body has historically been a mark of power and moral superiority for those who bear it (Dutton 1995). Thus, an interesting question remains: How might the mainstream American print media construct sports heroes' bodies once they announce they have a socially stigmatized disease, such as HIV/AIDS? Will the print media protect the widely celebrated virility of male sport heroes, or will it mark the athletes' bodies with symbols of "immorality" and "inappropriate" sexuality? Through an analysis of the different ways in which professional athletes with HIV/AIDS have been framed by print media, we will unpack the racialized, sexualized, and classed iconography of the body. In particular, we will explore how power relations, as expressed in public discourse, normalize certain sexual acts and identities while stigmatizing others.

The Historical Conflation of Sexual Act and Identity

In 1981, the first case of what is now known as Acquired Immune Deficiency Syndrome (AIDS) was reported (Patton 1990; Seidman 1992; Weeks 1985). The disease was first termed GRID or Gay-Relayed Immune Disorder (Patton 1990; Seidman 1992). Although the virus was known to be transmitted primarily through blood and "bodily fluids" in sexual acts, AIDS was automatically attached to a specific sexual identity—the gay identity. Ironically, the medical community did not immediately ask *which sex acts* were correlated to high risks, but rather, which sexual identities were high risk. Today, numerous mainstream media accounts jump to the same conclusion, so much so that being gay and having AIDS are nearly synonymous (Connell 1987; LePoire 1994; Patton 1990; Watney 1989; Weeks 1985). It is important to note that regardless of act or identity, if one's partners do not have the virus, one is not at risk of contracting HIV/AIDS.

Although millions of gay men have died from AIDS and currently constitute the largest category of deaths in the United States,[4] there is no reason to assume that being gay "causes" AIDS any more than being straight "caused" the international re-emergence of syphilis prior to the discovery of penicillin. In other words, it is inaccurate to conflate specific sexual identities with the performance of particular sexual acts. This point is exemplified by Alfred Kinsey's work (1948, 1953), wherein he revealed the wide range of sexual behaviors which are practiced by individuals across multiple sexual identity categories.[5]

A current example of the complex relationship between sex acts and sexual identity clarifies this point. For years, rumors have circulated about Magic Johnson's alleged bisexual activities. In 1996, several newspapers published articles claiming that Magic Johnson had numerous boyfriends as part of "life in the fast lane" (see Note 16). Magic Johnson self-identifies as a heterosexual man and publicly denies any accusations of same-sex activity. Whether he does so in fear of public stigmatization or because the "heterosexual" descriptor is accurate, sexual identity categories by themselves clearly provide little help in unfolding the complexities of HIV/AIDS transmission, behavior, and risk. In fact, there are potentially dangerous consequences of conflating act and identity, especially if the goal is to provide the public with accurate information about HIV transmission.

Equally dangerous is the conflation of sexual identity and risk. For example, gay men are assumed always to engage in high-risk activity. This error is repeated frequently by the medical community and the mass media (Watney 1989). Despite the dangers of such assumptions, the medical establishment for some time formed sexual "risk groups" largely on the basis of sexual identity. Several researchers (Duggan and Hunter 1995; Watney 1989; Weeks 1985) have highlighted how sexual act, sexual identity, and risk are not necessarily linked. These same researchers note how medicine, law, and the mass media have continued to make and enforce discourses on this basis.[6] As we will demonstrate, mainstream news media perpetuate myths about HIV/AIDS through the absence of any discussion of acts while implicitly fixing sexual identity in relation to specific acts. By assuming a "natural" and "fixed" identity which is assumed to include some acts and partners while excluding others, mainstream news media reinforce ignorance about both sexual practices and risk.[7]

Lastly, the mass media have historically problematized gay sexuality by marking it as inherently dangerous. While no longer assumed to be a problem solely for the gay community, HIV/AIDS is still solidly and consistently blamed on the gay community (Connell 1987; Grosz 1994; LePoire 1994; Patton 1990; Seidman 1992; Sontag 1989; Watney 1989; Weeks 1985). At the same time, members of the heterosexual community, especially heterosexual men in the athletic community who engage in high-risk behaviors, are largely absolved of the stigma of HIV/AIDS.[8]

Policing Bodies and Sexuality: The Role of the Mass Media

Foucault (1978) presents power as both repressive and constitutive. He describes how both forms of power operate simultaneously. One way in which power is exercised in a repressive manner is through the policing of deviant acts. Deviant acts and identities are defined in contrast to what is deemed normal. Deviant acts and identities require surveillance and policing so that what is "normal" can be reaffirmed. It is important to understand that what is normal could not exist without some form of deviance which sets the boundaries and limits on normality. At the same time, examples of normality and deviance demonstrate how power is constitutive (Foucault 1979), since only particular social formations are conceptualized and reproduced, while others are wholly unthinkable.

For Foucault, power is not a simple relationship between normal and deviant. Rather, there are multiple sets of hierarchicalized dualities which fragment identity around various social categories. For the purposes of this discussion, categories which fragment identity and constitute the social location of the individual, such as race, class, gender, and sexual identity, will be explicated. We argue that the mainstream news media are acting as a surveillance mechanism, not only through what is considered "newsworthy," but through hierarchical framings and interpretations of events. The dissemination to the public of a particular frame sends clear messages about the boundaries between normal and deviant behavior. As we will see, the mainstream American media survey and police sexuality by race, class, gender, and sexual identity. The analysis focuses primarily on sexual identity but takes these other axes of social organization into account as well.

Both Foucault (1978) and Rubin (1993) demonstrate how once a difference is named, it is hierarchicalized. Rubin's theories are especially relevant to our analysis when she focuses on the way sexual acts and identities are hierarchicalized. She suggests that U.S. culture has a hierarchical system of sexual value whereby there is a continuous contestation, challenge, and battle over what counts as "good sex" and what falls into the category of "bad sex." Generally speaking, good sex is that which is viewed and defined as natural, healthy, normal, and holy; while bad sex is viewed as sick, sinful, unnatural, and unholy. Good sex is viewed as heterosexual, monogamous, and reproductive; while bad sex includes such qualities as "homosexual sex," fetishes, promiscuity, and casual sex. Rubin notes a "middle ground" which is the site of major contestation and includes unmarried heterosexuals, promiscuous heterosexuals, and stable, long-term relationships between gays and lesbians. Simply put, sex is highly politicized terrain wherein some identities and acts are rewarded and encouraged while others are punished and suppressed (1993).

While both Foucault and Rubin speak in harmony on conceptualizations of normality and deviance, it is a Foucauldian contribution to view the body as the primary site where power is imposed and/or enforced.[9] Foucault (1978, 1979) provides numerous historical examples whereby bodies are policed and disciplined through surveillance mechanisms. Through the designation of institutional expertise, the normal body is defined in contrast to the deviant body. While both normal and deviant bodies may be subject to policing mechanisms such as surveillance, the normal body is elevated while the deviant body is stigmatized and disciplined. We explore the differential print media framings of athletes' HIV/AIDS announcements through three examples: Magic Johnson, Tommy Morrison, and Greg Louganis. While on some level all three men are condemned for "moral" failings, we hypothesize that the framing of the athletes will differ because the media polices and hierarchicalizes the athletes' (and, by extension, all individuals') sexual identities.

Methodological Considerations

We performed a textual analysis on all articles from the *Los Angeles Times (LAT)*, *New York Times (NYT)*, and *Washington Post (WP)* which immediately followed the HIV-positive announcements of Olympic diver Greg Louganis, professional basketball player Earvin "Magic" Johnson, and professional boxer Tommy Morrison. For Magic Johnson, we also collected all available articles for three months following his announcement and 10 percent of the articles which appeared the following year. These three mainstream newspapers were chosen from three major cities in the United States in order to represent the dominant or mainstream print media's treatment of HIV/AIDS. Indeed, other papers, such as *USA Today*, may have large circulations, and the gay and alternative presses may offer different framings of these events. However, the selected newspapers garner prestige and respect as reliable sources of accurate information.[10]

Numerous scholars discuss the importance of the mass media in social, political, and cultural life (DeFleur and Ball-Rokeach 1989; Fiske 1994;

McLuhan 1964; McQuail 1987). While media texts can be read by agents who construct meaning from the text in resistant and polysemic ways, power limits which texts are presented to a mass audience (Fiske 1994). As Herman and Chomsky (1988) discuss, relatively few corporations own, produce, and distribute most of our "news." Using textual analysis, we focus primarily on the cultural assumptions built into the text rather than the text itself. Cultural assumptions demonstrate how power constitutes certain practices as normal, while marking others as deviant (Foucault 1978). At the same time, these cultural assumptions also reveal what is completely left out of our mass cultural discourse, that is, what is unrepresentable.

Given the social importance of male team sports, it is hardly surprising that there were over one hundred articles about Magic Johnson, twelve articles about Greg Louganis, and six articles about Tommy Morrison. Perhaps the difference in the sheer number of articles highlights not only Magic Johnson's celebrity status within the basketball community, but also the popularity of basketball in our culture and its link to the symbolic production of masculinity. By contrast, the fewer number of articles about Morrison and Louganis may reflect their lower popularity as individuals or the status of the sports in which they participate.

The relative lack of coverage of Louganis likely reflects that diving, which involves no direct physical confrontation, is not linked to the construction of hegemonic masculinity. Where Morrison participates in a sport with heavy doses of physical contact, boxing's historic links to working-class blood sports (Gorn and Goldstein 1993) undermine it as an icon of middle-class masculinity. However, it is interesting to note that Morrison received almost as much coverage as Louganis despite his mediocre success as compared to Louganis, who dominated the sport of diving for most of his career.[11] Lastly, Greg Louganis's sexual identity may have been a key issue in keeping the media from covering him in greater depth.

While the focus of this analysis is on newspaper content, a mixed media analysis was considered where television transcripts and magazine articles were also collected and examined.[12] After our initial reading of the articles, four themes emerged. Articles were then coded around these themes. First, we explored whether or not the media conflated sexual identity with risk group. Second, we investigated whether the mainstream print media committed the historical error of conflating act with identity. Third, in order to uncover cultural assumptions in the texts, we analyzed frames which emphasized notions of family and/or relationships, personal responsibility, and "failure." Finally, we explicated how social location (consisting of multiple axes of power) led to a differential interpretation of an individual athlete's behavior depending upon which axis media coverage highlighted. The list of relevant articles is included in an appendix.

Findings and Analysis: "It's Not Just a Gay Disease!"
Shock and Silence

Consistent with the conflation of risk groups and HIV/AIDS status, the articles on Magic Johnson express overwhelming surprise that he contracted HIV/AIDS. Questions arise immediately as to how Magic Johnson could have contracted HIV/AIDS. Once we learn that he contracted HIV/AIDS through "heterosexual sex,"[13] articles report "shock" and "surprise" and repeatedly use exclamations such as: "startling," "totally mind blowing," "seems ridiculous," and "stunning." Forty-two of one hundred articles express the sentiment that the public is caught totally off guard by Johnson's announcement, such as: "Even Hearing News Was Not Believing It," (Bonk *LAT*, 11/8/91), "Hero's Shocker Leaves Teens *Grasping* For Answers," (Shen WP, 11/9/91), "A Jarring Reveille For Sports," (Lipsyte *NYT*, 11/10/91), and "A Day Later, It Remains a Shock Felt Around the World" (Thomas, Jr. *NYT*, 11/9/91).

The "shock" registered in these articles arises from the historic conflation of gay identity with risk of and blame for the disease. Essentially, Magic Johnson is lauded for showing the public that AIDS is not restricted to gays and that it in fact can be transmitted to "heterosexuals" through "heterosexual sex." What heterosexual sex consists of is never explained, since it is assumed that identity explains act. One phrase which appeared repeatedly is "it's not just a gay disease," generally followed by a discussion of how heterosexuals can also "get AIDS."[14] Media coverage does not highlight behaviors and the risks associated with those behaviors. The coverage focuses, instead, on sexual identity while assuming that sex is inherently risky. For example, one article is entitled, "Johnson's HIV Caused by Sex: Heterosexual Transmission Cited, Wife is Pregnant" (Cannon and Cotton *WP*, 11/9/91).

Ultimately, the shock directed at a heterosexually identified individual announcing that he has HIV/AIDS implies that if one is gay, he[15] is necessarily at risk regardless of his lifestyle. The articles ignore the reality that high- (and low-) risk acts, including intravenous drug use, are practiced across the spectrum of sexualities. The media's expression of shock and linkage of risk and identity (as opposed to act and risk), reinforce the conflation of identity and risk group. Specifically, the conflation of gay and HIV/AIDS is both reinforced (through an expression of shock) and destabilized (through the existence of a heterosexual with HIV/AIDS).

None of the articles mentioned the sexual acts which put Magic Johnson at risk. Rather, they stated that he contracted the disease through "heterosexual sex" and ended the inquiry there (e.g., Cannon and Cotton WP, 11/9/91; McNeil NYT, 11/10/91; see Note 13). The mainstream media overwhelmingly took as their focus a confirmation of Magic Johnson's heterosexuality and "surprise" that he contracted the virus. This is consistent with the findings of Gamson and Modigliana (1989) and Messner and Solomon (1993), who argue that mass media use "ready made" packages to construct meanings around stories. In this case, part of the ready made package is the affirmation of a hero's heterosexuality. The media center on Johnson's contraction of the "heterosexual disease," with Johnson claiming that he is "far from homosexual."[16] He immediately reassures the public that he contracted the virus through "heterosexual sex." Although "straights can get it too," media coverage continues to imply that gay men are primarily at risk. In other words, the conflation between risk (or the act which puts one at risk) and identity remains unchallenged.[17]

Rather than leading to a questioning of Magic Johnson's heterosexuality, his HIV-positive condition is framed by the media as a reaffirmation of his desirability to women. Magic Johnson's unprotected sexual activity is not problematized as his "responsibility" or his "risk," but rather, is blamed on female groupies. As McKay (1993) argues, the media privilege and protect virile male heterosexuality in sport while making consistent references to aggressive women who wait for the athletes. The implication is that any normal man would have done the same thing (e.g., "boys will be boys").

Magic Johnson's "promiscuity" is not only blamed on women, but he is painted as a kind man who says he tries "accommodating" as many women as possible. In one article Magic Johnson says, "There were just some bachelors that almost every woman in Los Angeles wanted to be with: Eddie Murphy, Arsenio Hall, and Magic Johnson. I confess that after I arrived in L.A. in 1979 I did my best to accommodate as many women as I could" (Editors *NYT*, 11/14/91). A second article agrees: "The groupies, the 'Annies.' They are the ancient entitlements of the locker room, the customary fringe benefits of muscles" (Callahan *WP*, 11/10/91). Such views are reminiscent of the Victorian Era whereby men's sexual appetites were assumed to be naturally more powerful and aggressive than women's. At the same time, women are expected to be the moral guardians of civilization by not eliciting or provoking male desire (Gilder 1973). Similar arguments are by no means confined to past history. Gilder's (1986) modern version substantially influenced Ronald Reagan during his presidency and other conservatives.

Even though over four years separate Magic Johnson's and Tommy Morrison's HIV announcements, the articles still expressed shock that a self-identified heterosexual man contracted the disease. Morrison says he thought he "had a better chance of winning the lottery than contracting this disease" (Romano *NYT*, 2/16/96) and that he thought it was a disease which only could be transmitted to homosexuals and drug users. The remaining articles on Morrison deal in some way with the risk of acquiring HIV/AIDS in the boxing ring. Over half the articles focus on the risk of transmission in the ring, even though all of the authors agree that the probability of acquiring HIV in the boxing ring is "infinitesimally small." While some articles simply use Morrison as a way to advocate new boxing policies, the articles which focus on Morrison note his "promiscuous lifestyle" and the fact that he was surprised, as no doubt were others, that a heterosexual man could contract the disease.

Rather than elevating Morrison to hero status for overcoming the stigma of the illness, the media more often treated him as a tragic figure who, through his ignorance about HIV transmission, cut short a promising career. Similar to the Johnson version, though, women are framed as pursuers, and Morrison is framed as one who is unable to resist temptation. For example, Romano framed as the problem the women who "wait outside the door fighting over who was going to get Tommy that night" (*NYT*, 2/16/96), not Morrison's pursuit of these women or his failure to practice safe sex. Though Morrison accepts some personal responsibility for contacting the "young ladies" and is blamed for making "irrational, immature decisions" in his "fast lane" life, he is not framed as the threatening pursuer but as the "world's biggest bimbo magnet."

While the articles hold Morrison accountable for his ignorance of HIV/AIDS transmission, he is not held responsible for the risk to which he may have subjected others. Romano highlights the way Morrison's "inner circle" sums up the situation: "It wasn't uncommon for me to go to his hotel room and find three or four women outside the door fighting over who was going to get Tommy that night. We had groupies all the way up to career women" (*WP*, 2/16/96). Similar to their treatment of Johnson, the media's confirmation of Morrison's heterosexuality serves to affirm his sexual desirability to women, his presumed "normal" sexuality, and his participation in only "normal" sexual acts.

Most importantly, the articles convey very little information about the transmission of HIV/AIDS. While most of the articles mention the small chance of contracting HIV in the ring, there is no mention of the types of specific activities that put one at risk outside the ring. "Promiscuity" and a "fast and reckless lifestyle" are implied risks, but promiscuity alone does not have to be risky (Watney 1989), and in fact no acts pose an HIV risk if none of the participants are HIV-positive. There is no focus in the Morrison articles on "safe sex" or the specific types of acts which are high risk. This type of omission likely contributes to the moral panic over AIDS and sex (Weeks 1985). Further, the assumed risk of promiscuity implies that heterosexual monogamy is the only imaginable moral and responsible alternative. Later, we will return to this point.

Silence Surrounding Gays and HIV/AIDS

In contrast to the coverage of Johnson's and Morrison's announcements, the print media make no mention of shock or surprise when Greg Louganis makes his announcement that he is HIV-positive. There is no discussion of promiscuity, no mention of a relationship, no indictment of a "fast lane" lifestyle, and no indication of surprise by Louganis or the public. Additionally, there are no questions as to how he could have contracted the disease. Apparently when "Louganis says he has AIDS," his homosexuality is a catch-all which signifies participation in high-risk activities, promiscuity, and inevitable contraction.

We argue that the lack of inquiry into how Louganis could have contracted the disease works to reinforce the undiscussed (assumed) inevitability of HIV/AIDS for homosexual men. This works to perpetuate the assumption that Greg Louganis's body is necessarily diseased, thereby exemplifying the conflation of gay identity with HIV/AIDS. As discussed, this stands in stark contrast to the way the mainstream print media informed the public that Magic Johnson and Tommy Morrison acquired HIV/AIDS through heterosexual activity, thus maintaining the illusion that identity explains act. In both cases, however, the specific high-risk sex acts are never discussed.

Sexual Hierarchies, Legitimate Relationships, and the Threat of Transmission

Cultural norms affect how one conceptualizes and hierarchicalizes relationships. We argue that these norms are reproduced in the discourse found in mainstream print media. This is revealed in how "straight" and "gay" men are framed differently with regard to the mention of long-term partners and/or spouses. Magic Johnson and Tommy Morrison are discussed vis-à-vis a wife and fiancée, respectively, while our previous discussion highlights the fact that no mention is made of Greg Louganis's long-term partner. Thus, by inquiring into Johnson's and Morrison's risk of infecting loved ones while never mentioning Louganis's partner, the media perpetuate the hegemony of heterosexual relationships, sex, and nuclear families. Consistent with Rubin's (1993) sexual hierarchy, we find that heterosexual relationships are more valued than homosexual relationships.

While the "blame" or responsibility for the pollution of the bodies of Magic Johnson and Tommy Morrison is placed on the aggressive women who pursued successful male sports stars, the print media offer no corollary absolution for Greg Louganis. There is no discussion about the aggressive men who may have pursued Louganis. Ironically, Greg Louganis stated in his television interview with Barbara Walters that he was in a monogamous relationship with a man who both cheated on him and abused him (*20/20*, February 24, 1995). However, none of the newspaper articles ask Louganis's partner who is responsible for transmission.

The athletes also are framed differently vis-à-vis the risk of transmission they present to others. Here, Magic Johnson and Tommy Morrison's threat to women is discussed nearly always in relation to their "legitimate" sex partners, while they are not presented often as a threat to their numerous other sex partners. Only three of the one hundred articles on Magic Johnson mention the risks he posed to the many women with whom he slept. Morrison by contrast, was said to be remorseful for putting other women at risk and urged any woman with whom he had sexual contact to "get tested." Yet he is not criticized specifically for putting these women at risk, because blame for the risk of transmission is placed on the women.

Morrison and Johnson are framed with a lifestyle which is consistent sexually with hegemonic masculinity. Their behavior may be judged as a bit "reckless," but indeed it is seen as nonproblematized heterosexuality— "female groupies" who have enticed and tainted them are the problem, and the men did what any "normal" man would do. However, the print media see no need even to ask about the men Greg Louganis may have infected, nor even to inquire about his long-term relationship, nor the risk each partner poses to the other. In this way, gay men and "promiscuous" women are problematized, while hegemonic masculinity is reaffirmed.

Class, Race, Sports, and AIDS: "Boys Will Be Boys"

Historically, African Americans and the working class have had their bodies constructed as hypersexualized, primitive, and "closer to nature" (Collins 1990). Similar to women in the mind/body duality, subordinated men are associated with the body. By contrast, white, middle-class men are defined by the mind or rationality (Synnott 1993).

This ideological belief has been reinforced and reproduced in the sports world through the disproportionate representation of men of color and working-class men (Edwards 1973; Messner 1990). A limited structure of opportunity disproportionately funnels men of color and working-class men into particular sports (Messner 1990). Articles which mention Morrison's and Johnson's class background praise these men for their current career success; yet their HIV announcements dangerously reify historical links between sexual excess and minority and working-class peoples.

Sports media tend to focus on those sports which reproduce hegemonic masculinity (Messner 1988). Since disproportionate numbers of black and working-class bodies are featured in professional sports, and since HIV/AIDS cases are well-publicized when sporting bodies are involved, it is implied that individual minority and working-class bodies are "excessively" sexual and "morally depraved." Rather than problematizing male sexuality in sport through an examination of its social norms, including the validation of masculinity through sexual conquest, the media focus on individual moral failings. In this way, the media preserve male (hetero)sexual privilege, including the conquest of women, while displacing the blame for the spread of HIV/AIDS onto black and working-class bodies.

The previous analysis revealed that Johnson's and Morrisons' social locations are simultaneously marginalized and privileged. While both men occupy marginalized race and/or class statuses, they occupy a privileged position through their contribution to the maintenance of hegemonic masculinity. However, they are also subordinated through the symbolic reaffirmation of the link between sexual immorality and socially marginalized race and class positions. Thus, while the sports-promoted norms of hegemonic masculinity are protected, the media potentially reinvigorate cultural ideas about the threatening and excessive sexualities of minority and working-class peoples.

Through such coverage, "bad" (gay, black, or working-class) sexuality is juxtaposed against the unstated norms of (heterosexual, white, middle-class) reproductive, monogamous, familial sex. White, middle-class, heterosexual men are left out of the picture and are absolved altogether from any involvement with HIV/AIDS or promiscuity. They are left out of the print media picture of sports, not because of individual differences in morality but because of a greater structure of opportunity whereby men are likely to pursue numerous career options ahead of a sports career (Edwards 1973; Messner 1990). These men are the invisible, mythical "good" or normal icons against which "bad" men and women are highlighted. In short, hegemonic masculinity is constructed as good and pure, while the bodies of women, gay men, and other subordinated masculinities are framed as corrupt.

Conservative rhetoric surrounding HIV/AIDS has emphasized abundantly the view that the sexual liberationist era of the 1960s and 1970s produced the individual moral failures of today. Here, gay men have been criticized rampantly for "fast lane" lifestyles and made to seem deserved of AIDS, no matter their sexual practices. Consistent with Eisenstein (1994), our analysis highlights how modern public discussions of HIV/AIDS have extended the signifier of AIDS beyond the gay community to include heterosexual minorities and the working class. Ultimately, as we shall see, the idea of heterosexuality is reinforced as "good," while these particular individuals are seen to have practiced "bad" heterosexuality by failing to meet dominant cultural norms of reproductive, monogamous, familial sex.

Challenging "Natural" Sexual Acts and Identities

Rather than seeing sexuality as a fixed inner essence or "natural," sexual identity categories are considered by some researchers to be a product of historical, social, and economic forces, and are the results of complex regimes of power (Foucault 1978; Katz 1995; Phelan 1994; Rubin 1993; Sedgwick 1990; Seidman 1992; Weeks 1985). Other theorists have suggested that instead of a simple dichotomy or trichotomy of sexual identity categories,[18] there is a continuum of fluid sexual identities which may shift over time. Here, researchers have challenged the insistence of placing individuals in a fixed manner into one of three groups: heterosexual, bisexual, or homosexual. In sum, certain researchers question whether there even are sexual identity categories with fixed essences or whether these are social constructions which support heterosexism and the nuclear family structure.

As previously discussed, there are a wide range of sexual practices enacted across a multitude of sexualities. Indeed, there are numerous sex acts in common between gays, lesbians, bisexuals, and heterosexuals. Rather than emphasizing the commonalities between identities, our culture and mass media tend to construct boundaries between these identities which in effect create and emphasize difference. Media discourse assumes that particular practices are limited by definition to certain identities;

however, actual practices transcend identity. In our analysis, we highlight how the media have made no mention of high-risk sexual acts the three men may have had in common. Instead, the media have focused on affirming, declaring, and reifying a fixed inner essence which our culture refers to as *sexual identity.*

The maintenance of discrete categories is one means through which power is exercised. In this way, some identities are privileged legally and socially, while others are excluded and/or condemned regardless of actual practices. Through the maintenance of these boundaries, good and bad sexualities are defined, and sexual identity is linked definitely to particular individuals and practices. By assuming that risk correlates to identity, not practice, the myth of dangerous and bad sexualities is maintained. In our analysis, the assumption that being gay "causes" HIV/AIDS, combined with the overwhelming inquiry into how a heterosexual could possibly have acquired HIV/AIDS, both reinforces and problematizes the conflation between act and identity. That is, the very fact that "straights can get it too" is destabilizing the assumption that only gays are at risk or that only acts associated with "being" gay create risk. However, by ignoring the common sexual practices of the three men and by focusing on fixed identities rather than acts, the media work to maintain discrete sexual identity categories that are thought automatically to correspond to specific acts and, hence, risk.

As a more accurate alternative, we propose analyzing these categories without the set boundaries imposed on them through the use of Haraway's (1991) metaphor of the cyborg. The cyborg metaphor demonstrates that individuals often transgress the "rules" or boundaries which mark their identities. Hence, we might expect a fusion and implosion of categories. While this appears to be occurring in lived experiences,[19] the mainstream print media's framing of these experiences attempts to maintain the distinction between these identities, acts, and risk groups.

Clearly, American discomfort with public discussion of specific sexual matters and acts contributes to the confirmation, policing, and hierarchicalization of sexual identity categories. More accurate information about AIDS/HIV transmission and human sexuality could be conveyed through the mass media if AIDS/HIV were associated with particular acts rather than particular fixed identities. Instead of destabilizing the conflation between risk and identity, our analysis has highlighted how the media merely broadened the definition of bad sexuality from gay identity to nonmonogamous, nonfamilial, heterosexual identity, while fully excluding discussions about actual behaviors and risks.

Who Can Be "Saved" From the Fate of HIV/AIDS: The Discourse of Individual Responsibility and New Right Ideology

As previously discussed, Foucault's insights demonstrate how certain ideas are imaginable, while others are unfathomable given our cultural discourse/framework. The assumptions embedded in the texts—specifically, the conflation of gay with promiscuity and the inevitability of HIV/AIDS—demonstrate how power is exercised. In terms of the way their sexual identities are framed, Magic Johnson and Tommy Morrison may be redeemed from the stigma of HIV/AIDS. Johnson and Morrison, as heterosexual "family men"—Johnson is married and has a child, Morrison is engaged—are framed as having made "mistakes." Johnson says, "Sometimes you're a little naive. . . . You think it can never happen to you" (Downey LAT, 11/8/91). Morrison says he "blew it with irresponsible, irrational, immature decisions" (Romano WP, 2/16/96). Johnson's current familial role is praised and held out as an example to young black men. In particular, he touts marriage and abstinence. Johnson asks "teenagers to be less promiscuous" and recommends they "remain virgins until marriage" (French WP, 1/14/92). The heterosexual, monogamous body is normalized, while nonmonogamous heterosexuals are labeled as deviant but redeemable through abstinence and/or by returning to the confines of heterosexual monogamy. In other words, self-identified heterosexual men are presented as temporarily lapsing from an otherwise "good" sexuality, and these lapses are presented as individual moral "failings." For these men, HIV/AIDS may be a "punishment" for transgressions, but not an irremovable stigma or "inevitable."[20]

By contrast, the homosexual body is framed as necessarily immoral, deviant, and stigmatized. Louganis is not framed as having the option of abstinence or monogamy which could have "saved" him from HIV/AIDS. Being gay conflates him with the "evils of promiscuity," a dangerous gay sexuality, and an inevitable HIV/AIDS outcome. This is accomplished through the absence of any comment about Louganis's sexual practices or any inquiry into the cause of his HIV-positive condition. Because gay sexuality is already marked as deviant and immoral, the gay body is assumed to be doomed necessarily. While Magic Johnson is given a presidential appointment as national spokesman and is lauded for being a public educator, a local senator attempts to ban Greg Louganis from speaking at a Florida university because of his "moral decadence" and for being "an embarrassment to the university community" (Associated Press *LAT*, 1/26/97).

Mainstream mass media often ignore how political and social ideologies and policies enforce a particular lifestyle and the public perception of a lifestyle. For instance, we see in our analysis how heterosexual relationships are legitimated when the mass media highlight Johnson's and Morrison's partners while ignoring Louganis's long-term partner. This is consistent with the hierarchy of sexual value which privileges heterosexual over homosexual sex and relationships (Rubin 1993). In addition, there was a definitive shift in the years between Johnson's and Morrison's HIV-positive announcements. Earlier media frames labeled certain behavior (safe sex, monogamy, and abstinence) acceptable and responsible, while later frames only included abstinence and monogamy. Numerous articles stress safe sex and Johnson's role in current and future safe sex campaigns. By contrast, media attention surrounding Tommy Morrison's announcement four years later included no discussion of safe sex. Instead, the focus was on Morrison's promiscuity, which is roundly condemned.

Such a shift is explained largely by the recent resurgence of the New Right, which offers "clear cut and familiar" moral strategies which are seen as best regulating "personal and social life" (Weeks 1985, 53). Historically, there have been three different approaches to regulating sexuality: liberal, libertarian, and absolutist (Weeks 1985). Rooted in Christianity, absolutist strategies are becoming increasingly popular in the United States in this post-sexual liberation era. Under these strategies, participants value limited notions of relationships and family forms, along with abstinence and monogamy. Here, our analysis has shown how the mass media act to promote as "moral," and hence safe, monogamous nuclear family forms. The media frame excludes a discussion of numerous viable forms of relationships and safe erotic pluralism across sexual identity categories. Given the current rise of a New Right ideology which stresses "family values" and which is obvious in its backlash against gay and lesbian political progress, it is not surprising that sexual liberation is not a part of the cultural discourse presented by the mainstream print media.

Conclusion

In sum, the media police sexuality by presenting the causes of and solutions to the HIV/AIDS epidemic by framing marriage, heterosexuality, and monogamy as "safe" and by condemning homosexuality, promiscuity, and casual sex as "dangerous." Here, we see male sporting bodies of "promiscuous" minority and working-class heterosexuals grouped with "immoral" gay men. Despite challenging the automatic conflation of gays and HIV/AIDS by adding heterosexuals to the list of those at risk, the mass media maintain the assumption that gays will get AIDS and that a gay lifestyle is synonymous with promiscuity. Because the lifestyles of only some heterosexuals are stigmatized, the "moral panic" surrounding sex is reinvigorated (Rubin 1993) and the stigmatization and fear about homosexuality being anti-family is reinforced subtly.

Invoking a moral panic through an emphasis on the "evils of promiscuity" falsely reinforces the idea that sex is inherently dangerous (Rubin 1993; Watney 1989; Weeks 1985). This occurs through the perpetuation of the myth that promiscuity is necessarily dangerous and risky. Watney (1989) predicted such tendencies when he posited that as we see more people with HIV/AIDS across social groups, we will see a more frantic push for monogamy and a denunciation of the promiscuous. It should be noted that AIDS is neither caused by promiscuity nor prevented by monogamy, as "one can contract AIDS if one has one sexual partner in one's life—with AIDS" (Watney 1989, 32). What needs to be emphasized if we are going to highlight individual solutions is not the lessening of sexual activities or "the demonology of sex" (Rubin 1993), but a discussion of the kinds of activities which put one at risk. The challenges posed by Segal (1994), Weeks (1989), Watney (1989), and Patton (1990) include creative ideas on how a safe and active erotic plurality could easily be highlighted and, in fact, already exists.

The print media coverage of HIV-positive athletes reveals how sports media are active in the reproduction of ideologies which privilege hetero-

269

sexual male behavior. How athletes are framed by the mass media with regards to their social locations reveals and reproduces cultural assumptions about normal and deviant behavior. Even when exemplars of hegemonic masculinity contract a highly stigmatized illness, print media coverage does not problematize norms of male sexual conquest in sport, norms which are consistent with hegemonic masculinity. Rather, print media coverage focuses blame on failed individual bodies and subordinate sexualities, specifically those of women, minorities, and working-class and gay men.

Social fears surrounding HIV/AIDS, a "moral panic" over sex, the spread of HIV/AIDS in sport, and concerns for a "dissipating" nuclear family structure make such an analysis especially timely. As Rubin notes, "It is precisely at times such as these" that "disputes over sexual behavior . . . become the vehicles for displacing social anxieties, and discharging their attendant emotional intensity" (1993, 4). We must be critical, however, of the media's role in forming erroneous links in the culture at large between HIV/AIDS, sexual identity, and risk. As noted by Weeks (1985), we tend to invent "new victims" in times of social apprehension. This may be true, but we are also finding new villains. Clearly, the media are playing an important role in the policing of bodies and acts and in the fixing of identities through a hierarchical sexual morality which is embedded in the "cultural anxiousness" of our time.

Notes

1. It is important to understand that men who are members of a subordinated racial group can still "do" and reinforce hegemonic masculinity.

2. At the turn of the century, as urbanization and industrialization led to an increase in the middle class and a decline in the traditional jobs which signified masculinity, sports were presented as a means to ensure that the "proper" values would be transferred to men. Further, success at sports came to replace physical labor as a cultural reaffirmation of ideologies of male physical superiority.

3. Female sexualities such as bisexuality and lesbianism appear to be largely excluded from the discourse altogether. This in and of itself exemplifies Foucault's (and numerous feminist theorists') discussion of the unthinkable (or the culturally invisible).

4. While gay men constitute the largest number of deaths in absolute terms, the largest growing categories of transmission are said to be heterosexuals (Chase *WSJ*, 11/11/91) and people of color (Specter *NYT*, 11/9/91).

5. Kinsey's research focused on sex acts rather than identities and found that 37 percent of men and approximately 20 percent of women had experienced at least one same-sex experience to the point of orgasm (1948, 1953).

6. Imagine a gay man who practices bondage on one hundred men a year but never exchanges any bodily fluids. Then let us think of a monogamous married woman who only has unprotected vaginal intercourse with her husband, who in turn has unprotected anal sex with a man who is HIV-positive. Popular perception, which focuses on identity and not acts, assumes that the gay man has a very high risk of transmission and that the heterosexual woman has a low risk. In reality, the gay man's risk is very low while the married monogamous woman's risk is higher.

7. In other words, sexual act and risk group can be dangerously conflated. For instance, numerous heterosexual women have anal and oral sex, sex acts which are frequently seen as acts which make HIV transmission for gay men highly likely. Here, heterosexual women share "high-risk acts" with gay men and yet generally have been viewed as a group not at risk, while gay men are generally viewed as very *high* risk. Recently, this perception has started to change as both groups are perceived as being at risk. Once again, no act is high risk unless one commits high-risk sex acts with someone who is HIV-positive.

8. Other analyses of media coverage reveal frames of Magic Johnson as a "hero" for living with a stigmatized illness with little to no mention of how his unprotected "promiscuity" posed a threat of transmission to women. Gay men, on the other hand, are not only held responsible for their illness but also are villainized as a threat to the heterosexual community (Wachs and Dworkin 1997). For example, Greg Louganis was framed by mass media as a "carrier" of the virus, which emphasizes his HIV-positive status as a threat to the heterosexual community.

9. Radical feminists such as Firestone (1970) predated Foucault in this respect. Even work as early as Mary Wollestonecraft's (of the late 1790s) is said to explicate concepts which are corollaries to modern terms such as "docile" and obedient bodies (Bordo 1993).

10. We recognize the use of the Associated Press by all three of these newspapers. However, most major newspapers use the Associated Press. In many ways, this strengthens our argument, as it demonstrates the homogenization of information dissemination among the mainstream print media.

11. Greg Louganis has won forty-seven national titles, five world championships, and five Olympic medals, winning consecutive double gold medals in 1984 and 1988. In addition, he had been favored to win two gold medals in 1980, the year the United States boycotted the Olympics.

12. Magazine articles and television transcripts were collected, and this informa-

271

tion does inform our analysis. However, in the interest of time and due to a lack of funding, a thorough analysis of these additional materials could not be performed.

13. One article notes that numerous AIDS hotline callers who had questions about HIV/AIDS transmission asked: What is "heterosexual sex?" (Lewis WP, 11/9/91). This supports our argument which stresses the need to focus on high-risk acts, not sexual identity categories, when discussing HIV/AIDS transmission.

14. As discussed in Note 10, the frequency of this line may be due to media reliance on the Associated Press or other newspapers as sources, thus limiting the discourse on an issue. Further, often the same sports reporters are assigned to stories with similar content, and, hence, these reporters' personal views may be overrepresented by newspapers. Regardless, the frequency of the occurrence still represents the dissemination of limited information and ideologies.

15. In many articles, it is simply gay identity which is framed as at risk. Thus, it is likely that lesbian and gay identities were both conflated with risk no matter what the sexual act or risk differences may be between the two groups. In general, "he" is used as the subject (therefore, we use he as the subject), since all of the articles covered had male subjects.

16. Significantly, most of the mainstream media chose to ignore long-time rumors of Johnson's participation in bisexual activities. Some exceptions include the *San Francisco Examiner* and *USA Today.*

17. While we are stressing the perceived link between act and identity with reference to sexual identity, this coverage indeed may contribute to a reinforcement of heterosexual panic surrounding tropes of black male promiscuity and sexual "excessiveness" (Cole and Andrews 1996; Cole and Denny 1994; Lule 1995).

18. Generally, there is an assumption that individuals are either gay/lesbian or straight. An additional category, bisexual, has recently been increasingly recognized to form a trichotomy (Klein 1993; Rust 1995; Weinberg, Williams, and Pryor 1994).

19. For example, some newspapers cover Magic Johnson's alleged "bisexual" activities, yet he maintains a self-proclaimed solidly heterosexual identity. Ultimately, this demonstrates the fluidity of sex acts across identities and perhaps points to the fluidity of identity itself. It is the naming and marking of these identities (and the fixing of sex acts to identities) which reifies the power of each identity category.

20. Magic Johnson currently asserts that "God saved him" (editors NYT, 4/5/97). Ignoring the fact that he is receiving the best medical care the world has to offer, Johnson attributes the decrease of the virus in his blood to his current monogamous family life.

References

Bordo, S. (1993). *Unbearable weight: Feminism, Western culture, and the body.* Berkeley: University of California Press.

Cole, C. L., & Andrews, D. L. (1996). Look, it's NBA Showtime!: A research annual. *Cultural Studies, 1,* 141–181.

Cole, C. L., & Denny, H. (1994). Visualizing deviance in post-Reagan America: Magic Johnson, AIDS and the promiscuous world of professional sport. *Critical Sociology, 20,* 123–147.

Collins, P. H. (1990). *Black feminist thought—Knowledge, consciousness, and the politics of empowerment.* London: HarperCollins.

Connell, R. W. (1987). *Gender and power: Society, the person and sexual politics.* Stanford: Stanford University Press.

———. (1990). An iron man: The body and some contradictions of hegemonic masculinity. In M. Messner & D. Sabo (eds.), *Sport, men and the gender order* (pp. 83–96). Champaign, Ill.: Human Kinetics.

Crosset, T. (1990). Masculinity, sexuality, and the development of early modern sport. In M. Messner & D. Sabo (eds.), *Sport, men and the gender order* (pp. 45–54). Champaign, Ill.: Human Kinetics.

Davis, L. (1997). *The swimsuit issue and sport: Hegemonic masculinity in* Sports Illustrated. New York: SUNY Press.

DeFleur, M., & Ball-Rokeach, S. (1989). *Theories of mass communication.* New York: Longman.

Duggan, L., & Hunter, N. D. (1995). *Sex wars: Sexual dissent and political culture.* New York: Routledge.

Duncan, M. C., Messner, M. A., & Jensen, K. (1994). *Gender stereotyping in televised sports: A follow-up to the 1989 study.* Los Angeles: The Amateur Athletic Foundation.

Dutton, K. (1995). *The perfectible body: The Western ideal of male physical development.* New York: Continuum.

Dworkin, S. L., & Wachs, F. L. (in press). The morality/manhood paradox: Masculinity, sport, and the media. In M. Messner, J. McKay, & D. Sabo (eds.), *Masculinities and sport.* London: Sage.

Edwards, H. (1973). *Sociology of sport.* Homewood, Ill.: Dorsey Press.

Eisenstein, Z. (1994). *The color of gender: Reimaging democracy.* Berkeley: University of California Press.

Firestone, S. (1970). *The dialectic of sex: The case for feminist revolution.* New York: Quill.

Fiske, J. (1994). *Media matters: Everyday culture and political change.* Minneapolis: University of Minnesota Press.

Foucault, M. (1978). *The history of sexuality.* New York: Vintage Books.

———. (1979). *Discipline and punish: The birth of the prison.* New York: Vintage Books.

Gamson, W., & Modigliana, A. (1989). Media discourse and public opinion on nuclear power: A constructionist approach. *American Journal of Sociology, 95,* 1–37.

Gilder, G. (1973). *Sexual suicide.* New York: Quadrangle.

————. (1986). *Men and marriage.* Gretna, La.: Pelican.

Gorn, E., & Goldstein, W. (1993). *A brief history of American sports.* New York: Hill & Wang.

Grosz, E. (1994). *Volatile bodies: Towards a corporeal feminism.* Bloomington: Indiana University Press.

Haraway, D. (1991). *Simians, cyborgs, and women: The reinvention of nature.* London: Free Association.

Herman, E. S., & Chomsky, N. (1988). *Manufacturing consent: The political economy of the mass media.* New York: Pantheon.

Kane, M. J. (1988). Media coverage of the female athlete before, during, and after Title IX: *Sports Illustrated* revisited. *Journal of Sport Management, 2,* 87–99.

Kane, M. J., & Snyder, E. (1989). Sport typing: The social "containment" of women in sport. *Arena Review, 13,* 77–96.

Katz, J. N. (1995). *The invention of heterosexuality.* New York: Penguin.

Kimmel, M. (1990). Baseball and the reconstitution of American masculinity, 1880–1920. In M. Messner & D. Sabo (eds.), *Sport, men and the gender order* (pp. 55–66). Champaign, Ill.: Human Kinetics.

Kinsey, A. (1948). *Sexual behavior in the human male.* Philadelphia: W.B. Saunders.

————. (1953). *Sexual behavior in the human female.* Philadelphia: W.B. Saunders.

Klein, F. (1993). *The bisexual option.* New York: Haworth Press.

LePoire, B. (1994). Attraction toward and nonverbal stigmatization of gay males and persons with AIDS: Evidence of symbolic over instrumental attitudinal structures. *Human Communication Research, 21*(2), 241–279.

Lule, J. (1995). The rape of Mike Tyson: Race, the press and symbolic stereotypes. *Critical Studies in Mass Communication, 12,* 176–195.

McKay, J. (1993). "Marked men" and "wanton women": The politics of naming sexual "deviance" in sport. *The Journal of Men's Studies, 2,* 69–87.

McLuhan, M. (1964). *Understanding media: The extensions of man.* Cambridge, Mass.: MIT Press.

McQuail, D. (1987). *Mass communication theory.* London: Sage.

Messner, M. A. (1990). Masculinities and athletic careers: Bonding and status differences. In M. Messner & D. Sabo (eds.), *Sport, men and the gender order* (pp. 97–108). Champaign, Ill.: Human Kinetics.

————. (1988). Sports and male domination: The female athlete as contested ideological terrain. *Sociology of Sport Journal, 12,* 197–211.

Messner, M. A., & Solomon, W. S. (1993). Outside the frame: Newspaper coverage of the Sugar Ray Leonard wife abuse story. *Sociology of Sport Journal, 10,* 119–134.

Metheny, E. (1965). *Connotations of movement in sport and dance.* Dubuque, Iowa: Wm. C. Brown.

Patton, C. (1990). *Inventing AIDS.* New York: Routledge.

Phelan, S. (1994). *Getting specific: Post-modern lesbian politics.* Minneapolis: University of Minnesota Press.

Rubin, G. (1993). Thinking sex: Notes for a radical theory of the politics of sexuality. In H. Abelove, M. A. Barale, & D. M. Halperin (eds.), *The lesbian and gay studies reader* (pp. 3–62). New York: Routledge.

Rust, P. (1995). *Bisexuality and the challenge to lesbian politics: Sex, loyalty, and revolution.* New York: New York Press.

Sedgwick, E. K. (1990). *Epistemology of the closet.* Berkeley: University of California Press.

Segal, L. (1994). *Straight sex: Rethinking the politics of pleasure.* Berkeley: University of California Press.

Seidman, S. (1992). *Embattled eros: Sexual politics and ethics in contemporary America.* New York: Routledge.

Sontag, S. (1989). *AIDS and its metaphors.* New York: Farrar, Straus, and Giroux.

Synnott, A. (1993). *The body social: Symbolism, self and society.* London: Routledge.

Wachs, F. L., & Dworkin, S. L. (1997). There's no such thing as a gay hero: Magic = hero, Louganis = carrier: Sexual identity and media framing of HIV positive athletes. *Journal of Sport and Social Issues, 21,* 335–355.

Watney, S. (1989). *Policing desire: Pornography, AIDS, and the media.* Minneapolis: University of Minnesota Press.

Weeks, J. (1985). *Sexuality and its discontents: Meanings, myths, and modern sexualities.* New York: Routledge.

Weinberg, M. S., Williams, C., & Pryor, D. (1994). *Dual attraction: Understanding bisexuality.* New York: Oxford University Press.

Appendix

Magic Johnson

11/8/91   Harris, S. Announcement hailed as a way to teach public, *Los Angeles Times,* A32.

11/8/91   Heisler, M. Magic Johnson's career ended by HIV-positive test, *Los Angeles Times,* A1.

11/8/91   Murphy, D. E., & Griego, T. An icon falls and his public suffers the pain, *Los Angeles Times,* AI.

11/8/91   Kindred, D. Magic's gift for inspiring us tests reality, *Los Angeles Times,* B7.

11/8/91   Bonk, T. Even hearing news was not believing it, *Los Angeles Times,* C1.

11/8/91   Downey, M. Earvin leaves NBA, but his smile remains, *Los Angeles Times,* C1.

11/8/91   Springer, S. Through the years, he stayed the same, *Los Angeles Times,* C1.

11/8/91   Stevenson, R. W. Basketball star retires on advice of his doctors, *New York Times,* A1.

11/8/91   Berkow, I. Magic Johnson's legacy, *New York Times*, B11.

11/8/91   Thomas, R. M., Jr. News reverberates through basketball and well beyond it, *New York Times*, B13.

11/8/91   Brown, C. A career of impact, a player with heart, *New York Times*, B11.

11/8/91   Araton, H. Riley leads the prayers, *New York Times*, B11.

11/8/91   Specter, M. Magic's loud message for young black men, *New York Times*, B12.

11/8/91   Aldridge, D. Lakers star put imprint on finals, records, money, *Washington Post*, C1.

11/8/91   Gladwell, M., & Muscatine, A. Legend's latest challenge, *Washington Post*, front page.

11/8/91   Cannon, L. Basketball star Magic Johnson retires with AIDS virus, *Washington Post*, front page.

11/8/91   Castaneda, R., & Sanchez, R. Johnson's AIDS virus revelation moves teenagers, fans, *Washington Post*, D1.

11/9/91   Bonk, T., & Scott, J. "Don't feel sorry for me," Magic says, *Los Angeles Times*, A1.

11/9/91   Lacey, M., & Martin, H. Student's cry a bit, learn life lessons, *Los Angeles Times*, A26.

11/9/91   Gerstenzang, J., & Cimons, M. Bush calls Johnson a hero, defends administration's policy on AIDS, *Los Angeles Times*, A26.

11/9/91   Horovitz, B. Sponsors may use Magic in ads to encourage safe sex, *Los Angeles Times*, D1.

11/9/91   Editors, A magical cure for lethargy, *Los Angeles Times*, B5.

11/9/91   Thomas, R. M., Jr. A day later, it remains a shock felt around the world, *New York Times*, 33.

11/9/91   Specter, M. When AIDS taps hero, his "children" feel pain, *New York Times*, front page.

11/9/91   McMillen, T. Magic, now and forever, *New York Times*, 23.

11/9/91   Stevenson, R. W. Johnson's frankness continues, *New York Times*, 33.

11/9/91   Mathews, J. Los Angeles stunned as hero begins future with HIV *Washington Post*, A1 2.

11/9/91   Cannon, L., & Cotton, A. Johnson's HIV caused by sex: "Heterosexual transmission" cited; wife is pregnant, *Washington Post*, front page.

11/9/91   Lewis, N. Apprehensive callers swamp hotline, *Washington Post*, A12.

11/9/91   Shen, F. Hero's shocker leaves teens grasping for answers, *Washington Post*, front page.

11/10/91   Callahan, T. What it boils down to is playing with fire, *Washington Post*, D2.

11/10/91   Jones, R. A. A shock that shifted the world, *Los Angeles Times*, A3.

11/10/91   Lipsyte, R. A jarring reveille for sports, *New York Times*, S1.

11/10/91   McNeil, D. On the court or off, still Magic, *New York Times*, E9.

11/10/91   Muscatine, A. Magic's revelation transcends sports, *Washington Post*, D1.

11/10/91 Aldridge, D. For moments like these, *Washington Post*, D4.

11/11/91 Horovitz, B. Advertisers try to handle this Magic moment carefully, *Los Angeles Times*, D1.

11/14/91 Editors, Sorry but Magic isn't a hero, *New York Times*, B19.

11/14/91 Editors, Converse's AIDS efforts feature Magic Johnson, *New York Times*, D1.

11/18/91 Almond, E., & Ford, A. Wild ovation greets Magic at Lakers game, *Los Angeles Times*, A1.

11/30/91 Editors, Keep Magic in the mainstream, *New York Times*, B7.

1/1/92 Araton, H. Advertisers shying from Magic's touch, *New York Times*, 44.

1/14/92 French, M. A. Magic, rewriting the rules of romance, *Washington Post*, B1.

11/11/91 Chase, M. Johnson disclosure underscores facts of AIDS in heterosexual population, *Wall Street Journal*, B1.

4/5/97 Editors, Johnson's HIV level drops, AIDS virus in Earvin "Magic" Johnson is significantly reduced, *New York Times*, 36.

Greg Louganis

2/23/95 Weyler, J. Olympic diver Louganis reveals that he has AIDS, *Los Angeles Times*, A1.

2/23/95 Sandomir, R. Louganis, Olympic champion, says he has AIDS, *New York Times*, B11.

2/23/95 Longman, J. Doctor at games supports Louganis, *New York Times*, B15.

2/24/95 Boxall, B., & Williams, F. Louganis disclosure greeted with sadness, *Los Angeles Times*, B1.

2/24/95 Editors, Louganis: Breaks his silence, another world-famous athlete disclosed he has AIDS, *Los Angeles Times*, B6.

2/24/95 Vecsey, G. Tolerance, not blame, for Louganis, *New York Times*, B7.

2/24/95 Longman, J. Olympians won't have to take HIV test, *New York Times*, B7.

2/26/95 Longman, J. Olympian blood: Debate about HIV tests sparked by diver with AIDS. *New York Times*, 2.

2/28/95 Quintanilla, M. The truth shall set you free, *Los Angeles Times*, E11.

3/5/95 Alfano, P. The Louganis disclosure: AIDS in the age of hype, *New York Times Magazine*, E1.

5/5/95 Ammon, R. Gay athletes, *Los Angeles Times*, M5.

1/26/97 Senator seeks to ban Louganis, *Los Angeles Times*, C11.

Tommy Morrison

2/12/96 Eskenazi, G. Morrison suspension: An HIV concern, *New York Times*, B6.

2/13/96 Springer, S. Magic Johnson plans to call boxer, *Los Angeles Times*, A9.

2/13/96 Springer, S., & Gustkey, E. Boxer's HIV test heats up debate over risk to others, *Los Angeles Times*, A1.

2/13/96 Eskenazi, G. Morrison confirms positive HIV test, *New York Times*, B13.

2/14/96   HIV test for Morrison ref, *New York Times*, B11.

2/16/96   Vecsey, G. Morrison didn't pay enough attention, *New York Times*, B20.

2/16/96   Eskenazi, G. Remorseful Morrison has words of caution, *New York Times*, B7.

2/16/96   Romano, L. Heavyweight deals with serious blow, *Washington Post*, A1.

9/20/96   Kawakami, T. HIV-positive Morrison says he'll fight again, *Los Angeles Times*, C9.

10

SUSAN BIRRELL AND CHERYL L. COLE

Double Fault
Renee Richards and the Construction
and Naturalization of Difference

● In July of 1976, a reporter covering a local tennis tournament in La Jolla, California, became suspicious when the defending champion in the women's division was soundly thrashed by a 6-foot 2-inch newcomer by the name of Renee Clarke. Searching further, the reporter discovered that Renee Clarke was actually Renee Richards, a constructed-female transsexual[1] who less than a year before had been Richard Raskind, a man ranked highly by the United States Tennis Association in the thirty-five-and-over men's division. The media clamor that ensued might have died down had Richards not accepted an invitation to play in a national tournament in South Orange, New Jersey, that his/her[2] old friend Eugene Scott was organizing as a warm-up to the United States Open. The United States Tennis Association (USTA) and the Women's Tennis Association (WTA) promptly withdrew their sanctions from the South Orange tournament. In protest of Richards's participation, twenty-five of the thirty-two women originally scheduled to play in South Orange withdrew to enter an alternative tournament hastily arranged and sanctioned by the USTA and the WTA. Undaunted, the forty-one-year-old Richards advanced through

This essay originally appeared in and is reprinted by permission of *Sociology of Sport Journal* 7(1)(1990): 1–21.

three rounds before losing in the semifinals to seventeen-year-old Lea Antonopolis. Thus begins one of the more sensational and most illuminating incidents in contemporary sport.

A few days later, Richards announced his/her intention to play women's singles in the 1976 US Open at Forest Hills, and the antagonism between Renee Richards and the women's tennis world was formalized. The USTA, the WTA, and the United States Open Committee (USOC) responded by requiring that all women competitors take a sex chromatin test known as the Barr body test. Richards refused, and the US Open went on without him/her. One year later, s/he took the case to the New York Supreme Court, which ruled that "this person is now female" and that requiring Richards to pass the Barr body test was "grossly unfair, discriminatory and inequitable, and violative of her rights" (*Richards* v. *USTA*, 1977, 272). The court's decision cleared the way for Richards to play in the women's singles at the 1977 US Open where s/he lost in the first round to Virginia Wade, 6–1, 6–4. Richards's modest professional career continued until 1981, when s/he retired from competition at age forty-seven. After a successful year as Martina Navratilova's coach, s/he left professional tennis and returned to his/her ophthalmology practice.

The entrance of Renee Richards into women's professional tennis created confusion and controversy for the players, the fans, organized tennis, and the public. Adding drama to the general controversy over the sexual status of transsexuals was Richards's decision to participate as a woman in a cultural activity still accepted as legitimately divided into two sex categories. The confusion that followed Richards's action illuminates sport as an important element in a political field which produces and reproduces two apparently natural, mutually exclusive, "opposite" sexes.

The controversy over Richards's contested entrance into women's sport was addressed at length in the press and later re-examined in Richards's autobiography *Second Serve* (1983) and the television movie, *Second Serve*. These sources framed the Renee Richards story within traditional liberal rhetoric as a story about fairness and human rights focused around the problematic status of the transsexual. By focusing on the question of individual sex legitimacy, that is, whether Renee Richards is a man or a woman, the media obscured the broader political and social issues.

The purpose of our analysis is to show how our culture constructs woman and produces particular notions of gender, sex, and difference by examining a case where these ideological processes are literally enacted: the construction of a "woman," Renee Richards, from a man. In Richards's rather spectacular case, the construction can be examined on two dimensions: the relatively private technical construction of Richards accomplished by an array of medical and legal experts; and the more public construction of Richards accomplished through the discursive practices of the print media and the autobiographical construction offered by Richards in the book and television movie *Second Serve*. In this essay we examine the media's construction of the controversy surrounding Renee Richards; we offer a critical reading of discursive practices which construct and control transsexualism, sexuality, sex, and gender; and we explore the particular problematic posed by Richards's entrance into the highly gendered world of professional sport. Moreover, by asking how it is possible to "change" sexes, what it means to want to change, and what it means to be able to change, we argue that transsexualism simultaneously illuminates and mystifies the cultural constructions of woman and man by positioning a seemingly anomalous case within hegemonic discourses of sex difference, sex and gender identity, and the gendering of bodies.

Although initially Renee Richards appears to be newsworthy because s/he is a sexual anomaly who challenges taken-for-granted assumptions about sex and gender, our critical reading suggests how the various media frames invoked to explain the meaning of Renee Richards reproduce rather than challenge dominant gender arrangements and ideologies, specifically the assumptions that there are two and only two, obviously universal, natural, bipolar, mutually exclusive sexes which necessarily correspond to stable gender identity and gendered behavior. And while the media coverage of the controversy surrounding Richards's desire to play women's professional tennis is seemingly confined to the immediate event, we will suggest that the media enter into and depend upon a broader discourse produced by a constellation of institutions empowered to enforce boundaries between woman and man based on essential conceptualizations of gender, sex, and difference.

Transsexualism and the Technological Construction of Woman

Within the dominant discourse of sex research, the category of trans-sexual is assigned to a person who believes that he or she was born into the wrong body, a belief Jan Morris describes as "a passionate, lifelong, ineradicable conviction" (1974, 8). The anatomical structure of the body which indexes sex, particularly the genitals, is in direct conflict with the pre-operative transsexual's sense of self as a gendered individual. In contrast to transvestites, who habitually cross-dress, "true transsexuals feel that they belong to the other sex, they want to be and function as members of the opposite sex, not only to appear as such" (Benjamin 1966, 13). Such an identity depends on the belief that there are two neatly distinct and absolute categories of sex-gender. As Jan Morris understands it, "I was born into the wrong body, being feminine by gender but male by sex, and I could achieve completeness only when the one was adjusted to the other" (1974, 26).

Anxieties constructed through sex, gender, and sexuality in our culture reside ultimately in the body and our attitudes toward our own body as well as the bodies of others. Foucault (1979) suggests, "The body is directly involved in a political field; power relations have an intimate hold upon it: they invest it, train it, and torture it, force it to carry out its tasks, to perform ceremonies and emit signs" (25–26).

The gender dysphoria that transsexuals suffer often drives them to seek "sex reassignment," a lengthy process which requires the services of a number of experts in normalizing disciplines: surgeons, gynecologists, endocrinologists, plastic surgeons, psychiatrists, speech therapists, and lawyers. These experts enact a discourse which legitimates sex reassignment by working together to alter what is presented as the unalterable. In this sense, gender dysphoria and transsexualism are not neutral categories but elements in a social system that controls and regulates the body and sex.

For the constructed-female transsexual—estimated as comprising about 80 to 90 percent of the ten thousand transsexuals in the United States (Grimm 1987)—the sex reassignment process begins with extensive psychotherapy to ensure that surgery is advisable. This is followed by a lengthy period during which the preoperative transsexual must live as a member of the opposite sex as proof of his or her ability to accomplish appropriately gendered behavior. Finally, a series of operations is performed during which the sex signifiers are exchanged: Male sex organs are removed and an artificial vagina is constructed and implanted. Massive doses of female sex hormones, breast implants, cosmetic plastic surgery on the face and adam's apple, and speech therapy further sustain the apparent change.

The knowledge which organizes our understanding of transsexualism has been divided into two major approaches (Bolin 1987): clinical approaches which characterize the psychiatric and psychological research and are based on a medical model in which transsexualism is constituted as an individual problem, "a syndrome subject to treatment" (41); and sociocultural approaches taken by ethnomethodologists and anthropologists, which focus on "the relationship of . . . transsexualism to the culture at large" (47).

Clinical approaches (e.g., Benjamin 1966; Money and Ehrhardt 1972; Money and Tucker 1975; Stoller 1975), are concerned with transsexual etiology or the biological and/or psychological variables which have caused transsexualism.[3] They subscribe to some form of sexual essentialism while locating the problem within the individual and the dysfunctional family, "with the family as the largest unit of external etiological influence" (Bolin 1987, 59). However, by focusing on the individual as the pathological victim of a disconcerting sexual syndrome, the body and transsexualism are removed from the technologies of gender[4] and the broader network of social relations in which we live and understand our lives. In this view, the transsexual is blamed for failing to adjust to a rigid system of gender stereotypes. Therapeutic management programs designed to create gender reversal and surgical treatment, though an object of some dispute, are viewed as legitimate treatments to cure transsexuals. Gender dysphoria is represented as a state which can be most effectively corrected through the combination of biomedical and legal authorization of the exchange of the material signifiers that reconstitute sex status.

Sociocultural approaches view transsexualism not as an individual malady but as an epiphenomenon which can be understood only within the context of a particular culture. Sociocultural researchers (e.g., Bolin 1988; Garfinkel and Stoller 1967; Kando 1973; Kessler and McKenna 1978;

Williams 1986) are interested in "what transsexualism reveals about the cultural construction of gender and the sex/gender system" (Bolin 1977, 47). For example, while the disproportionate number of transsexuals are male to female, historically, the reverse was true (Bullough 1975), testimony to the cultural and historical specificity of transsexual emergence.[5] And the ethnocentricity of our two-sex/two-gender paradigm is revealed through analyses of different sex/gender arrangements in other cultures such as the berdasch and the amazonia (Williams 1986).[6]

The existence of transsexualism is discomforting because it simultaneously disrupts and confirms our commonsense about the nature of sex, gender, and the relationships between them. Transsexualism unravels and rebinds our cultural notion that there are two and only two, mutually exclusive, naturally occurring, immutable, opposite sexes. The acute gender dysphoria that impels a transsexual to consider surgical remedy suggests that radically reconfiguring the body through the removal and construction of sex signifiers is easier than living in a culture in which rigid gender ideologies do not permit men to act in stereotypically female ways.

The transsexual's solution to gender dysphoria is to change sexes: an individual solution to a systemic problem. Gender dysphoria is the personal manifestation of a larger cultural problem, in this case, the institutionalization of a system that reduces sex to two mutually exclusive, natural categories. By seeking surgical remedy, the transsexual acquiesces to a system which locates individuals as either male or female subjects. Ironically, the transsexual's personal relief reinforces the very system that produces transsexualism.

Contesting Sex: The Legal Construction of Woman

In her critique *The Transsexual Empire*, Jan Raymond (1979) raises important critical issues: Who is empowered to legitimate transsexual surgery as a valid medical procedure and treatment? Who is authorized to decide who qualifies for sex reassignment, and what will the "proof" of qualification be? Who will determine the legal status of the postoperative transsexual? Raymond bases her argument on the cultural construction of gender identity and transsexualism.[7] The successful male candidate for sex reassignment surgery, for example, must demonstrate stereotypical female behavior patterns and attitudes to the men who hold the power to reconstruct his body.

By conceptualizing transsexualism within a scientific-clinical discourse as an exceptional pathological condition traceable to early childhood abnormalities, and by dealing with it on a case-by-case basis, those who control the technologies of gender, especially the transsexual empire, give themselves license to offer a technological solution to the cultural problem of inflexible gender role prescriptions. For a culture organized around rigid gender roles and for the individuals most discomfited by those demands, the transsexual empire prescribes the small but expensive Band-Aid of reconstructive surgery.

The Renee Richards case offered a particularly public opportunity to examine Raymond's thesis, but the power of the transsexual empire is one of the major issues obscured by the news media in that case. The coverage of Richards's entrance into women's tennis fails to acknowledge the existence of the male-dominated transsexual empire of surgeons, lawyers, and psychologists whose technological and discursive practices make it legally and, Raymond would argue, morally possible to change one's body/sex. While medical technology makes sex reassignment possible, the legal system insists upon and is the final arbiter of sex identity.[8] Renee Richards was positioned as a woman through legal discourses and was granted the legal right to play tennis as a woman because the New York Supreme Court accepted as its criterion of womanhood a female-appearing phenotype brought about by cosmetic surgery and sustained by massive amounts of female hormones.

In formulating their decision, the court was persuaded by the argument of the expert witnesses Richards called on his/her behalf: the surgeon who performed his sex reassignment operation; his gynecologist; and John Money, a psychologist from Johns Hopkins who is considered the most prominent sex reassignment expert in the United States and a major architect of the transsexual empire. In effect, the court accepted as voices of legitimation those very people responsible for producing Richards as a postoperative transsexual in the first place.

Opposing Richards in court were the defendants, the USTA, the WTA, and the USOC, who argued that "there is a competitive advantage for a male who has undergone 'sex-change' surgery as a result of physical train-ing and development as a male" (*Richards* v. *USTA* 1977, 269). To support their case, they submitted affidavits from an expert witness defending the validity of the Barr body test; from three women professional tennis play-ers, Francoise Durr, Janet Newberry, and Kristien Shaw; and from the Director of Women's Tennis for the USTA, Vicki Berner. Those who would articulate oppositional discourses, however, lacked access to both the institutions and the means of challenging them directly. Thus, the Renee Richards case offers literal and dramatic evidence that when an individual's sex is contested, and when the discourses of womanhood are contested, male-dominated institutions have disproportionate power to decide what is and is not a woman. Acting in concert, the medical and legal institutions have the power to authorize, regulate, and control the body and sex.

Media Conventions and Frames, and the Construction of Woman

The construction of Renee Richards began with the transformation of Richard Raskind to Renee Richards through extensive psychological and medical procedures. Thus, Renee Richards exists as Renee Richards at least partially because it is technologically possible. The construction continues more publicly in the news media's coverage of the controversy and in Richards's autobiography *Second Serve* (1983) and the made-for-television movie adaptation of the autobiography which aired in 1985. By drawing upon examples from both the news media and the autobiographies we will show how dominant liberal conventions shape the narrative and thus public understandings of Renee Richards and transsexualism.[9]

The media produce news, not truth. While the media appear simply to report "what happened," they actively construct news through frames, values, and conventions. Having made the initial decision that an incident is worthy of treatment as news, reporters and editors make a number of choices which foreground some elements of the potential narrative and obscure others, and they define and delineate issues through a series of choices including headlines, descriptive word choices, photographs, whom to authorize with an interview, and what to report (Hartley 1982). Gitlin (1980) suggests that the hegemonic frames, codes, and conventions in U.S. news include an emphasis on elements of drama and personality; conventions of "balance," brevity, and stereotyping in which the complexity of an event is collapsed into two opposing positions and authorities representing each side are offered the opportunity to comment; temporality; and suspicion of difference and disorder as threat. In the production of news, the frame constructed and choices made offer a preferred reading of the events. As Hall (1977) summarizes the effect:

> It is masked, frequently by the intervention of the professional ideologies—those practical-technical routinizations of practices (news values, news sense, lively presentation, "exciting pictures," good stories, hot news, etc.) which, at the phenomenal level, structure the everyday practices of encoding and set the encoder within the bracket of a professional-technical neutrality which, in any case distances him [sic] effectively from the ideological content of the material he is handling and the ideological inflections of codes he is employing. Hence, though events will not be systematically encoded in a single way, they will tend, systematically, to draw on a very limited repertoire: and that repertoire . . . will have the overall tendency of making things "mean" within the sphere of the dominant ideology. (344)

Following convention, the newspapers recognized the tennis controversy as news because its immediacy and finiteness mark it as newsworthy within the media's ideological code. The coverage of the Renee Richards story began in the national news media on July 24, 1976, the first news mention of Richards during the South Orange tournament, and it ended on August 18, 1977, the date the papers reported the court decision that granted Richards the right to participate as a woman in the 1977 US Open. By using the official proclamation of the law to provide closure for the story, the newspapers implied that the end of the tennis controversy marks the logical resolution to the issue of transsexualism itself.

To the newspapers, the threshold of newsworthiness had passed. Indeed, only Richards's intentions to enter women's sport had qualified the story as news in the first place: The mere existence of a transsexual in society has not been news since Christine Jorgensen (1967). Thus, the newspapers focus on what seems to be a concrete event: the controversy surrounding Renee Richards's decision to enter women's tennis. But by isolating the event in the present, the historical and cultural context and significance are excluded from the frame. In other words, the ideological codes that journalists follow in their apparent impartiality actively mystify the ideological determinants of the story.

The media identified two issues which guided their coverage: Is it fair to allow Renee Richards to play women's professional tennis? and Is Renee Richards a man or a woman? Both issues are clearly embedded in ideological frames of liberalism and sexual essentialism. The central narrative was constructed around liberal notions of human rights, and fairness clearly was defined in terms of Richards, not in terms of the women players who had to accommodate him/her as one of them. Richards was represented as the central character within a drama of heroic confrontation between an individual and the tennis bureaucracy. Richards was thus positioned within a familiar cultural discourse of heroic narrative, a story worthy of Frank Capra, about an individual's struggle to prevail against the tyranny of the system.

Generally obscured in the newspapers' construction of this drama of human rights were: any serious consideration of the women players' case, particularly the social and historical context within which sport in North America has developed as an activity that privileges males; the meaning of the sex test ordered by the USTA; the meaning of the anti-feminist sentiment which was packaged as pro-Richards rhetoric; and the wider implications of the Richards controversy, including the cultural meaning of transsexualism, sex, and gender, and the power of the male-dominated medical and legal professions to construct and legitimate the female.

The news coverage and the autobiographies differ in the relationship between the issues of whether Richards should be allowed to play women's tennis and whether Richards is a man or a woman. The news media focused on the former and implicated the latter, while the autobiography and film used the former as an occasion to focus on the latter. The news media clearly defined the issues in terms of tennis, and the Renee Richards story unfolded as news almost entirely on the sport pages of newspapers and the sport sections of magazines. In contrast, the autobiographies rely on the familiar autobiographical convention of exposing personal truths to address broader issues of transsexualism. In the entire book of 373 pages, tennis comprises only 46 pages, a proportion that is matched in the film as well. Tennis, it is clear, is merely the occasion for the unfolding of a deeper personal narrative.

Yet even taken together, the news media's exposition of the tennis controversy and the autobiographies' analyses of transsexualism as personal history do not offer a critical understanding of transsexualism. Both accounts work within the constraints of a dominant discourse which constructs two essential, universal and opposite sexes. By maintaining a tight frame around Richards and by presenting Richards as an isolated case, they endorse an individualistic, clinical model, and they neglect the larger cultural context of gender arrangements. Beneath the surface of their narratives, the ideology of gender relations lies undisturbed, and important questions go unasked: What is a woman? On what basis should we make our decision? Who shall be empowered to decide? How have women been constructed? What is the connection between sex and gender, since transsexual gender identity makes it clear that one cannot necessarily be mapped from the other? These issues are not centralized in the narrative; they are too controversial and complex to be treated within the media conventions of balance, immediacy, objectivity, and appeals to authority.

The Gendering of Renee Richards

The news media focused primarily on whether Richards should be allowed to play women's tennis, but the issue of whether Richards is a man or a woman formed an implicit frame for their narratives. Indeed, the most significant framing device the papers used in their construction of the story was the gendering of Richards as a female. The framing of Richards as female was accomplished through their choice of personal pronouns and through the descriptions of Richards they drew for their readers.

While there was some doubt in their minds about what sex category Richards belonged in and whether Richards was a transvestite or a transsexual (*New York Times* July 24, 1976), in fact they resolved the problem for themselves and their readers by referring to Richards as "she" from the very first day of coverage. This choice of personal pronoun was made a full year before a legal decision was made,[10] and it is one of the primary ways that the public came to know Richards. By framing Richards as "she" the press resolved the very issue it was purporting to cover: the contest over his/her sex. In a similar manner, the casting of Vanessa Redgrave to portray Richards in the television movie tells viewers from the very first minute that Renee Richards is truly and naturally a female.

An individual contesting his or her sex creates a linguistic dilemma in cultures where pronouns and adjectives denote gender. The dilemma is reflected in the quotes from women protesting Richards. Glynnis Coles was quite consistent: "I don't think he should be playing . . . As far as I'm concerned he's just a man who's had an operation" (*Washington Post* January 1, 1978). But Diane Fromholtz's complaint captured the ambiguity most protesters could not work through: "People are laughing at us, at the way she walks on and acts like a female" (*Washington Post* January 1, 1978). With the very act of refuting Richards's claims to be female, Fromholtz genders Richards's female. The most telling statement was Roz Reid's protest on behalf of his wife, Kerry Melville Reid: "We don't believe Renee is a woman. Kerry will never play her again" (*Washington Post* January 1, 1978).

Officials also had difficulty with the ambiguity. Early in the controversy, W. E. Hester, vice-president of the USTA, stated, "I don't know on what grounds we could admit her and on what grounds we can refuse to admit him" (*Los Angeles Times* August 12, 1976). The USTA first described Richards as "a man [who had] won a woman's tournament" (*New York Times* July 24, 1976) and "a biological male" (*New York Times* August 14, 1976), then, as more sophisticated discourses developed, as a "person not genetically female" (*New York Times* August 15, 1976). Phillippe Chatrier of the International Tennis Federation, determined to bar Richards from international competition, said "Mr.-Miss Richards should not be allowed to play" (*Winston-Salem Journal* October 22, 1977).

Richards was also gendered by the press in terms of the descriptions they offered of him/her, many of which captured the ambiguity the press and the public were trying to resolve. The *New York Times* noted: "Dr. Richards displays traits associated with both sexes. The soft husky voice is mostly male but the high cheekbones, shapely legs, graceful gold pierced earrings and peach nail polish . . . are distinctly female" (August 19, 1976).

And Neil Amdur reported Richards's declaration that "I'm as much a woman as anyone on the US tour" and added:

> At 6 feet 2 inches, Dr. Richards who weighs 147 pounds is consider-
> ably taller than most women, even women athletes. She has tight
> muscles in her calves, the kind you might expect to see on a male
> sprinter or a halfback in football. Yet her facial features, the high
> cheekbones, the brown eyes and the sharply defined eyebrows—are
> distinctly feminine. She carries herself considerably smoother than
> many female athletes . . . Her voice is soft, somewhat raspy but firm
> in the manner of a confident professional. (*New York Times*, August
> 21, 1976)

Elsewhere, the press followed their convention of mentioning details of physical appearance of women athletes they generally ignore in male athletes. By reporting on physical appearance, the press legitimates physi- cality as a valid means for assessing one's sex status, thus confusing the issue of the sex/gender relationship and obscuring the cultural production of such relationships.

Richards's autobiography makes even more explicit the cultural con- fusion about sex, gender, and sexuality. Throughout the book, Richards dwells on his/her appearance and the confirmation of his/her true female self, his/her "success as a girl," that is reflected in male attention to his/ her female-appearing body: "Renee fed on [the attention] because [it] represented a casual and ready acceptance of her femaleness. Men held doors open for me, young boys and sometimes older men looked me over appreciatively" (31). On a trip to Casablanca, Richards was mistaken for a woman and picked up for the first time. His/her suitor had "eyes that appraised me with obvious interest. This was the first time I had ever been openly, unreservedly ogled by a man. I quite liked it . . . The more he appreciated me the more I felt like a girl" (220).

Elsewhere in the autobiography Richards enacts male-defined concep- tions of feminine behavior. These include the almost total objectification of his/her new body, an exhibitionism evident throughout the book and symbolized by sitting naked for an hour in the locker room while being interviewed by reporters after the South Orange tournament (*Washington*

Post August 22, 1976), and his/her desire to relate to men in submissive ways. Of one male friend who had known him/her only as Renee, s/he says, "He'd always treated me with overtones of male superiority, and I loved it, considering this treatment a compliment of my validity as a woman" (321).

His/her submission to men is most marked in his/her accounts of intimacy in which s/he clearly equates sexuality, specifically sexual passivity and submission, with being a woman. In his adolescent years, for example, he enacted mock rapes with a male high school friend under the guise of wrestling naked on his bed:

> Eventually I would have to surrender to his compelling strength. There was something about this situation that pleased me . . . I struggled like hell because that was crucial to my feeling. I had to know that his dominance was real . . . It was very sensual to surrender like that. (45)

His trip to Europe was full of sexual encounters with strange men: a truck driver who helped him by scraping ice off the windshield of his Maserati, then made sexual advances ("After all, he had done me a favor and deserved something for his trouble . . . It's not every day that a truck driver gets to make out with a classy dame in a Maserati" [237]); a dangerous episode with a stranger in Marrakech; and a menage à trois in Majorca. Finally, after the reconstructive surgery, Richards "waited three months, resigning myself to a lengthy virginity" (287) before being "deflowered" by a former homosexual lover:

> I got a real sense of satisfaction out of being the object of his desire . . . Tremendously exciting also were his encompassing size, the smell of him, his hairiness, and his weight pressing down on me . . . [H]e finished quickly, and I loved that as well. I was warmed by his sense of urgency and the forceful thrusts that accompanied his climax. I didn't have an orgasm myself . . . Nonetheless, I loved it. I was at last fully capable of the woman's role. (294–296)

By offering his/her body as a source of sexual pleasure for men, Richards apparently believes s/he has been re-sexed as a woman. S/he has clearly incorporated the dominant cultural discourse on femininity, gendered bodies, and femaleness into his/her consciousness.

Constructing the Oppositions

Since conventions limit journalists's abilities to deal with the complexity of the issues posed by controversy, and since reporters are required to cover and present only two sides of a story, the controversy over Renee Richards's entrance into women's professional tennis was reduced and assembled into two mutually exclusive and opposing positions. Support for Richards came from his old male tennis friends, such as Gene Scott and Bobby Riggs, and from two prominent women, Gladys Heldman, who provided several opportunities for Richards to play on a women's tour she was promoting, and Billie Jean King, who invited Richards to play women's doubles with her on that tour.

Opposition came from the rank and file of the women's tour, some of whom refused to play Richards. Their position was represented by Beth Norton in a letter to the WTA quoted in the *Winston-Salem Journal* in which she protested

> the unfairness of forcing young girls to compete with a middle-aged transsexual who previously has been a nationally ranked men's player . . . [and who had] 30 years experience playing men's and boy's tennis . . . It is only fair that her rights should not impose upon the rights of girls earning a professional living in the women's tour. The rights of all of us as individuals should be taken into consideration. (February 14, 1978)

However, the voices of the individual women tennis players who opposed Richards were generally silenced by the media[11] who represented opposition to Richards as "the tennis establishment," "organized tennis," or most often by the impersonal device of initials: the WTA, the USTA, the USOC. The use of initials and the fact that most spokespersons for these groups were men not only depersonalized the opposition but obscured sex and gender in a situation which is in fact about sex and gender. Richards's sex status was constantly foregrounded while the sex of his/her opposition was obscured.

The autobiographies obscure the opposition even more, never acknowledging adverse reaction from anyone other than the USTA and the
WTA. Richards claims "most of the women . . . were on my side" (1984,
346). S/he reports receiving forty thousand letters after the La Jolla tournament, of which "nine-tenths was positive" (324), and s/he notes a pattern
of support from the fans: "I was treated respectfully and if there were
hecklers I never heard them" (350). The newspapers confirmed this impression (*New York Times* August 28, 1976).

Thus, opposition to Richards was framed as organizational impulses
to protect the carefully nurtured image of women's tennis by protecting
the women players from unfair competition.[12] What might have been reported as a series of individual dramas that paralleled the structure of the
sport itself—Richards vs. Antonopolis, Richards vs. Smith, Richards vs.
Evert—was instead packaged as Richards vs. The Establishment. The controversy was framed within the classic American liberal tradition of the
heroic struggle of one individual against the bureaucracy. Given such a
plot, the American tradition is to root for the beleaguered underdog.

Richards solidified his/her role as an underdog by positioning him/
herself as a spokesperson for a minority group. S/he first discovered this
possibility at the La Jolla tournament when a woman of color said:

"Renee . . . I don't want you to withdraw. I am a member of a
minority myself . . . I've found that when people don't know what
pigeonhole to put you in, your only alternative is to show them what
you are and act as if you have the right to be that. You won't be
doing yourself a favor if you run away from this tournament. You'll
be giving in to stupidity. Hold your head up and play." (317)

Richards noted "This was the first time anybody had ever put the
issues in broader perspective," and s/he began to consider him/herself "a
kind of standard bearer" (317). S/he was deluged with letters of support
from "people who were members of minorities. Among others, I heard
from blacks, convicts, Chicanos, hippies, homosexuals, people with physical handicaps and, of course, transsexuals (325). Notably absent from his/
her list of oppressed groups is women. The support surprised Richards
who admitted

I've never even been political [but] . . . I was susceptible to this flood of sentiment. Until you have pawed through thirty thousand letters pleading with you to stand up for you rights and, in so doing, stand up for the rights of the world's downtrodden, you don't know what pressure is. Left to my own devices, I probably would have resolved my personal pique at being summarily barred from competition— but, my god, the whole world seemed to be looking for me to be their Joan of Arc. (325)

The broadened support an identity as Joan of Arc could provide him/ her was not lost on Richards, who returned to that theme throughout the book and regularly spoke to it during interviews with the press. In a story headlined "Renee Richards Pursuing Tennis Career for a Cause" (August 19, 1976), the *New York Times* positioned Richards as a champion for all transsexuals, and later they broadened Richards's underdog status by quoting him/her: "[The USTA] have done the same thing with me that they've done with every other minority" (September 1, 1976).

However, Richards's inability to recognize women as a political group whose interests must be protected, or whose interests might, indeed do, interfere with his/her own undermines his/her stance as a spokesperson for human rights. Richards acknowledged in the autobiography that much as s/he desired to live life as a woman, s/he had little sensitivity to the political implications of that life: "My idea of how a lady is treated was formed prior to women's liberation . . ." (291). Like many transsexuals, s/he displays an exaggerated, stereotypical notion of feminine behavior drawn from male-defined notions of gender. This attitude was exacer- bated by the requirement that s/he prove to male psychiatrists and medical experts that s/he was ready for the drastic surgical step of sex reassignment by demonstrating almost hyperfeminine behavior.

Moreover, Richards is clearly unaware of the advantages of Raskind's life of male privilege, including attendance at a boys's prep school, gradua- tion from Yale, completion of medical school, a successful surgical prac- tice, the thrill of being approached by a scout from the New York Yankees, and access to highly competitive tennis which s/he took as his/her natural right as a male. His/her own sister, who so longed for such opportunities, was summarily denied them. Yet Richards never acknowledges the implications for women of his/her entrance into their world. As one colleague has suggested to us, "Renee Richards should have had his consciousness raised before he had his sex changed."

Support for Richards as Suspicion of Women

Richards's apparent inability to recognize the political position of women problematizes the media's construction of him/her as a symbol for human rights. But while Richards was being positioned by the press as a symbol of human rights, support for him/her can be read for meanings overlooked by the media: Indeed it is difficult to read the support for Richards as anything other than opposition to women. Richards's entrance into women's professional sport occasioned an outburst of anti-feminist sentiment that was unexamined by the press.

The vehemence of this opposition to the women players can be read within a Foucauldian (1979) context of anxiety, suspicion, and surveillance. Terry (1989) has argued that "we witness daily technological developments designed to keep a watchful eye on those entities considered suspicious . . . in an effort to contain 'danger' and restore 'security' " (14). Given the challenges transsexuals pose to the dominant gender system, medical and legal surveillance systems work together to contain what they consider to be dangerous. In a similar manner, growing anxiety about changes in women's social positions and participation in traditional masculine practices such as sport have intensified suspicion of women.

The historical struggles of women and sport are particularly important in locating the sources of the tension around the women players, since Richards entered women's sport in the wake of the women's liberation movement and dramatic gains for women and for women in sport throughout the 1960s and 1970s. Billie Jean King's defeat of Bobby Riggs in "The Battle of the Sexes" (1974) and the success of Gladys Heldman and King in organizing resistance to male control of the women's tennis circuit in the early 1970s marked the end of men's complete dominance in tennis. Ironically Richards's desire to play on the women's tour depended upon the recent struggles of women players and organizers whose successes gave the tour increased economic viability. Thus, Richards stood to benefit directly from the hard-won opportunities for women in sport at the very moment s/he was challenging them.

While the media's narratives make general references to the history of sex discrimination in tennis and to past confrontations, in effect they provided space for male voices to frame women's successes within an atmosphere of suspicion, and readers were not given a context in which to understand these challenges to the women's integrity. By directing attention to the event's immediacy and presenting the controversy apart from its historical context, the origins of opposition are obscured. Jameson (1983) notes:

the disappearance of a sense of history, the way in which our entire contemporary social system has little by little begun to lose its capacity to retain its own past, has begun to live in a perpetual present and in a perpetual change which obliterates traditions of the kind which all earlier social formations have had in one way or another to preserve . . . One is tempted to say that the very function of the news media would thus be to help us forget, to serve as the very agents and mechanisms for our historical amnesia. (125)

The support for Richards can be read within a context of anxiety and suspicion of women's recent successes in sport. Gene Scott's support of Richards was particularly revealing of this suspicion: "The women players are always talking about sex discrimination but when it comes to a real issue they run and hide. If we followed them we'd still be reading by candlelight" (quoted in Kennedy 1976, 19).

Although Scott's comments allude to a history of struggle around women and sport, to him the "real" issue is not the hard-won rights of the women players, but the rights of constructed-female transsexuals. Equally telling was Scott's comment to the *Washington Post*:

I think the women players today are basically sheep followers. They have worked hard and gotten a terrific recognition factor and lots of spectators. The prize money has escalated out of all proportion. But they did all this by cultivating a reputation of being in a mood of change and imagination. [Their reaction to Renee Richards] shows this is all bunk. They're actually afraid of new ideas. (August 21, 1976)

This quote betrays Scott's feelings about women's equality when he complains that "the prize money has escalated out of all proportion." He dismissed the women players's opposition to Richards as childish whimpering: "I've heard the women whine for years about Chris Evert's dominating on clay" (*Washington Post* August 21, 1976).

Ilie Nastase's comment also reveals more disdain for the women players than support for Richards: "If she wears a dress, why not? Now you see how strong the women players are. She could be their mother, yet they complain. They're afraid" (quoted in Kennedy 1976, 18).

Richards was proud to report that Nastase "was one of my earliest supporters; he once made a remark that I was more feminine than some of the women already on the tour" (332). Such comments cast suspicion on the women players as imperfect women and belittle the historical struggles of women in sport. Through similar homophobic comments about the women players, Richards attempted to establish his/her own claim to female status. Explaining why s/he refused to take the sex chromosome test, for example, Richards argued "in my case such tests were irrelevant. Of all the potential competitors my sex was the least in doubt. It was a matter of public record based on legal documentation" (343). Admitting that at 6'1" "I looked so damn fearsome," Richards continued, "Still Betty Stove was six feet tall and hefty besides. So were some lesser known pros, yet their sexuality had never been questioned" (344). Throughout the autobiography, Richards used the concepts sex status and sexuality interchangeably. That confusion reveals the homophobia that also forms the basis for the men's anxieties. Elsewhere the confusion can be understood as a central feature in Richards's construction of him/herself as a gendered being.

In all the coverage of the Renee Richards controversy, not one mention was made of a male player who did not support Richards, a rather extraordinary detail which may indicate either the press's reluctance to report opposition among male players or the depths of anti-woman sentiment on the tour. As one woman player who opposed Richards complained, "They want to see anybody beat us, even a transsexual" (quoted in Steinem 1977, 85). Thus, "support" for Richards came in a form which simultaneously cast suspicion on or discredited the women players. Steinem pointed out the tactic as well:

When the women players themselves questioned the fairness of their facing someone trained physically and culturally for forty years as a man, they were ridiculed as poor sports, anti–civil libertarians, or cowards who feared they couldn't win. (85)

The press sometimes joined in the trivialization of the women's opposition. The *Washington Post* acknowledged "Few on Tour Support Richards" and "Opposition to Richards Apparently Growing" (January 1, 1978). They estimated that 80 percent of the women opposed Richards: "some of it friendly, some impersonal, some viciously hostile." Yet in one of the few stories dealing with the reactions of individual women players, the *Post* chose to report instances of "downright cruel" behavior, including two British players who appeared at a tournament wearing T-shirts with the message, "I am a real woman."

A final example of producing sympathy for Richards by casting suspicion on or blaming women can be found in Richards's autobiography. The book is an extended narrative of personal etiology in which Richards recounts in detail the anguish of gender dysphoria, his/her analysis of the causes, and his/her forty-one-year search for remedies, including the mutilation of his/her penis in a denial of the signifier of manhood; vivid accounts of sexual adventures into hyper-heterosexuality, transvestism, homosexuality, and quasi-lesbianism; and the cruel series of promises and rejections from the medical establishment, the psychiatric community, and family and friends as s/he finally sought sex reassignment.

In the book and movie a major focus of blame and suspicion was Richards's mother. The book begins, for example, with the words, "My mother was a headstrong woman" (1) and within two pages the reader has been acquainted with the sex role reversals traditionally believed to be the root of transsexualism and male homosexuality: the domineering mother, the submissive father. Richards paints a picture of a childhood full of gender confusion—an older sister named Michael who wanted to be a boy, and his mother's and sister's habit of dressing him in girl's clothes, including a traumatic incident at age four when he was humiliated by being made to appear in public dressed as a girl. Richards argues that "my early life is strewn with unsubtle touches that beg to be seen as reasons for my sexual confusion. If they aren't the true cause they ought to be" (5).

Most of these incidents are depicted in the film as well, and a rather foreshortened analysis is offered by his/her psychiatrist mother (Louise Fletcher in a tight performance reminiscent of her portrayal of Nurse Ratched in *One Flew Over the Cuckoo's Nest*). When confronted by her son's admission of deep sexual confusion, she prescribes psychiatric therapy and states simply, "Maybe it's my fault . . . You probably identified with me instead of your father. Quite *natural* really. I was so strong" (our emphasis). To underscore her strength, she is portrayed in her first scene as a feminist, and her first line, delivered to someone on the phone while her son awaits her attention, is "But women have always had to fight." In both the book and the film, strong women come in for more than their share of blame for Richards's condition while cultural constructions of rigid gender and sex ideologies go unaddressed.

Competitive Equality and the Natural Inferiority of Women

Opposition to Richards was framed in terms of the issues of competitive equality and the domino effect. As the USTA saw it, "The entry into women's events . . . of persons not genetically female would introduce an element of inequality and unfairness into the championships" (*New York Times* August 15, 1976). USTA counsel Peter Leisure argued in court, "It would be unfair to have women who have worked hard and prepared for this tournament beaten by a person who is more than woman (*New York Times* August 11, 1977). Added to the fear that Richards's male body provided an insurmountable natural advantage over the women players was the fear that Richards would "open the way to problems in the future from young male players with transsexual tendencies" (*New York Times* December 31, 1976). As Richards viewed the issue:

> If I was allowed to play, then the floodgates would be opened and through them would come tumbling an endless stream of made-over Neanderthals who would brutalize Chris Evert and Evonne Goolagong . . . Some player who was not quite good enough in men's tennis might decide to change only in order to overpower the women players. (345)

These debates over fairness were translated into issues related to the body and power. The body, one of the most seemingly natural elements of social life, was foregrounded by the press. Descriptions emphasizing Richards's/women's physical appearance and women's physical inferiority were presented uncritically and circulated by the media. The logic they employed seemed to say that if Richards is weaker than s/he was or if s/he adorns his/her body in stereotypical feminine ways, then Richards is weak enough and feminine enough to be allowed to play.

Because the media focused on men's "natural" ability rather than the years of privileged access to sport that Richard Raskind had enjoyed, they foregrounded physical definitions of sex and gender and obscured cultural ones. Richards also constructed the argument in physiological and biomechanical terms. S/he noted with characteristic humor, "they think of me as a bionic woman" (*New York Times* August 18, 1976), but s/he refuted this view. Noting the changes in his/her body as the result of hormonal treatments, s/he said "The tone of the muscles . . . seemed to be softer now" (172). Of his/her tennis game s/he remarked "I didn't notice much decrease in my general abilities though I was definitely less strong. After six months of hormone therapy I estimate that I had about four-fifths of my previous strength" (178). In fact Richards argued that his/her heavier male bone structure and hormonally reduced muscle mass actually meant "I was playing with a handicap" (344). S/he argued that his/her losses proved a point: "(T)hey served to inform the public that I was not an unbeatable behemoth out to prey on helpless little girls" (350).

The discourse on bodies within the Richards's controversy demonstrates the cultural significance of constructing women's bodies as different from and representing them as physically inferior to men's bodies. The challenge of Richards's presence in women's sport works to naturalize women as physically inferior, and that assumption of the natural inferiority of women is evident in Richards's thinking throughout the autobiography. Playing social tennis in Europe while undergoing hormonal treatment preliminary to his/her operation, Richards was pleased at his/her partners's reaction to his/her superior skill but "when I missed a ball, they were quick to blame it on my being a woman. I didn't mind these jibes because they affirmed my womanliness" (238).

Richards's mediocre performances on court were also used by the

press to suggest his acceptability as a woman. After Richards lost to Antonopolis in South Orange (August 28, 1976) the *Times* asked, "So what was
all the fuss about?" Billie Jean King argued in Richards's defense, "she
does not enjoy physical superiority or strength so as to have an advantage
over women competitors in the sport of tennis" (*Richards v. USTA* 1977,
272). And the USTA eventually decided against an appeal because Richards
"did not represent the physical threat that officials and players once
feared" (*New York Times* August 18, 1977). Richards himself noted that
"none of the fears that drove them to ban me ever proved warranted. I
certainly haven't dominated the world of women's tennis" (365).[13]

Richards's inability to "dominate" women's tennis is offered as proof
of his/her status as a woman. Radically reconfiguring his/her body
through the exchange of material sex-signifiers has apparently cost Richards his/her natural superiority as a (former) male. Through reference to
his weakened condition, the news media and Richards construct Richards
as less-than-male and thus an acceptable challenge for women players.

Representation and Constraint

In this essay we have tried to show how meanings of sex, gender,
difference, and power are literally inscribed onto the body and then how
that body is represented through the discourse of news and the autobiographical constructions of individual subjectivity. The ambiguity of
Richards's constructed-female transsexual body triggered a crisis in representation in terms of sport and the body. However, the media not only
ignored the contradictions posed by Richards but positioned him/her as a
hero and a signifier of resistance while women as a group became targets
for the exercise of power through criticism. Homophobic and sexist discourses were constructed to contain women as suspicious. Dyer (1982)
reminds us that

> a major legacy of the social and political movements of the Sixties
> and Seventies has been the realization of the importance of represen-
> tation. The political chances of different groups in society—powerful
> or weak, central or marginal—are crucially affected by how they are
> represented, whether in legal and parliamentary discourse, in educa-
> tional practices, or in the arts. The mass media in particular have a

crucial role to play, because they are a centralised source of definitions of what people are like in any given society. How a particular
group is represented determines in a very real sense what it can do
in society. (43)

The Renee Richards case provides a dramatic moment for examining these
issues.

Our examination of the media's representation of the controversy
around Renee Richards is an attempt to illuminate the everyday practices
of the media and the processes through which representations define femininity. In this case, the media accepted as unproblematic the assumptions
of liberalism, dominant images of femininity, and ideologies of sport.
While the contradictions embedded in and through the processes of transsexualism potentially trigger a crisis in representations of sex and gender,
the conventions of the media make it difficult to articulate and interpret
the controversy outside of dominant discourses.

This is not to suggest that all readings are symmetrical with encodings
or preferred readings. The varied and complex lived experiences of social
actors no doubt produce readings which depart from the frame constructed by the commercial media. But the tight frame and the narrative
constructed around the controversy combined with a neglect of the historical position of women and sport, the meaning of the possibility of transsexualism, and the technologies of gender work to constrain the possibility
of alternative readings. These conventions produce what Hall (1977) has
suggested is the endemic tendency of the media: support of the status quo.

Renee Richards, Sport, and the Production of Difference

Renee Richards's determination to enter women's sport, the support
and opposition to that move, and the representation of the controversy
that the media constructed provide fascinating insight into our cultural
understandings of sex difference, gender behavior, and the role that sport
plays in their production and reproduction.

The entrance of a transsexual into women's sport posed an interesting
dilemma which was symbolized by the fact that Richards had to sue to
gain the legal right to enter sport as a woman. After all, Jan Morris did

not have to sue to be allowed to be a writer, Christine Jorgensen did not have to sue to become an entertainer, and Richards continued his/her career as an ophthalmologist. The particular difficulty of this dilemma reveals sport not only as a gender-producing, gender-affirming system, but as a difference-producing system. For sport works to differentiate winners from losers, the men from the boys, the men from the women. As a significant gendering activity, sport not only reproduces gender and sex differences but it produces a logic of differentiation.

Because sport celebrates physicality within a competitive frame, working to determine winners based on physical superiority, it is a major site for the naturalization of sex and gender differences. Moreover sport's logic continually reproduces men as naturally superior to women (Willis 1982; Connell 1983). The sex test instituted for the 1968 Olympic Games is a clear example of the manner in which sex categories are vigilantly maintained in sport. The sex test arose from the suspicion that superior female athletic performances, such as those of Ewa Klobukowska, were actually accomplished by women who were not truly women or by craftily disguised men. The implication is that superior athletic prowess is the natural domain of males.

The prestige of athletic victory, the "natural" inferiority of women constructed through sport's power as metaphor, and thus the easier competition assumed in the women's division all lead to the logical conclusion that enterprising men might try to pass as women. Renee Richards represented one form that challenge might take. Although Richards asked, "How hungry for tennis success must you be to have your penis chopped off in pursuit of it? How many men would do it for a million dollars?" (345), in fact the U.S. obsession with sport makes it not at all unlikely that some man would willingly sacrifice his penis for victory; drug abuse, steroid use, blood doping, urine transplants, overtraining, and ignoring life-threatening or crippling injuries are all a part of the modern sport scene.

A critical reading of the Renee Richards incident illuminates the part sport plays in the reproduction of an ideology of sex difference/power, gender and sex identity, and the regulation of the body. As Willis and others argue, sport is a central site for the naturalization of sex and gender differences, that is, sport produces a narrative structured around physical superiority in which sex differences are understood as, and thus reproduced as, real and meaningful. Transsexualism appears to challenge the neatness and logic—indeed the "reality"—of a sex/gender system marked by biological difference. This reveals not only the social construction of gender, but the social construction of the sex-gender connection. Moreover, transsexualism demonstrates that it is not only the categories of difference that are culturally produced but the notion of difference itself.

It would seem as though the re-sexing of an individual such as Richards deconstructs notions of natural sex identity, but in fact, by remaining gendered, Richards reaffirms the concept of difference. By apparently changing sex, Renee Richards appears to upset our dominant ideology of gender relations, but in fact he stabilizes that ideology by merely shifting categories, by demonstrating dramatically that we must have a gendered home and that the "mistakes of nature" can be technologically corrected by man.

As Joan Scott and other poststructuralists point out, "meaning is made through implicit and explicit contrast" (1988, 36), through antithesis and difference. Primary among these binary oppositions that structure our discourses and thus our consciousness, indeed the archetype of that ideological practice, is sexual difference. When sex difference is contested, the entire ideological enterprise of meaning through difference is shaken. While Renee Richards demonstrates the disproportionate power that male-dominated institutions have in the construction and legitimization of woman, even more profound is the illumination the Renee Richards incident casts on our cultural mandate to maintain difference. There are no alternative categories for Richards or other nonconforming subjects to inhabit in the law, medical science, language, or sport. Their order depends upon the maintenance of the familiar binary opposition of male/female. The Renee Richards case is not only about tennis and transsexualism, not only about the construction of woman, but also about the construction of difference itself.

Notes

This essay was written during a developmental leave provided by the University of Iowa and generously supported by the staff and colleagues at University House. The senior author gratefully acknowledges this collegial support. We would also like to thank Nancy Theberge, Linda Yanney, and Nancy Romalov and the reviewers for the *Sociology of Sport Journal* for bringing important sources to our attention and for useful critical feedback.

1. A major purpose of this paper is to problematize one fiction of science, the discourse of transsexualism, including the assumptions about the ontological status of sex and femininity, and to ask how sex reassignment or sex change is possible. We problematize some terms through the use of quotation marks at first mention. We use the phrase "constructed-female transsexual" because it reflects the constructedness of sex and gender.

2. The pronoun used to describe Richards is a significant political move. We have opted to refer to Renee Richards as s/he to denote Richards's bisexed lived experience and his/her difference from those who have lived only one sexual identity. Had we countered the mainstream positioning of Richards as female by repositioning him as male, the choice of a singular pronoun would deny either Richards's past or present positioning.

3. This is true, as well, of the autobiographies of transsexuals (e.g., Martino 1977; Jorgensen 1967; Morris 1974; Richards 1973) which struggle to comprehend their own personal etiology, which dwell on the personal anguish of gender dysphoria, and which end on a note of personal triumph.

4. According to de Lauretis (1987), the concept of technologies of gender "takes . . . its conceptual premise from Foucault's theory of sexuality as a 'technology of sex' and proposes that gender, too, both as a representation and self-representation, is the product of various social technologies, such as cinema, as well as by institutional discourses, epistemologies, and critical practices; [meaning] not only academic criticism, but more broadly social and cultural practices" (ix).

5. According to Bullough (1975) strict religious sanctions and "a kind of mystic view of the inferiority of the female" made it almost impossible for men to assume the female role without harsh reprisals. Thus the majority of preoperative transsexuals, or transvestites, prior to the nineteenth century were women.

6. We persist in our two sexes/two genders paradigm despite the existence of counterexamples in our own culture: tomboys and sissies, transvestites, female impersonators, drag queens, gay men, lesbians, gender blending women (Devor 1987). These anomalies are repositioned within dominant discourse through a variety of cultural practices: labeling homosexuals as queers whose behavior "goes against human nature," refusing to take transvestites and drag queens seriously, patiently waiting for tomboys to grow out of their inappropriate behavior, and completely misunderstanding the meaning of the berdasch by imposing ethnocentric models on them (Williams 1987).

7. Raymond's book clearly illuminates the relationship between sex stereotypes and the medical empire's understanding and treatment of transsexuals. Although her argument is based on an understanding of the cultural constructedness of gender, she contradicts her explanation of the cultural construction of gender identity and transsexualism when she argues that female-transsexuals can never be real women because women's biology makes females unique.

8. While a number of criteria traditionally have been available to distinguish between the sexes—including chromosomes, anatomy or morphological structure, genital or gonadal evidence, endocrine or hormonal balances, and psychological factors (Money and Earhardt 1972)—the law accepts genital anatomy as its means of "official sex designation" (Dunlap 1979, 1132).

9. Our analysis is of three metropolitan newspapers of national reputation: the *New York Times,* the *Washington Post,* and the *Los Angeles Times.* We analyzed all news stories, editorials, photographs, and cartoons featuring Renee Richards which appeared between July 24, 1976, the first news mention of Richards during the South Orange tournament, and August 12, 1982, when Richards returned to his/her medical practice. We also included articles in popular magazines such as *Sports Illustrated, Time,* and *Newsweek.*

10. The legal system also accomplished gendering through language. In the very case which was to determine Richards's legal sex status, the court referred to Richards as "she" in the very first sentence: "A professional tennis player who had undergone sex reassignment surgery which allegedly changed her sex from male to female . . ." (*Richards* v. *USTA* 1977, 267).

11. Reactions of feminists outside of tennis were not covered by the news media. Writing in *Ms.* magazine, Gloria Steinem (1977) noted the deeper cultural meaning of transsexualism underlying the Richards story and she decried the diversionary effect that attention to Richards had on women's issues. Marcia Seligman (1977), by focusing upon the promotional efforts launched in Richards's behalf and the opportunism he displayed, raised serious doubts about his sincerity and commitment.

12. The USTA's opposition to Richards represented male protectionism, not of women's rights but of commercial profit. The economic rationality of the tour depends upon a clear division of competitors by sex because one tenet of profit maximization is to provide a product that clearly differentiates itself from the competition. Richards had to be challenged because s/he problematized the division of sport into two separate markets.

13. Richards's dominance of the tour is not the point. None of the top players ever lost to Richards, but many of the less experienced players did. Allowing Richards to play in the US Open in 1977 did not displace King or Evert but some lower ranked professional woman player whose interests were equally worthy of protection. The USTA's action makes it clear that it was not the rank and file players they sought to protect but the top stars, and thus the economic vitality of the tour.

References

Axthelm, P. (1977, September 12). Only human. *Newsweek*, pp. 77–78.

Benjamin, H. (1966). The transsexual phenomenon. New York: Julian.

Bolin, A. (1988). *In search of Eve: Transsexual rites of passage*. South Hadley, Mass.: Bergen & Garvey.

Bolin, A. (1987). Transsexualism and the limits of traditional analysis. *American Behavioral Scientist 31*, 41–65.

Brod, H. (1987). Cross-culture, cross-gender. Cultural marginality and gender transcendence. *American Behavioral Scientist 31*, 5–11.

Bullough, V. L. (1975). Transsexualism in history. *Archives of Sexual Behavior 4* (5), 561–571.

Connell, R. (1983). *Which way is up?* Sydney: George Allen and Unwin.

de Lauretis, T. (1987). *Technologies of gender: Essays on theory, film and fiction*. Bloomington: Indiana University Press.

Devor, H. (1987). Gender blending females: Women and sometimes men. *American Behavioral Scientist 31*, 12–39.

Dunlap, M. C. (1979). The constitutional rights of sexual minorities: A crisis of the male/female dichotomy. *Hastings Law Journal 30*(4), 1131–1149.

Dyer, R. (1982). The celluloid closet. *Birmingham Arts Lab Bulletin 1*, 43.

Foucault, M. (1979). *Discipline and punish: The birth of the prison*. New York: Vintage, 197–203.

Garfinkel, H., & Stoller, R. J. (1967). Passing and the managed achievement of sex status in an "intersexed" person. In H. Garfinkel (ed.), *Studies in ethnomethodology* (pp. 116–135). Englewood Cliffs, N.J.: Prentice Hall.

Gitlin, T. (1980). The whole world is watching. Berkeley: University of California Press.

Grimm, D. E. (1987). Toward a theory of gender. *American Behavioral Scientist 31*, 66–85.

Hall, S. (1977). Culture, the media and "ideological effect." In J. Curran, M. Gurevich, & J. Woollocott (eds.), *Mass communication and society*. London: Edward Arnold.

Hartley, J. (1982). *Understanding news*. New York: Methuen.

Jameson, F. (1983). Postmodernism and consumer society. In H. Foster (ed.), *The antiaesthetic: Essays on postmodern cultures* (pp. 111–125). Port Townsend, Wa.: Bay Press.

Jorgensen, C. (1967). *Christine Jorgensen: A personal autobiography*. New York: Bantam.

Jones, J. (1976). The economics of the NHL revisited. In R. Gruneau & J. Albinson (eds.), *Canadian sport: Sociological perspectives* (pp. 249–258). Don Mills, Ont.: Addison-Wesley.

Kando, T. (1973). *Sex change: The achievement of gender identity among feminized transsexuals*. Springfield, Ill.: Chas. C. Thomas.

Keerdoga, E. with Foote, J. (1978, October 23). Tennis transsexual. *Newsweek*, pp. 28, 33.

Kennedy, R. (1976, September 6). She'd rather switch—and fight. *Sports Illustrated*, pp. 16–19.

Kessler, S. J., & McKenna, W. (1978). *Gender: An ethnomethodological approach*. New York: Wiley.

Kroll, J. (1976, November 22). The transsexuals. *Newsweek*, pp. 104–105.

Los Angeles Times. (August 12, 1976–August 12, 1987). Selected articles.

Lothstein, L. M. (1982). Sex reassignment surgery: Historical, bioethical and theoretical issues. *American Journal of Psychiatry* 139(4), 417–426.

Martino, M. (1977). *Emergence: A transsexual autobiography*. New York: Signet.

Money, J., & Ehrhardt, A. (1972). *Man and woman, boy and girl*. Baltimore: Johns Hopkins University Press.

Money, J., & Tucker, P. (1975). *Sexual signatures: On being a man or a woman*. Boston: Little, Brown.

Morris, J. (1974). *Conundrum*. New York: Henry Holt.

New York Times. (July 24, 1976–August 18, 1977). Selected articles.

Raymond, J. (1979). The transsexual empire. Boston: Beacon Press.

Richards, R. with Ames, J. (1983). *Second Serve*. New York: Stein and Day.

Richards v. United States Tennis Association, 400 N.Y.S. 2d 267, (1977).

Seligson, M. (1977, February). The packaging of Renee Richards. *MS*, pp. 74–76, 85.

Steinem, G. (1977, February). If the shoe doesn't fit, change the foot. *MS*, pp. 76, 85, 86.

Stoller, R. (1975). *Sex and gender, vol. 2: The transsexual experiment*. New York: Jason Aronson.

Szasz, T. (1976, October 2). Male women, female men. *New Republic*, pp. 8–9.

Terry, J. (1989). The body invaded: Medical surveillance of women as reproducers. *Socialist Review 19*, pp. 13–45.

Washington Post (August 12, 1976–January 1, 1978). Selected articles.

Williams, W. L. (1986). *The spirit and the flesh: Sexual diversity of American Indian culture*. Boston: Beacon.

———. (1987). Women, men, and others. *American Behavioral Scientist 31*, 135–141.

Willis, P. (1982). Women in sport in ideology. In J. Hargreaves (ed.), *Sport, culture and ideology* (pp. 117–135). London: Routledge & Kegan Paul.

Winston Salem Journal. (August 5, 1977–February 14, 1978). Selected articles.

Contributors

DAVID L. ANDREWS
Associate Professor
Department of Human Movement Sciences and Education
University of Memphis

SUSAN BIRRELL
Professor
Departments of Sport, Health, Leisure and Physical Studies, and Women's Studies
University of Iowa

CHERYL L. COLE
Associate Professor
Departments of Kinesiology, Women's Studies, and Criticism
and Interpretive Theory
University of Illinois

LISA DISCH
Associate Professor
Department of Political Science, Center for Advanced Feminist Studies
University of Minnesota

SHARI LEE DWORKIN
Ph.D. candidate
Department of Sociology
University of Southern California

ABIGAIL M. FEDER-KANE
Labor Operations Department
Metropolitan Opera

KATHERINE M. JAMIESON
Assistant Professor
Department of Exercise and Sport Science
University of North Carolina, Greensboro

CONTRIBUTORS

LEOLA JOHNSON
Assistant Professor
Department of Communication Studies
Macalester College

MARY JO KANE
Professor and Director
Tucker Center for Research on Girls and Women in Sport, School of Kinesiology
University of Minnesota

MÉLISSE LAFRANCE
Master of Studies candidate
Faculty of Modern Languages
University of Oxford

MARY G. McDONALD
Assistant Professor
Department of Physical Education, Health and Sport Studies
Miami University

GENEVIÈVE RAIL
Associate Professor
Women's Studies Program and the School of Human Kinetics
University of Ottawa

DAVID ROEDIGER
Chair and Professor
American Studies Program
University of Minnesota

SAM STOLOFF
Independent Scholar

NICK TRUJILLO
Associate Professor
Department of Communication Studies
California State University, Sacramento

FAYE LINDA WACHS
Visiting Assistant Professor
Department of Sociology
University of North Florida

Index

Aaron, Henry, 33, 43
Abdul-Jabbar, Kareem, 46, 59, 71 n. 37 (*see also* Alcindor, Lew)
absolutionist strategies, 268
advertising (*see also* celebrity endorsements): in African American markets, 49; ape images, 94–95; black athletic style marketing, 54–57; counter-cultural personalities, 101–2; Jordan's baseball career, 193–94; Nike promotional images, 172–73, 174–75; Olympics as prelude to commercial success, 228; physical attractiveness of models, 229; racial caricatures, 180–81; racial politics, 174–75; racial sign systems, 179–80; racism, 43–44; safe sex symbolism, 31; Simpson's crossover appeal, 41–42, 44, 49–50, 52, 54, 64–67; U.S. Postal Service and Olympics, 223–24; Western motif, 27
African American Otherness, 169, 173, 181–83, 190
African Americans: black male sexuality, 90–93; blackness, 93–95, 116, 167, 178; economic conditions of, 176; "failed" black family, 98; "good black"/"bad black," 96–98; males as pathologically deficient, 184–85; media celebrations of sporting prowess, 170; media representation of, 181; police repression, 45; rebellion in San Francisco, 52; as role models, 50; sporting activities as essential to community, 98; success tied to male responsibility, 54; toleration of with assimilation, 178–79; transcendence of color, 40–43, 50, 64–67, 115; vicarious identification with, 66
African Otherness, 92–93
Agassi, Andre, 219
aggressiveness, 82–84
AIDS: association with identities rather than

acts, 253–54, 258, 266–67, 271 n. 7, 272 n. 17; concern with epidemic, 87–89; conflation with gay sexuality, 253–54; conservative rhetoric surrounding, 265; and drug users, 259, 260; first reported case, 253; focus on high-risk acts, 272 n. 13; as framed by print media, 252–53; origin of virus, 104 n. 6; popular myth, 271 n. 6; risk assumptions, 254, 258–59, 272 n. 15; and sexual hierarchies, 262–63; silence surrounding, 261–62; social class, race, and sport, 263–65; transmission information conveyed by media, 259–61; transmission threat, 259–61, 262–63, 271 n. 4
Aikens, E., 78, 80–82, 85
Air Jordan promotion, 174–75, 180
Alcindor, Lew, 43, 46 (*see also* Abdul-Jabbar, Kareem)
Ali, Muhammad, 43, 45–46, 47, 55–56
Allen, Lucius, 46
Altman, Robert, 47
Alvarez, A., 158, 159
amazonia, 284
Amdur, Neil, 291
American dream, 97–100, 104 n. 7, 152, 175–76, 192
American meritocracy, 98–100, 175
Anderson, Dave, 22, 30, 184–85
Andrews, S., 123
Antonopolis, Lea, 280, 302
Anzaldua, G., 161
apartheid, 46
ape images, 94–95, 104 n. 6
apologetic posturing, 129–35, 135–37, 140 n. 15, 208–9
Araton, Harvey, 191
aristocracy, 240
Arledge, Roone, 59–62, 63, 71 n. 39, 72 n. 43

313

Patton, P., 176
peeking excessively, 111, 118, 120, 122, 125
penis, relationship to phallus, 120–21
performativity, 78–79, 103 n. 3
Perkins, Sam, 170
phallic power, 129–30
phallic symbolism, 32, 121–22
phallocentric politics of spectatorship, 118
phallocentrism, 91–92
phallocratic reality, 118
phallus: mystique of, 123; relationship to penis, 120–21
Phoenix Suns, 186
Pierce, Charles F., 197
Pippen, Scottie, 180, 181
pitching records, 22–23
Pitt, D. E., 114
play, tension with display, 245
post-Reaganite American imaginary, 166
Potrero Hill (San Francisco), 50, 51–52
power: body as primary site of enforcement, 256, 282; as both repressive and constitutive, 254–55; cultural assumptions about, 257; decisions regarding sexual identity, 286; defined as physical force and control, 15; dynamic nature of, 124; in locker room, 131; and objectification, 213; of white, heterosexual, middle-class men, 149
power lines: articulation through sport, 7–10; exploring, 4–6; limits in popular discourse, 6–7
Powers, Ron, 71 n. 39
Presley, Elvis, 99
professional-managerial class, 239
promiscuity: emphasis on evils of, 269; and HIV/AIDS risk, 261; of Magic Johnson, 259–60, 271 n. 8; of Morrison, 260–61
Pronger, B., 161
Protestant work ethic, 21
protests, 45–46

queer chic, 87
queer theory, 6
queerness, working definition, 82

race: as distinguishing characteristic in sport, 147–48; ideologies of, 151; social class, sport, and AIDS, 263–65; structuring of, 167–68; transcendence of, 176–77, 179
racial caricatures, 180–81

racial discourse: examination of, 168; media narration of 1982 NCAA championship, 170–71; mind-body dualism, 169
racial discrimination, 53, 116–17
racial displacement, 179, 196
racial hegemony, 29
racial identity, 40–43, 166–67, 177–79
racial narratives, in Olson-Patriot incident, 113–17
racial Otherness, subversion of, 174, 176
racial paranoia, 183
racial politics, 174–75, 175–77
racial scholarship, 5–6
racial signifiers, 167, 177, 195
racial stereotypes, 43–44, 46–47, 64
racism: in advertising, 43–44; black athletic ability descriptions, 46–47; classical, 170; commodity racism, 56–57; in courtroom, 67; ingrained within American society, 178; in network television, 62; taunts, 40–41; white and black, 104 n. 8; in Yamaguchi coverage, 215
racist discourse, 173
radical tactics, 156
Ragtime (Doctorow), 47
Rare Air (Vancil), 193
Raskind, Richard, 279, 286, 295, 300 (see also Richards, Renee)
Raymond, Jan, 284–85, 307 n. 7
reading sport, 10–13
Reagan, Ronald, 45, 174, 198, 260
Reeves, J. L., 166–67
regendering, 128
Reid, Kerry Melville, 290
Reid, Roz, 290
Reinsdorf, Jerry, 166
reproductive control, 160
Republican party, 195
Richards, Renee: about Birrell and Cole essay, 10, 281, 306 n. 2, 307 n. 9; antagonism with women's tennis world, 280; appearance, 279–80; autobiography, 280–81, 286–89, 291–93, 295, 298, 299–300; benefit from women's struggles, 296; as champion for transsexuals, 295; competitive equality, 300–301; construction of, 286; court case, 280, 285–86, 307 n. 10; examination of Raymond's thesis, 285; gendering as female, 289–93; inability to dominate women's tennis, 302, 307 n. 13; Lopez's media representa-

voyeurism, 119–20, 136
vulnerability, 131–32, 220–21

Walk on the Wild Side (Rodman), 83, 86–87, 88–89, 90–91, 99, 104 n. 8
Walters, Barbara, 262
Wang, Vera, 211
War, Battering and Other Sports (McBride), 63
Warren, Mike, 46
Washington Redskins, 130
Watney, S., 261, 269
Wayne, John, 27, 45
Webber, Chris, 195
Weeks, J., 268, 270
Weems, Robert, 49
Whannel, G., 211
white feminist movement, 156
"white man's Negro," 49–50
white masculinity, 113
white racism, 104 n. 8
white trash, 239, 248
whiteness, 115–16
Wide World of Sports, 60, 62
Wideman, John Edgar, 176
Wieden and Kennedy agency, 175
wilding, 114, 138 n. 6, 139 n. 7
Williamson, Fred, 62
Willigan, G. E., 180–81
Willis, P., 207, 210, 213, 217, 304
Wills, Maury, 54
Witt, Katarina, 211–14, 216, 219, 227
Wolf, Naomi, 210, 215
Wollestonecraft, Mary, 271 n. 9
women: abuse of, 62–64; acceptance in feminine sports, 212; athleticism belittled, 218; blame for HIV/AIDS infections, 254, 262;

conquest of, 264; cost of access to patriarchal power, 123; cultural constructs, 281; dividing and silencing through fear, 159–60; legal construction of, 284–86; marginalization of, 17; minorities, status in sport, 149; natural inferiority of, 301–2, 304; as sexual aggressors, 252, 259–61; suspicion of, 296–300, 302; victimized by figure skating system, 221–23
women athletes: avoidance of coding as masculine or lesbian, 210; ghettoized into selected sports, 212–13; sex-ID testing, 210; as sex objects, 213
women sports reporters: accommodations to locker room culture, 132; adversarial presence in locker rooms, 121–22; ambiguous position of, 119; apologetic posturing, 132–35, 135–37; baiting of, 120; black, 139 n. 9; eye-to-eye contact, 133; gender-neutral locker room access rights, 109, 110, 119–20; gender relations in locker room, 111–12; in locker rooms, 109, 113; as percentage of total reporters, 110
Women's Tennis Association, 279–80, 285–86, 293–94
Woods, Tiger, 144, 145
Woolf, Virginia, 118
work, division along gender lines, 15
work ethic, 21
working class, 237, 239
Worthy, James, 170
Wright, Erik Olin, 242
Wylie, Paul, 208

Yamaguchi, Kristi, 215–20, 222–25, 229–30, 231 n. 4